ReFocus: The Films of Ken Russell

ReFocus: The International Directors Series

Series Editors: Robert Singer, Stefanie Van de Peer and Gary D. Rhodes

Board of advisors:
Lizelle Bisschoff (Glasgow University)
Stephanie Hemelryck Donald (University of Lincoln)
Anna Misiak (Falmouth University)
Des O'Rawe (Queen's University Belfast)

ReFocus is a series of contemporary methodological and theoretical approaches to the interdisciplinary analyses and interpretations of international film directors, from the celebrated to the ignored, in direct relationship to their respective culture – its myths, values, and historical precepts – and the broader parameters of international film history and theory.

Titles in the series include:

Susanne Bier Edited by Missy Molloy, Mimi Nielsen and Meryl Shriver-Rice

Francis Veber Keith Corson

Jia Zhangke Maureen Turim

Xavier Dolan Edited by Andrée Lafontaine

Pedro Costa: Producing and Consuming Contemporary Art Cinema Nuno Barradas Jorge

Sohrab Shahid Saless: Exile, Displacement and the Stateless Moving Image Edited by Azadeh Fatehrad

Pablo Larraín Edited by Laura Hatry

Michel Gondry Edited by Marcelline Block and Jennifer Kirby

Rachid Bouchareb Edited by Michael Gott and Leslie Kealhofer-Kemp

Andrei Tarkovsky Edited by Sergey Toymentsev

Paul Leni Edited by Erica Tortolani and Martin F. Norden

Rakhshan Banietemad Edited by Maryam Ghorbankarimi

Jocelyn Saab: Films, Artworks and Cultural Events for the Arab World Edited by Mathilde Rouxel and Stefanie Van de Peer

François Ozon Edited by Loïc Bourdeau

Teuvo Tulio Henry Bacon, Kimmo Laine and Jaakko Seppälä

João Pedro Rodrigues and João Rui Guerra da Mata Edited by José Duarte and Filipa Rosário

Lucrecia Martel Edited by Natalia Christofoletti Barrenha, Julia Kratje and Paul Merchant

Shyam Benegal Edited by Sneha Kar Chaudhuri and Ramit Samaddar

Denis Villeneuve Edited by Jeri English and Marie Pascal

Ken Russell Edited by Matthew Melia

Antoinetta Angelidi Edited by Penny Bouska and Sotiris Petridis

edinburghuniversitypress.com/series/refocint

ReFocus:
The Films of Ken Russell

Edited by Matthew Melia

EDINBURGH
University Press

This book is dedicated to the memory of Philip Aaronson

Edinburgh University Press is one of the leading university presses in the UK. We publish academic books and journals in our selected subject areas across the humanities and social sciences, combining cutting-edge scholarship with high editorial and production values to produce academic works of lasting importance. For more information visit our website: edinburghuniversitypress.com

© editorial matter and organisation, Matthew Melia, 2023, 2024
© the chapters their several authors, 2023, 2024

Edinburgh University Press Ltd
The Tun – Holyrood Road
12 (2f) Jackson's Entry
Edinburgh EH8 8PJ

First published in hardback by Edinburgh University Press 2023

Typeset in 11/13 Ehrhardt MT by
IDSUK (DataConnection) Ltd

A CIP record for this book is available from the British Library

ISBN 978 1 4744 7765 9 (hardback)
ISBN 978 1 4744 7766 6 (paperback)
ISBN 978 1 4744 7767 3 (webready PDF)
ISBN 978 1 4744 7768 0 (epub)

The right of Matthew Melia to be identified as editor of this work has been asserted in accordance with the Copyright, Designs and Patents Act 1988 and the Copyright and Related Rights Regulations 2003 (SI No. 2498).

Contents

List of Figures	vii
Notes on Contributors	ix
Acknowledgements	xiii
Foreword by Bernard Rose	xv
Introduction	1

Part 1 Contextualising Ken Russell

1 Ken Russell: The Boy behind the Man   23
 Elize Russell
2 Performed Masculinities: Oliver Reed in Ken Russell's Films of the 'Long 1960s'   48
 Caroline Langhorst
3 Ken Russell's Gothic Modernism   69
 Matthew Melia

Part 2 Ken Russell and Television

4 Ken Russell and Television Advertising   95
 Richard Farmer
5 Quartet: Ken Russell's Painter Biopics and How they Anticipate the Later Cinematic Work   109
 Paul Davies
6 'An Authentic Part of the History of European Painting': Ken Russell's Early Engagement with the Pre-Raphaelites   125
 Jo George

Part 3 Design, Staging and Stardom

7 Shirley Russell and the Role of *The Boy Friend* in 1970s Retro   145
 NJ Stevenson

8 'No Better Director to Learn From': The Collaboration and
   Parallel Careers of Ken Russell and Derek Jarman   162
   Brian Hoyle
9 The Hermeneutics of Noise: The Sounds of Salvation in
   Ken Russell's *Tommy*   180
   K. A. Laity
10 Mythologising Valentino: Stardom, Biography and Performance
   in Ken Russell's *Valentino*   195
   Jade Evans

Part 4 Transgression and the Russell Legacy

11 An Extraordinary Parallel: Ken Russell and Dennis Potter Side by Side 213
   Mateja Đedović
12 Ken Russell and the Sexual Dimension of the Outsider Artist:
   An Exploration of *Elgar: The Erotic Variations* and *Delius:
   A Moment with Venus*   228
   Kevin Fullerton
13 A Short History of Ken Russell's Films in Japan   242
   Sawako Omori
14 Nicolas Winding Refn and the Ken Russell Style   260
   Adam Powell

Part 5 A Word from the Editor . . .

15 Ken Russell's *Song of Summer*: The Virtue of Restraint   281
   Roger Crittenden

Index   298

Figures

1.1	Ken and his mother, Ethel	25
1.2	Ken Russell on *The Boy Friend* sofa	28
1.3	Ken Russell, the young ballet dancer	42
1.4	Ken Russell in the 'ball chair' from *Tommy*	45
2.1	Father Mignon (Murray Melvin) at the orgy	49
2.2–2.5	Chamberlain as Tchaikovsky in *The Music Lovers*	52
2.6	Michael Caine as Harry Palmer in *Billion Dollar Brain*	53
2.7	Oliver Reed as Rossetti	57
2.8–2.9	Grieving and haunted: Reed's tormented Rossetti	60
2.10	Alienated, detached and conflicted: Reed as Gerald Crich in *Women in Love*	62
2.11	Grandier's stigmatised body as fetishised spectacle in *The Devils*	63
3.1	Rock 'n' roll Frankenstein	73
3.2	'Something created that night . . .'	74
3.3	China Blue	75
3.4	Rev. Shayne	76
3.5	Camel on the beach in *French Dressing*	78
3.6	Bartók	85
5.1	The Two Roberts	111
5.2	Pauline Boty and Peter Blake	112
6.1	*The Spear of Ithuriel*	128
7.1–7.2	Shirley Russell's storyboards for *The Boy Friend*	148
9.1	Young Tommy in the mirror	187
9.2	The family	188
9.3	Fighter planes	192

10.1	Rudolph Valentino's funeral	202
10.2	Valentino as a faun	204
14.1	*The Birth of Venus*	270
14.2	Roger Daltrey and Rick Wakeman in *Lisztomania*	272
14.3	Tom Hardy as *Bronson*	273
15.1	Fenby and Delius	285

Notes on Contributors

Roger Crittenden, after a distinguished career as a film editor at the BBC, was recruited to the newly established National Film School as Head of Editing in 1971, eventually becoming Director of the MA programme. He has lectured around the world and published several books including two devoted to interviews with European film editors entitled *Fine Cuts*. This has led to curating symposia around the world from São Paulo to Tokyo. He was recipient of the first international teaching award by CILECT, the International Association of Cinema, Audiovisual and Media Schools (2014). He is Adjunct Professor of Film at Griffith University in Brisbane, Australia.

Paul Davies is an English language instructor at the University of Passau in Germany where he teaches essay writing and area studies as well as seminars on comparative American and British cinema. In German literature he holds a BA from Leicester University, an MA from the University of Manitoba and a PhD from Queen's University. Apart from publications in German literary studies, he has presented several conference papers and written articles on a variety of film topics. He also runs the University of Passau's World Cinema club and has a website on the intermedial use of paintings: http://paintings-in-film.com.

Mateja Đedović is a film scholar and practitioner with a number of short films, documentaries, plays and a children's opera to his name. His topics of research include the works of Dennis Potter, Ken Russell, Stanley Kubrick and John Cassavetes, the adaptations of the novels of the Brontë sisters and John le Carré, with a special interest in Yugoslav film history.

Jade Evans is an AHRC funded PhD candidate at QMUL researching the creation, exhibition and exportation of British film stars in a collaborative project with the BFI National Archives. She examines archival objects to consider what they reveal about the ways in which the British film industry worked to promote its actors as stars, the hidden creative labour of female film stars and the players behind the scenes whose creative work shaped British stardom, and the promotion of national identity between 1920 and 1970.

Richard Farmer is Research Associate on the ERC-funded STUDIOTEC project at the University of Bristol. He has published extensively on British cinema and popular culture and is the author of three monographs: *The Food Companions: Cinema and Consumption in Wartime Britain, 1939–45* (2011); *Cinemas and Cinemagoing in Wartime Britain, 1939–45: The Utility Dream Palace* (2016); and the co-authored *Transformation and Tradition in 1960s British Cinema* (2019), which contained his chapter on the extensive intersections between television advertising and popular cinema in the 1960s.

Kevin Fullerton is a writer, academic and researcher in Literature and Film at the University of Dundee. He has special interests in transgressive film and literature; the relationship between cityscapes and cinema; and British class structure of the 1960s. His current research focuses on the intersection between social class, architecture and Ken Russell's films of the 'long 1960s'.

Jo George is a Senior Lecturer in English and Theatre Studies at the University of Dundee, where she also runs the JOOT Theatre Company. Her research interests include Old English poetry, early drama, translation studies, the Pre-Raphaelites and the films of Derek Jarman.

Brian Hoyle is a Senior Lecturer in Film Studies and English at the University of Dundee. He has a particular interest in British art cinema and has published on John Boorman, Derek Jarman, Peter Greenaway and others. His work on Ken Russell includes several publications on his amateur films and full-length DVD commentaries for the BFI releases of *Always on Sunday* and *Dante's Inferno*, and he is currently researching a monograph on Russell for Manchester University Press. He is co-editor of *British Art Cinema: Creativity, Experimentation and Innovation*.

K. A. Laity is an award-winning author, scholar, critic, editor and arcane artist. Her film *A Fire Ritual for the Heart* was featured in the 2021 Silent Fire exhibition co-curated by the Yale Institute of Sacred Music and Nasty Women Connecticut. Her fiction includes literary, crime, fantasy, Gothic and historical tomes. She has edited a variety of anthologies and written many short stories, songs, poems, as well as scholarly essays on film, medieval literature, historical magic, and modern fantasy and crime fiction. Her 2011–12 Fulbright Fellowship at the National University of Ireland, Galway, focused on Digital Humanities. She is Associate Professor of English at the College of Saint Rose (New York).

Caroline Langhorst holds a BA in Film Studies and British Studies and an MA in Film Studies from the University of Mainz. She is currently working on her PhD thesis on rebellious actors in 1960s British cinema at the Cinema and Television History Research Institute, De Montfort University Leicester. Her main research interests include British and American cinema, television, popular music and culture, acting/performance and star studies (especially British, Classical Hollywood and European stardom), gender studies, as well as the 'long 1960s' and the counterculture.

Matthew Melia is a senior lecturer in film, media and literature at Kingston School of Art, Kingston University. He is co-editor of *The Jaws Book: New Perspectives on the Classic Summer Blockbuster* (2020) and *Anthony Burgess, Stanley Kubrick and A Clockwork Orange* (2022). His current research focuses on Ken Russell's unmade projects and he is writing a monograph on *Gothic* for Liverpool University Press (Auteur/Devil's Advocates). He has written widely on the work of both Ken Russell and Stanley Kubrick. He has contributed audio commentaries with Elize Russell for the Lionsgate/Vestron Blu-ray releases of *The Lair of the White Worm* and *Gothic*.

Sawako Omori is a film journalist in Japan with a special interest in British cinema. She writes for one of Japan's foremost film journals, *Kinema Junpo*. She is the author of three books and the translator of four others including *Woody Allen on Woody Allen*. She is the author of *Tokyo Arthouses Revisited*, a nonfiction history of arthouses in Tokyo. She has interviewed many British directors including Ken Russell, Nicolas Roeg, Derek Jarman, Peter Greenaway, Mike Leigh, Stephen Frears and Danny Boyle.

Adam Powell is writer on cinema and currently a film scholar at Kingston University, carrying out research into the international metteur en scène in the twenty-first century, with a focus on Nicolas Winding Refn. He contributes to the *Senses of Cinema* website and has conducted extensive interviews with Carlos Reygadas, Nicolas Winding Refn and Pedro Costa.

Elize Russell was happily married to Ken Russell for ten years. She has degrees in Dramatic Art and Creative Writing from UNC-Chapel Hill, with graduate studies in Medieval Thought and Learning. She worked at CBS News for Dan Rather and has acted in nine films and two TV broadcasts directed by

Ken Russell between 2001 and 2010, including *The Fall of the Louse of Usher* (2002), *Boudica Bites Back* (2009) and *Elgar: Fantasy of a Composer on a Bicycle* (2002). She has appeared in films by Andrew Logan, Jon Jesurun, Spookey Ruben, Loudon Wainwright and Bob Porco, and in Shelby Coe's documentary *Theatre of Desire*. Lisi is active now as a professional theatre and film actor and published poet. She is also a produced playwright and book editor for the Smithsonian Museum, a recording singer, and regular film presenter of Ken Russell films at cinema houses in NYC and NC 2012–17 as well as a film festival presenter. Lisi was a participant in the Ken Russell Retrospective at London's Cinema Museum (2017), and a presenter at the Ken Russell Film Festival in Lymington and Ken Russell Movies at the Edinburgh Festival (both 2016). She has contributed commentaries with Matthew Melia on Vestron's Blu-ray releases of *The Lair of the White Worm* and *Gothic*.

NJ Stevenson is a fashion curator, author, lecturer in fashion history and digital copywriter. She is a researching for an exhibition on period film costume and fashion to be held at the Fashion and Textile Museum, London. She is also Director of the Fashion Foundation, Port Eliot Festival, and Curator and Presenter of the Tim Yip Cloud Project at the Southbank Centre.

Acknowledgements

I would like to extend my heartfelt thanks to the following for their help and support in putting this book together: the staff of Edinburgh University Press for their unlimited patience and support, especially series editors Robert Singer, Stefanie Van de Peer and Gary D. Rhodes as well as publisher Gillian Leslie, and assistant commissioning editor Sam Johnson and Eddie Clark for readying the book for publication; to Dr Simon Brown, Associate Lecturer in Film at Kingston University whose friendship and whose moral and financial support as founder and coordinator of the Kingston University Popular Culture Research Group provided the foundation and funding for the 2017 conference *Ken Russell: Perspectives, Reception and Legacy*, a springboard for this book; and to the staff of the British Film Institute Archives, the archives of the Bill Douglas Centre, Exeter, and the BBC Written Archives Centre in Caversham.

I would especially like to extend my thanks to the following members of the Russell family for their support: Ken's wife, Elize Russell, for her unwavering faith in the project, his daughter, Victoria Russell, and his granddaughter, Amelia Russell. In thanking the Russell family, I would of course like to express my thanks to Ken himself whose films changed my life and way of thinking about cinema.

I would also like to thank director Bernard Rose for taking the time from his busy schedule to write the foreword to this book.

I would like to thank Stewart Williams, who, unfortunately, was forced to withdraw his chapter but who has remained a constant source of support. Thank you as well to James Fenwick and Nathan Abrams for reviewing the book and for their testimonials.

I would especially like to thank all the contributors to this volume for their incredible work and patience over the long gestation of this book. You've all been amazing!

Several of the contributors have asked me to extend their thanks. I have added this to the end of their chapters.

Finally I would like to express my love and gratitude to my partner Nikki and daughter Charlotte for their patience and generosity in the time taken away from the family to produce this book.

Foreword

Bernard Rose

The first Ken Russell film I saw was *Mahler* (1974), and from the opening sequence I knew I was in the presence of something utterly different: a chalet sits peacefully by the side of an idyllic lake – birdsong – and then a sudden fireball engulfs the wooden hut; we don't hear an explosion but the grandiose, terrifying orchestral sounds of Gustav Mahler. I was instantly hooked. But before I could settle into whatever doomy but grand film this was obviously going to be, Russell had segued to a strange ballet: a naked woman lies encased in a cotton chrysalis, stretching and tearing at her strange wrapping, lying on a volcanic rock formation, trying to 'be born'. How do I know that's what was happening? Because Georgina Hale (as Alma Mahler) explained it as her dream in the next scene, suddenly a naturalistic costume drama in a train.

Russell said many times that he learned how to begin something starting from his BBC days. He wanted to shock and arouse the audience before his Dad could get up off the couch and shuffle over to the TV to turn the dial to the (only) other channel. In this opening Russell gives himself permission to do anything; to 'explode' the concept of a classical music biography, to express ideas in dance rather than dialogue, to make a film that is more about Alma Mahler than Gustav Mahler (the title is just *Mahler*). And of course to make a film that was as much about his troubled marriage to Shirley Russell as it was any sort of biography of a third party.

I remember my first screening of this film vividly: it was at the Odeon Haymarket on its first run, presented in four-track stereo. I was thirteen and ran to tell anyone I could that this was a movie they simply had to see. Most did not agree, some vociferously, and I heard the epithets that were often hurled at Russell; he was 'vulgar', 'childish', 'obscene' and, the most common, 'over the top'. As if he didn't mean to be. I soon realized that my love of Ken

Russell (and I sought out every one of his films after that) was considered pretty unacceptable in mainstream cineaste circles. They would praise Fellini (only the early films, of course) and admire Visconti, but Ken Russell was beyond the pale.

Time has made fools of these opinions, but way too late for Russell. He knew that would eventually happen, but I think the dismissals and derision got to him more than he admitted. So it is with great pleasure that I see this book as further evidence of Russell's work being taken as seriously as it should be, vulgar humour and all. Because it is a deeply serious body of work about the spiritual investigation of the artist and the healing process by which suffering is turned into art. In those terms Russell is a card-carrying Romantic, but formally his work is Brechtian and uses alienation with as much rigour as Godard.

Russell was also a flamboyant showman and I will leave you with my enduring memory of him, at the premiere of *Salome's Last Dance* (1988), which I attended as the guest of producer Dan Ireland. Ken was about to drive down Shaftesbury Avenue in an open-topped Bentley, dressed in giant costume rings and swathed in a fur coat. On either side of him were seated two of the ladies who act as the 'soldiers/brothel workers' in the film. Ken yelled out (as the paparazzi took his picture), 'Okay ladies – tits out!' They bared their breasts and drove off into the night.

Introduction

Matthew Melia

PERSPECTIVES: KEN RUSSELL, AN 'ENFANT TERRIBLE'?

> His taste is as broad as the subject matter of his films, neither square nor hip; he has a passion for the thirties; for offbeat things like musical boxes and pianolas, and for celluloid in any shape or form. He's the sort of man who will drive 200 miles to buy a fifty-year old 35mm projector . . . he's got an uncanny knowledge of music – he can't read a note, but he can sing you the theme from pretty well any piece you care to mention. He is married, has three sons aged 4, 3 and 2. He never ties his shoelaces, and he drives like a madman.[1]

This is how Ken Russell described himself to the *Radio Times* in 1962 ahead of the broadcast of his BBC film *The Lonely Shore* (BBC, 1962) – a documentary film narrated from the perspective of alien archaeologists discovering the detritus of humanity, millennia after its extinction. It's an apt and offbeat summary of a man whose work is among the most idiosyncratic and powerful in British cinema and television. Few, if any, other British directors have polarised critical and public opinion quite so much, and as film director and standard bearer for the Russell legacy Bernard Rose points out in the foreword to this book, Russell's status as an auteur of world art cinema à la Fellini or Visconti has been unjustly neglected. Nevertheless, since his death in 2011, there has been a gathering momentum in the critical re-evaluation and reaffirmation of Russell's rightful place within British film and indeed world cinema. This volume aims to contribute to the growing corpus of critical literature on Russell by presenting a range of the most recent research from established and emerging scholars of his work as well as personal reflections from those who knew him, worked with him and loved him, offering new perspectives and insight into Russell's extensive, diverse, iconic and often iconoclastic body of work, and into his persona and working practices.

The book has several aims but let's start with what it aims not to do. First and foremost, it aims not to buy into or indulge the decades-old habit of referring to Russell as the 'Enfant Terrible' or 'Madman'/'Wild Man' of British cinema. The first reference to Russell as 'Enfant Terrible' is in MGM's marketing material for *The Boy Friend* (MGM-EMI, 1971),[2] and archived press cuttings from the mid-1960s show his reputation as the 'Wild Man of the BBC' predate his graduation to cinematic 'madman'.[3] This book rejects these terms (although chapters across this book will necessarily critically engage with them as part of the wider discussion). He and his work deserve better. Russell's reputation suffered throughout his career under these lazy media sobriquets – but they were also something of a double-edged sword. On the one hand they became a distinguishing feature of his auteurist persona, a brand, and something that he would increasingly and knowingly play up to as his career progressed. Conversely we should note, while this was the popular image of Russell, there was also a body of critics who viewed Russell as both an artist and poet and someone who was essential to the legitimisation of the emerging and experimental medium of television as an art form in the post-war years. Emerging from a background in dance, photography and amateur film-making, between 1956 and 1970 he produced an extraordinary body of work for the BBC Arts documentary programme *Monitor* and its replacement (in 1967), *Omnibus*. This body of work included innovative, experimental and *cinematic* documentaries about (predominantly) the (similarly innovative, experimental and romantic) artists, performers and composers with whom he was enamoured.[4] During his years at *Monitor*, he would enjoy a fruitful and sometimes combative relationship with the (Reithian) producer Huw Wheldon – a figure who must be held at least in part accountable for shaping and evolving Russell's career.

Russell would return to the medium of television again during the 1990s, this time working predominantly for ITV with his old screenwriting collaborator Melvyn Bragg, with whom he had previously worked with on *The Debussy Film* (BBC, 1965) and *The Music Lovers* (United Artists, 1970) – his film about the composer Pyotr Ilyich Tchaikovsky's (Richard Chamberlain) turbulent inner life. During this period he also made a return to the BBC for the first time since his controversial *Omnibus* film about the composer Richard Strauss, *Dance of the Seven Veils* (BBC, 1970) with *The Mystery of Dr Martinu* (BBC, 1992) – a surrealist-inspired film about the Czech composer Bohuslav Jan Martinů – as well as an adaptation of D. H. Lawrence's *Lady Chatterley's Lover* (BBC, 1993).

Russell developed an outward-facing public persona to match the public perception of his films, a defence mechanism perhaps, and one he knowingly played up to. During his tenure as a contestant on Channel 4's *Celebrity Big Brother* in 2007, he claimed in his introductory VT roll:

I am the most famous English film director! [. . .] I'm called controversial because I occasionally choose controversial subjects [. . .] I used to be described as the 'Enfant Terrible' of British films, now I am regarded, I think, as the *Grand-Père* terrible![5]

Behind this often flamboyant and theatrical public persona, however, was a Romantic, a deeply cultured man who had a great love for and an encyclopedic knowledge of classical music and film, and who was both shy and sensitive – as his wife, Elize Russell, records in Chapter 1. 'Madman'/'Wild Man' and 'Enfant Terrible', however, became journalistic shorthand for dismissing both the man and his work as a vulgar embarrassment to the alleged prestige and increasing conservatism of the British film industry. These terms contributed to his pariah status later in his career and to years of industrial and cultural dismissal and neglect, serving to obscure and obfuscate the ground-breaking, experimental, artistic and challenging nature of his extensive canon.

Rather than thinking of Ken Russell as the 'Madman' or 'Wild Man' of British cinema, maybe we need to think of him as the 'Renaissance Man' of British cinema and television (like his contemporaries and collaborators Jonathan Miller, Humphrey Burton and Melvyn Bragg) whose work strove to disassemble cultural boundaries and hierarchies, and whose many accomplishments ran the gamut of visual media: from ballet and photography, through television, advertising, film, theatre, radio and music video to novels and opera productions. While Ken Russell's role as a film-maker is, of course, what he is most known for, the authors in this book deal with and recognise the importance of Russell's other creative endeavours as well – those which perhaps have not been given significant critical focus elsewhere and which offer a framework for better understanding his work with film. Richard Farmer, for instance, discusses Russell's early and formative pre-BBC work in advertising; while Kevin Fullerton focuses attention on Russell's late career divergence as a novelist, and Matthew Melia considers his early photography as part of a discussion around his 'Gothic imagination'.

RECEPTION: THE CRITICS

Ken Russell was widely regarded in the media as a purveyor of camp, kitsch, excessive, perverse and sometimes cult cinema. He was perceived as a director whose work within the genre of film biography was an affront to the cultural sacred cows (romantic composers, artists, poets, etc.) he sought to depict. Cries of historical inaccuracy, irreverence and cultural blasphemy ricocheted around much of the more conservative critical discourse, not least from Russell's nemesis, the *Evening Standard* film critic Alexander Walker. Walker famously responded to *The Devils* (Warner Bros., 1971) by attacking Russell's 'taste for visual sensation that makes scene after scene look like the masturbatory fantasies of a Catholic boyhood',[6] provoking an on-air debate on the BBC between the two which ended with Russell hitting Walker on the head with a rolled-up copy of his own review. Nevertheless, these critics' responses either unwittingly or otherwise ignored the fact that Russell's films were not conventional biographies or hagiographies but rather, as he was at pains to point out, deeply personal impressionistic responses to his own sublime experiences of the artist through their work. Russell was unafraid to depict and tackle the more problematic side of the subjects: Strauss's Nazism or Frederick Delius's vampiric self-centredness and bullying personality, for instance (*Delius: Song of Summer*, BBC, 1968).

Russell's own work is itself highly experiential and seeks to overwhelm all of the viewer's senses first and foremost (as K. A. Laity discusses later in this book in relation to *Tommy* [Columbia, 1975]).[7] The author Anthony Burgess, writing about *The Debussy Film* in *The Listener*, said:

> For this particular work, Ken Russell gave us balloons in a garden and Pierre Loti lying on a studio couch. I know that the aims of his Elgar and Debussy films represented the ultimate bringing low of the daughters[8] – music in the service of biography [. . .] The Elgar film, beautiful to look at though it is, had little to say about the great Elgar – the Elgar of the Symphonies.[9] *The Debussy film*, was a technical tour de force, a genuine traducement of the composer. It was also perverse, using *La Mer* to accompany Debussy's dream about himself as Roderick Usher instead of *Ce qu'a vu le vent du Ouest* (originally written as a prelude to an unwritten opera of Poe's story).[10]

In the *Observer* (October 1977), critic Nigel Gosling 'profiles the enfant terrible of British cinema'. Gosling's article chastises Russell, who:

> Cheerfully tramples on the most cherished of our traditions, our celebrated instinct for fair play and good taste. The enfant terrible of British cinema lays about him with a billboard vigour and rebellious relish. He regards our addiction to moderation as feebleness and cowardice and is defiant in the face of accusations of good taste and vulgarity.[11]

Russell's response to such accusations was:

> It's strange that people can't reconcile vulgarity with artistry [. . .] They're the same thing to me. By vulgarity I mean an exuberant, over the top, larger than life and slightly bad taste, red blooded but essentially human thing. If that's nothing to do with art, let's have nothing to do with art.[12]

Few, if any, film directors have balanced and harmonised the sacred and the profane, the romantic, the sublime and the vulgar quite as consciously, effectively and strategically as Russell. The writer Jonathan Meades connects Russell's more bawdy tendencies to his Southampton background and temperament, noting that:

> There were the houses where Ken Russell and [British comedian] Benny Hill had grown up. They might have been twins sired by Donald McGill. There wasn't a house in Southampton that didn't rock with bawdy laughter [. . .] The city lacked decorum.[13]

In an email correspondence with this author, Meades reflected that Russell's was a calculated vulgarity typical of that city.

In Russell's 1993 book *Fire Over England: The British Cinema Comes Under Friendly Fire*, in which he casts a personal eye over the history and the then current state of British film, he begins by recalling:

> Cycling down the smouldering remains of Southampton High Street the morning after our worst Blitz. Gone were most of the old familiar landmarks. Gone was the Cadena Café where a lady's string trio had played 'Tea for Two' as Mum and I took some light refreshment after a matinee at the Picture House. Gone was the Picture House![14]

Ken Russell was thirteen during the Blitz (nowhere in his work is its impact on him more evident than in *Tommy*), and the image painted here provides a useful metaphor. Cinema, as he records in both *Fire Over England* and his autobiography, *A British Picture*, was a catalytic force in his journey from childhood to adulthood. He emerged as an amateur film-maker and evolved to become part of a 'year zero' moment in British cinema in the late 1960s, an era which also saw the emergence of other auteur directors such as Nicolas Roeg, John Boorman and Lindsay Anderson.[15] Amateur film-making and his amateur roots remained vitally important to him (as Brian Hoyle has noted), and it was a state to which he would return in his final years, bringing his career full circle.[16]

These 'year zero' film-makers were transgressive innovators who embodied a resetting of the aesthetics, style and identity of British cinema, propelling it out of the post-war parochialism of the 1950s, looking towards both European and American art film and experimentalism. Sue Harper and Justin Smith link the emergence of these auteurs to the opening of a new cultural space, the result of the 'retrenchment' of American funding in British cinema at the end of the 1960s, a space which was:

> Filled by opportunistic independent auteurs (such as Losey, Russell and Roeg), whose modestly budgeted art films of this period had an exposure

they might not have achieved in healthier economic climes . . . It is possible to argue that the success of Ken Russell's films in the first half of the 1970s provide evidence not of an increase in the market for art-house films, but of the attractiveness to popular tastes of sexual liberalism.[17]

In *Fire Over England* Russell clearly identifies with the climactic sequence in Anderson's public school drama *If. . .* (Paramount, 1968), in which Malcolm McDowell (as the rebellious Mick Travis) and his friends open fire on the old guard of the (school) establishment.[18] Archived press articles housed at the British Film Institute in London also reveal how critically divided in response the press were to Russell. *Films and Filming*, for instance, was 'rare in its praise it gave to Ken Russell',[19] while:

> Gordon Gow, a regular writer, presciently found *Tommy* 'a milestone in British cinema, which will go down as either the film which stopped the slide into mediocrity and mindlessness, or it may turn out to be the lone, gloriously defiant stand against apathy and indifference'.[20]

Nigel Gosling compared Russell to 'our other cultural shocker, the painter Francis Bacon'.[21] Despite being intended as a negative comparison, it is also rather an appropriate one. As with Russell's work, Bacon's paintings of dissolving human subjects and melting flesh strive to dissolve traditional ways of representing the subject, to challenge perceived notions of beauty and taste and to confront the viewer's culturally conditioned perceptions of art.

One of the aims of this collection is to consider Russell's work within the legacy of certain other artistic and cultural traditions. Jo George, for instance, discusses Russell's preoccupation with, and immersion in, the work of the Pre-Raphaelite Brotherhood; while Matthew Melia's chapter considers how Russell's work engages both Gothic and modernist traditions (often simultaneously), and in his own edited collection Kevin M. Flanagan positions Russell as a 'Mannerist' director.[22] Maybe another apt art historical comparison would be with the Flemish painter Rembrandt van Rijn (another subject of Bacon's), whose images evade an idealised and even a romanticised form of figuration and representation, and whose fleshy and un-sentimentalised renditions of the human body are echoed in Russell's approach to the biographical format and the representation of hallowed historical and cultural figures.[23] Russell's films, and especially his biographical films, are vulgar only in the sense that they do not conform to the style and conventional standard of idealised reverence and representation required of 'tasteful' high art and beauty. As musician (and friend and collaborator of Russell's) David Massengill recently commented in a Facebook post commemorating what would have been the director's ninety-fourth birthday, Russell's films 'enlightened the public and at the same time reminded us that artists had pimples and balls and that they were very human'.[24]

What Gosling and other critics failed to realise is that for Russell, the artist's work is directly connected to who they are, to their beliefs, and to their lived experience. With *Dance of the Seven Veils*, for instance, Russell interrogates the balance between the beauty of Richard Strauss's music and the ugliness of his fascist inclinations. We live, today, in a media culture where, in an ideologically reversed echo of the anti-permissiveness of the 1970s public figures – actors, musicians, writers, etc. – are frequently 'cancelled': removed from the artistic roll call for their publicised controversies, behaviour, actions, politics or statements made.[25] The debate rolls on – can you love the art and not the artist? Russell's film addressed and interrogated this issue back in 1970 and as Elize Russell suggested in 2020 at the Keswick Film Festival when introducing the film, 'Ken loved Strauss's music but not his politics or personality.'

Dance of the Seven Veils (broadcast on the BBC on 15 February 1970) was protested by the Strauss family and Russell was accused of pornography. Media campaigner Mary Whitehouse tried to sue the Post Office for letting it go out across the broadcast signal, questions were raised in Parliament the next day and the film was shelved by the BBC, never to be broadcast again. Behind closed doors at the BBC the debate raged at a General Advisory Council meeting ahead of the broadcast over the film's content and whether it constituted pornography. The archived minutes show that it was then controller of BBC 2 David Attenborough who mounted a defence of Russell's film, saying that the film met the expectations of viewers of 'seriousness and sophistication' who would be watching during the 10.15 p.m. broadcast slot. In a letter from 28 January 1970, Attenborough referred to it as a 'remarkable and accomplished film of great merit'.[26] It was nevertheless not seen publicly again until (just over) fifty years later to the day in Russell's beloved and adopted home of the Lake District, to a sold-out house – immediately before the world went into the Covid-19 lockdown.[27]

LEGACY

Critical Engagement

What has been the Russell legacy? In terms of scholarly touchstones for understanding Russell's work, film critic Ken Hanke's 'Red Book' – *Ken Russell's Films*, John Baxter's *An Appalling Talent* and Joseph Gomez's *Ken Russell: The Adaptor as Creator* remain foundational texts.[28] However, since Russell's death there has been a growing critical and scholarly interest (both academic and otherwise) in his extensive back catalogue of work. The most significant of these are two major academic collections. The first (and the last published within Russell's lifetime), Kevin M. Flanagan's *Ken Russell: Re-Viewing England's*

Last Mannerist (2009), was a game-changing publication that opened the door for a new era of scholarly engagement with the work. The second is a special edition of the *Journal of British Cinema and Television* (2015).[29] It emerged out of a 2014 academic conference, 'Imagining the Past: Ken Russell, Biography and the Art of Making History', which took place at Cinema RITCS, Brussels as part of the 2014 Offscreen Film festival, and which programmed a complete retrospective of Russell's work. Edited by conference conveners Christophe Van Eecke and Karel Vanhaesebrouck along with British television scholar John Hill, this collection was the first body of scholarship to reflect on Russell's work *after* his passing, and aimed to rethink and readdress Russell's 'awkward' and peripheral position 'within British film studies'.[30] More recently Matthew Melia has shed light on Russell's early unmade work for the BBC, the first part of a project that considers the importance of the unmade and abandoned projects to the Russell filmography.[31]

It's useful here to compare the resurgence of critical interest in Russell's work with that of his contemporary Stanley Kubrick (in whom there has been a much more sustained level of academic interest). Since the opening of the Stanley Kubrick Archive (at University of the Arts London: London College of Communication) in 2007, interest in Kubrick has yielded a huge amount of innovative and scholarly research and critical writing. There is gathering momentum in the archival study of Russell's work too (something that this collection hopes to illustrate). However, whereas the Kubrick Archive, which stands as the main port of call for primary material (scripts, correspondences, production materials, etc.), is all under one roof, archival materials pertaining to Russell's work are far less centralised and much more dispersed across a variety of different sites including the British Film Institute, the BBC Written Archive Centre, the Bill Douglas Centre at Exeter University, the Special Collections at Southampton Solent University, and the Melvyn Bragg Archive in Leeds. A lot of material also remains in private collections. A devastating fire at the Russells' home in 2006 destroyed decades' worth of material from his personal archive. That there is no central archive for Russell has affected his legacy within film academia – historically putting him at a distance from critical and archival study. However, Russell did donate material to the Special Collections at Southampton Solent University, and in the 1970s (according to the trade press) attempted to establish a Ken and Shirley Russell collection for posterity;[32] it is therefore interesting to observe Russell's own attempts to safeguard his legacy through self-conservatorship.

Several more recent publications have brought new critical and popular attention to Russell's work and consolidated a renewal of interest from both scholars and fans alike, such as Christophe Van Eecke's wide-ranging PhD thesis *Pandemonium: Ken Russell's Artist Biographies as Baroque Performance*, Chris Wade's *Ken Russell: On Screen*, Joseph Lanza's *Phallic Frenzy: Ken Russell and*

His Films, and Paul Sutton's conversational aggregation of interviews with Russell, his actors and production staff *Talking About Ken Russell*.³³ Lanza's book seems to have appealed to Russell, who, in his column in the *Times*, wrote:

> *Phallic Frenzy* reads like an overblown, outrageous, biographical film script by Ken Russell, full of myth masquerading as fact. And as usual the finished product is bright, irreverent, camp and cacophonous. Lanza has managed to disguise his masterful research as a near-neo-novel with gothic and surreal overtones. I have to applaud the man, having done the same with my own biographies on composers.³⁴

There have also been several recent monographs dedicated to single films in the Russell repertoire. Leading UK film scholar and Russell authority Professor Linda Ruth Williams has written extensively on Russell's relationship with D. H. Lawrence and *Women in Love* (United Artists, 1969).³⁵ While Richard Crouse's *Raising Hell: Ken Russell and the Unmaking of The Devils*, and Darren Arnold's monograph *The Devils* for Auteur (part of the Devil's Advocates horror series) focus on Russell's most (in)famous film, others have looked elsewhere, such as Kit Power's recent personal reflection on *Tommy* and Matthew Melia's forthcoming monograph devoted to *Gothic* (Virgin Vision/Vestron, 1986).³⁶

So where does this *Refocus: The Films of Ken Russell* fit in to this roll call of publications? In 2017 a collection of scholars from around the globe gathered at Kingston University, UK, for a three-day conference, 'Ken Russell: Perspectives, Reception and Legacy', shortly after what would have been Russell's ninetieth birthday. The aim was to bring together fresh and emerging scholarship around Russell's work from both new and established researchers and to offer fresh critical perspectives across the range of Russell's work as well as to consider the Russell legacy and the ways in which his work has been received.

While this is not a 'book of the conference' or 'conference proceedings', the scholarship of several of the papers given at the conference is developed here alongside work which was not included as part of the event emerging independently of it. It aims to build on the precedent set by Flanagan's collection, and to continue the momentum in critical scholarship around Russell's work, furthering the recuperation of Russell as a pivotal figure in not only British but global cinema. This is also the first edited *book* collection of critical writing published on Russell since his death; it includes contributions from those close to Russell and who worked and collaborated with him, including his wife and film-making partner Elize Russell and BBC editor Roger Crittenden. It aims to take a widescreen approach to discussing Ken Russell's varied and diverse career, offering a range of new perspectives on Russell's work which have gone undiscussed in other critical writing: his reception in Japan, for instance, or his influence and legacy in the work of contemporary Danish film-maker Nicolas Winding Refn. This book hopes to be as comprehensive as possible, but given the enormous scope of Russell's output (over fifty-five films made for the BBC alone!), it begs the reader's forgiveness for any omissions and hopes that the scholarship and range of perspectives on the material covered in the book will make up for this.

While it is published in the wake of the fiftieth anniversary of *The Devils*, the book aims to look beyond this much discussed and rightly celebrated masterpiece. To some extent *The Devils* (and to a slightly lesser degree *Women in Love* and *Tommy*) has come to dominate a popular and critical understanding of Russell and his work. Hence it is the aim of this book to turn its attention to work which, to a greater or lesser extent, has existed in its shadow. That's not to say that discussion of this film will be omitted entirely (Mateja Đedović uses it as a key point of reference and discussion in his critical and comparative study of Russell and transgressive TV dramatist Dennis Potter – another first), simply that this collection chooses to focus on aspects of Russell's work which deserve further critical attention.

Within the field of auteur studies, more recent research (by scholars like Manca Perko or James Fenwick) has complicated the persistence of this term by considering the role that collaboration and collaborative working practices play in understanding a body of work and director. This collection also crucially strives to understand the importance of collaborative working practices and relationships in the production of Russell's films considering the roles of family, editors, set designers, writers, costume designers, and so on. This is a recurring line of inquiry and in pursuing it this book hopes to open out and broaden critical inquiry into Russell's work.

Ken Russell in the Twenty-first Century

The Internet and social media have opened new pathways to Russell, offering a digital point of access for new (and old) sets of admirers and enthusiasts. Video streaming sites like YouTube or Daily Motion have become repositories for films which have been withdrawn from or even evaded distribution, uploaded from old out-of-print VHS tapes or off-air recordings. Such sites have become useful sources for accessing Russell himself via his various television interviews and appearances (which became more frequent from the 1990s as he fought to maintain visibility in the public eye) – which included a five-day stint in the Channel 4 *Celebrity Big Brother* house in 2007.[37]

Russell's work has also undergone a renaissance via the restoration and re-release of his films. In fact, given the laserdisc release of *Lisztomania* (Goodtimes Enterprises, 1975) in 1993, and before, those releases of his work on VHS as well as his relationship with Vestron Video, Russell's work has for some time existed at the frontier of new forms of media distribution. In 2012 the British Film Institute began a run of re-releases with the momentous release of the 'director's cut' of *The Devils* (the version of the film that Russell conceded to for the British Board of Film Censors and the most complete version available). It was followed up by BFI Blu-ray restorations and re-releases of *Women in Love* and *Valentino* (United Artists, 1977) in 2016. In 2017 the BFI also released two DVD/Blu-ray sets of Russell's BBC films – *The Great Composers* (*Elgar* [1962], *Delius: Song of Summer* and *The Debussy Film* [1965]) and *The Great Passions* (*Always On Sunday* [1965], *Isadora* [1966] and *Dante's Inferno* [1967]) – which had previously only been available on Region 1 DVD via BBC America. The 1962 BBC documentary *Pop Goes the Easel* was included in the first volume of the collection *Visions of Change: The Evolution of the British TV Documentary*; and both *A House in Bayswater* (BBC, 1960) and *A Poet in London* (BBC, 1959) have enjoyed extended stays on the BBC iPlayer. Russell's work has also been re-released in recent years via prestigious distributors such as Criterion (*Women in Love* and *Mahler* [Goodtimes Enterprises, 1974]), and cult distributors (no less prestigious) such as Arrow Films (*Crimes of Passion* [New World Pictures, 1984]) and Lionsgate/Vestron (*The Lair of the White Worm* [Vestron, 1988] and *Gothic*). All these releases point to a posthumous reniassance of interest in Russell's films.

In 2019 *Tommy* was restored and re-released in cinemas via the British Film Institute in anticipation of its forty-fifth anniversary, and in February 2020 the Keswick Film Festival screened *Dance of the Seven Veils* – the first public showing of the film in the fifty years since its first and only broadcast and its subsequent ban (see earlier). In the US, the Alamo Draft House in New York regularly programmes Russell's films, and in 2017 the Cinema Museum in London programmed a sold-out three-night retrospective showing *The Debussy Film*, *The Music Lovers*, *Mahler*, *Savage Messiah* (MGM-EMI, 1972) and *The Devils*. The screenings were accompanied by talks, introductions and Q and As by such Russell luminaries as Melvyn Bragg and Mark Kermode, and stars such as Robert Powell, Judith Paris, Georgina Hale and Glenda Jackson.

Russell has also found dedicated spaces on social media sites like Facebook (with flourishing groups such as 'The Ken Russell Discussion Group' and 'The Devils Appreciation Society'); Twitter has provided a platform for fan-driven online campaigns such as #FreeTheDevils (a campaign to get Warner Brothers to relax its fifty-year grip on the full cut of the film) – consolidating the reception of Russell and his work as a 'cult' property. He has found a new home and new fandoms in this contemporary digital landscape. One wonders what he would have made of the new lease of life given to his work via digital platforms such as Amazon Prime Video and the horror streaming site Shudder (which more recently has played host to the US cut of *The Devils*). We might presume he would have approved of such access (especially to his more unavailable work); after all in the final decade of his life he himself turned to the internet as a space to distribute his own films, which were made on his own terms outside of studio interference during a period of criminal cultural neglect throughout the 1990s and up to 2011, during which time he was routinely unable to secure funding for mainstream distribution.

These later films, known as the 'Gorsewood Productions' (after the production company he set up, Gorsewood Films) or 'Garagiste' films (due to their DIY nature), were a conscious attempt to return to his amateur film-making roots using production technology (digital video/camcorder) which had been unavailable to him at the start of his career. Russell was an early advocate of the home camcorder since the 1980s and before (video playback was used in *Valentino*), even appearing as himself in the 1995 Channel 4 programme *I-Camcorder*, in which he set about filming a young couple's wedding.

This late body of films present a knowing and ironic self-commentary. If no studio was going to fund him to make films, then he would just do it himself! Their self-referentiality is in keeping with an increasingly self-reflective persona Russell developed in the last decade of his life, during which time he also took up a post as a columnist for the *Times*, reflecting over his life as a film-maker (archived press cuttings at the British Film Institute reveal that Russell made frequent use of the press to look back over his life between 2000 and 2011), and made a variety of knowing cameo roles in other people's film.

The Gorsewood films combined consciously amateur aesthetics and performances with new domestic digital recording technologies. They also constitute a return to the freedom of amateur film-making (and as Melia indicates later in this collection, provided a way of finally making previously unrealised films). They constitute a final attempt to regain control and are fiercely independent, made wholly on his own terms and, maybe for the first time in his career since his early amateur films, without interference. These films were self-funded and made use of shop-bought and home-made props and cast from across a circle of his close friends and family. In the short film *A Kitten for Hitler* (a 2007 film made for a wager with his old friend Melvyn Bragg, who said that Russell could not make a film so offensive even Russell would want it banned!) and *Boudica Bites Back* (A Gorsewood Production, 2009), his last completed film, Russell employed his long-time editor Michael Bradsell, connecting this late period of film-making with his earlier and more celebrated work. Russell also became an early (and uncredited) pioneer of the digital film movement and an early exponent of the Internet as a means of self-distribution with the following films: *Lion's Mouth* (A Gorsewood Production, 2000); *The Fall of the Louse of Usher* (Gorsewood

Films, 2002) – his last film to be given an official release; the *Hot Pants Trilogy* ('Revenge of the Elephant Man' [A Gorsewood Production, 2004]; 'The Mystery of Mata Hari' [A Gorsewood Production, 2004]; and 'The Goodship Venus' [A Gorsewood Production, 2006]); and *Boudica Bites Back*. In an interview on *The Directors* radio programme with film critic and heroic defender of Russell and his work, Mark Kermode, Russell stated:

> I think of myself as just about to be at the beginning of something new and something big, at the beginning of a new concept in programming. There's the Internet, there's the availability of equipment which now is so user friendly, and getting cheaper and cheaper and cheaper, that one can do marvels with, and which would cost a fortune in the normal terms of feature films. So, I feel like an old Christopher Columbus about to discover a new world.[38]

Jacqueline Maley noted how Russell had adapted to a new, more economical way of making and distributing films:

> The controversial film director Ken Russell has turned his back on the conventional movie business, launching a cottage industry in his back garden . . . He used a studio built from his garage and collaborated with friends and neighbours. 'I hope to distribute it through eBay or the internet or my own website,' he said . . . Russell said he was also working on a feature film, entitled *Bravetart Versus the Loch Ness Monster*, which was shot on video. 'I hope [it] will have massive distribution and will cost me £100,' he said.[39]

Influence

While the public recognition afforded contemporaries like Stanley Kubrick may have evaded Russell, there have been a host of younger directors ready to publicly claim his work as an influence and to publicly defend it – not least Guillermo del Toro (who has been outspoken in his defence of *The Devils* and the need for Warner Bros. to release the full cut), Anna Biller (whose film *The Love Witch* [Oscilloscope, 2017] consciously borrows the typeface and opening iconography of *The Lair of the White Worm* in its titles, Peter Strickland and Carol Morley.

Russell relocated for a period to the US at the end of the 1970s, moving away from artist biographies into 'genre cinema' with films like *Altered States* (Warner Bros., 1980) and *Crimes of Passion*. It was through his association with the video production company and distributor Vestron Video and its head of film acquisition Dan Ireland that Russell's reputation as a director of cult horror was consolidated with both *Gothic* and *The Lair of the White Worm*. Chris Wade notes his legacy in this field:

> Ken's influence is present whenever someone fuses sex and religion, from a Madonna live show (both the religious imagery she portrays in concert and specifically one particular backdrop for her song 'Get Together' was inspired by *Tommy*) to the asylum series of *American Horror Story*. And it's clearly there in the more chaotic work of Ben Wheatley, David Cronenberg, Guillermo del Toro and even the great Nicholas Roeg.[40]

Both Luca Guadagnino's *Suspiria* (Amazon Studios, 2018) and Gaspar Noé's *Climax* (Wild Bunch, 2018) bear the imprint of *The Devils* in their orgiastic and hysterical dance sequences. Noé's *Enter the Void* (Wild Bunch, 2009) might also be said to carry the legacy of *Altered States* in its psychotropic and 'vivid depictions of altered states of consciousness (most notably out of body experiences and the experience of dying)'.[41] In a 2019 interview, Noé revealed, with some hubris, that he had considered a remake of Russell's film:

> They sent me the script and I said, 'You know what? I loved *Altered States* when I was younger. I'd rather do a remake because there's scenes I really like in the movie. I can make the movie better than the original.' But at the same time, I was putting more of my own attention on *Enter the Void*. I told my producers who couldn't raise money for *Enter the Void* that I was probably going to do the remake of *Altered States*, and it triggered some financial stuff. 'We can get the money to do *Enter the Void*.'[42]

It is, however, the director Bernard Rose, who dedicated his Paganini biopic *The Devil's Violinist* (Arte, 2013) to Russell, whose work most evidently segues with Russell's own. At the time of writing, Rose is drip releasing a series of Russell-inspired short films via the social media site Vero. His gothic short *The Hurdy Gurdy Man* (Bernard Rose Productions, 2018) tracks the final days of the syphilitic composer Franz Schubert (about whom Russell had also earlier intended to make a film, according to Elize Russell, with the singer Rufus Wainwright in the lead role) as he is stalked by the figure of death in shape of the titular musician. A follow-up short, *Danse Profane* (Bernard Rose Productions, 2019), combines Claude Debussy's 1904 orchestral composition of the same title with a Busby Berkeley dance routine. In 2008 Rose wrote:

> François Truffaut once said that if you love a man's work, you love all of it. That's how I feel about Ken Russell. Of the British directors active in

the 1960s and 1970s who inspired me, Nic Roeg and Jim Henson were mentors in a very direct way (I worked for them), while Stanley Kubrick and Lindsay Anderson were remote, mythical figures. But Russell was my hero, the heir to Michael Powell's peculiarly emotional Englishness and vivid visual rhapsodies. And, sadly, a controversial figure more loved abroad than here.[43]

Rose's Beethoven film, *Immortal Beloved* (Columbia, 1995), is a truly Russellian exercise. It was not only based on Russell's own unmade film *The Beethoven Secret* (1981),[44] but also employed several of Russell's own production staff including cinematographer Peter Suschitzky and costume designer Leonard Pollack. The bravura sequence in which a young Beethoven floats face up in a pond looking up into the night sky, the stars' reflection in the water giving the appearance of the boy adrift in the cosmos as 'Ode to Joy' floods the scene, is pure Russell.

Perhaps, though, the person most responsible for this collective reawakening of awareness was Russell himself, who, even as ill health and old age crept up on him, tirelessly produced films and wrote screenplays and novels. He toured globally, attending film festivals with his wife Elize (who has been a tireless campaigner for the Russell legacy both before and since his passing), made television appearances, and worked with and taught young film students at both Southampton Solent University and the International Film School of Wales.

In the last decade of his life Russell made a series of knowing and self-aware appearances in a range of films by younger directors. He had habitually inserted himself in Hitchcock-style cameos in his own work since the 1960s (e.g. as a waving rambler in the background of a shot in *The Lair of the White Worm*). From the 1990s he increasingly took roles in other people's films (e.g. as Walter in Fred Schepisi's adaptation of John le Carré's *The Russia House* [MGM, 1990]); he also increasingly became front and centre in his own films (as the composer Arnold Bax in *The Secret Life of Arnold Bax* [ITV, 1992]), taking starring roles in his later Gorsewood productions – usually in an ironic 'mad scientist role' – such as Dr Calahari in *The Fall of the Louse of Usher* or as the cross-gendered Dr Lucy in his section ('The Girl with the Golden Breasts') of the horror compendium *Trapped Ashes* (Filmflex, 2006). Bernard Rose cast Russell in a cameo role in his adaptation of the Howard Marks autobiography *Mr. Nice* (Rose, 2010); he had a further cameo in the film *Colour Me Kubrick* (Brian W. Cook, Canal+, 2005); and in *Brothers of the Head* (Keith Fulton and Louis Pepe, Film4 Productions, 2006), an adaptation of Brian Aldiss's sci-fi horror novel, Russell plays a version himself in a complex documentary/drama meta-narrative which also plays to his own Frankenstein preoccupations.[45]

STRUCTURE OF THE BOOK

Part 1: Contextualising Ken Russell

In Chapter 1 Elize Russell opens her private journals, her diaries of a life lived with her husband Ken Russell. She presents both an intimate and personal reflection as well as providing historical background for understanding both man and director. Elize was a constant collaborator in the last decade and a half of his life (having first met him in the mid-1970s). Drawing upon personal conversations and private and public reminiscences, she chronicles how the circumstances and events of Russell's childhood came to have a direct bearing on his films and film-making method.

In Chapter 2 cultural historian Caroline Langhorst considers the issue of performed masculinities in his cinema. She focuses on the collaborative relationship between Russell and actor Oliver Reed, maybe the actor who is most associated with Russell's work. This is the first study to look in detail at the Reed–Russell relationship, offering a critical contextualisation of Russell's work as it emerges against the backdrop of the counterculture of the 1960s.

Matthew Melia discusses the many and varied approaches to representing the Gothic in Russell's work in Chapter 3. He explores how Russell allies the Gothic with modernist and postmodernist European (and American) artistic and cultural traditions. The chapter also necessarily takes into consideration a range of Russell's unmade films, including, for the first time, his collaboration with the producer Michael Nolin on the unmade scripts *Ten Times Poe / Horrible Beauty* in the early 1980s.

Part 2: Ken Russell and Television

In Chapter 4 television scholar Richard Farmer sets out a detailed and comprehensive analysis of Russell's advertising films and how they not only helped inform the aesthetic approach of the later television and theatrically released films, but also provided Russell with a production base of film workers with whom he would collborate across his career.

Art historian Paul Davies then turns to Russell's often overlooked BBC artist films in Chapter 5, considering how Russell frames and presents the work of his subjects within the diegesis of the films themselves. Focusing on these early film biographies and documentaries – including *Scottish Painters* (BBC, 1959), a film about the painters Roberts MacBryde and Colquhoun (the first of Russell's films to deal with queer subjects) – Davies explores Russell's evolving stylistic technique and approach to the form of biographical film-making, through the representation of art and the painters.

In Chapter 6 Jo George turns to Russell's immersion in the work of the nineteenth-century Pre-Raphaelite Brotherhood. The chapter takes a new approach to looking at Russell's engagement with the Pre-Raphaelites: not only does it examine the framing and presentation of the work, but also, through them, it considers how Russell's approach to the Brotherhood in *Old Battersea House* can be viewed against the backdrop of the evolving television documentary format and style as well as drawing stylistic comparisons with European modernism.

Part 3: Design, Staging and Stardom

In Chapter 7 NJ Stevenson focuses on the 1971 postmodern musical *The Boy Friend*. This is the first study to consider the role and contribution played by Russell's first wife, costume designer Shirley Russell (née Kingdon). Stevenson argues that *The Boy Friend* is a defining moment in the story of the interplay between nostalgia, film and fashion, and that their relationship was crucial in informing the idiosyncratic 'Russellian' visual style.

Brian Hoyle then turns to set design in Chapter 8, discussing the collaborative relationship between Russell and film-maker, artist, gardener and designer Derek Jarman. Through an examination of Jarman's sets for *Savage Messiah* as well as for *The Devils*, Hoyle argues that the two men were kindred spirits whose neo-baroque aesthetic flew in the face of the dominant British preference for realism and understatement. Hoyle offers an analysis of Jarman's own work, illustrating the formative influence working with Russell had on him.

Chapter 9 turns a critical eye on Ken Russell and sound design. Here K. A. Laity examines the 1975 rock opera *Tommy* and what she terms the 'hermeneutics of noise'. The chapter unpacks the layered or palimpsestic sound design of the film and the intersection of the sonic and the visual, considering how it contributes to the viewer's/listener's immersive aural experience of the film.

Jade Evans discusses the much-maligned 1978 biopic *Valentino* in Chapter 10. She examines Russell's textual and visual deconstruction of the Valentino star persona as both unreachable and mythological. The chapter discusses the ways in which the representation of Valentino in Russell's film contributes to the construction and our reading of his star image.

Part 4: Transgression and the Russell Legacy

In Chapter 11 writer, journalist and theatre/opera director Mateja Đedović offers a highly original comparative analysis between Russell and his contemporary, the similarly controversial and transgressive British TV dramatist and screenwriter Dennis Potter. The chapter explores cross-over in themes, motifs and filmic (and televisual) approaches. The chapter takes in a wide comparative range of their work, their statuses as 'gun for hire' directors, and their approaches to the process of cinematic and televisual adaptation and transgression.

In Chapter 12 Kevin Fullerton turns to a discussion of Russell's published novels – an area of his work that has gone unremarked upon in existing critical discussions. While the chapter initially offers a broad overview of Russell as a novelist, intertextually engaging with the earlier BBC films, it also examines how the novels engage thematically with the notions of the outsider artist and outsider/transgressive sexualities. Fullerton discusses how Russell was propelled to execute previously unmade ideas and films in other forms during a mature period dogged by lack of funding and financial backing.

In Chapter 13 journalist Sawako Omori, a writer for Japan's oldest film publication *Kinema Junpo*, offers a detailed and comprehensive 'short history' of how Russell was received by both critics and audiences in Japan between the 1960s and the 1990s, his legacy within Japanese film-making, and the legacy of the first major retrospective of Russell's work in the country in 1987.

Finally, Chapter 14 sees auteur scholar Adam Powell charts the legacy of Russell in the contemporary Danish director Nicolas Winding Refn. Offering a surprising comparison between Refn's 2008 film *Bronson* (Vertigo) and Russell's *Women in Love*, he proposes that both Refn and Russell approach biography, history and culture in distinct and overlapping ways: making use of a high camp visual style and combining music and image to provide narrative examinations of religion, art, fashion, media and cinema itself.

Part 5: A Word from the Editor . . .

If this book begins with Elize Russell's personal reflection on a life spent married to and collaborating with Ken Russell, then it ends in a similar reflective vein and in Chapter 6 Jo George considers Russell's documentary films in relation to Kenneth Clark's epic series *Civilisation* (BBC, 1969). One of the editors who worked on that series, Roger Crittenden, was also central to the production and editing of some of Russell's major work for the BBC. In Chapter 15 he recalls in detail his work on *Delius: Song of Summer* and his work with Russell in editing the film, offering valuable first-hand insight into Russell's approach to editing and to cutting and framing.

NOTES

1. BBC Written Archives Centre, Radio Times Material, 14 January 1962, *The Lonely Shore* production file, 'Ken Russell of Monitor' (Communication from Humphrey Burton to Dennis Dick), T32/1016.
2. *The Boy Friend*, BFI Press Cuttings, Reuben Library, British Film Institute, London.

3. Julian Holland, 'Striking Again Tonight . . . The Wild Man of the BBC', *Daily Mail*, 29 June 1965, BFI Press Cuttings. This is the first recorded reference to Russell using this term.
4. Documentaries whose scope and cinematic ambition challenged the limited frame and dimensions of the medium of post-war television.
5. *Big Brother*, Channel 4, 2007, available on *YouTube*, <https://www.youtube.com/watch?v=jW-t3LzZZd8> (last accessed 22 February 2022).
6. Alexander Walker, 'Review of *The Devils*', *Evening Standard*, 22 July 1971, Press archive, British Film Institute.
7. The 'Trip' sequences in his science fiction/horror film *Altered States* (Warner Bros., 1980) are as powerful and immediate (perhaps more so) even than Dave Bowman's (Keir Dullea) journey through the Starfield in Stanley Kubrick's *2001: A Space Odyssey* (1968).
8. 'the daughters of music'.
9. Russell would later return to Elgar's story with the unmade script for a feature film, *Elgar: Land of Hope and Glory* (British Film Institute Archive, 1986, SCR-20506).
10. Anthony Burgess, 'Reflections on a Golden Ring', *The Listener* (London), Thursday, 28 December 1967, issue 2022, 838.
11. Nigel Gosling, 'Trampling on Our Traditions', *Observer*, 9 October 1977.
12. John Baxter, *Ken Russell: An Appalling Talent* (London: Michael Joseph, 1973), 131.
13. Jonathan Meades, *An Encyclopaedia of Myself* (London: Fourth Estate, 2015), 57.
14. Ken Russell, *Fire Over England: The British Cinema Comes Under Friendly Fire* (London: Hutchinson, 1993), 1.
15. Anderson in fact had enjoyed the critically privileged status of auteur since the 1950s and his association with the Free Cinema movement, during which time Ken Russell was emerging out of the shadows of amateur film making.
16. Brian Hoyle, 'In Defence of the Amateur', in Kevin M. Flanagan (ed.), *Ken Russell: Re-Viewing England's Last Mannerist* (Plymouth: Scarecrow Press, 2009), 40–65.
17. Sue Harper and Justin Smith, *British Film Culture in the 1970s: The Boundaries of Pleasure* (Edinburgh: Edinburgh University Press), 211.
18. Russell, 8.
19. Harper and Smith, 219.
20. Ibid.
21. Gosling.
22. Flanagan (ed.).
23. At the finale of *Altered States*, during the final and almost total regression of Dr Eddie Jessup (William Hurt) to an amorphous state of primordial being, bodily prosthetics are used to transform Jessup into something closely resembling Bacon's dissolving bodies.
24. David Massengill, Facebook, 4 July 2021, <https://www.facebook.com/photo?fbid=10222330130216924&set=a.1716635070501> (last accessed 24 May 2022).
25. The ideological ground here has shifted in the twenty-first century from conservative right to liberal left as critics of 'permissiveness'.
26. BBC Written Archives Centre, Minutes of General Advisory Board Meeting, 27 April 1970; Memo from David Attenborough, 28 January 1970, *Dance of the Seven Veils* file, TX 70/02/15.
27. Saturday, 29 February 2020, Theatre by the Lake, Keswick, UK. The original BBC broadcast was on 15 February 1970.
28. Ken Hanke, *Ken Russell's Films* (Metuchen, NJ: Scarecrow Press, 1984); Baxter; Joseph A. Gomez, *Ken Russell: The Adaptor as Creator* (London: Frederick Muller, 1976).
29. *Journal of British Cinema and Television*, vol. 12, no. 4, October 2015.
30. Ibid.

31. Matthew Melia, 'Ken Russell's Unfinished Projects and Unmade Films, 1956–68: The BBC Years', in James Fenwick, Kieran Foster and David Eldridge (eds), *Shadow Cinema: The Historical and Production Contexts of Unmade Films* (New York: Bloomsbury Academic, 2021), 91–109.
32. Shirley was Russell's first wife and the costume designer for his films during the first half of his career. Their collaboration is the subject of NJ Stevenson's chapter in this collection.
33. Christophe Van Eecke, *Pandemonium: Ken Russell's Artist Biographies as Baroque Performance*, Maastricht University, 2015, <https://www.academia.edu/28985516/Pandaemonium_Ken_Russells_Artist_Biographies_as_Baroque_Performance> (last accessed 6 November 2021); Chris Wade, *Ken Russell: On Screen* (Leeds: Wisdom Twin Books, 2015); Joseph Lanza, *Phallic Frenzy: Ken Russell and His Films* (London: Aurum Books, 2008); Paul Sutton, *Talking About Ken Russell* (Cambridge: Buffalo Books, 2015).
34. Ken Russell, 'Can It Really Be Me Who Lived That Life?', *Times*, 3 June 2008, <https://www.thetimes.co.uk/article/can-it-really-be-me-who-lived-that-life-ftsx82pszgg> (last accessed 22 February 2022).
35. Linda Ruth Williams, 'Bad Sex and Obscene Undertakings: Ken Russell's Women in Love', Journal of Adaptation in Film & Performance, vol. 6, no. 3, 2013, 341–54.
36. Richard Crouse, *Raising Hell: Ken Russell and the Unmaking of The Devils* (Toronto: ECW Press, 2012); Darren Arnold, *The Devils* (Leighton Buzzard: Auteur/Devil's Advocates Series, 2019); Kit Power, *Tommy* (Hornsea: PS Publishing/Midnight Monographs, 2019); Matthew Melia, *Gothic* (Liverpool: Liverpool University Press/Auteur/Devil's Advocates Series, forthcoming 2023).
37. The then seventy-nine-year-old Russell quit the show in a principled stand against the racist abuse of another cast member.
38. BBC Radio 2, 30 November 2000.
39. Jacqueline Maley, 'The Future of Films Is on the Net, Claims Ken Russell', *Guardian*, 28 January 2006, <https://www.theguardian.com/uk/2006/jan/28/digitalmedia.film> (last accessed 6 November 2021).
40. Wade, 168.
41. Jon Lindblom, 'Beyond the Myth of Experience, Part 2: Deviant Phenomenal Models in Gaspar Noé's *Enter the Void*', *Modernism Unbound*, 5 November 2018, <https://modernismunbound.com/essays/beyond-the-myth-of-experience-part-2-deviant-phenomenal-models-in-gaspar-noes-enter-the-void/> (last accessed 22 February 2022).
42. Larry Fitzmaurice, 'Gaspar Noé on his psychedelic horror trip, *Climax*', *Fader*, 20 March 2019, <https://www.thefader.com/2019/03/20/gaspar-no-on-his-psychedelic-horror-trip-climax> (last accessed 4 June 2022).
43. Bernard Rose, 'Hi Ken, Sorry I Stole Your Movie', *Guardian*, 15 September 2008, <https://www.theguardian.com/film/2008/sep/15/biography> (last accessed 6 October 2021).
44. Ibid.
45. Matthew Melia, 'Ken Russell, the Gothic and *Brothers of the Head*', *ArtTVFilm*, 7 October 2021, <https://arttvfilm.wordpress.com/2021/10/07/ken-russell-the-gothic-and-brothers-of-the-head-fulton-and-pepe-2005/> (last accessed 22 February 2022).

PART I

Contextualising Ken Russell

CHAPTER 1

Ken Russell: The Boy behind the Man

Elize Russell

INTRODUCTION

I lived with film-maker Ken Russell for twelve years and we were married for ten, until his death in 2011. We met by correspondence during his filming *Dance of the Seven Veils* (BBC, 1970), exchanging a few letters with one another about scriptwriting. This led to an unexpected meeting in 1975, when he appeared at my door at 9 a.m., this beaming chrysanthemum of a man, bearing tickets to the *Tommy* premier (1975). I missed it, but he subsequently cast me in *Lisztomania* (Goodtimes Enterprises, 1975). My mother refused to allow it. 'Over my dead body,' she said. Ken's first statement to me when we re-met over the phone in 1999 was, 'Is your mother dead yet?'[1] As it happened, she was.

We are all aware of the reputation of Ken as 'l'enfant terrible', of someone who wove wildly interpretative fantasy interludes and dramatic scenes of alternately passionate and subtle conflicts into his films. Because most of his films include an element of baroque, extravagance or buffoonery, they were not considered a source for historical accuracy or textbook directing, even by him, though he could identify historical references for each questioned image (the kites and tea trays in *Elgar* [BBC, 1962]; the human blackbirds in *The Devils* [Warner Bros., 1971]; the issue of Nazi collusion in *Dance of the Seven Veils*). Ken created by imagining his way through a subject, using daydream, technical agility, painstakingly detailed research and an innate sensibility. He invented a visually rich, unexpectedly charming and precise structural edifice and storytelling arc on which to hang the practical and emotional dilemmas of his films' central characters: flawed individuals with whom he felt a kinship. Ken wanted to use images and movement to provide impressionistic glimpses into a higher truth, the place where inspiration breaks through convention and speaks straight from its archetypal source.

Ken integrated the two opposing urges, logos and eros, into an expressive and mutually supportive style. One can hardly tease apart the place where music meets action, fantasy meets biography in his films, like gold leaf exaggerating the message. One doesn't just see a Ken Russell film; one surrenders to it. The proliferation of imagery, the welding of high and low art, the heightened emotional atmosphere are designed to engender in a viewer a corresponding emotional experience, whether positive or negative. He was bold and fearless. He extracted an emotional truth from a stimulating array of complicated relationships. Ken was acutely aware of emotional weather.

He never intended to shock. When the public or critics reacted with shock, he could defend himself vigorously. 'I believe in what I'm doing wholeheartedly, passionately . . . I suppose such a thing could be annoying to some people.'[2] He wanted to engender a visceral response. To keep people awake. When Ken joined the creative team of the seminal BBC Arts television program *Monitor* in 1958 and was able to share his first biographical documentary films with a wider audience, he said the impetus for establishing the unanticipated, dramatic 'opening sequence' (which became a signature mark of Ken's, along with his surprise endings) was not to dazzle the audience, but to keep his father from changing the channel after the first minute.[3] He was making films for the slightly weary househusband in Southampton as well as for the intellects and creatives. He was making films for his mother, and for all women who used bitter wisecracks or silent suffering to keep their stiff upper lips in place, in circumstances of emotional deprivation. For someone who was intuitive and increasingly self-educated, he was both interactive with the milieu of his times and individualistically idiosyncratic. He followed his dreams through a circuitous and unpredictable route, as people without funds often do. It's that touch of serendipity that seems to have affected his life over and over that bled into his films. One feels that things are possible after seeing a Ken Russell film. It's a bravura performance and reaches into both the lowbrow and highbrow aspects of culture and the social fabric.

CHILDHOOD AND BACKGROUND

Ken came from a typically conservative lower-middle-class household in suburban Southampton, Hampshire. His father was a shoe merchant with a canny and successful interest-making loan business on the side. ('He preferred to call himself a "footwear retailer,"' Ken laughed ruefully.[4]) His mother was a housewife who had trimmed hats before her marriage; there was a maid, as was customary in aspirational families; always a dog. Not much religion except in the most obligatory way: memorised hymns, the Ten Commandments, Sunday dinners. He loved his parents and family but entertained no illusions about

Figure 1.1 The young Ken Russell with his mother, Ethel.
Photo: held by Elize Russell.

their sharing his own childlike obsessions with adventure, heroism, danger and romance. During World War II, safety and propriety would have been preoccupations for the less well-off couples whose responsibilities were to Queen, parents and children. The elder son of two by several years, he lived primarily a solitary life as a young child. Culturally, he was not exposed to higher art. He was his mother's constant companion to the movies, outings that were routinely followed at the arcade by 'a pot of tea with two cups and a plate of iced fancies'; or 'a stroll through Tyrell's to the tea dances'.[5] Yet his fertile imagination and curiosity knew no bounds. I daresay that's a recognisable component of almost anyone's childhood, given enough reliable security and freedom to daydream. Ken was artistic. He was likely an undiagnosed synaesthetic, for whom picture and sound were amplified and inseparably linked. He was sensitive. 'I'm like Roddy in the *House of Usher*, reacting to every stimulus in a heightened way and terrified of death,' he told me in that first phone call in 1999. 'I can hear the sound the sugar makes falling into a cup of tea from two rooms away.'[6]

When he heard a sound, he experienced it visually as a path to follow intently. Sound would bring a story to him, image after image. Later he would claim to me that his pen wrote his work, not himself. He said:

> Having extrasensory referencing gives me an insight into other people that they may not have themselves. I seem to register everything, sensorily and on several levels. I'm a truth-detector. Of course, people are

likely to disagree with my perceptions, which is natural, and I'm just as liable to change my opinions. People grow, and I'm no exception. But I'm resourceful and steadfast.[7]

Those are qualities that were particularly crucial to develop in the war years, and as actress Glenda Jackson has said, 'Ken has a third eye.'[8] Essential to understanding Ken's work is that World War II and the subsequent Southampton Blitz of 1940 changed Ken's life when he was twelve. A munitions factory down the road made his neighbourhood particularly vulnerable. The Luftwaffe made 57 attacks on the city; 1,500 air raid warnings sounded; 30,000 incendiary devices were dropped; and 45,000 buildings damaged. The water supply was ruined and fires were left to burn themselves out. Bombing raids continued there till 1942.[9]

The conker tree in the back garden became his refuge and stage set and had been from an early age. His favourite book, he said once, was Italo Calvino's *The Baron in the Trees* (1957). Ken related to the tale of a child who refused to eat snail soup and so disappeared into the branches with a vow never to come down. 'When I was a child I spent many happy hours at the bottom of the garden up in our conker tree – a galleon if I'd just read *Treasure Island*, or a medieval castle if I'd just read *Robin Hood*.'[10]

His personal war was in yearning for approval from his father, a ship's detective and fire warden, whose constantly expressed disappointment in young Ken registered keenly in such a sensitive child. He repeated many times the horror of his father's having flung a freshly caught live eel at his feet in the car, his screaming in reaction, and his father angrily labelling him a coward.[11] The other incident he would relate for my amusement and to make me squirm was his being terrorised by the king ragworm with which his father expected Ken to bait the fishing hooks on the family boat. The sight of the huge worm wriggling, with its mouth opening on a ferocious set of daggerish teeth, and his father screaming at him that he was to pierce its body with the hook, made its way into his psyche.[12] Grotesque and repulsive vampiric teeth sinking into unsuspecting (innocent) skin were highlighted most obviously in *The Lair of the White Worm* (Vestron, 1988), his sequence, *Girl with the Golden Breasts*, from the portmanteau film *Trapped Ashes* (Independent Film Fund, Cinema Investment, 2006), where nipples are toothy lamprey eels, *Gothic* (Virgin Vision, 1986) and *Lisztomania* (Goodtimes Enterprises, 1975).

Worse perhaps than his father's tests of steeling him to be a man was his mother's telling him she had wanted a daughter, having miscarried a girl-child before his birth. He was born on the kitchen table, as was customary in those days of 1927, at 12.15 in the morning; and he was expected to soothe his mother's frustration with an inattentive husband and longed-for and lost baby. He was compliant. Except when he wasn't. How often did I hear Ken's first cousin

June, a year younger, who lived so close by as to qualify more as a sister, reiterate the old complaint, 'You pushed me into the roaring fire when I was three!' Like a call-and-response, Ken would answer without shame, 'I only wanted to see what would happen.'[13] Curiosity was justification enough for a four-year-old, he insisted. And it is. But the expectations of his parents were made very clear indeed. 'Ken is 90 per cent good and 10 per cent very bad,' his mother would reiterate, like a mantra; and Ken would repeat it to me throughout our marriage, relishing the label. And so, I found him so.

The part of Ken that was pure mischief was not intended maliciously, nor with a target in mind, but was an irresistible impulse to provide the excitement he felt in the privacy of his enthusiasms. For all his habitual routines at home, the 6 a.m. to 12 p.m. rituals, making movies, answering letters, writing scripts, studying books, walking, cooking, watching a movie, tea, tea, tea; it was all for movies. 'I tried to break into movies as a teaboy. I knew no one; they wouldn't have me.'[14]

The movies gave him his first food. 'I was eaten up with the image,' Ken would say as an adult, explaining his history and film technique. Ken and his mother went to the many picture palaces of Southampton, especially the Broadway in Portswood, every day. She had to promise first, though, that it wouldn't be a love story. 'It's not love, Mum; is it?' 'No, Ken; it's not love,' she would swear; and little Ken would pipe up, outraged, tears in his eyes, after the first giant embrace onscreen, 'You said it wouldn't be love, Mum!'[15] Ken's ambivalence about love was something he outgrew. But you can see it in his films. In the scripts he was attracted to or wrote, in portraying romantic moments and alliances or lofty goals, the stories were intentionally punctuated by reality, with the haphazard messiness and fleshliness of life and congress intruding into ideas of perfect bliss. Ken held a mirror to traditional notions of perfection and beauty, which much of his artistic nature could be said to share ('pattern, form and texture', he called it, mimicking his lessons at Walthamstow Technical/Arts College); and the mirror would inevitably and intentionally be a little cracked or distorting and the reflection fraught. See, for example, the honeymoon scene in *The Music Lovers* (United Artists, 1970), the hallucinatory sex in *Gothic*, the Gudrun–Gerald and Hermione–Rupert mix of repulsion, savagery and passionate desire in *Women in Love* (United Artists, 1969). Life could be savage as well as pure, and sometimes the juxtaposition of the two created satire, something he imbibed as a youth at the movies from Chaplin, the Marx Brothers, Felix the Cat and Betty Boop. (He started a script on Betty Boop in 2007.[16]) He lapped up the Busby Berkeley musicals like *42nd Street* (given tribute in *The Boy Friend* (MGM-EMI, 1971).

Sex was an ecstatic part of life, suggested on the movie screen by Hedy Lamarr and Dorothy Lamour. Any mention of sex was suppressed at his childhood home, however. Ken recalls that a certain provocative relative was whispered about, with accompanying sorrowful looks, as having (sotto voce): 'glands'.[17] The family dog, Fido Rum-Eared, was a randy sort who made vigorous attempts to help himself to any visitor's lap, his mother pretending that it was not happening. Ken's mother 'broke his father's heart', Ken said, by moving to another bedroom to avoid his father's snoring.

It was impressed upon young Ken that it was forbidden to sit upon a divan, like the one at a café he and his mum visited (once). 'You don't know if someone's been *reclining* on that,'[18] she frowned, conjuring lurid seductions by her tone of voice. *Salome's Last Dance* (Vestron, 1988), *Gothic* and *Variations on a Mechanical Theme* (BBC, 1959) took delight in sexual innuendo from overstuffed furniture with tales to tell. In *The Boy Friend*, Tony (Christopher Gable) and Polly (Twiggy) find imaginary wedded bliss in two giant overstuffed chairs.

PROFESSIONAL CAREER

> I'm not sex mad. I'm just not afraid to include it on screen, or its undercurrent. It's an essential element of people's drive. I was kept so in the dark about sex as a youngster that when a kind gentleman named Herbert repeatedly came on to me, after ballet school, saying 'I won't touch you if you don't touch me,' it never occurred to me it might be an invitation.[19]

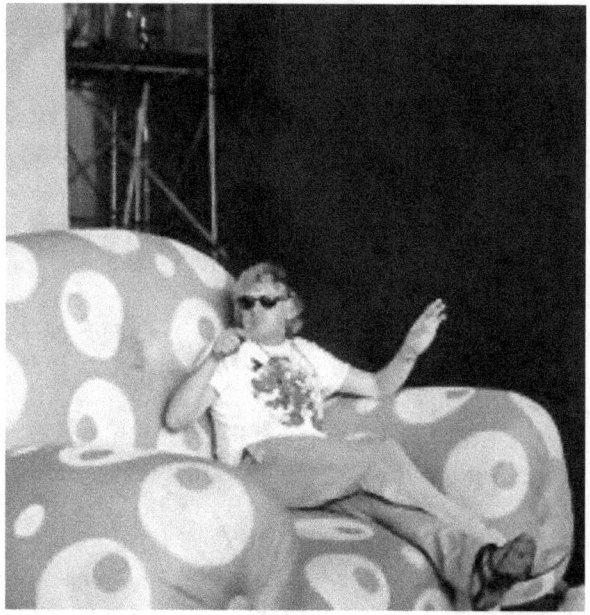

Figure 1.2 Ken Russell on the set of *The Boy Friend*.
Photo: held by Elize Russell.

Ken began his professional career making dense, delicate and emotionally rich and buoyant films, beginning with the one that got him noticed, *Amelia and the Angel* (BFI Experimental Film Fund, 1958). He believed that to be human is to entertain angels but not be able to fix them in place to do one's bidding, that the crude and unredeemable aspects of living were due their acknowledgement. 'All we really want, as humans,' he pondered aloud to me once, 'is to have sex with angels.'[20] (He was speaking metaphorically, not literally.) That was the alchemical task of an artist, in Ken's opinion: to give birth to some spark of greatness in oneself or to inspire it in others (as he had been inspired by classical music, painting and dance) out of the cauldron of the primal substance, the earth, air, fire and water; the blood and belligerence, the sweetness and simplicity, the reversals and paradoxes, the failures of moral courage in self and others and the dedicated mastering of one's calling, whether the route was pretty or not. He was catalyst, with a substantial reservoir of energy at hand. Ken had a commitment to participating fully and to completion.

All the great artists and composers whose works he admired, portrayed and respected were at their worst locked in a struggle with their own birth pangs or desire to create a perfect and ultimately harmonious or moving expression of the complexity of their perception and vision. The art, the vision was all; the universe enfolded in it. 'Mahler and Elgar are the two whose inner lives are most like mine,' he'd say.[21]

To live with him was to listen to classical music, and he certainly resembled living with Henri Gaudier-Brzeska (Scott Anthony) as portrayed in *Savage Messiah* (MGM-EMI, 1972). Ken was always racing ahead physically to catch the future on the trail of his singular, boisterous dream. Ken would run outside to address the thunder as his father, and like Gaudier-Brzeska, 'the Louvre, mother.' In portraying the lives of his heroic composers, poets and painters he can be seen to be a romantic idealist with the eye of a realist. His films went from moments of enchanted grace to instances of comic absurdity, for instance in *Dante's Inferno* (BBC, 1967) with its bone dust, *Dance of the Seven Veils'* cakewalks, *Diary of a Nobody* (BBC, 1964) and Lupin's (Murray Melvin) tumble downstairs into blancmange, *The Boy Friend* and *The Preservation Man* (BBC, 1962).

Ken had antennae for the tragic nuance, as well. The tragic in his films always concluded with an element of redemptive grace. To him both perspectives, light and dark, were important to explore. A life included the whole of human experience, as lived with a powerful emotional body, with its disillusionments, arguments, separations, betrayals and ultimately, its alignments, epiphanies, ecstasies and redemptive trajectory. *Salome's Last Dance*, *Lisztomania*, *Crimes of Passion* (New World Pictures, 1984), *Valentino* (United Artists, 1977) and *Whore* (Trimark Pictures, 1991) were perhaps his most cynical depictions of mating, but they too are not without their own sequences of tenderness, vulnerability and transcendence.

Ken was astonishingly ahead of his time in casting people with disabilities (in *Tommy* [Columbia, 1975] and in *Salome's Last Dance*, where lead actress Imogen Millais-Scott went blind three weeks before shooting due to glandular fever) and in treating them equitably. As a boy he was acutely aware of the veterans returning broken from World War II, as shown vividly in his *Elgar* and *Composer on a Bicycle* (ITV, 2002). He was rattled by British comedian Benny Hill's father's shop (on the same street as his own father's), where artificial limbs hung from the ceiling. (He never spoke to Benny Hill, a boy three years older; Ken was too shy.[22]) And he was haunted by the phrase, oft repeated by his mum, that his uncle 'never got a chance to take his boots off for the last six months of the War'.[23]

His anger, perhaps, he saved for the plots of *The Devils* in 1971 (adapted from Aldous Huxley's historical novel *The Devils* and from John Whiting's play of the same name) and *Dance of the Seven Veils*. Ken could be even-tempered and focused, calming everyone. He needed concentration to approximate his next vision on film. He could also explode when unable to communicate what he wanted, or from stress. So did his films explode at times, as in *The Music Lovers* when Tchaikovsky's (Richard Chamberlain) brother Modeste (Ken Colley) fires the cannon that takes the heads off the soul-sucking others who keep Modeste from profiting off his brother's work. The righteous indignation Ken felt on behalf of his beloved Catholic Church, which he joined as a young adult, surfaced in *The Devils*. It had promised and delivered much in the form of the perfect Mother Mary, a belief he sustained. It was She who provided the 'major minor miracles',[24] as Ken called them. But the dark side in the Church's history, even the Church increasingly could not deny. He once said, 'I want to meet the Pope. I think he'd understand me.'[25] He hired Simon Boswell for his last commissioned film, *Alice in Wonderland: The Musical* (2011) and was delighted to find Boswell had composed for the Pope.[26] Ken also engaged Sean Lennon for the project.

The Church was not Ken's main target in *The Devils*, since he was a believer, who had occasional consultations with monks; his anger was, as has been stated so often, against the misuse of power: 'A film about blasphemy is not blasphemy.'[27] Ken was a social justice warrior with a sharp distaste for political machinations, manipulation, misuse of power and snobbery. His father had looked down on his mum, Ken said, for no reason. Ken was willing to accept, along with Blake and Wordsworth, that innocence might be reborn as enlightened experience; but he was not going to accept the sanctioning of evil under the façade of expediency or the spell of greed. Here we can see the child who discerns very clearly the truth of a situation shorn of its embellishments, the face (or farce) under social convention. He might play along, but only so far.

WAR

Sir Oswald Mosley's symmetrical costumes dazzled me as a boy, but I was ultimately loyal to the values of the tales of King Arthur and his knights, and the atmosphere of fighting for a noble cause and the sanctity of family – the values of the War.[28]

Ken had a chance to illustrate his anger at the Holocaust amid the hypocrisies of religion and fascism, most pointedly in *Mahler* (Goodtimes Enterprises, 1974), *Dance of the Seven Veils* and *Lisztomania*. Ken insisted World War II did not traumatise him. He was young and took it as normal, he said; as something to adapt to.[29] He carefully described the eerie whistling sounds of the bombs dropping, which went silent for a moment before they landed in the garden, and the house next door disappearing in a blaze. He did not remember being frightened, but he may have been disassociating to a degree; it's a survival mechanism:

> I was scared of the naked plucked chicken I saw in the big reveal in *Monster of the Loch* playing at the Variety. I jumped up and ran all the way home, leaving my coat behind. The heroic diver who discovered the Monster under the flowerpot looked exactly like my little underwater diver toy that I played with in the bathtub. I know it's said it's an iguana, but to me it was an enormous fleshy, grotesque plucked chicken, haltingly walking and pecking its way to its human meal underwater! And now I preserve it intact as one of my Monsters of the Id . . . The other horrific for me was Mr Brain next door. He was probably a nice older man who didn't get out much, but because he had that name, I would go out of my way to avoid his front steps. I was traumatised by the gas mask I discovered by accident in the hall closet. All rubbery and goggley-eyed and warped, like a giant malevolent creature or squid, alive and meaning me harm.[30]

He swore he was not frightened by his father's being gone at all hours to put out fires, nor by he and his mother getting into the Morrison cage when the sirens blasted:

> My dad was also a ship's detective and was the last person off the *Titanic* at its stop on the Isle of Wight, before it launched into the ocean. I trusted he'd be back. My mum and her sister, June's mum, reassured me enough. I remember the relief, not the interim uncertainty.[31]

The best depiction of Ken's life as a war child would be in the prologue of his film *Tommy*, with the frightened parents, the shattered houses, the fallen child, the half-naked women in gas masks, one astonishingly confronting the camera; the Morrison cage Tommy's mother takes shelter in, the broken glass on the photo frame synchronising with bad news for her pilot husband. Young Ken, like Tommy, liked to get dizzy on carnival rides. The romantic dances in the Brighton Pier ballroom were very like Ken's description of the tea dances he'd attend with his mum.

Ken's mother wasn't with him when a Scoutmaster fondled him in the movie theatre while he watched one of his favourite films, Disney's *Pinocchio* (1940). Though he joked about it as an adult, it also disturbed him and sent him running out of the cinema.[32] Perhaps Boy Scout Kevin had to die a prolonged and bloody death in *The Lair of the White Worm* to even that score, or Uncle Ernie had to feel his own guilt in *Tommy*. Ken described it with the benefit of hindsight: 'I didn't understand what was happening to me, but the part of the movie I saw was brilliant.'

Young Ken was sent away at one point on the train, with his home address tagged to his coat, leaving behind his mum, dad and little brother. It had become too dangerous for an active child in Southampton. Kind strangers in Bournemouth were opening their homes to extra children. Ken said he got there and started screaming: 'They were nice people, but I didn't know them. I opened my mouth and screamed so loud and so long, they sent me back. I never apologised. I was content. I was back home.'[33]

I speculate that Ken's intermittent roar while filming as a grown-up is the same one he exploded with as a youngster scared of being left among strangers, while his loved ones were in danger miles away. In his roar, you could hear bombs shattering the sky, planes diving and the pavement breaking apart. He tried to explain his always unexpected explosions of anger:

> It's always when I think I've made a mistake, not someone else. I get frightened, that I won't be able to realise my vision or communicate what I want. An instant rush of adrenalin envelopes my brain with a red curtain – a red cloud. It drops and smothers all rational thought. I experience myself as though Erich Von Stroheim or my Mariinsky ballet master Konstantin Sergeyev were barking at me. I only know that my life is in utter peril and I must yell, must defend myself, to keep imagined predators from killing me. The red recedes in a minute and I hardly remember what I've said. It's always been that way. I had a lot of yelling and ridicule aimed at me in my life – certainly at Pangbourne Naval College, and in the Merchant Navy. I'm no good at fighting; I can yell, and I'm fighting my own mistakes. To have made a mistake can ruin things I have hopes of achieving. I let go my anger relatively quickly. I know it's wrong, and people get frightened or cross or run away. Anger is catching. Dick Bush (director of photography) had a ritual of always

quitting on each film he worked on for me and then coming back after a few days. When I'm momentarily beyond control, I'm fighting for my life and for my work (which is the same thing to me). I'm expressing how important it is for me to be in control of my material and the map in my head (and on paper). I have painstakingly built the whole picture over months of listening to music and locating the corresponding exact image that my imagination delivers to me. I am as surprised as the other person or people are at the force of my voice in those instances. Have you seen the film *The Shout*?[34]

RITUAL, MADNESS AND THE SUPERNATURAL

Ken had incredible projection and vocal strength. He used it to our advantage or for my amusement when he decided to banish the ghost in our sixteenth-century cottage and stood at the top of the stairs naked. ('That will get rid of it,' he said.[35]) He let loose his mighty bellow in the direction of the wraith who had reportedly haunted the house since its purchase. The cottage was an old Presbyterian meeting house, and any ghosts that appeared or grabbed the blankets, I was confident I could handle, but Ken was determined to protect me. He roared. I am certain that the ghost departed.

Ken was conscious of and wary of ghosts as a child, and his fascination with the supernatural was most perfectly realised in scripts that others wrote for him, Stephen Volk's *Gothic* and Paddy Chayefsky's *Altered States* (Warner Bros., 1980). He choreographed and filmed a ballet of Charlotte Brontë and her haunted life, with Jane Eyre's Mr Rochester portraying a dual role as the Spectre of Death.[36] In 1978 he wrote a script for *Dracula* and after years of failed attempts to finance it, made further inroads by casting it anew in Toronto in 2010. (It never came to fruition.) Having painted the Poe stories as a twelve-year-old, Ken wrote his amalgam of Poe stories, enlisting our dog to play the part of The Black Cat (not in costume, as the dog was not sympathetic to dressing up), and made a pilgrimage to Poe's house in Philadelphia in 2002. (*The Debussy Film* [BBC, 1965] and *The Fall of the Louse of Usher* [A Gorsewood Production, 2002] honoured Poe.)

He was fascinated by the imagery of shamanic ritual and the witches in nearby Burley, whom he interviewed for the *Times* under promise of keeping them anonymous.[37] Ken would absorb his research into art books, museums, magicians of the Victorian age, composers; and then for his films invent his own imagery out of his imagination. 'It's my impression of a subject; how I see it.' He used his fascination most overtly in *The Debussy Film*, *Louse of Usher*, *Aria* (Egyptian healing and Book of the Dead rituals [Virgin Vision, 1987]), the séance in *Gothic*, *Bravetart* (an unfinished film about Aleister Crowley being bested by a scrappy female Scottish punk-rocker [A Gorsewood Production, 2008])[38] and in his last finished film, the mini-opera *Boudica Bites Back* (A Gorsewood Production, 2009), in which the Celtic folk tribes of the pre-British Isles worship Astarte.

Like a child, Ken's respect for magic meant he had no desire to try it out himself. He could portray it in a film, and have it be messy, precisely choreographed, frightening, transcendent, ineffectual or humorous, without tempting any darkness. 'Satan's boy I could never be!' was a line he invariably bellowed uninhibitedly, in concert with Oliver Reed as Father Grandier, when the line arrived on-screen during *The Devils* in a cinema. He enjoyed the audience's surprise, and in later screenings would enlist people to do it en masse and sing along with 'The D'Ampton Worm' song in *The Lair of the White Worm*. But Ken did not experiment with any dark arts. Maybe inadvertently: when Alexander Walker died, the critic who had slammed *The Devils* (reporting there were 'crushed testicles in the film' when there aren't), Ken came to me with a downcast face. 'I killed him,' Ken confessed. 'I thought him to death. It took me forty years.'[39]

As an adult Ken fondly remembered the terrors of the haunted house on the boardwalk, with its bowls of grapes becoming eyeballs in the dark, and its hall of mirrors (as in *Tommy*). Everything was magic. His bike speeding downhill in the Commons near St Mary's was a flying plane. The smoke that enveloped him from the steam engines at the train station at St Denys was a transformative mist, a benevolent and liminal dragon's breath. He could not adequately explain the world or himself to his parents. 'I can't tell you, I have to show you.' I think it's highly possible he would have been diagnosed with ADD in a contemporary world. (A young Ken tried to be clever and market himself as 'Young aesthete suffering from ennui' in a newspaper ad for work.[40] 'Send him down the mines!'[41] came the published reply. And to film *The Miners' Picnic* [BBC, 1960] and *Women in Love*, that's exactly where he went, befriending the miners and trying out drilling.)

As an adult, Ken submitted to analysis several times, as performance. He did *Russell on the Couch* (radio) for the BBC and a BBC TV documentary, *Southern Visions*,[42] took him through the rooms of his childhood Southampton house to trigger memories. It ended comically with my mock psychoanalysis of him in a hammock in the garden in East Boldre, with Ken pratfalling out of the sling to avoid answering questions. (I have never seen this film, only the shoot; it may not have aired.) Ken enjoyed acting in the promo for a season of his films on Channel 4, with actor Rusty Goffe dressing up in a moulded latex Ken-head to re-enact costumed characters of Russell films, each wearing Ken's face. 'I went privately to a psychiatrist, once,' he told me. 'He said I was the most mentally healthy patient he'd ever had, and it would do no good to see me further.'[43] It was certainly an expedient solution to the task of probing the

Neptunian psyche of Ken Russell. When his back went into spasm, he claimed it was a kiss from the pretty physiotherapist that cured him; just as in his film *The Strange Affliction of Anton Bruckner* (London Weekend Television, 1990).

Madness in others fascinated him, but Ken himself did not seek to derange his senses, pared back drinking with time, and was not keen to get involved with fans he believed might be unbalanced (a subjective opinion, to be sure, but I remember how frightened he was of a woman who wrote that she slept with a stuffed leopard, had a million dollars and naked photos of herself). His parents were not drinkers, and he was not tempted as a youth. His detour as a young adult into snuff, originally attracted by the tin boxes, was relieved by one particularly fervent prayer to Mother Mary, while riding a bus. Ken had his own imagination to wrestle with; his own dreams to decipher; no extras required. 'Every night I dream I rescue immigrant children who have fallen overboard into the sea. It's my second job,' he told me as an adult.[44]

Pictures and stories would reel out in his mind like fully formed films while he played the phonograph. Little Nemo, The Yellow Kid, The Katzenjammer Kids, Baby Horace, Tiny Town were part of his fertile subconscious, and their lines or scenarios would come bubbling out of him at times. (The trademark punchline: 'What does Horace say?' 'SCHWRYTREPF!'[45]) Ken the kid listened to serials on the radio at home. ('The Shadow knows,' Ken would say, mimicking Orson Welles, who ironically had been the voice entertaining a ten-year-old Ken on the radio.) Ken's later, unmade, *Pretty Boy Floyd* script is peppered with voice-over radio announcements of the 1930s and focuses in part on Floyd's little innocent son defending his father.[46]

Ken's films are very soberly constructed to investigate and penetrate the mystery of madness. *Tommy* will 'surely take your mind where minds don't usually go.' *The Mystery of Dr Martinu* (BBC, 1992), about Czech composer Bohuslav Martinů, is a psychologically drenched, *Vertigo* style, Daliesque study, as is *The Strange Affliction of Anton Bruckner*, a film dealing with numeromania. *Crimes of Passion* features a mad priest (Anthony Perkins). Along with directing, writing, camera operating, set building, set dressing, lighting and camerawork, he tackled with zest the roles of mad doctors Calahari in *The Fall of the Louse of Usher* and Henry Horenstein in *Revenge of the Elephant Man* (A Gorsewood Production, 2004). Ken hilariously played a madman in an asylum in Brian Cook's film *Colour Me Kubrick* ([Magnolia Pictures, 2005], originally to be directed by Bresson), yelling 'I'M Stanley Kubrick!' For Granada Television, ITV, Ken filmed an unforgettable, serious portrayal of Coleridge's hallucinatory laudanum addiction in 1978's *Clouds of Glory* ('The Rime of the Ancient Mariner'). The soul-searching visions of Dr Jessup in *Altered States* were psychological windows into the archetypal realm of father issues, blood sacrifice, souls doomed in a fiery hell and, always, crucifixions and Catholic imagery. 'Not too many bloody crucifixes, Russell!' shouted his BBC mentor Huw Wheldon.[47]

'In Paddy Chayefsky's script where the hallucinations begin, were only two words: "The Void." He wanted the screen to go black for that,'[48] Ken laughed in disbelief. Despite his fears, Ken took mushrooms as research during the development of *Altered States*, at Shelley Winters's house in LA. He claimed he was terrorised by giant, murderous palm trees and an aggressive lilo.[49] Ken retained his fear of gigantic leaves his whole life and would automatically give them a wide berth when encountering them in any botanical garden or on the neighbour's pavement: 'Trust me, big-leafed plants do not wish us well.'[50]

Madness was most explicitly and gruesomely depicted in his 2007 book *Brahms Gets Laid* (in the person of Robert Schumann), *Mahler* (in Hugo Wolf), *Women in Love* (Mrs Crich and in the end, Gerald Crich) and *The Music Lovers*, where Nina Tchaikovsky is driven mad by her desperate need for validation and her husband's disinterest in her (and her mother's manipulation). Ken had a conscious need to redeem his own mother's loneliness and neglect by her husband, Ken's father, Henry, whom Ken described (whether fairly or not) as having 'put her away' probably for his convenience when Ken himself was fully into his successful career and with family of his own.[51] Ken told me many times about the horror of seeing her without shoes in the rest home, given that her husband's business was to make shoes.[52] Alma Mahler's own composing in *Mahler* was suppressed by her husband's fame and preoccupation, and her loneliness and insecurity are poignantly suggested in impressionistic sequences, as is her anger. In *The Boy Friend*, a side thread is the wife with the baby whose husband takes every opportunity to avoid her.

'3–6–5 – never a kind word – hello, how are you?' his mother would repeat every day like a mantra to Ken's father, sulking.[53] Ken's father would remind her that his social status was a class above hers, back when those things were acutely felt. Ken jubilantly peppered his speech at home to make me laugh with repeated snatches of songs and poetry he'd memorised as a youth (Longfellow, Tennyson and Sitwell),[54] random lines from his movies ('I'm so TI-rred!' – *Savage Messiah*) and with sayings his mother would repeat over and over.

FAMILY

Ken's family of origin were a constant companion in his mind. Every night he prayed, 'God bless Mummy and Daddy and all of the family.'[55] His almost-sister June took me aside early on to explain what she called the mystery in Ken's operational style. 'His father was obsessed with clocks. With being on time. It's a nautical thing, that relentless urgency.'[56] Ken kept giant clocks all over the house, their audible ticks carefully muffled (as in *Mahler*, the cow bells silenced by Alma [Georgina Hale]), like totems to his father and symbols of infinite time. Clocks emerged as a feature in *Mindbender* ([Major Motion Pictures, 1996], a film which Ken personally disowned as having been re-edited) and in the exquisite BBC short film from 1962 *The Lonely Shore* (set in the future). The metronome and a giant clock feature in *Lisztomania*. Ken wrote a script called *Trees* about a grandfather clock, out of which a feral woman who'd grown up in the trees emerges.[57] His fondness for transformational chambers which can effect a change on the body was with him since his beginning, imagining the hall closet full of mysteries.

His father's displays of temper and sternness were intermittent and frightening, according to Ken, and though Ken as an elder never altered in his love for and fond memories of him, there is little question that the scene where a crying Mahler hides in the outdoor toilet drew on memories of a fiercely reprimanded young Ken in his own history. A sensitive boy registers everything more deeply. His mother over-protected him from the worst. The projectionist at the theatre in Bournemouth told a mature Ken in 2008 that he'd started his career at the time when Ken's presence in British cinemas was at its height, and he became friends with Ken's mother Ethel, who he said came every day to see Ken's films, over and over, quietly slipping in by herself to watch. Ken was astonished and touched. He'd never known.

He and his brother were always together as children, merged into one entity by the family nickname 'Ray-Ken', and young Ken was devoted to him, playing with him happily on family holidays in Calshot and perhaps taking him for granted. 'Ray was the "favourite" of the family.' Humorously, Ray in his seventies insisted with a little resentment that Ken was the favourite.[58] The fluidity of different points of view is the sea we all swim in, and Ken more than most. But his biggest and earliest love, his first true love, was for his sunny and brave cousin Marian, whose presence in his life from birth to age thirteen was a source of unconditional love and joy, according to a mature Ken.

'It's the one tragedy of my life,' he said on Sky TV's interview *Living the Life*, one week before his demise, speaking in a whisper:

> Marian's death is the one thing I have never reconciled. She was playing alone on the beach age thirteen and for some unknown reason, ignored the warning signs and climbed a fence into a forbidden zone. A buried landmine went off and she was instantly killed. Her father, uncle Jack, immediately came over to tell us. For me, a light went out.[59]

He kept a photograph of the two of them together, age four, and you can see a shy boy beaming, dressed like a little Fauntleroy in velvet jacket, while he holds the hand of a little bonneted girl.

Although he would portray the death of children in his films, notably in *Mahler* and *Lisztomania*, Ken said he buried the pain of Marian deeper than could be accessed consciously for films. He did his best to resurrect the image of her thirteen-year-old self in the lead character Ursula, in *The Rainbow* (Vestron, 1989).

SOUTHAMPTON

Growing up in the Shirley district of Southampton, young Ken knew every alternate path in the woods to get to the cinema. As a grown man, he startled me by insisting he knew a shortcut to get to the movies, and suddenly drove the car straight up the stone steps through the newly redesigned quadrangle of Solent University, where he taught. His students took great and raucous delight in seeing Professor Russell navigating confidently down the concrete pathways. Southampton's puzzling roads with 'no left turns' were memorialised in Ken's 1991 TV mini-movie *Road to Mandalay*. By taking his shortcut, he got to the Odeon in time for the film, using his mental map for bicycling in Southampton in the thirties. He always preferred the direct route through any maze, and sometimes his third eye got him into trouble. He was a completest from the earliest days. 'Whatever is the most direct route to getting it done,' he would say to me, although his direct route was not always accommodated by other people. Act first, explain later.

For *Aria*, Ken showed up with a simple description of his plans and said, 'I've got it. It's all in my head.' Producer-director Don Boyd protested, 'Ken, you have to give me more than this.' Immediately Ken wrote out a second-by-second shot list timed to each note of the music, astounding in its detail and precision.[60] He really *did* have it all in his head.

His attraction to Tesla, culminating in a film he developed, *Charged* (2004), with the help of the Serbian government, was partly based on his appreciating Tesla's proclivity for designing his inventions to the last detail in his head, electronically complicated, imaged to three or more dimensions, before committing it all to paper. For *The Debussy Film*, a cameraman-in-training relegated to clapper board duties, was thrilled when asked to take over the reins at the camera for a shot. 'Yes!' he said. The sequence was to focus on Oliver Reed as Debussy by the open fire, but the flame was dying out. 'More fire!' roared Ken, and the clapper boy said in defence, 'There's no more wood.' 'That's wood, isn't it?' said Ken, indicating the clapper board. 'Not the clapper board,' protested the apprentice cameraman-clapper boy. 'It's essential!' Ken's answer was to take it and toss it on the fire. The flames roared up, and they got the shot.

Many years later, the now grown man ran into Ken at a function. 'I remember you,' Ken surprised him by exclaiming. 'You do?' said the erstwhile camera operator, not believing such a thing were possible. 'Yes! You're the idiot who threw the clapper board into the fire!'[61]

KEN RUSSELL'S RECIPE FOR FILM-MAKING

Ken's methods of expedient filming, learned as a youth, he gave to me in short form:

1. Make the weather your friend. The script can accommodate whatever it's up to.
2. Check your ego at the door. We can't afford lorries to carry the egos.
3. Use what equipment is at hand. Necessity is the mother of invention.
4. Be able to step outside your prescribed role and take on another, as circumstances require. Be flexible.
5. As crew, you are expected to become an actor in an emergency.
6. Filming two comedies to one serious film is a healthily balanced diet; or vice versa.
7. The talent is the least important facet of film-making, though it imagines it's the most important. Humour them. Fuss over them, love them, feed them well; they're sensitive creatures. Then give them space to do what they do.
8. Always go for the low-priced option on set dressing and extras and make it work. You can fake opulence.
9. 6 a.m. call, break for lunch 2–4 p.m., resume alertly after lunch.
10. Always start with a script. Don't imagine you can make it up as you go along. The script must be solid.
11. Eat, live and breathe films during shooting. When you break off work, see one film before bed to relax your mind, a good one. Or watch *Have I Got News for You*.
12. The sparks (lighting directors) are your most valuable players on the team. If you have the head lighting director on your side, he can get the others on board when the possibility of mutiny arises.
13. The director is only one of many making the film come true, but he's the captain.[62]

SCHOOLDAYS AND BALLET

Young Ken came to a crossroads when he came of age to go to a public school. His parents enrolled their first-born, age fifteen, at Pangbourne Nautical College, a trajectory ill-suited to a boy who liked best pasting collages into scrapbooks with his glue, screening movies for the neighbourhood, going to the movies, riding his bicycle, playing with miniature trains and his deep-sea diver, chasing steam trains, playing with his little brother, June and the dog, climbing trees and digging in the sand. Young Ken was immediately singled out for derision. 'Aitch Ki-y Aye Russell'[63] (HKA), they'd tease him, mocking his strong Hampshire accent. He set to work improving his accent. He perfected 'square-bashing', marching in the hot sun for hours in full gear.

His masters were savage, believing corporal punishment was the shortest distance to obedience and sometimes enjoying it rather too much, according to Ken. He told stories of sitting on a headmaster's lap after being whipped soundly, and obligingly enduring his cuddling, as did all the other boys.[64] He made friends with a young fellow sailor who shared with him the coveted assignment of playing records for musical performances in the canteen. Ken irrepressibly and precociously made a film with his only friend Robin and staged the first drag performance for his fellow students. There were repercussions from the masters, even though he swore some of them were chuckling. Ken was becoming used to being told he was 'out of bounds'. He would sneak out on weekends to see movies. He was tongue-tied whenever the time came to explain or defend himself. That was not what a shy boy could manage, and the best course was to take his punishment in silence.

Ken was not one to hold a grudge. 'I was never a tit-for-tat person,' he insisted,[65] and I personally found that to be true (notwithstanding the rolled newspaper on head reserved for critic Alexander Walker on TV), and *Savage Messiah* is a kind of tone poem to forgiveness as the ultimate expression of love. When he graduated from Pangbourne's bed-making, clock-watching, knot-tying, flag semaphore, Morse Code practising, impeccable obedience-to-authority and pride-in-presentation school, it was time for his national service. World War II was still sputtering in the Pacific, so he chose the Merchant Navy:

> I had dreams of meeting Dorothy Lamour in a sarong on the South Seas. I really was quite naïve. It never occurred to me that *Aloma of the South Seas* might have been made on an MGM back lot. Getting to her was my sole intent, and this was my means to free passage.[66]

Alas, it was not to be so. His ship was headed by a man Ken called 'Captain Bligh' (of *Mutiny on The Bounty*) who was a martinet and whose punishments were impulsive, cruel and random:

> He had me stand watch in the hot sun for double shifts and would leer over my skinny legs in their regulation short trousers. He was always on the lookout for any sign of threatening Japanese warships (we found none) and did his best to transfer his paranoia to all of us who were under orders to do his bidding.[67]

When he got to the South Seas and there was no Dorothy Lamour, and no let-up from the captain's neurotically sadistic nature, young Ken broke down with an anxiety disorder. He was invalided out and sent home, and proceeded to sit as a semi-invalid, 'a bemused vegetable',[68] in Ken's words, as his mum and the maid Olive vacuumed around his feet for three months (sometimes described as six months).

It was then, semi-comatose in the living room chair, that he had an epiphanic awakening that would lead him to his rightful path and his source of emotional sustenance:

The radio was on. Suddenly, I was struck by the most beautiful confluence of sound. I waited for the BBC announcer's identification of the music, and memorised it. Energy returned to my limbs. I urgently pumped up the flat tyres on my bike, took my savings in coins and rode to the shop, where I read out to the clerk, 'Tchaikovsky's *Piano Concerto in B-flat minor* performed by Solomon and the Hallé Orchestra.' I received a big brown album with four shellac records.[69]

As soon as Ken was captivated by classical composers, he was on his way. He knew his place. Images poured forth in his head to accompany the music. His internal dialogue, flattened by nervous exhaustion, was reinvigorated by music. His depression was vanquished. Unfortunately, he found he had no talent for playing music on an instrument. 'You have pianer fingers,' his mum Ethel encouraged him, as usual, referring to his long fingers, but they would not recreate the sounds he heard on the records, no matter how closely he practised following music scores along with his records. Instead, he became a regular at the record shop, devouring classical composers' work and memorising the instructional booklets that came with each album. Listening to Stravinsky at weekends home, aged 13, he first felt inspired by the spirit of dancing. He threw off all his clothes and danced around the room naked. At that moment, his mother and her friend poked their heads in. She never blinked an eye. 'Tea, Brush?' she said. (Brush meant 'Brother'.) It was like her inattention to Fido Rum-Eared's excesses.

So much for the budding Nijinsky. It was back to the Service, to finish out his commitment and be assigned to another branch of the Service. 'What are you interested in?' they rather sympathetically asked. 'Pictures,' he ventured. 'Right.' When he examined his record, it read, 'Picture framing.' He was misunderstood again.[70] He was sent to the Royal Air Force, where he recharged dead batteries in a military shed in Marchwood, not far from his home of origin.

The dream of dance incubated and after his service was ended, he enrolled in classes in the outskirts of London for ballet. He announced to his father and mother his intention to become a professional ballet dancer. 'You will not,' his father stated. 'I'll never be able to hold up my head in St Mary's Street again.' (St Mary's Street, Southampton, was where the Russell Brothers' main shop was.)[71]

Ken was determined. ('*Billy Elliot* is my story,' he whispered to me after its cinema debut, tears in his eyes.[72]) Young Ken was so determined, in fact, that he landed a place in the Norsk Ballet Company under the tutelage of the Russian maestro Konstantin Sergeyev of the Mariinsky Ballet. 'He chose me because I could jump the highest. "Jump," he'd bark and I would fly straight up in fear.'[73] Ken described very closely his experience of the way fear and shyness would react in him physically in his book *Brahms Gets Laid*: 'He panicked and turned red with embarrassment . . . those big hands fluttering about like

Figure 1.3 Ken Russell, the young ballet dancer.
Photo: held by Elize Russell.

oversized cabbage white butterflies . . . whereupon something burst through (his) SHY BARRIER, enabling him to burst into song.'[74]

His ballet career was not long-lasting (five years). Starting at age twenty hindered him, although he gamely and proudly performed in ballets, such as in the role of the Toymaker in *Coppélia* and in *Swan Lake*. (Dance is featured heavily in all his films.)[75] And always, he said, his mother would shout out from the audience where she sat with his father and brother, 'There's our Ken!' He learned the wise-cracking and suggestive Polari lingo of the dressing rooms, and the choreography to masterworks of classical music. He remained an elegant dancer his whole life, and would often re-enact playfully for me his 'most distinguished solo role', that of the hunter who would take the spotlight to mime in silent dance and gesture, upon meeting the Prince in the Forest, 'What? You? Here? In these clothes? Why?'[76]

He toured in the chorus of *Annie Get Your Gun* and would re-enact all the musical steps for me. After the ballet, he tried his hand at selling art, another passion of his. His lack of cultural education was a handicap. He went to the library and learned everything about Walter Sickert, chosen at random, and Turner, Raphael and the Pre-Raphaelites (*Dante's Inferno*). He got a job at a gallery. But he was not good at it, and found purpose in roaming the streets, taking pictures with his Rolleicord camera.

He enrolled in Walthamstow art school (film-maker-to-be Peter Greenaway was also enrolled there as was Ken's future first wife Shirley Kingdon and designer Zandra Rhodes). With his remarkable and imaginative post-war photo essays of London life, he was able to freelance for Picture Post, Illustrated Magazine and Pictorial Press and eventually see his photos turn up at TopFoto:

> I wasn't cut out for commercial photography at the time. The subjects that interested me were considered eccentric. I was on assignment to photograph Audrey Hepburn and Mel Ferrer on their honeymoon. Sitting behind them on the plane, I couldn't bear to invade their privacy. They were so in love. I didn't take the shot.[77]

His BBC films *A House in Bayswater* (BBC, 1960) and *Watch the Birdie* (BBC, 1963), featuring his housemate David Hurn, anticipated Antonioni's *Blow-Up* (MGM, 1966) and the recognition of the photographer as significant cultural figure. He'd wander Notting Hill and Portobello and on his kitchen table develop his photo essays of post-war Teddy Girls, Portobello bombsites, sandwich men, nurses, the Royal Guard, dancer Helen May, the Troubadour Café, the hip bath, the pogo stick, children playing in the street ('poor little sods'), housewives on stoops, his landlady, penny-farthings, skating rinks, friends in dress-up in Hyde Park. All viewed in sequence could have been films.

His sensitivity to his own embarrassment made him insist on not attending parties except once a year in later life (a rule that he readily broke when feeling welcomed). He genuinely liked people; yet he was genuinely self-conscious in their company. ('I'm an old British film director you won't have heard of.' *Big Brother*, Channel 4.[78]) It was a treasure when he'd meet someone with whom he resonated and could relax. Journalist Tim Teeman, actor Ben Kingsley, fellow directors from *Monitor* and *Omnibus*; his much-loved producers Roy Baird, Melvyn Bragg, Humphrey Burton, Dan Ireland, Si Litvinoff were cherished friends. Cinematographers Billy Williams, David Watkin, Dougie Slocombe, Dick Bush were likewise extended family; as were editors Mike Bradsell, Roger Crittenden, David King and Stuart Baird. (Mike was editor on most of Ken's films, from *Monitor* to the 'Garagiste' home movies, earning from Ken the nickname 'my psychic twin'.) Ken enjoyed seeing directors he felt close to, like Roeg, Boorman, Ridley and Tony Scott, Don Boyd, Mick Garris (who threw a commission his way[79]); conductors, musicians or composers he worked with, like Peter Maxwell Davies, Vasily Petrenko, Pete Townshend, Roger Daltrey, Barry Lowe and David Massengill. Critics Derek Malcolm and Mark Kermode were close pals. His shyness was relieved when directing, or when in the company of film or music lovers. He even played a director in *Valentino* and a photographer in *Salome's Last Dance*. In 2005 actor William Hurt recalled of his work with Ken on *Altered States*, 'What I most vividly recall of the shoot was Ken's incredible knowledge of classical music.'[80]

Ken also recalled:

> I got the job with Huw Wheldon on BBC's *Monitor* because I was mute. Huw liked my little amateur film, *Amelia and the Angel*, inspired by Cocteau and therefore different to other submissions, and thought I might add something to the mix of talented filmmakers he oversaw working at *Monitor*. I'd found the water I was born to swim in. I still remember Huw yelling after I'd fumbled my way through the first week: 'Russell! I hired you because you were quiet, standing there eating your sandwich with hardly an answer to my interview. I thought you were contemplative and wise. And now I find you know F— all!'[81]

Huw was his mentor. Ken looked up to him. Huw, broadcaster, presenter, film editor, good friend to William Faulkner, genuinely understood Ken, worked with him and nurtured his talents.

CONCLUSION

That Ken had found a language and people who understood it was a source of enormous satisfaction: 'I could not make myself understood properly, except with other film-makers.' (And not always with them: years later, in 2005, when Ken booed at *Little Britain*'s South Bank Awards win, Ken was upsetting protocol:

> I realised it a second later. I was impulsively protesting that they had used the sight gag of spitting in Vanessa Feltz's face. I always watched the show. But it's wrong to spit on a woman! Melvyn would understand that![82]

But of course, Ken never explained his faux pas. He just hoped it would go away.

It was painful for him to endure the critics. So many critics. He took to his bed once after yet another publication seemed to revel in dismissing his work. 'Is that what they think of me?'[83]

'I have one purpose, to make films,' Ken affirmed to me. 'I have no social skills. I am new to this planet. This is my first life. I came in to make films. And "to sit with my beloved in a field with daisies all around us,"'[84] quoting from D. H. Lawrence, *Women in Love*. Stéphane Mallarmé, nineteenth-century French poet, described the process of adjusting to the world as 'a child abdicating his ecstasy'. I think it could be said that Ken Russell never abdicated his ecstasy.

Ken, for all his genius and intellect, remained at heart the affectionate boy who proudly brought his mum chocolate on Valentine's Day. 'What have you got there behind your back?' she scolded. 'What is it?'[85]

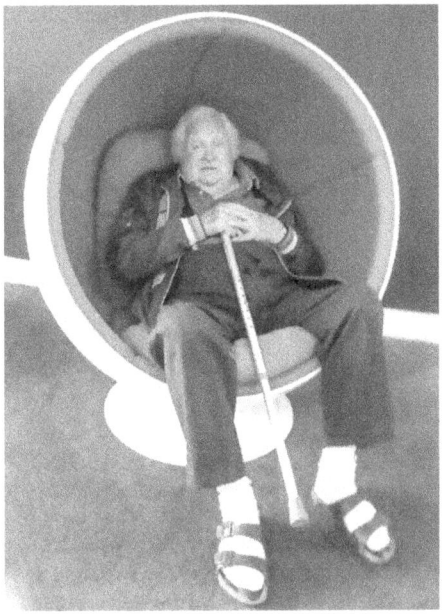

Figure 1.4 Ken Russell in the 'ball chair' from *Tommy*.
Photo: held by Elize Russell.

He was afraid to say. It melted in his clutched grip.

'That's all I ever tried to do with my films,' Ken told me. 'To give the world a sweet they weren't expecting. To make my mum accept the chocolate.'[86]

NOTES

1. Elize Russell, Personal Notebooks 1999–2011 (Unpublished). All quotes by Ken Russell. All images are from Elize Russell's personal archive.
2. John A. Riley, 'Ken Russell', *Senses of Cinema*, July 2009, <https://www.sensesofcinema.com/2009/great-directors/ken-russell/> (last accessed 9 February 2021).
3. Elize Russell, Personal Notebooks (Unpublished), March 2006.
4. Ibid., February 2000.
5. Ibid., July 2006.
6. Ibid., October 2009.
7. Ibid., February 2007.
8. 'Ken Russell: Tributes Paid to Film Director', BBC, Entertainment & Arts, 28 November 2011, <https://www.bbc.co.uk/news/entertainment-arts-15920491> (last accessed 25 May 2022).
9. Jez Gale, 'Southampton Blitz – City Remembers on Its 75th Anniversary', *Southampton Daily Echo*, 30 November 2015, <https://www.dailyecho.co.uk/news/14112339.photos-southampton-blitz-city-remembers-on-75th-anniversary/> (last accessed 5 February 2021).
10. Ken Russell, 'The Lifelong Reading Spree That Inspires My World ', *Times*, 16 December 2008.

11. Elize Russell, Personal Notebooks (Unpublished), February 2000.
12. Ibid., March 2002.
13. Ibid., September 2001.
14. Ken Russell, *A British Picture: An Autobiography* (London: Southbank Publishing, 2008), 21.
15. Elize Russell, Personal Notebooks (Unpublished), February 2000.
16. Ken Russell, *Boop-Oop-a-Doop* (unmade script, Russell personal archive), 2008.
17. Elize Russell, Personal Notebooks (Unpublished), January 2002.
18. Russell, *A British Picture*, 46.
19. Ibid., 32–4.
20. Elize Russell, Personal Notebooks (Unpublished), December 2006.
21. Ibid., November 2001.
22. Ibid., December 2002.
23. Ibid., March 2003.
24. Ibid., December 1999.
25. Ibid., November 2006.
26. Simon Boswell is a British film composer who has scored (among others) *Shallow Grave* (Boyle, 1994) and *Santa Sagre* (Jodorowsky, 1989).
27. Ken Russell, 'Nun Lust, Torture Porn? Ken Russell's Devils are Back', *Times*, 12 March 2012 (posthumous), <https://www.thetimes.co.uk/article/nun-lust-torture-porn-ken-russells-devils-are-back-h2dm9ljholm> (last accessed 2 February 2021).
28. Elize Russell, Personal Notebooks (Unpublished), March 2000.
29. Ibid., 2001.
30. Russell, *A British Picture*, 5–6.
31. Elize Russell, Personal Notebooks (Unpublished), June 2001.
32. Russell, *A British Picture*, 6–7.
33. Elize Russell, Personal Notebooks (Unpublished), January 2001.
34. Ibid., December 2007.
35. Ibid., November 2004.
36. 'A Brontë Burlesque', *BrontëBlog*, September 2006, <http://bronteblog.blogspot.com/2006/09/bront-burlesque.html> (last accessed 25 May 2022).
37. Ken Russell, 'My Friendly Neighbourhood Witches', *Times*, 8 July 2008.
38. Ken Russell, *Bravetart vs. The Loch Ness Monster* (unfinished script, Russell personal archive), 2007.
39. Elize Russell, Personal Notebooks (Unpublished), July 2003.
40. Tim Martin, 'Ken Russell's Postwar London', Economist, 2 December 2016.
41. Ken Russell, 'Send Him Down the Mines', *Times*, weekly arts column, 28 August 2009.
42. 'Ken Russell – Southern Visions', BBC, 12 May 2005, updated 3 April 2008, <http://www.bbc.co.uk/dorset/content/articles/2005/05/12/pictureofbritian_russell_feature.shtml> (last accessed 25 May 2022).
43. Elize Russell, Personal Notebooks (Unpublished), October 2001.
44. Ibid., May 1999.
45. Harry Hemsley, 'Ovaltiney's Concert Party. 1934–1939', Lambiek Comiclopedia, <https://www.lambiek.net/artists/l/larkman_g.htm> (last accessed 3 March 2021).
46. Ken Russell and Elize Russell, *Pretty Boy Floyd* (unmade script, Russell personal archive) 2006.
47. Russell, *A British Picture*, 24.
48. Elize Russell, Personal Notebooks (Unpublished), October 2005.
49. Russell, *A British Picture*, 176.
50. Elize Russell, Personal Notebooks (Unpublished), July 2010.
51. Ibid., February 2002.

52. Ibid., January 2002.
53. Ibid., November 2011.
54. Henry Wadsworth Longfellow, 'The Song of Hiawatha', 1855; Alfred, Lord Tennyson, 'Charge of the Light Brigade', 1854; Edith Sitwell, 'Scotch Rhapsody', 1922.
55. Elize Russell, Personal Notebooks (Unpublished), April 2006–February 2010.
56. Ibid., September 2001.
57. Ken Russell and Elize Russell, *Trees* (unmade script, Russell personal archive), 2006.
58. Elize Russell, Personal Notebooks (Unpublished), 2007.
59. 'Sir Peter Blake & Ken Russell', *Living the Life*, Season 1, Sky Arts, 15 January 2012.
60. Conversation with Don Boyd and Ken Russell, Southbank, London, 9 June 2009.
61. Stefan Sargent, 'Ken Russell Threw My Clapper on the Fire', Creative Planet Network, 2016, <https://www.creativeplanetnetwork.com/news/ken-russell-burned-my-clapper-z-cars-it-ain-t-613977> (last accessed 3 March 2021).
62. Elize Russell, Personal Notebooks (Unpublished), dictation from Ken Russell, June 2008.
63. Russell, *A British Picture*, 36.
64. Ibid., 37–8.
65. Elize Russell, Personal Notebooks (Unpublished), March 2006.
66. Russell, *A British Picture*, 35.
67. Ibid., 52.
68. Ken Russell, 'A Film about Tchaikovsky? You Must Be Joking', *Guardian*, 1 July 2004, <https://www.theguardian.com/film/2004/jul/01/1> (last accessed 24 June 2022).
69. Russell, *A British Picture*, 55.
70. Elize Russell, Personal Notebooks (Unpublished), February 2002.
71. Russell, *A British Picture*, 73.
72. Elize Russell, Personal Notebooks (Unpublished), October 2000.
73. Ibid., April 2006.
74. Ken Russell, Brahms Gets Laid (London: Peter Owen Publishers, 2007), 114.
75. Jasper Rees, 'Q & A: Director Ken Russell', *The Arts Desk*, 28 November 2011.
76. Elize Russell, Personal Notebooks (Unpublished), December 2006.
77. Ibid., March 2006.
78. Sally Churchward, 'Director Ken Enters the Big Brother House', *Daily Echo*, 4 January 2007.
79. Editor's note: Garris offered Ken an instalment of his 'Masters of Horror' series but owing to ill health it was never made. The section made its way with a different script into his sequence for the anthology film *Trapped Ashes*.
80. William Hurt in conversation on Christopher Street, NYC, 1998.
81. Elize Russell, Personal Notebooks (Unpublished), February 2002.
82. Ibid., January 2006.
83. Ibid., May 2007.
84. Ibid., August 2010.
85. Ibid., March 2006.
86. Ken Russell, conversation, August 2010.

CHAPTER 2

Performed Masculinities: Oliver Reed in Ken Russell's Films of the 'Long 1960s'

Caroline Langhorst

INTRODUCTION: PERFORMING AS A RUSSELLIAN MALE

Ken Russell's cinema features polymorphous manifestations of sexuality and encompasses a diverse spectrum of sexual desires. Although this chapter will interrogate the film-maker's collaborations with younger male actors who embody different forms of masculinity and sexuality through their individual performance styles, it focuses primarily on Russell's collaboration with Oliver Reed and considers the actor's 'Byronic' performances in *Dante's Inferno: The Private Life of Dante Gabriel Rossetti, Poet and Painter* (BBC, 1967), *Women in Love* (United Artists, 1969) and *The Devils* (Warner Bros., 1971). These performances paradigmatically merge self-destructive Romantic/ Gothic elements with the contemporary cultural, sexual landscapes of the 'long 1960s'. Throughout the 1960s and 1970s, Russell depicts a variety of complex male desires that repeatedly subvert an alleged cultural heteronormativity. He exposes the (male) human body in all its frailties in *The Music Lovers* (United Artists, 1970), *Mahler* (Goodtimes Enterprises, 1974) or *Tommy* (Columbia, 1975), for instance, as well as the intricacies of human behaviour.

Writing about the body on-screen, Stephen Heath argues that it consists of 'moments, intensities, outside a simple constant unity of the body as a whole; films [contain] bits of bodies, gestures, desirable traces, fetish points'.[1] Russell's films reveal a set of complex, nuanced layers of fragmented masculinity *and* corporeality which deviate from the contemporary English realist tradition and refuse to shy away from explicit depictions of frontal male nudity à la *Women in Love*'s wrestling scene. The scene offers a stripping away of preheld notions of masculinity in the disrobing of Gerald Crich (Reed) and Rupert Birkin (Alan Bates): from buttoned-up, stoic manhood to raw, naked self. This act of 'undressing' and the revealing of a more primal, 'natural' self also thematically anticipates Eddie Jessup's (William Hurt) tapping of the primitive self in *Altered States* (Warner Bros., 1980), becoming a Russellian trope.

Dante's Inferno combines medieval and Romantic ideals of spiritual love with necrophiliac and obsessive-neurotic Gothic (Poe-esque) tendencies, while *The Devils* demonstrates a visceral kaleidoscope of sexual desires and (Catholic) fetishes. These feature King Louis XIII's (Graham Armitage) initial *Birth of Venus* drag performance; Sister Jeanne's (Vanessa Redgrave) unrequited, sadomasochistic amour fou and her fetishistic utensils of self-punishment; the exorcism and orgy scenes; the repressed sexuality of Father Mignon (Murray Melvin); Urbain Grandier's (Oliver Reed) equally sado-masochistic and self-destructive urges that combine hedonistic excess with corporeal and spiritual pain; and Baron de Laubardemont's (Dudley Sutton) sadistic-cynical demeanour and his fetish-laden spurred boots. *The Devils* offers a range of polyvalent sexualities that are juxtaposed and connect narratively with Grandier's virile (hyper)masculinity (deemed by the female characters as 'worth going to hell for').

There are various forms of masculinity depicted within the plague-ridden microcosm of the film which are continuously paired with (or offset against) each other: the androgynous monarch and effeminate, scheming Cardinal Richelieu (Christopher Logue) who travels around in a mechanical mobile chair pushed by a coterie of nuns; Mignon's ambiguous repression that manifests itself in compensatory intrigue-scheming and (erotically charged) voyeurism (in a shot of him furiously masturbating from on high over the orgy of nuns during the censored 'Rape of Christ' sequence) (Figure 2.1); the androgynous and hyperbolic hippie exorcist Father Barré (Michael Gothard) who visually resembles a

Figure 2.1 Father Mignon at the orgy.
Source: Warner Bros., 1971.

fair-haired Mick Jagger and sports glasses that are reminiscent of John Lennon; and the sadistic Baron de Laubardemont. When Grandier is later turned into a martyr, his virile masculine body (denoted by his vainly groomed facial hair) is first shaved then, symbolically and literally, reduced to ash; another example of Russell's figurative and literal deconstruction of manhood.

Russell's male characters are beset by crisis. They succumb to self-destructive urges and feelings of uncertainty in relation to their own role in the narrative. This is illustrated, for instance, by Tchaikovsky's (Richard Chamberlain) 'pathétique' suicide or Gerald Crich's (Oliver Reed) alienated snowbound suicide in *Women in Love*. Sue Harper and Justin Smith note of Oliver Reed's on-screen portrayal of conflicted, alienated masculinity that the actor 'glowered through a range of 1970s films, but the stillness and social isolation he displayed as early as *Women in Love* make for a spatial balance between himself and other protagonists'.[2] The performer's recurring depiction of male crisis is symptomatic of Russell's approach to physicality defined by feelings of anxiety and an ongoing inner struggle[3] (the tension between the outer and inner self is also central to the narrative of *Altered States*, of course). I have previously examined Reed's raw performance style and the transformation of his star image from 'Byronic' teenage horror idol and 'alienated young male'[4] to hyper-virile rebel-rouser, stating: 'Reed performs a version of hypermasculinity that is, however, as conflicted and contradictory as his earlier performances of his male characters' personal (existential) crises. By this means, (heteronormative) (hyper)masculinity and its macho connotations are likewise exposed as fragile cultural constructions.'[5]

MURRAY MELVIN, RICHARD CHAMBERLAIN AND MICHAEL CAINE

Before turning in more detail to Reed's performance style, I would like to offer a brief comparative discussion of three other male actors in Russell's films. Murray Melvin's frequent collaborations with Russell, from *Diary of a Nobody: Domestic Jottings of a City Clerk* (BBC, 1964) to *Prisoner of Honour* (Dreyfuss-James Productions/HBO, 1991) depart from and contrast directly with Reed's hypermasculinity. Melvin had trained under theatre director Joan Littlewood, whose workshop and company is credited with 'the development of a new British performance style'.[6] Its range of influences encompass Meyerhold, 'Rudolf Laban's system of body language notation, ... and the sixteenth-century Italian Commedia dell'Arte with its radical troupe of travelling players'.[7] As a result, 'Joan Littlewood's disciples were rigorously trained in the art of movement, encouraged to strip themselves of their accumulated layers of social conditioning, to absorb themselves in the background to the play they were performing and to improvise.'[8]

Melvin's performative ambiguous sexuality and androgynous physicality are therefore accentuated in his on-screen performances by means of a self-aware performance style that displays an understated 'ironic disavowal'.[9] Harper and Smith propose that in 1970s British cinema:

> An extremely mannered acting style emerges, which is restricted to certain female styles and to camp or gayish roles. This style uses minimal shifts in facial expression or vocal tone to imply that the material or the proposition is not worth taking seriously ... There is a knowingness and a jokiness in a whole range of performances, and this resides in a range of genres, production contexts, acting abilities and character types; there is a perceptible gap between the role and the subjectivity of the performer.[10]

They cite Melvin as one of the key male examples of this style: he

> excels in a downward gaze and a raised pitch, and the effect of his acting in *The Boy Friend* [Ken Russell, MGM-EMI, 1971], *Joseph Andrews* [Tony Richardson, Paramount, 1977] and *Barry Lyndon* [Stanley Kubrick, Warner Bros., 1975] is to make the audience disbelieve the script's assertion of his heterosexuality.[11]

Whilst masculinity in Russell's films manifests itself in different forms, ranging from virile to more androgynous and sexually ambiguous, the common denominator is the ongoing inner tensions simmering below the surface. Richard Chamberlain's casting and performance as the tormented, closeted composer Tchaikovsky in *The Music Lovers* diverges from the (at first glance) (hyper)virile physicality of the likes of Reed, but nonetheless shares the underlying inner conflict of the Russellian Romantic male. The American actor delivers a nuanced performance comprised of recurrent and varied anguished facial expressions and troubled, pensive gazes (Figures 2.2–2.5), similarly employed by Reed in his Russellian performances. These are often shown in close shots and from angles that visually heighten the composer's inner turmoil and the pressures of his artistic, personal and spiritual struggles.

Chamberlain's sensitive portrayal of Tchaikovsky shifts between corporeal and emotional containment and repression, and it serves as another poignant visual reminder of how masculinity is performed, put on display and interrogated in Russell's films of the period. Like Crich, his male identity is reasserted and affirmed in his 'pathetic' but ultimately heroic suicide.

Furthermore, there is an ironic self-awareness to Russell's use of Michael Caine's swinging sixties star persona in *Billion Dollar Brain* (United Artists, 1967) (Figure 2.6).

Figures 2.2–2.5 Richard Chamberlain as Tchaikovsky in *The Music Lovers*.
Source: United Artists, 1970.

Figure 2.6 Michael Caine as Harry Palmer in *Billion Dollar Brain*.
Source: United Artists, 1967.

It forms the third part of the Harry Palmer trilogy after *The Ipcress File* (Sidney J. Furie, Rank Films, 1965) and *Funeral in Berlin* (Guy Hamilton, Paramount, 1966) and was released a year after Caine's role as carefree *Alfie* (Lewis Gilbert, Paramount, 1966). Caine had approached Russell to direct (on the strength of his BBC films), whilst the director had originally intended to make a film about Nijinsky for Harry Saltzman (and here Russell deals with two forms of diverging masculinity in the figure of spy and ballet dancer). Whereas Caine's bespectacled Palmer, based on the spy novels by Len Deighton, was generally regarded as the anti-007,[12] his hedonistic pleasure seeker Alfie epitomised the womanising swinging sixties bachelor lifestyle. South-east London-born Michael Caine and contemporaries such as Salford-born Albert Finney embody a 'specific notion of masculinity in which rebellion against the constraints of more traditional versions . . . is articulated both through gender representation and the mobilisation of a certain definition of class identity'.[13] Sixties Caine then 'becomes a "hero" for an alternative system of dominant values'.[14] Robert Shail acknowledges that Caine's 'cocky disruptiveness though has its dark sides'.[15] Yet even this darker side does not match the Byronic moodiness exuded by Reed who, despite his privileged upper-middle-class background, similarly set out to rebel against restrictive class hierarchies.[16]

OLIVER REED, BYRONIC MASCULINITIES AND THE LATE 1960S

It was Oliver Reed's irreverent attitude and physical magnetism that proved apposite for Russell's neo-Romantic, excessive aesthetics and embrace of liberated forms of sexuality, sensuality and corporeality which incorporate 'madness, morbidity, monstrosity and violent eroticism'.[17] The English actor had already starred in various Hammer productions, building up a star persona originally based on his brooding charisma and matinee-idol looks. Barry Forshaw considers mid-1960s Reed at the time of *The Party's Over* (Guy Hamilton, Monogram Pictures, 1965), for example, as being 'at the height of his self-destructive Byronic period as an actor'.[18] In her examination of screen manifestations of the Byronic hero, Atara Stein notes the type's liminal position as rebellious social outcast who follows his 'own rules and his own moral code'.[19] Importantly, 'The attitude of the hero toward society is paradoxical and ambivalent, rarely if ever as pure and unequivocal as it is usually said to be.'[20] This may be applied to Reed's characters and performances as an artistic and cultural outsider in *Dante's Inferno*, alienated, uprooted loner in *Women in Love* and defiant, hedonistic rebel priest in *The Devils*. However, whilst Reed portrays Byronic characters in both *Dante's Inferno* and *The Devils*, his take on Crich in *Women in Love* articulates Lawrence's modernist sensibility, addressing the individual's existential alienation from his surroundings. Russell would later depict Lord Byron in *Gothic* (Virgin Vision/Vestron, 1986), played by Irish actor Gabriel Byrne in a role and performance which homages Reed's roles in Russell's cinema.

Reed's first collaboration with Russell, *The Debussy Film*, turned out to be a 'pivotal point of his career'.[21] He recalled, 'I regard Debussy as the turning point of my career. It was the point at which I began to shoot upwards, sometimes, though not always from the cast of villain that I was poured into for my earlier roles.'[22] Reed 'captured the brooding sensuality and threatening calm that is so characteristic of the man and his music'.[23] Accordingly, the actor's portrayal of 'brooding sensuality' is a point of departure for his performances as poet/painter Dante Gabriel Rossetti in *Dante's Inferno*, *Women in Love*'s Gerald Crich and Urbain Grandier in *The Devils*.

Of Reed's performance in *The Debussy Film*, Russell observed that 'It wasn't actor Oliver Reed portraying Debussy ... it was Oliver Reed portraying himself preparing to play the part of Debussy.'[24] This observation is important as Russellian male characters, especially in the artist biopic films, frequently embody Russell's own approach to deconstructing the artistic persona. Reed's 'period' roles in Ken Russell's films of the era articulate some of the cultural tensions of the mid- to late 1960s. In *Dante's Inferno*, for instance, the depiction of the vicissitudes of the artistic life and sexual, romantic and interpersonal relationships of the Pre-Raphaelite Brotherhood resonate with late 1960s hedonistic excess. This becomes apparent by means of a brooding Gothic aesthetic and atmosphere, various anachronisms (contemporary song choices), and the rock star–muse (groupie) relationship portrayed via the artist–muse connection between Rossetti and Miss Siddal (Judith Paris) in the film. Yet the black-and-white aesthetic of the BBC production and the omniscient voice-over narrator lend the production as well as Reed's performance style an altogether more detached tone than in the later films, largely eschewing the excessive production and performance style of the 1970s films (and Reed's performance in *The Devils*).

Reed's Crich and Grandier point to a sense of emptiness and a threatening abyss, Crich's inner 'void' and Grandier's 'vortex', in which 'spin images of horror and lust' (see the downward spiralling architectural production design of his house) and which he claims he needs 'to turn against himself'. Crich is an emotionally damaged and alienated male, and Reed exposes the character's inner torment and vulnerability more openly than in his previous roles as evidenced towards the end of the film via his isolated death march into the snow.

The actor's performances in these films feature a heightened display of spectacular corporeality and sexuality. This focus on the body in its natural state further articulates a (counter)cultural return to less technocratic and more agricultural, pagan systems.[25] There was a widespread cultural affinity for occultism and mysticism to be detected that coincided with the countercultural penchant for communal living and an agrarian, nature-loving lifestyle. Leon Hunt notes that 'there was a growing interest in pre-Christian pagan cults allegedly representative of a more "authentic", prelapsarian national culture.'[26] In *Women in Love*, Birkin (Alan Bates), for instance, enthuses about leading a communal life and is linked throughout to both a oneness with nature and 'natural' sexuality (as demonstrated on numerous occasions: in the schoolroom lesson, in the love scene with Jennie Linden, in his demonstration of how to eat a fig, and in his cabin home set within the woods).

BYRONIC REED, THE COUNTERCULTURE AND THE LATE 1960S

Dante's Inferno resonates with the counterculture's reappraisal of Romantic poetry and decadent (pre-)fin-de-siècle writings by the likes of Joris-Karl Huysmans (*Against Nature*, 1884) and Oscar Wilde (*The Picture of Dorian Gray*, 1890), who combine hedonistic, obsessive-compulsive and ultimately self-destructive male tendencies with an aesthete's or dandy's worldview.

Russell's interest in Wilde is demonstrated via *Salome's Last Dance* (Vestron, 1988), which incorporates Aubrey Beardsley's famous illustrations for this occasion and in which Nickolas Grace's Wilde provides another post-Reed Byronic performance (à la Gabriel Byrne in *Gothic*). Both Russell and Beardsley eclectically fused the classical with their own respective viewpoints, thus pushing artistic and erotic boundaries.[27] Beardsley succeeded in 'revolutionizing the reception of classical heroes and heroines'.[28] Russell admired Beardsley and had planned a biopic on him, starring Melvin in the lead.[29] *Salome's Last Dance* significantly modifies excerpts from the life and art of Wilde and presents a (private and purely fictional) staging of the play at a London brothel (a self-reflexive play-within-a-play device which recurs across Russell's work). Wilde is associated with a 'Victorian sexual counter-culture',[30] reinforcing Russell's repeated engagement with various countercultural forces that are not confined to the 1960s but take on a much more flexible time frame.

Dante's Inferno contains scenes of civil unrest in 1848 (the 'year of revolutions'), depicting the burning of 'old' paintings. As the omniscient narrator declares in a factual manner, 'in England, rebels conspire to overthrow the Royal Academy of Arts. The rebels are students and idealists. They are against industry, state religion and official art.' These idealists also break with the old masters, desiring to leave their own individualistic mark on the art scene (not unlike the aims of the four 1960s pop artists Derek Boshier, Peter Blake, Pauline Boty and Peter Phillips in *Pop Goes the Easel* [BBC, 1962]). The film's twin themes of passion and death symbolise the merging of Eros and Thanatos (death drive) that are introduced at the very beginning, setting the stage for a Gothic atmosphere which pervades the second half of the film. After Miss Siddal's death, Reed's Rossetti is haunted by feelings of guilt and her spectral presence, obsessively drifting into addiction and madness. Reed is first shown in the film holding a burning torch. He is then presented in a close-up with flickering light surrounding him, further visually accentuating the Gothic scenery and setting.

This opening echoes the late 1960s' increased social unrest against social and racial inequalities within the establishment that grew more heated from 1968 onwards, extending from the US to Europe and the UK. The voice-over narrator continues, 'They would replace these with notions of honour, truth and beauty, quite unsuited to our times', corresponding to the countercultural back-to-nature ethos and its suspicion of the establishment's technocratic fervour. Theodore Roszak maintained that the counterculture was a direct reaction to 'technocracy', which he defined as 'a society in which those who govern justify themselves by appeal to technical experts'.[31] However, the counterculture did not fully depart from heteronormative structures. Certain traditional hegemonic patterns particular in terms of gender roles were upheld, with an emphasis on

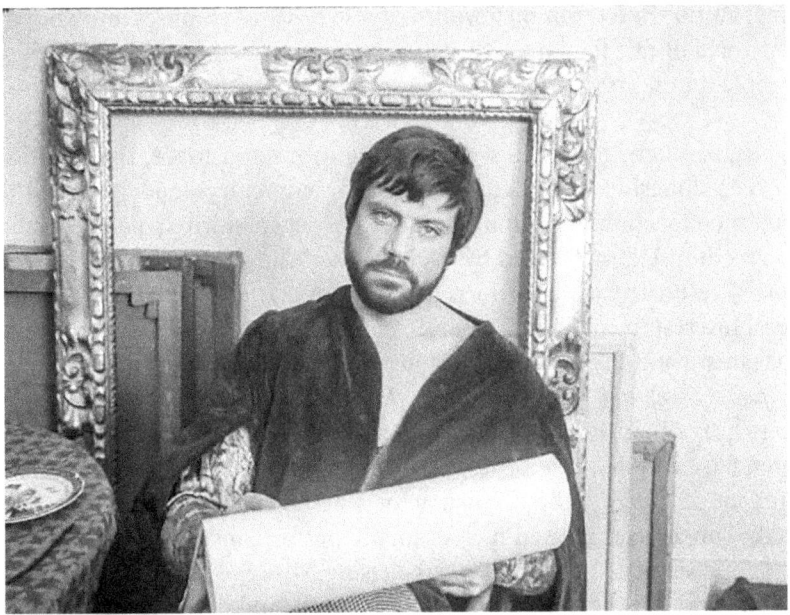

Figure 2.7 Oliver Reed as Rossetti.
Source: BBC, 1967.

the promiscuous gratification of male sexual urges. In *Dante's Inferno*, the Pre-Raphaelites are presented as an alternative community that pursues alternative lifestyles inspired by Romanticism, medieval culture, spirituality and nature. Initially, the audience is introduced to Reed's Rossetti (Figure 2.7) who acts as the focal point, then presented with his interactions with the rest of the circle (William Holman Hunt, John Everett Millais) and close associates such as John Ruskin (Clive Goodwin), William Morris (Andrew Faulds) and poet Algernon Charles Swinburne (Christopher Logue).

Like the countercultural revolutionaries and artists of the 1960s, the Pre-Raphaelites lamented the loss of spirituality and mankind's disconnection from nature, aggravated and accelerated by the Industrial Revolution. Moreover, on an extra-diegetic level, this may be said to reflect Russell's own feelings exhibited in *John Betjeman: A Poet in London* (BBC, 1959), where the obliteration of poetic architecture is replaced by new, utilitarian post-war architecture. Russell further presented a torn portrait of pre-swinging London in his short *London Moods* (1961), which depicts British traditions, affluence, and high and street culture:

> Russell's film . . . does reconcile two competing views of the post-war city. While containing buildings, people, and practices . . . aligned with

high culture and traditional wealth, it also features glimpses into a popular world of fast food, novelty exercise, youth subcultures, and ordinary people on the street.[32]

Thus, as often in Russell's work of the 1960s and 1970s, the traditional/past exists alongside and merges with the contemporary/modern. The Brotherhood's connection with the likes of the pagan-spirited poet Swinburne (who was, himself, influenced by Charles Baudelaire and French decadent literature[33]) resonates with the increasing late 1960s and early 1970s (counter) cultural interest in, and neo-Romantic tendency towards, mysticism, spirituality, paganism and the occult as seen in folk horror films of the period such as *Witchfinder General* (1968), *Cry of the Banshee* (1970) and *The Blood on Satan's Claw* (1971), a British cinematic milieu amongst which scholars, such as I. Q. Hunter, have counted *The Devils*.

In *Dante's Inferno*, the English actor's performance as Rossetti occasionally takes on an exaggerated melodramatic performance mode à la silent cinema: in one sequence he is presented chasing Miss Siddal amidst nature until he catches her. His beloved is painted as virtuous and inexperienced, although this is later exposed as a romanticised fallacy. A close-up shows Rossetti's enduring affection for her. Yet Reed's Rossetti does not confine himself to a celibate lifestyle just because he is being teased and kept waiting by her. She acts as his muse and 'personification of a spiritual ideal'. This idealistic and introverted fantasising disposition echoes the counterculture's and the hippies' preference for subjective (altered) states of consciousness that transcend realism. Reed's poet/painter is enthralled to Elizabeth and artistically inspired by her serene, tranquil beauty, yet, as she playfully proves by stabbing him with a needle when he makes a pass at her, she is a rose with a thorn that pricks. He is frequently shown in close-up with a dreamy, gazing expression in her presence. In the film, Elizabeth Siddal is occasionally given some female agency, but she remains nonetheless reduced to her status as muse and lover.

Oliver Reed's facial expressions and performance are nuanced and subtle (with the exception of the exaggerated farcical bawdy romp-style scenes). As Rossetti, his character 'drifts [between] being a poet and a painter, whatever impresses most, is least effort and pays best'. There is the enamoured artist in the presence of Miss Siddal, painting or spending time with her in pastoral surroundings with a certain degree of playfulness and reciprocal teasing. Then there is also the Byronic hedonist. In these scenes, Reed plays Rossetti as a rake but at certain moments (particularly in the second half) Reed's facial expressions convey the character's inner torment and conflicted emotions. John Baxter comments, 'Oliver Reed's vision of the pre-Raphaelite poet Dante Gabriel Rossetti is that of a man tortured by his remorse at the maltreatment of lovers and friends, and by the failure of his life to equal a vaulting imagination.'[34]

Reed was the only actor not selected on the basis of his physical resemblance to the character he was supposed to play, thus cast on the grounds of his screen presence and personality rather than historical accuracy.[35] Rossetti's inner torment is further demonstrated in the second half of the film, in which Reed portrays the character's transition into an eccentric, semi-reclusive crippled pariah and addict. Here the narrative focus is entirely placed on his character and performance as conflicted and guilt-ridden artist caught up in an irrevocable downward spiral of inner conflict and excess. Reed's character crystallises the late 1960s' hedonistic excess and fragmented psyche as similarly portrayed via Chas's (James Fox) downward spiral and the polyamorous and psychedelic ongoings in Turner's (Mick Jagger) abode in Donald Cammell and Nicolas Roeg's *Performance* (Goodtimes Enterprises, 1970). After the suicide of his by-then-wife Siddal, Reed's Rossetti starts to fall apart. The deliberate differentiation between the female mind being dominated by emotion and rational thought reserved for the male members of society is then also partly mirrored in *Dante's Inferno*. Ultimately, however, this is subverted as Rossetti's gradual decline into madness is portrayed in a more harrowing fashion by Reed that ultimately deprives the character of his own male agency. Reed's Rossetti is coping with his grief by withdrawing into himself, turning away from the company of others, growing more detached. He is shown with a pensive, despondent and brooding gaze, being visibly uncomfortably numb (Figures 2.8 and 2.9).

Reed's poet/painter is driven by guilt and experiences visions of his deceived wife's spectral presence. Eros and Thanatos merge very strongly in the burial scene, in which Rossetti places his poetry book in Elizabeth's coffin, calling it 'my heart' and thus showing more sincere reverence than during her lifetime (although he later intends to retrieve the book). This brings to mind Mary Shelley, who kept Percy Bysshe Shelley's 'heart', which is now thought to have been his liver,[36] as a token of remembrance. In *Dante's Inferno*, love, death and natural settings are likewise merged. As the narrator declares, Rossetti's mind is increasingly 'Sodden with insomnia, whisky and a new drug, chloral'. Nonetheless, addiction is still linked with poetry and artistic creation, thus playing to the stereotype of the self-destructive young artist who burns himself out too quickly that was prominent in the late 1960s in the form of the excessive, hedonistic 'life in the fast lane' attitude embodied by (rock) musicians of the time. By the end of the film, Reed's poet/painter is looking back at 'the lost days of his life' with regret and through the muddled haze of 'a mind clouded with chloral'. He cannot connect with anyone or anything and condemns himself endlessly.

Figures 2.8 and 2.9 Grieving and haunted: Oliver Reed's tormented Rossetti.
Source: BBC, 1967.

INNER VOIDS AND THE ABYSS: REED'S CONFLICTED MASCULINITY IN *WOMEN IN LOVE* AND *THE DEVILS*

Billy Williams's cinematography and Shirley Russell's costume design in *Women in Love* fuse 1920s and 1960s aesthetics, linking the screen adaptation to the roaring 1920s spirit and the 1960s bohemian/countercultural mindset: 'We set the film in 1920, which was a time of disillusionment, of change.'[37] Jack Fisher notes:

> There are two artistic consciousnesses at work: the vision of Lawrence which provides most of the words and actions, and Russell's which provides the shape, size, colour and rhythm – the visual attitude . . . With Russell the attitude inclines towards very pronounced forms: a remarkable range of colours from pastels to primaries and an increasingly restless rhythm in editing.[38]

By this means and through 'rigid control of the surrounding atmosphere, he presents us with the nature of the sexual experience being observed'.[39] The film was made nine years after the Lady Chatterley obscenity trial, which brought the author back into the headlines and into public consciousness, associating him with the nascent permissive society.

Women in Love's focus on two men and two women (Glenda Jackson and Jennie Linden as the Brangwen sisters, Gudrun and Ursula) structurally allows scenes to alternate between interactions between the two sisters and the male characters, Crich and Birkin. As the narrative unfolds, both male and female perspectives are given equal space and on-screen time. Linda Ruth Williams states that 'the seeing eye is specifically blind to the darkness of the self' and the 'conscious, visually fixated modern soul is denigrated'.[40] Lawrence invites the reader to 'abandon the priorities of human visual perception, and embrace other ways of knowing and touching the world'.[41] This rejection of ordinary perception in favour of sensual-tactile experimentation and related modes of perception corresponds to the 1960s countercultural fervour for breaking 'on through to the other side'. In his study of Russell and Stanley Kubrick as contemporaries, Matthew Melia draws a comparison as 'portals and thresholds also play a pivotal role in the work of both Russell and Kubrick . . . Across their bodies of work there are revealing instances of characters' crossing thresholds that are "alternate", "threatening" and "unreal".'[42] However, in the case of Crich, Reed shies away from breaking through perceptual, moral or sexual dimensions, whereas his self-indulgent Grandier endeavours to transcend these very thresholds.

Jackson's sassy portrayal of the free-spirited Gudrun, in turn, is of an explorative, curious nature, accentuated by her flapper haircut and the style that

Figure 2.10 Alienated, detached and conflicted: Reed as Gerald Crich.
Source: United Artists, 1969.

merges 1920s and 1960s bohemia and permissiveness.[43] The actress's performance throughout Russell's film is that of active female agency with a certain drive and grit as opposed to Reed's passive character, who rather reacts to other characters' actions and musings than acting himself, let alone driving the narrative. Reed is the dominant character in the first halves of *Dante's Inferno* and *The Devils*, but not in *Women in Love*. After the death of his father, Reed's estranged Gerald reaches an even more emotionally and physically passive state, not even reacting to his mother's abusive mockery. Whilst Reed's Grandier is staged as the epitome of imposing, assertive manhood in the first part of *The Devils*, Gerald Crich is muted and disrespected by his own family. A Freudian nightmare, his mother constantly humiliates him by attacking his manhood. Reed's Crich feebly reacts to this situation but does not attempt to regain his agency or balance, thus delivering a very modulated, contained performance. He is emotionally inarticulate and cannot connect with the outer world, which is conveyed via Reed's often clipped, stifled vocal delivery, his pauses, and his alienated, brooding and at times detached gazes and repressed bodily comportment.

He briefly opens up to Rupert and Gudrun, but eventually feels misunderstood by both on account of their oppositional mental and emotional dispositions. In a fatalistic mood, he tells Gudrun, 'you seem to be reaching at the void . . . then you realise . . . that you are a void yourself'. Visually, the emotional distance between them is enforced by their on-screen positioning: Gerald situated in the foreground, reflected in a mirror and Gudrun placed in the background. Gerald and Gudrun's dysfunctional relationship is also characterised by a constant sadomasochistic struggle for power, resonating with *The Devils*' multiple power struggles that encompass the domestic and the political (and with the nihilistic sexual and cultural conflicts at the end of the era).

Grandier is omnipresent in *The Devils*, even when physically absent, as the disfigured Mother Superior, Sister Jeanne of the Angels, nurses an ill-fated, unrequited amour fou where he is viscerally present in her erotic daydreams. Reed's repeatedly exposed body is shown covered in sweat and blood in one of Jeanne's sadomasochistic, erotic hallucinations. He is elevated to a fetishised Christ whose body is also shown in fragmented close shots (Figure 2.11). Body and gaze act as the two key signifiers of Reed's performance. It is not only her delusional, obsessive character, but the other female characters, too, who place their female gazes on Grandier, reducing him to a corporeal object of desire, shown in objectifying shots and close-ups that foreground and expose his other-worldly virility. During an early sequence, the nuns of the convent are depicted voyeuristically peeping through a grating at Grandier bedecked in his ecclesiastical finery (not unlike the depiction of Anthony Perkins's deranged street preacher – another religious figure – depicted leering through the peephole of a strip joint in *Crimes of Passion* [New World Pictures, 1984]).

Reed's passive protagonist in *Women in Love*, in turn, is eventually left behind by Gudrun, who opts for a more liberated, bohemian lifestyle. In both films, however, Reed's character ends up suffering: either committing suicide or turning into a martyr. The actor's recurrent portrayal of male crisis is symptomatic of Russell's already highlighted use of corporeality as being defined by feelings of anxiety, physical and spiritual pain and a lasting inner conflict.[44] Reed's Gerald also displays a Byronic moodiness, and despite his emotional repression and inner torment, is still depicted as a masculine captain of industry, as demonstrated by the violent thrashing of his horse at the railway crossing.

The Devils ranks as a pre-eminent film in a milieu of nihilistic late 1960s British cinema that articulates the decline of the counterculture and the

Figure 2.11 The body of Christ: Grandier's body as fetishised spectacle in *The Devils*.
Source: Warner Bros., 1971.

sobering revelation that the hippie dream was a naïve fantasy, where identity, sexuality and the 'free love' mantra are all refocused through a nihilistic, disillusioned lens. As David Simonelli observes, 'the highs of Swinging London were hangovers by 1972'.[45] Films of the time, including *The Devils*, then may be read as a reaction to the sociocultural upheavals of the 1960s and the resulting search for identity in a world descending into violent, excessive outbursts.[46] As Melia notes, *The Devils* presents 'stylised, enclosed, dystopic, gothic brutalist world building and architectures, as well as a deviant, violent and transgressive libertine sexuality'.[47] Moreover, 'The book [by Aldous Huxley] (as with the film) deals with sexual hysteria, the fear of permissiveness, state control over the individual, moral panic . . . – it's a film which repurposes its source material for the time.'[48]

Ken Hanke aptly states that 'Russell's concept of *The Devils* is as a film of and for its time, not Huxley's time.'[49] The film features the prevalent anti-establishment 1960s conflict between the individual and the state or system and the self-destructive and unstable individual disposition of the main protagonists (Grandier and Jeanne) that is set against the volatile backdrop of a plague-ridden city. In *The Devils*, Reed's defiant rebel priest first demonstrates some political and individual agency as his actions and decisions determine the course of the narrative before he is turned into a passive martyr and victimised scapegoat of the power struggle between monarch and the Church. Reed's Grandier's initial agency is highlighted by medium shots, depicting him holding a powerful rebel speech with a self-assured voice and intonation, from a slightly low angle and close-ups that stress his masculine authority, bodily comportment and personal narcissistic vanity.

In *Women in Love* Reed tones down his Byronic and excessive performance, whereas in *The Devils*, the actor's Grandier transcends the diegetic constraints. Reed's emotionally stunted Crich, in turn, remains within the narrative, having built his own cage, behaving in a repressed, ill-at-ease and taciturn manner. He is not as seductively eloquent and persuasive as the womanising priest in *The Devils*, but much more self-aware and guarded. Gerald's inhibitions are manifested and exposed during his interactions with Bates's Rupert. These serve to contrast both men, and performers, whilst at the same time highlighting their homosocial bonding, epitomised in the wrestling scene (although Reed's Crich rejects any potential queer reading of their brotherhood in the scene). This performance both subverts and reinforces Reed's 1960s virile star persona. In these encounters as well as throughout the film, Bates's Rupert comes across as much more outspoken and playfully curious than Reed's comparatively timid Gerald. Their first longer conversation juxtaposes their views on love and life. Preceding their wrestling match, a pensive and moody Gerald is depicted in profile and positioned in front of a fireplace, being (once more) spatially and emotionally cut off from the environment and its inhabitants.

Williams states that Lawrence's Gerald Crich is staged as a 'spectacle of masculinity' in the novel,[50] which is demonstrated in Russell's film in the sequence where Crich is shown swimming naked. Like Rupert Birkin, Gerald is also linked to animals and nature yet associated with a forced mastery over it (rather than in harmony with it à la Birkin), further signifying a Godlike virility – evidenced not only by his treatment of the horse but also in his handling of the Highland cattle. Whereas Birkin is part of nature, Crich 'subjugates the body to the purpose of work' and seems to only allow sexual intercourse – no real passion – when 'he has become "part of the machine" to such an extent that this fusion has split off desire as a waste product, extrinsic to his functioning'.[51] Crich's brutalisation of the horse (an image as cathartic and masturbatory as Murray Melvin's Mignon at the orgy in *The Devils*) in front of the two sisters to prove his authority and virile sportsmanship is depicted in shots accentuating Reed's physical prowess; later he gently caresses a rabbit, oscillating between rough, mechanical and awkwardly gentle bodily movements and gestures. In discussing Lawrence's novel and its portrayal of Gerald and the horse, Linda Ruth Williams writes:

> Gerald engulfs the horse, both become one spectacle, one single being with two halves, violator and violated . . . what we see, then, is subjection as spectacle, a violent image of mutuality of the interdependence of sadism and masochism in the act of power.[52]

Gerald and the horse enter 'a pact which finds each other's need as dominant and submissive'.[53] Reed's Rossetti also strolls and drifts through nature, either chasing a love interest or alone. He is associated with both natural impulses (sexuality) as well as the spiritual (art). Gerald's behaviour towards animals in *Women in Love* also exposes different sides to his contradictory character as does the recurrent association with fire and snow; Reed's initially philandering Rossetti is also visually linked with fire. Similarly, Grandier's (predatory) virility and power are also connected with nature and animals when duelling with a stuffed (phallic) crocodile. Later he is staged alone in nature, next to a mountain lake, quietly offering communion whilst lamenting in solitary musing that he is a man who 'has always been lost'.

In *Dante's Inferno*, Reed's Rossetti shifts between bawdy-hedonistic and dreamy, being smitten with his muse, whereas his Grandier oscillates between hedonistic (self-)indulgence and gentle caresses in the scenes with the previously worldly innocent Madeleine (Gemma Jones). The first sexual encounter between Gerald and Gudrun, for instance, is brought on by his awkward Byronic moodiness after his father's death when he abruptly arrives at her parents' home in the middle of the night with a muddy clenched fist. During the lovemaking scene, shots of Gerald's derisively laughing mother are inserted, accentuating his problematic relationships with women (he is previously only shown with several tarts), the emotional wound caused by an abusive mother and linking his mother to Gudrun (she likewise verbally abuses him at times). The thoughts and mental images of his abusive, cold mother then trigger an aggressive and mechanical behaviour and bodily movements. In all three roles, there are awkward moments emerging from Reed's respectively embodied troubled, contradictory male characters who at times do not really know how to (re)act.

CONCLUSION

As has been previously examined, performed masculinities in Ken Russell's films of the 1960s and 1970s are multi-layered and conflicted and resonate with their time(s), as is paradigmatically, albeit not exclusively, exemplified via the case study of Oliver Reed's Russellian performances. In *Dante's Inferno*, *Women in Love* and *The Devils*, Reed's troubled males are repeatedly subjected to the status of a corporeal spectacle that is both 'violator and violated' on account of their innate self-destructive and masochistic dispositions. This is further enhanced in performative terms by the actor's distinctive physical screen presence that does not shy away from presenting a broken male physique – the artist-turned-reclusive-addict in *Dante's Inferno*, the alienated Gerald who commits suicide by curling up in an embryonic, broken position in the snow in *Women in Love*, and the rebel priest who is elevated to martyrdom by burning at the stake after losing his physical signifiers of virility – moustache, hair and even eyebrows – in *The Devils*.

Reed's Rossetti, Crich and Grandier are all somewhat caught up in themselves and their own inner conflicts but in different ways (Rossetti and Grandier are both self-absorbed in an egocentric, vain manner) and therefore struggle to relate to the outer world. They further ultimately direct their aggressive potentials against themselves. Reed's Crich, for instance, eventually succumbs to his emotional apathy expressed by the inner void and his general weariness, which is evoked by detached facial expressions and stiff body language. At last, he gives in to his desire for self-annihilation in the cold snow; like Richard Burton's disillusioned and world-weary Alec Leamas in *The Spy Who Came in from the Cold* (Martin Ritt, Paramount, 1965), Reed's Crich realises that he cannot come in from the cold as he carries it within him.

NOTES

1. Stephen Heath, *Questions of Cinema* (Bloomington: Indiana University Press, 1981), 183.
2. Sue Harper and Justin Smith, *British Film Culture in the 1970s: The Boundaries of Pleasure* (Edinburgh: Edinburgh University Press, 2012), 187.

3. Barry Keith Grant, 'The Body Politic: Ken Russell in the 1980s', in Kevin M. Flanagan (ed.), *Ken Russell: Re-Viewing England's Last Mannerist* (Plymouth: Scarecrow Press, 2009), 32.
4. Andrew Spicer, *Typical Men: The Representation of Masculinity in Popular British Cinema* (London and New York: I.B. Tauris, 2001), 155.
5. Caroline Langhorst, '"Rebel Rebel"?: Oliver Reed in the 1960s', in Duncan Petrie, Melanie Williams and Laura Mayne (eds), *Sixties British Cinema Reconsidered* (Edinburgh: Edinburgh University Press, 2021), 42–3; see also 40–1.
6. Ruth Barton, *Acting Irish in Hollywood: From Fitzgerald to Farrell* (Dublin and Portland: Irish Academic Press, 2006), 126.
7. Ibid.
8. Ibid., 127.
9. Harper and Smith, 188.
10. Ibid.
11. Ibid.
12. Spicer, 76.
13. Phil Powrie, Ann Davies and Bruce Babington, 'Introduction: Turning the Male Inside Out', in Phil Powrie, Ann Davies and Bruce Babington (eds), *The Trouble with Men: Masculinities in European and Hollywood Cinema* (London and New York: Wallflower Press, 2004), 6.
14. Robert Shail, 'Masculinity and Class: Michael Caine as "Working-Class Hero"', in Powrie et al. (eds), 73.
15. Powrie et al., 'Introduction', 6.
16. Reed notably lacked formal acting training as he neither attended drama school nor joined a repertory theatre company. Instead, he started as an extra and then became a youthful Hammer horror idol.
17. Jack Fisher, 'Three Masterpieces of Sexuality: *Women in Love*, *The Music Lovers*, and *The Devils*', in Thomas R. Atkins (ed.), *Ken Russell* (New York: Monarch Press, 1976), 42.
18. Barry Forshaw, *British Crime Film: Subverting the Social Order* (Basingstoke: Palgrave Macmillan, 2012), 94.
19. Atara Stein, *The Byronic Hero in Film, Fiction, and Television* (Carbondale: Southern Illinois University Press, 2004), 1.
20. Ibid., 2.
21. Cliff Goodwin, *Evil Spirits: The Life of Oliver Reed* (London: Virgin Books, 2001), 98.
22. Oliver Reed, *Reed About Me* (London: Virgin Books, 1979), 124.
23. Goodwin, 98.
24. Joseph Lanza, *Phallic Frenzy: Ken Russell and His Films* (London: Aurum Press, 2007), 43.
25. Justin Smith, 'British Cult Cinema', in Robert Murphy (ed.), *The British Cinema Book*, 3rd edn (London: BFI, 2009), 59.
26. Leon Hunt, 'Necromancy in the UK: Witchcraft and the Occult in British Horror', in Steve Chibnall and Julian Petley (eds), *British Horror Cinema* (New York: Routledge, 1999), 84.
27. Emma Sutton, *Aubrey Beardsley and British Wagnerism in the 1890s* (Oxford: Oxford University Press, 2002), 189.
28. Richard Warren, *Art Nouveau and the Classical Tradition* (London and New York: Bloomsbury Academic, 2017), 66.
29. Matthew Melia, 'Ken Russell's Unfinished Projects and Unmade Films, 1956–68: The BBC Years', in James Fenwick, Kieran Foster and David Eldridge (eds), *Shadow Cinema: The Historical and Production Contexts of Unmade Films* (New York: Bloomsbury Academic, 2021), 93.
30. Petra Dierkes-Thrun, *Salome's Modernity: Oscar Wilde and the Aesthetics of Transgression* (Ann Arbor: University of Michigan Press, 2014), 162.

31. Andrew Kirk, '"Machines of Loving Grace": Alternative Technology, Environment, and the Counterculture', in Michael William Doyle and Peter Braunstein (eds), *Imagine Nation: The American Counterculture of the 1960's and 70's* (London and New York: Routledge, 2001), 359.
32. Kevin Flanagan, 'Whitehead's London: Pop and the Ascendant Celebrity', *Framework*, vol. 52, no. 1, 2011, 287.
33. Thomas J. Brennan, 'Creating From Nothing: Swinburne and Baudelaire in "Ave Atque Vale"', *Victorian Poetry*, vol. 44, no. 3, Fall 2006, 251–71.
34. John Baxter, 'The Television Plays: *Poet's London* to *Dance of the Seven Veils*', in Atkins (ed.), 33.
35. Ibid.
36. John Worthen, *The Life of Percy Bysshe Shelley: A Critical Biography* (Hoboken, NJ: Wiley, 2019), 438.
37. Louis K. Greiff, *D.H. Lawrence: Fifty Years on Film* (Carbondale: Southern Illinois University Press, 2001), 241, quoting Russell being interviewed by John Baxter.
38. Fisher, 42.
39. Ibid., 45.
40. Linda Ruth Williams, *Sex in the Head: Visions of Femininity and Film in D.H. Lawrence* (London: Routledge, 2017), 20, 1.
41. Ibid., 1.
42. Matthew Melia, 'Altered States, Altered Spaces: Architecture, Space and Landscape in the Film and Television of Stanley Kubrick and Ken Russell', Cinergie: Il Cinema e le Altre Arti, vol. 6, no. 12, 2017, 145, <https://cinergie.unibo.it/article/view/7352> (last accessed 19 February 2022).
43. See NJ Stevenson's chapter on costumer designer Shirley Russell and the influence of 'retrochic' on *The Boy Friend* in this volume.
44. Grant, 32.
45. David Simonelli, *Working-Class Heroes: Rock Music and British Society in the 1960s and 1970s* (Minneapolis, MN: Lexington Books, 2012), 147.
46. Smith, 59.
47. Matthew Melia, 'Stanley Kubrick's *A Clockwork Orange* and Ken Russell's *The Devils*: A Comparative Study of Two Parallel Texts', paper given at 'A Clockwork Symposium: New Perspectives in A Clockwork Orange', December 2018, University of Arts, London: London College of Communication.
48. Ibid.
49. Ken Hanke, *Ken Russell's Films* (Metuchen, NJ: Scarecrow Press, 1984), 120.
50. Williams, 80.
51. Petra Rau, *English Modernism, National Identity and the Germans, 1890–1950* (London and New York: Routledge, 2009), 145.
52. Ibid.
53. Ibid.

CHAPTER 3

Ken Russell's Gothic Modernism

Matthew Melia

INTRODUCTION

Critical scholarship surrounding Ken Russell's work and career has tended to privilege his Romantic preoccupations and sensibilities. There has been considerably (and somewhat surprisingly) less critical discourse devoted solely to the looming presence of either the Gothic or Modernism, or their intersection in his work. Recently, however, Kevin M. Flanagan has bridged the gap between the Gothic and the Romantic by interrogating the adaptive nature and (modernist) intertextual relationship between Russell's two major 'Frankentexts' *Lisztomania* (Goodtimes Enterprises, 1975) and *Gothic* (Virgin Vision, 1986). Flanagan observes that

> *Lisztomania* and *Gothic* are adaptations of a sort. They use intertextual references from Gothic horror culture to build apparently original commentaries on the act of creation as understood by the Romantic artists they profile . . . these two films express this discourse of creative invention through a paradox: originality and individualized expression via the quoting and repurposing of the Gothic mash-up mode.[1]

He also notes that

> Both films share a narrative fascination that aligns with the Romanticist discourse on artistic creation, with its nascent obsession with the idea of individual originality and concurrent exploration of the process of adaptation . . . each emerges as a kind of Gothic mash up or 'Frankenfiction'.[2]

Gothic, with its phantasmagorical, Henry Fuseli-inspired imagery, is perhaps the most direct example of Russell's Gothic imagination at work and it provides a later juncture between his earlier Gothic and Romantic preoccupations – such as a concern with the female Gothic and its representations of internalised monsters and hysteria, as in *Crimes of Passion* (New World Pictures, 1984), *The Music Lovers* (United Artists, 1970) and *Isadora Duncan, the Biggest Dancer in the World* (BBC, 1966) – and points the way forward to the final 'Garagiste' work, the films of his later (homemade) 'Gorsewood Productions'.

Russell's position as a modernist has also been overlooked, especially as his career frequently intersects with the cultural history of Modernism with adaptations of D. H. Lawrence (*Women in Love* [United Artists, 1969], *The Rainbow* [Vestron, 1989], *Lady Chatterley's Lover* [BBC, 1993]); filmic and televisual studies of modernist figures like the composer Béla Bartók (see below), and unrealised plans to make films about the lives of Bloomsbury authors Virginia Woolf and Lytton Strachey.[3]

Other modernist *cinematic* influences include Fritz Lang's *Metropolis* (UFA, 1927) with its utopian, futuristic set design and cityscape (a model for Derek Jarman's own set design in *The Devils* [Warner Bros., 1971]) and Gothic narrative of monstrous scientific creation. The image of Lang's Rotwang (Rudolph Klein-Rogge) as both scientist and sorcerer is rooted in Gothic and Romantic narratives of creation and perverted scientific ambition, which are thematically present across Russell's work (as in *Lisztomania* or *Altered States* [Warner Bros., 1980]). Other modernist points of reference include visual references to the work of Sergei Eisenstein (the restaging of the Battle on the Ice from *Alexander Nevsky* [Mosfilm, 1938] in *Billion Dollar Brain* [United Artists, 1967]) as well as the Hollywood Modernism of 1930s Busby Berkley Hollywood musicals and Universal horror films (in *The Boy Friend* [MGM-EMI, 1971], *Tommy* [Columbia, 1975] and *Lisztomania*).

The intersection of the Gothic and Modernism can be observed as far back as Russell's early career in photography (an area around which there has also been little critical discussion). The decaying past and the modern, progressive future collide in these images from the mid-1950s which depict the bombed, decaying and evanescent ruins and wastelands of post-war London. From out of this landscape emerge images of a subcultural milieu – the 'Teddy Girls', embodiments of youth and contemporaneity, standing amid the rubble and decomposition. 'In Your Dreams' (1955), part of the *Last of the Teddy Girls* series, depicts fourteen-year-old Jean Rayner staring defiantly (and transgressively) into the camera's lens, dressed in the style of a fashionable (male) Victorian dandy: the epitome of the late nineteenth-century modernist (and a figure connected through writers like Oscar Wilde to nineteenth-century neo-Gothic culture).[4] In another image, seventeen-year-old Grace Living is framed by the decaying and shadowy architecture of a derelict doorway and window – which resembles a ruined Gothic arch.[5]

In a previous study I presented an archive-based survey of Russell's unmade work from between 1956 and 1968 ('the BBC years'), and argued that these lost and abandoned projects are as valuable to a complete understanding of Russell's career as the extant ones.[6] Hence in this chapter, by drawing from across a range of completed *and* unmade work, I hope to better understand and to critically interrogate Russell's Gothic-modernist imagination, to observe his journey from early career modernist to late career postmodernist, and to observe how his approach to Modernism is mediated through the Gothic (and vice versa).

KEN RUSSELL'S *GOTHIC* 1980S

From the end of the 1970s and throughout the 1980s Russell turned away (mostly) from the biographical film-making which had defined the first half of his career, and towards Gothic genre cinema, literary adaptation and author/screenwriter collaboration. The Gothic itself increasingly became the subject rather than the spectre lurking in the background. Flanagan observes that after *Valentino* (United Artists, 1977), 'Russell entered a more commercial phase' of his career, leaving Britain to work (at least temporarily) in the US. *Valentino* and *Altered States* were 'both made with the backing of major funding and distribution'.[7] Their commercial failures, however, meant Russell became persona non grata with the major studios and was adopted by a series of 'Minimajors' – New World Pictures, Virgin Vision and Vestron Pictures – during which period he 'became something of a maestro of horror cinema' and the object of renewed cult interest.[8]

During the mid-1980s Russell found himself in the right place at the right time, the fates aligning him with the growing popularity of the home video market. Joseph Lanza observes:

> That a movie as literary and idiosyncratic as *Salome's Last Dance* got made at all has much to do with Russell's temporary turn of good fortune after Vestron Video profited from American VHS sales of *Gothic*. As a result, its subsidiary Vestron Pictures (who also made a killing on the 1987 romance *Dirty Dancing*) was impressed enough to offer Russell a three-movie deal. *Salome's Last Dance* would be the first (followed by *The Lair of the White Worm* and *The Rainbow*).[9]

Russell began the decade with a cycle of Gothic adaptations, beginning with *Dracula* (an ultimately unmade script from 1978), followed by *Altered States* (from Paddy Chayefsky's script based on his 1978 science fiction novel, a 'tightly written and technically radical overhaul of Robert Louis Stevenson's *Dr Jekyll and Mr Hyde*'[10] (a comparison widely made in the critical reception of the film at the time), the presence of which also imprints upon *Crimes of Passion*. *Gothic* emerged out of a collaboration with the British screenwriter and author Stephen Volk. It was Volk's first script, which he had first drafted in 1981 when working in advertising (as Russell had done). It is a text with two 'creators': Russell's visual cinematic language synchronised with Volk's script ideas, which they subsequently worked on collaboratively.

Both John Kenneth Muir and Barry Keith Grant contextualise Russell's genre output of the 1980s against the backdrop of body horror cinema and a revived cultural interest in Gothic horror during the period.[11] *Gothic* was funded and produced by Virgin Films and distributed by Vestron Video, and takes its place among the Gothic renaissance of the 1980s, owing much in terms of style and Gothic aesthetic to the emergent medium of the music video which Russell had indirectly helped with *Tommy*, and a medium in which he had worked in directing videos for Elton John, among others. In 1989 he would direct the music video for Jim Steinman's 'It's all Coming Back to Me Now', which Steinman had scripted based on Russell's 'Nessun Dorma' sequence from Don Boyd's *Aria* (Virgin Vision, 1987).[12]

Gothic's postmodern approach to the Frankenstein mythology references a host of cinematic, literary, theatrical and art historical Gothic sources. Leaving out the creature altogether (its presence is indirectly felt), it focuses instead on the frenzied crucible of the novel's own birth: the fateful meeting of haunted minds at the Villa Diodati in 1816, the 'Year Without Summer', out of which emerged not only *Frankenstein* but Polidori's *The Vampyre* (1819), a key influence on Stoker's *Dracula*. This is a film about the birth of Gothic popular culture. It is also illustrative of what Roger Luckhurst has termed 'Corridor Gothic'.[13] The Villa Diodati, Byron's (Gabriel Byrne) rented home on the shores of Lake Geneva, Switzerland, is a haunted funhouse (again this featured heavily as a description in the critical reception of the film after its release) full of mechanical automatons, disorienting corridors and passages – metonyms for the haunted and traumatised Gothic psyche – where the viewer is drawn ever further into its nightmarish complexities as the frenzy of the evening crescendos, growing ever more surreal and horrifying. Christophe Van Eecke has noted that

> The phantasmagoria of the opening titles connects Gothic to the context of Victorian popular entertainment . . . the film is structured as a ride through the booby-trapped funhouse of the Villa Diodati. Just like a dark ride in a modern theme park, where spectators move from one view to the next, so too the spectacular geography of the Villa Diodati is that of a series of rooms furnished with attractions that await us.[14]

The Frankenstein mythology and its cultural iconography are embedded in the fabric of Russell's work, not only in the textual preoccupation with the act of creation (facets of both Romantic and modernist discourse) but also observed elsewhere in Gerald Crich's (Oliver Reed) lonely death march into the snow in *Women*

Figure 3.1 Rock 'n' roll Frankenstein.
Source: Columbia, 1975.

in Love (like the Creature's own lonely retreat into the snowy wastes in Shelley's novel); or young Sally Simpson's (Victoria Russell) rock musician husband in *Tommy* (1975): a child actor in a Boris Karloff mask (Gary Rich) (Figure 3.1).

Gothic is as much an homage to the popular culture surrounding *Frankenstein* and to the cultural history of the Gothic as it is to Shelley's novel. Frankenstein's monster is absent from the film; however, in the closing moments the present day Frankentourists swarm the villa and its grounds, and a tour guide/voice-over tells us, 'Something created that night 170 years ago lives on – still haunting us to this day: Mary Shelley's *Frankenstein*' (Figure 3.2). In the final freezeframe Russell depicts a monstrous foetus floating beneath the water of Lake Geneva, its head seemingly square and elongated like that of Boris Karloff's iconic creature.

Gothic is also Volk's homage to the costumed Gothic of the British Hammer horror films, and Byron 'enters the film in exactly the way the haughty, aristocratic Christopher Lee enters Dracula (Terence Fisher, Hammer, 1958): gliding down a staircase to greet his guests, a deliberate signal that this is a Hammer film, in all but name'.[15] *The Lair of the White Worm* (Vestron, 1988), on the other hand, is Russell's camp parody of Hammer. He admitted that the film emerged out of the failure of the *Dracula* project (1978), quipping that he couldn't make Bram Stoker's best novel, so he made Stoker's worst. It is

> both a self-parodying exercise with comic adaptation (a deliberately ridiculous version of a very bad novel) and a pastiche of the allegories of

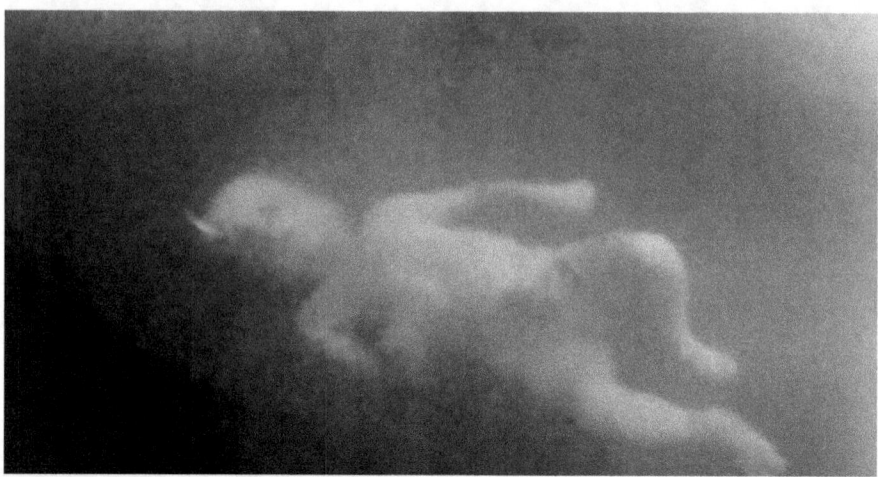

Figure 3.2 'Something created that night . . .'
Source: Virgin Pictures/Vestron, 1986.

England we encountered in 1970s horror . . . Russell retrofits the programmatic trash film, to a very English style of Baroque high camp, as he also did in the follow up *Salome's Last Dance*. Russell's *The Fall of the Louse of Usher* [2002] continues this signature style of puckish high camp in what is essentially a home movie.[16]

Crimes of Passion may initially seem like the odd one out during the first half of the 1980s. Based solely on an original script idea from screenwriter Barry Sandler and set amid the neon-drenched night-time streets of LA, it was Russell's most explicit and transgressive film since *The Devils*, and the casting of Anthony Perkins as the sexually depraved preacher Rev. Peter Shayne draws intertextually on the Gothic horror of Hitchcock's *Psycho* (Paramount Pictures, 1960). Its protagonist Joanna/China Blue (Kathleen Turner), fashion executive by day/sex worker by night (Figure 3.3), is a female Jekyll and Hyde figure operating within a noirish world of sexual transgression and deviance – (In one scene she pleasures a cop with his own nightstick). The China Blue side of the persona an externalisation of interior and transgressive sexual desire, very much in the historical and cultural tradition of the female Gothic.

Russell juxtaposes the shadowy, Gothic and exotic attractions of the night-time world of the city with the more mundane aesthetic of the suburbs. China Blue's dual identity and her movement between the daytime world of the professional suburban middle class to the darker temptations of night-city are rooted in various Gothic narrative traditions (not least film noir). Oscar Wilde explores similar urban transgressions in *The Picture of Dorian Gray* as Dorian transgresses between worlds to satiate his pleasure, roaming

Figure 3.3 China Blue.
Source: New World Pictures, 1984.

into the less salubrious East End of London, an 'othered space' diametrically opposed to the (supposedly) polite world of West End society.

George Haggerty notes in his definition of the Gothic that

> Catholicism emerges from the historical setting to play an active role in most gothic novels. In Walpole's *The Castle of Otranto* (1764), a Catholic chapel provides one of the key sites of the action, and the unassuming Father Jerome, the local cleric, himself holds a significant position in the denouement of the action. More to the point, however, is the mood of religious sentiment that suffuses the whole.[17]

Russell converted to Catholicism in the 1950s and Catholic imagery (often subverted) is part of the defining iconography of his work. Deviant, libertine clerics and nuns abound in Russell's cinema: images of ravaged, uninhibited and orgiastic nuns occur not only in *The Devils* but also in *Dance of the Seven Veils* (BBC, 1970), *French Dressing* (Associated British Picture Corporation, 1964), *Watch the Birdie* (BBC, 1963) and *The Lair of the White Worm*. While *The Devils* adapts Aldous Huxley's historical narrative of real-life events (1952), and John Whiting's play (1961), it also bears the Gothic weight of both Walpole's novel and Matthew Lewis's *The Monk* (1796). Anthony Perkins's sexually deranged preacher in *Crimes of Passion*, with his horrifying killer dildo ('The Superman') and hold-all of bizarre sex toys, is another example of this Gothic trope. When we first meet Shayne, he is high on poppers and leering through the peephole of a strip show (Figure 3.4).[18] Screenwriter Barry Sandler described how Shayne

Figure 3.4 Rev. Shayne.
Source: New World Pictures, 1984.

was originally written as a psychiatrist and the film was a 'two-hander' with China Blue. Russell's collaboration with Sandler expanded this vision, creating the wider noirish contemporary Gothic setting. Shayne's transformation from shrink to street preacher, however, was a decision made between Sandler and Perkins, and was influenced by the hypnotic, pervasive influence of TV evangelists like Jimmy Swaggart.[19]

Russell's Gothic imagination is rooted in both a childhood love of cinema and the wartime trauma of the Southampton Blitz (evident in the early childhood scenes in *Tommy* in which, like in his photography, Russell presents the bombed, collapsed ruins of the city). In his autobiography Russell recounts being traumatised by a tentacled, eldritch creature haunting a cupboard at his childhood home, which turned out to be nothing more than a gas mask left over from the Great War. It is an image incorporated into *The Debussy Film* (BBC, 1965): immediately prior to the 'House of Usher Sequence' (discussed below) Debussy's war requiem plays over the images of horrifying gas-masked soldiers, emerging from the mustard gas hell of the Somme. Russell would find further 'monstrous' trauma at the cinema. He recounted his experience of the 1934 British horror film *The Secret of the Loch* ('The most horrific film I ever saw'[20]) in which the monstrous creature turned out to be a 'naked chicken, plucked and very much alive'.[21] The 'make-do-and-mend' DIY expediency of this image imprints itself on his early amateur films as well as his final homemade Garagiste films. Russell would later (almost) return to this subject. In 1979, as reported in *Variety*, he was set to direct *The Monster of Loch Ness*, 'a contemporary tale of the 300ft monster, in this case mutated by ecological disaster and radiation'.[22] The film was never made but Russell might have looked back here to 1950s American B-movies and their combination of Gothic atomic monstrosity and mid-century Modernism.

European expressionist cinema provides yet another source for Russell's Gothic imagination, and he references the influence of the 'bold imagery of Jean Cocteau and Fritz Lang'.[23] Furthermore, a shot in *The Devils* of a nun furiously masturbating with a candlestick recalls a similar shot from Swedish director Benjamin Christensen's film essay on the history of witchcraft, *Häxan* (Scandia's Fimbria, 1922), in which a demon is shown pulverising a baby during a Sabbat; and the coffined figure of the somnambulist Cesare from *The Cabinet of Dr. Caligari* (Robert Wiene, UFA, 1920) is also imprinted upon the confined and coffined bodies which populate Russell's films. In *Mahler* (Goodtimes Enterprises, 1974), *Tommy* and *Altered States*, characters and subjects are presented encased in cocoons or chrysalises from which the coffined body emerges transcendent and transfigured. This is a repeated Russell trope: in *Tommy* during the 'Acid Queen' sequence, trauma and ecstasy are symbiotic with transfiguration and metamorphosis.[24]

The depletion of the senses elevates and transcends the self, and *Tommy* exhibits stylistic Gothic excess in both its expressionist mise en scène and cinematography. During the sequence Tommy emerges as a messianic figure from a Paolozzi-esque (post)modernist pop art/Gothic iron maiden (lined with heroin needles rather than spikes); the kineticism of the sequence and the wide angle close-up of the Acid Queen's face contribute to a sense of Gothic hysteria and frame her as a cloistered monster or 'madwoman in the attic' – both exotic ('I'm the gypsy, the acid queen'), transgressive and sexually aggressive monster and agent of sublime change ('Give us a room, close the door / Leave us for a while / You won't be a boy no more / Young, but not a child'). The nightmarish coffin sequence in *Mahler*, in which the composer is placed in the coffin alive, is also an homage to a similar sequence in Carl Dreyer's influential dreamlike, expressionist Gothic horror *The Vampyr* (Vereinigte Star-Film, 1932) in which the central protagonist has a nightmare about being buried alive – calling to mind another literary Gothic preoccupation of Russell's: the work of Edgar Allan Poe.

GOTHIC SPACES AND LOCATIONS

Lakes, beaches and boats

Lakes, beaches and boats are images which are associated with death across Russell's work, and they call to mind the Greek mythology of Charon, the ferryman of Hades, transporting souls to the underworld. *Gothic* opens with the party of the two Shelleys, Mary and Percy (Natasha Richardson and Julian Sands), and Clair Clairemont (Myriam Cyr), Mary's half-sister, arriving at Byron's Villa

Diodati on the shores of Lake Geneva by rowing boat. This is bookended by the film's epilogue where we learn of Percy Shelley's later death by drowning. In *Mahler* the composer responds to his young daughter's questions about the afterlife, while out rowing on a lake, by denying the existence of heaven or hell; shortly thereafter she dies. In *Isadora Duncan, the Biggest Dancer in the World* the dancer's (Vivian Pickles) daughters are also drowned, and in *Women in Love* a newly married couple are drowned in the boating lake of the Crich home during their own wedding party.

Shores, coasts and beaches are also traditional spaces in Gothic culture: Count Dracula making landfall in Whitby Bay, or the haunted beach of M. R. James's *Oh Whistle and I'll Come to You, My Lad* (1904) (and its accompanying 1968 BBC adaptation directed by Jonathan Miller), for example. They are liminal, haunted sites and contested spaces between land and sea; frontiers between the known and the unknown, the familiar and the unfamiliar; disorienting spaces where past and present collide. The seaside, however, was also 'the setting for some of Britain's first and finest ventures into Modernism' (architecturally speaking), 'a new movement [in the 1930s] that espoused the benefits of sunshine, simplicity and space'.[25] *French Dressing* (Associated British Picture Corporation, 1964), a seaside comedy and Russell's first film made for theatrical release, was filmed in Herne Bay (standing in for 'Gormleigh-on-Sea'), Kent. Russell combines the modernist space of Herne Bay with a sense of Gothic decay; his shore is a bewildering, bizarre, *surrealist* site where, in one sequence, the viewer is presented with a tatty, out-of-place stuffed camel on a beach during a photoshoot (a symbol of the decay and decline of Empire?) (Figure 3.5). It is a space locked in a decaying past (occupied by geriatrics on mobility scooters) but filmed looking outwards (like its central protagonist, Jim

Figure 3.5 Camel on the beach in *French Dressing*.
Source: Network DVD.

[James Booth]) to the progressive, modern and modernist Continent, through the filmic eye of the French New Wave.

This would certainly also not be the last time that Russell would look to French cinematic Modernism as a reference point. His 1966 BBC film *Don't Shoot the Composer* focused on the composer Georges Delerue who had scored films for Truffaut; *The Debussy Film* would also draw on Alain Resnais's *Last Year in Marienbad* (Cocinor, 1961), not least in its depiction of Debussy's château in the final act. Furthermore, the impressionism of Jean Vigo is present in the final moments of *A House in Bayswater* (BBC, 1960) where dreamlike superimpositions and dissolves evoke the memories of the house which are about to be buried in its rubble.

The displaced ephemera on the beach looks back to Russell's 1962 BBC film *The Lonely Shore* (filmed on Camber Sands, East Sussex). The film combines modernist aesthetics with dystopian science fiction and is indebted to another Mary Shelley novel, *The Last Man* (1826), in its narrative and thematic structure. In the film's dreamlike, dystopian, surrealist landscape, the shore is littered with the decaying ephemera of contemporary consumer culture. It is also possible that Russell's film influenced Chris Marker's 1981 short film *Junkopia* (Argos Films), whose 'meditative, eerie images reappropriate pieces of detritus, turning them into objects of strange beauty'.[26]

The BBC synopsis for *The Lonely Shore* reads:

> Inspired by an idea by Jacquetta Hawkes, a BBC Camera team has made a film, 'the Lonely Shore' which visualises a future civilisation exploring the left-over fragments of our present day. From these fragments, what, if anything, can be gleaned of our way of life? Does the pre-holocaust age look as strange to those who came after as prehistoric monsters do to us? Will our possessions reveal anything of the causes which led to our annihilation?[27]

The production files at the BBC Written Archives Centre contain a large body of correspondence between Huw Wheldon and archaeologist Hawkes. Wheldon had been impressed by lecture given by Hawkes for the Society of Industrial Artists in 1960 on the archaeology of the future, entitled 'Patterns and Future', in which she discussed the future destruction of civilisation by man and how humanity will be understood in the future. It was Wheldon who presented the idea of a *Monitor* film based on the lecture and who introduced Hawkes to Russell in 1961. The three would then collaborate on the project, with Hawkes writing the script.[28]

The film, as Michael Brooke indicates, looks to the modernist influence of the surrealist artists Giorgio de Chirico for its imagery '(for the use of incongruous props and a disconcerting sense of space and perspective) and Yves

Tanguy (for the many images of inexplicable objects strewn on an otherwise barren landscape)'.[29] Brooke also highlights the employment of electronic music, which, during the early 1960s, was being pioneered at the BBC by the likes of Delia Derbyshire. Again, the production files offer evidence of experimental and avant-garde music choices for the film, including Edgard Varèse and an 'Electronic Music Anthology'. Russell would turn to the electronic score again in his 1980s Gothic films: Thomas Dolby's score for *Gothic*, for instance, harmonising both the Gothic and modernist (and scientific) and fitting within the wider frame of 1980s synth-based electronic music.

Russell returned to the shore (Eastbourne) for *The Debussy Film*, to film the 'Martyrdom of Saint Sebastian' sequence in which Catholic imagery intersects with the Gothic and the modernist, inverted through a distinct pop art aesthetic, and later in 1992 for *The Mystery of Dr Martinu*. The latter was to be Russell's first film at the BBC for twenty-two years. The first half is a nightmare sequence taking place on a shoreline. The twentieth-century Czech composer Bohuslav Martinů is caught in a disorienting circularity of repetition and Buñuelian–Freudian imagery (for instance, a hand covered in ants à la *Un Chien Andalou* Luis Buñuel, Les Grands Films Classiques, 1929). A set of figures (Martinu and his bride; a group of crab-fishing schoolgirls) are depicted along a rocky shoreline reminiscent of the surrealist-Gothic of *L'Age d'Or* (Luis Buñuel, Corinth Films, 1930) and its skeletal bishops in a similar locale. The film locates part of this nightmare in the disorienting architecture of an isolated lighthouse, whose looming staircase seems to spiral upwards infinitely. During the sequence Russell depicts this single coastal location over and over in a loop, varying it each time, further estranging Martinů's (and our) familiarity with it each time.

Asylums

While we might not consider *The Music Lovers* to be a film in the popular or traditional Gothic mode (although there are no eldritch supernatural creatures or haunted castles, there are vampiric characters who feed off the composer in other ways), American film critic Ken Hanke suggests that the film 'can only be viewed as Russell's most horrifying view of life, black and terrible'.[30] Haggerty notes that 'Transgressive social-sexual relations are the most basic common denominator of gothic' and that

> Terror is almost always sexual terror: fear and flight, as well as incarceration and escape, are almost always coloured by the exoticism of transgressive sexual aggression. It is no mere coincidence that the cult of gothic fiction reached its apex at the very moment when gender and sexuality were beginning to be codified for modern culture.[31]

This 'terror' is perhaps most clearly visualised during the nightmarish train carriage sequence in which the closeted composer Tchaikovsky's (Richard Chamberlain) horror at his new wife Nina's (Glenda Jackson) aggressive sexuality is magnified in the claustrophobic, cloistered and confining space (another example of a character's being 'entombed alive') through frenetic camera work, a cacophony of music (spliced together from the composer's Manfred and Pathétique Symphonies), and the monstrous, devouring vaginal 'mouth' of Nina's petticoat. Elsewhere the film contains a variety of Gothic horror imagery: the immersion of Tchaikovsky's mother in boiling water and Nina's own descent into madness. In her final asylum incarceration, during her molestation at the hands of lunatic inmates groping her from beneath a dungeon grill, she cries, 'Oh I have so many lovers!' This associates her sexuality with mania, madness and a final purging of irrepressible desire. We are left with a final shot of her peering from the confines of a cell, through a barred window, recalling similar shots in both *The Devils* and *Crimes of Passion* (see earlier).

The script for the unrealised film sequel to *Elgar* (BBC, 1962), *Elgar: Land of Hope and Glory* (1976), opens with two Russellian, Gothic images: a rowing boat carrying 'The Woman', and the Gothic Powick asylum where Elgar is conducting the band while the lunatics dance.[32] It begins in 1935, a year after Elgar's death, and flashes back to his younger years as leader of the Powick asylum house band. In the present, a young mechanic goes on a tour of Elgar country with a mysterious woman – potentially the late composer's lover (Russell recycles and adapts this device in his unmade script from 1982, *The Beethoven Secret*).

Dancing, madness and hysteria is another often repeated trope of Russell's work. In *Mahler*, for instance, the composer and his wife, Alma (Georgina Hale), waltz through the palace of Emperor Franz Joseph (David Collings), which is revealed to be an asylum, and the 'Emperor' – Mahler's friend, the composer Hugo Wolf – believes himself to *be* the Emperor. *Isadora Duncan, the Biggest Dancer in the World* opens with a sped-up sequence of the unruly, uncontainable body of the naked Isadora Duncan (Vivian Pickles) dancing wildly and publicly on stage in New York before being carted off. It is one of Russell's most kinetic films. Isadora rarely stops dancing throughout the film (as if she has 'St Vitus's dance') and in the closing moments dances joyously right to her death to the sound of 'Bye Bye Blackbird'.

GOTHIC ADAPTORS: POE, DEBUSSY, BARTÓK AND RUSSELL

Russell's subjects during his BBC years include modernist figures who were, like him, intertextual adaptors and interpreters of the Gothic: the French and

Hungarian composers Claude Debussy and Béla Bartók, for instance. *The Debussy Film* depicts the composer's struggle to compose his (uncompleted) opera *The Fall of the House of Usher* (1917) and his descent into 'isolated communion with himself'. Edgar Allan Poe is a lynchpin for understanding the presence of the Gothic in Russell's work. In an archived draft of an article written for the *Radio Times*, Russell writes of Debussy:

> During the remaining years of his life [he] worked intermittently on Poe's *Fall of the House of Usher* turning it into an opera until it became an obsession with him. Roderick Usher lived in a very large and lonely house, engrossed in his artistic experiments and with his sister. She dies, he incarcerates her in one of his vaults. 'If Roderick Usher's sister was to suddenly walk into my room', said Debussy, 'I wouldn't be the least surprised.' And again. 'Roderick Usher sees and feels everything in the world and tries to force these impulses into his work'. Finally, Debussy identified so completely with Usher that he could say 'I am Roderick Usher'. He worked on the opera for many years but when he died only a few sheets where found – why?[33]

Debussy is a tormented creator and adaptor, and composing music, a traumatic, monstrous and abortive act of birth. *The Debussy Film* also foregrounds the phenomenon of the incomplete or abandoned project. Russell's own career contains a large number of unbirthed projects but rarely during his career was a project ever fully lost or left to die, rather it would frequently be resurrected in some other form. The unmade project in Russell's case becomes the raw material for a new 'creature' (or text). Russell also reconstructs his subjects like a Frankenstein, using 'Letters, facts, legends about the composer, but in order to suggest the emotional states of the historical figures rather than to depict the events that occurred'.[34] From the base of these raw materials he creates an impression or interpretation of the subject (just as the Russell scholar may use archived materials to construct an understanding of the director himself). Like his subjects he is, as Joseph A. Gomez recognises, 'adaptor as creator'.[35]

The *Usher* sequence in *The Debussy Film* incorporates references to a variety of Gothic-modernist sources other than Poe. Oliver Reed, playing an actor playing Debussy, moves silently and spectrally through the empty space of his Gothic château – a combination of Roderick Usher and Charles Foster Kane traipsing the spaces and hallways of Xanadu. The shot of 'the director' watching the images back in *The Debussy Film* recalls the screening room scenes in *Citizen Kane* (Orson Welles, RKO, 1941), a film with its own Gothic identity and which has a pervasive influence across the broader canon of Russell's work. Russell presents three-dimensional shots of corridors, rooms and staircases and the spectral image of Usher's sister. John C. Tibbetts notes that

> In a beautifully composed deep focus shot, with Roderick's figure occupying the foreground, facing the camera, Madeline's shrouded figure slowly advances from the background toward him. She falls lifeless at Roderick's feet, blood flowing from her mouth. Another female figure appears and also falls to the floor. We recognise the figures as Gaby and Lilly, the women whom Debussy had driven to attempted suicide.[36]

The haunted stairways and corridors in the sequence anticipate those in *Gothic* and recall Alain Resnais's dreamlike modernist exploration of identity and memory, *Last Year in Marienbad*: an architecturally and three-dimensionally disorienting film which assimilates aspects of Gothic and baroque style and aesthetics but is also considered one of the key moments in the post-war modernist avant-garde cinema – a comparison also made in the archived transcript for a BBC critics forum around the broadcast of Russell's film.[37]

Poe's influence is evident in the earlier *A House in Bayswater*. In the final shot the histories and memories of the house are entombed and buried beneath the rubble of its own demolition. Producer, academic and former Russell collaborator Michael Nolin asserts that prior to embarking on his (unmade) *Dracula* project, Russell had 'always wanted to make a Gothic film',[38] but in many respects he had been making Gothic films since his days as an amateur filmmaker and his earliest years at the BBC. Russell films the interiors and inhabitants of his then (condemned) lodgings in Bayswater, London. The landlady, Mrs Collins, is introduced as a spectral figure with long, flowing white hair to below her waist. Towards the end she recounts to one of the tenants the horrific story of a murder/suicide which had occurred in the house. She is a remnant from the past, an embodiment of the crumbling building that is reduced to dust at the end of the film after a montage of ghostly, Jean Vigo-inspired imagery. Her voice-over commentary is disembodied as she emerges from a basement and climbs a shadowy staircase to deliver the milk to her tenants. Archived production correspondence shows the title for Russell's original treatment had been 'A House in Bayswater, A Story of Five Floors Told by a Body in the Basement'– a title with clear Gothic intimations (which he was forced to change by the BBC's programme planning department).[39]

The production files for Russell's film *Béla Bartók*, about the Hungarian modernist composer, describe the film as an 'evocation' rather than a biopic.[40] Again Russell presents the composer as a Gothic adaptor during the staging of his opera *Doctor Bluebeard's Castle* (1911), and through this medium presents us with his *own* interpretation of Bartók's opera. Writing in *The Listener* in 1973, George Steiner unpacks the components, the 'sources and strands', which comprise and impact upon cultural understandings of the Bluebeard mythology and which are present in Russell's own interpretation via the composer.[41] The first strand is the story of Gilles de Rais (1404–40), maréchal de France, companion-in-arms of Joan of Arc, and alleged mass child murderer, occultist and sadist. In 1994 *Variety* reported that Russell was attached to film a version of the Joan of Arc story for producer Phillip Emanuel which may have potentially depicted or dealt with the death of Rais. The second thematic 'strand', according to Steiner, is 'that of labyrinths, minotaurs and secret mazes' (see also *Mahler*) and strange, disturbing architectures.[42] The third strand is the notion of the 'prohibited', the 'forbidden'.[43] Hence Russell is depicting a composer whose own Gothic preoccupations and interests are like his own.[44]

During the *Bluebeard* sequence the representation of Gothic architecture is brought into tension with the depiction of contemporary towering, utilitarian and modernist architecture. Brooke notes how it is 'staged in the starkly modernist setting of London's New Zealand House, its doors leading to visions of hi-tech weaponry and a row of unnervingly blank-faced women (Bluebeard's previous wives)'.[45] John Hill observes that it 'fuses pre-existing footage (Phillip Donnellan's 1961 steelmaking documentary *Men of Corby*, "made strange" through juxtaposition) with imaginative fantasy (Bluebeard's former wives in blank face-masks apparently imprisoned inside a "beauty parlour")'.[46] The BBC production files also refer to the *Bluebeard* sequence as being about living entombment (recalling Poe again), and the locations for the film consolidate its Gothic identity: a *basement* lecture room at the BBC for part of the *Bluebeard's Castle* sequence; West Norwood Cemetery;[47] and the Greenwich tunnel in London.[48] At the film's opening we learn that the composer, now an émigré in exile in the US, spent his early life travelling through Eastern Europe – Hungary, and Romania (countries historically associated with Gothic stories) – for folk tales and songs, capturing them on his Edison cylinders (the props of which, so the files tell us, were lent to the production by another Russell subject, the inventor Bruce Lacey).

The film opens with a shot of the towering cityscape of 'New York 1942'. The composer is cloistered away in exile and presented as a haunted, sick and diminished figure: a victim of 'neglect' and 'public indifference'. Wheldon's voice-over narration tells us that Bartók worked for Columbia University cataloguing record collections and folk songs, closeted away in his empty room, forgotten. Bartók stares vacantly in his decrepitude, in a bare, minimalist room, sitting in front of a table with a gramophone, like Samuel Beckett's Krapp in front of his tape recorder (Figure 3.6). The score for the 1919 ballet *The Miraculous Mandarin* fills the empty space of Bartók's room. As with *The Debussy Film*, we then enter a meta-narrative. A young prostitute (played by pop artist Pauline Boty, subject of a previous Russell BBC film, *Pop Goes the Easel* [1962]) is profiled, smoking, in chiaroscuro, New York

Figure 3.6 Bartók.
Source: BBC, 1964.

City visible through the window. Russell experiments with the palette of the Gothic, colliding expressionistic film noir, folk Gothic, and the modernist avant-garde.[49]

UNMADE AND FINAL FILMS

A further connection may be made between *The Debussy Film* and *The Fall of the Louse of Usher* (Gorsewood Films, 2002) via a largely unremarked upon unmade project from 1978 entitled *Ten Times Poe*. Tibbetts comments:

> *The Debussy Film* afforded Russell his first opportunity to translate Poe to the screen. Like Debussy, he has been preoccupied from an early age with Poe's famous tales. 'When I was twelve, I painted scenes from "The Tell-Tale Heart" and "Usher" and other stories, much in the manner of the horror movies I was seeing.'[50]

This childhood drive to recreate Poe, to readapt and to 'collage' his stories, asserts itself in this unmade project, later developed by and in collaboration with Michael Nolin. *Ten Times Poe* is an anthology film which collects and modernises several of Poe's stories, stitching them together (à la Frankenstein) in one 'portmanteau' and 'picaresque' narrative (typical of British horror studio Amicus). The stories are reimagined via the characters in the script – the inmates of an asylum who are encountered by the protagonist Roderick Usher, here an LA rock star who has been committed for the murder of his sister. It was

> A contemporary treatment of ten works by Edgar Allan Poe – poems and short stories – some famous, some obscure, plus allusions to many more. Russell appears to have selected these works for they, as well as any other pieces in the Poe Canon, reflect the nineteenth century writer's obsession with the grotesque and the arabesque.[51]

Nolin's collaborative relationship with Russell began when he was asked to produce *Dracula* (his first executive job) by Robert Littman, then head of Columbia Pictures. *Ten Times Poe* was pitched to film producer Alan Ladd Jnr (then head of Fox) as if it was a Roger Corman Poe production. He hated Russell's approach and the idea was abandoned until Nolin took it with him to Fox, where he and Russell worked on the project, now retitled *Horrible Beauty* (1980). Although ultimately the script remained unmade, its ideas were later imprinted on and revived in the narrative of *The Fall of the Louse of Usher*, the last film by Russell to secure an official release and the most famous of the homemade Gorsewood or Garagiste films.

Ten Times Poe/Horrible Beauty was a postmodern homage to Poe's work – a collage of various stories – and it exhibits Russell's increasing interest in self-reference, and self-adaptation also. In *The Fall of the Louse of Usher* he adapts Poe via himself (it's another example of Russell returning to earlier projects he was originally unable to make). The brief collaborative relationship with Nolin is an important and overlooked work. Nolin comments that 'It's easy to see why Russell was attracted to Poe: both writers share fascinations with death, disease, human aberration, physical deformity, and the relationship of the artist to society/man to the universe.'[52]

Russell's Gothic imagination is rooted in a variety of different cultural sources which are synthesised into the fabric of his work, including the work of the Pre-Raphaelites (William Holman Hunt's *The Awakening Conscience* [1853] epitomises the tensions illustrated by Haggerty: sexual terror, flight and transgressive sexual aggression) and the transgressive sexuality and excessive abandon of the nineteenth-century Decadent movement – especially Oscar Wilde and scandalous artist Aubrey Beardsley, both of whose influence is present across his work and are imprinted on his own aesthetic of 'excess'. Russell's Vestron films, especially *Gothic* and *Salome's Last Dance*, may also be viewed against the backdrop of a Victorian/Gothic cultural revival during the 1980s. Van Eecke writes that '*Gothic* offers a neo-Victorian way of looking at contemporary appropriations of nineteenth-century culture in the heritage industry and the heritage film. The film is situated on the intersection of these concerns, which were very much alive in British culture of the 1980s.'[53]

In an interview, stalwart Russell actor Murray Melvin revealed how Russell had even been keen to cast him in an (unmade) film about Beardsley in the 1970s.[54] The artist's sexually provocative nineteenth-century images are intercut into the editing of *Crimes of Passion*; they adorn the walls of the salon where Wilde watches *Salome* in *Salome's Last Dance* and in the unmade *Dracula* script.

Russell's unmade *Dracula* was the first project that Nolin worked on with him as an executive at Columbia (he facilitated Russell's transition to working in the US) but, according to Nolin, it was ultimately abandoned in the face of John Badham's *Dracula* (Universal, 1979).[55] Here Jonathan Harker is invited to sleep in 'The Beardsley Room':

Beardsley Room, Cont'd
Judging by JONATHAN's expression he has never seen anything like it. Life size reproductions of Beardsley's more erotic works adorn the walls and the furniture also is moulded on that artists phallic style while the drapes and fabrics are in stark black and white

     Dracula
Beardsley was surely one of your
Finest artists. It is to my ever-
Lasting regret that I never met him.
So talented and to die so young.
A tragedy! I might have helped him[56]

Russell's *Dracula* updates Bram Stoker's novel to the modernist 1920s, incorporating the cutting-edge and contemporary European design aesthetics of the era into the mise en scène of Castle Dracula:

INT. CASTLE DRACULA. RECEPTION ROOM. DAY.
JONATHAN and DRACULA are seated in angular chairs of the Bauhaus School before a table fashioned from a chunk of highly polished black marble. The general effect resembles a gallery of modern art rather than a reception room as was obviously the designer's intention. Schubert's Unfinished Symphony plays incongruously in the background.[57]

Russell's Dracula feeds off the cultural, aesthetic and artistic milieu he has encountered through time. He is an aesthete embodying the intersection of Modernism and the Gothic. Nolin described to me how the exploration of vampirism in *Dracula*, in which genius is both vampiric and vampirised, emerged directly out of *Lisztomania*'s depiction of composer Richard Wagner (Paul Nicholas) as a vampire who bites Liszt (Roger Daltrey), feeding off his ideas.[58]

Not only does *Ten Times Poe* illustrate Russell's preoccupation with Poe, its postmodern structure – the refashioning and stitching together of Poe's stories – also points back to Russell's immersion in the Frankenstein mythology and to an increasingly self-referential disposition. This is most evident in the final homemade Gorsewood productions. These films, which include *The Fall of the Louse of Usher*, *Boudica Bites Back* (2007, his last commissioned film) and the *Hot Pants Trilogy* (*Revenge of the Elephant Man* [2004], *The Mystery of Mata Hari* [2004] and *The Good Ship Venus* [2005] – all Gorsewood Productions), were shot at home on digital camcorder, and are often dismissed by critics as a frivolous and inconsequential coda to his career, an embarrassing aside. However, they must be recognised for what they are: an important and valuable body of work which ends his career on a note of complete self-determination and control. *Revenge of the Elephant Man* references Victorian Gothic folk mythology in its title and presents a narrative detailing the 'strange history' of Ella (Russell's neighbour Barry Lowe), 'A truly remarkable subhuman being' with an unusual appendage (a penis-trunk! – 'without CGI, a plastic toy elephant's trunk covered in lubricant').[59] *Louse of Usher* also engages contemporary late nineteenth- and early twentieth-century Gothic culture, casting musical ensemble Mediaeval Baebes as well as James Johnston, lead singer of the group Gallon Drunk (as Roddy Usher), who had toured as part of Nick Cave and the Bad Seeds in the early 2000s.[60] Musical motifs resembling Cave's music also occur in the film.

The Gorsewood films are ironic and highly self-aware examples of punk cinema, sending up the clichéd media perception of Russell as the 'Madman of British cinema', circumnavigating his own cultural and industrial marginalisation, deliberately returning to his amateur roots. These films are defined through their raw DIY aesthetic and are made up of 'raw materials' – shop-bought and homemade props and costumes, with actors and crew cast from family and friends[61] – and filmed at home, and they reflect playfully on his past Gothic preoccupations. These films are Ken Russell's ultimate Frankenstein texts and he the (self-referentially and ironic) 'mad' creator.

The earlier BBC film *The Preservation Man* (1962), a short documentary about the British eccentric and countercultural icon, artist, collector, inventor and film-maker Bruce Lacey, is an early example of Russell's fixation with monstrous creation and the *Frankenstein* lore. Lacey's bric-a-brac mechanical automatons are presented as whimsical, cobbled together, homemade, Frankenstein-style DIY creations which anticipate the ethos of Russell's final

Gorsewood or Garagiste films. Mechanical automated toys also reappear in *Gothic* in the form of a mechanical piano player and a mechanical belly dancer, and through them Van Eecke positions *Gothic* as a 'neo-Victorian meta-heritage' film, which as part of the Gothic revival of the 1980s 'recuperated' modes of Victorian culture in that decade.[62]

CONCLUSION

Ken Russell's Gothic imagination is diverse, expansive, self-reflexive and self-interrogatory; his Garagiste films are self-referential and ironically deconstruct the folkloric, Gothic and (post)modernist preoccupations which shaped his career. The Gothic is not simply a stylistic quirk of Russell's film-making, it is an inherent structural principle of it, and no other director in British cinema balanced these two modes quite as comprehensively or effectively.

ACKNOWLEDGEMENTS

I would like to thank both Michael Nolin and Murray Melvin for taking time out of their schedules to be interviewed, as well as Stewart Williams and Brian Hoyle for their support.

NOTES

1. Kevin M. Flanagan, 'Adapting Monstrous Creation: *Lisztomania* and *Gothic* as Gothic Mash-Ups', in Natalie Neill (ed.), *Gothic Mash-Ups: Hybridity, Appropriation, and Intertextuality in Gothic Storytelling* (Lanham, MD: Lexington Books, 2022), 22.
2. Ibid., 21.
3. Matthew Melia, 'Ken Russell's Unfinished Projects and Unmade Films, 1956–68: The BBC Years', in James Fenwick, Kieran Foster and David Eldridge (eds), *Shadow Cinema: The Historical and Production Contexts of Unmade Films* (New York: Bloomsbury Academic, 2021), 91.
4. Ken Russell, 'In Your Dreams', 1955, from *Last of the Teddy Girls* series, *TopFoto*, <https://www.topfoto.co.uk/asset/2172> (last accessed 14 April 2021).
5. Ken Russell, Untitled, 1955, from *Last of the Teddy Girls* series, *TopFoto*, <https://www.topfoto.co.uk/asset/3249532> (last accessed 14 April 2021).
6. Melia, 'Ken Russell's Unfinished Projects and Unmade Films', 91–109.
7. Kevin M. Flanagan, 'Introduction', in Kevin M. Flanagan (ed.), *Ken Russell: Re-Viewing England's Last Mannerist* (Plymouth: Scarecrow Press, 2009), xxi.
8. Ibid.
9. Joseph Lanza, *Phallic Frenzy: Ken Russell and His Films* (London: Aurum Press, 2008), 72.
10. Mark Pilkington, 'What Was the Inspiration for Paddy Chayefksy's Hallucinatory Novel?', *Frieze*, 2 June 2018, <https://www.frieze.com/article/what-was-inspiration-paddy-chayefskys-hallucinatory-novel> (last accessed 26 May 2022).

11. John Kenneth Muir, 'As the (White) Worm Turns: Ken Russell as God and Devil of Rubber-Reality Horror Cinema', in Flanagan (ed.), 179–94; Barry Keith Grant, 'The Body Politic: Ken Russell in the 1980s', in Flanagan (ed.), 24–39.
12. 'An apocalyptic S&M orgy, with leather-clad demons and angels fighting over the soul of a woman (portrayed by Elaine Caswell) who hovers between life and death after a fiery motorcycle crash in a graveyard.' Ben Herman, 'Jim Steinman: 1947 to 2021', *In My Not so Humble Opinion: The Writing and Ramblings of Ben Herman*, 22 April 2021, <https://benjaminherman.wordpress.com/tag/ken-russell/> (last accessed 26 May 2022).
13. Roger Luckhurst, 'Corridor Gothic', *Gothic Studies*, vol. 20, nos. 1–2, December 2018, 295–310.
14. Christophe Van Eecke, 'Phantasmagoria: Ken Russell's "Gothic" as a Neo-Victorian Meta-Heritage Film', *Journal of Neo-Victorian Studies*, vol. 12, 2019, 135–56.
15. Stephen Volk, 'Villa Diodati', in James Bell (ed.), *Gothic: The Dark Heart of Film* (London: BFI, 2003), 63.
16. I. Q. Hunter, *British Trash Cinema* (London: BFI, 2013), 152.
17. George Haggerty, 'The Horrors of Catholicism: Religion and Sexuality in Gothic Fiction', *Érudit*, 27 July 2005, <https://www.erudit.org/en/journals/ron/2004-n36-37-ron947/011133ar/> (last accessed 19 February 2022).
18. An image which also recalls a moment in *The Devils*, in which a group of amorous nuns are depicted ogling Father Grandier, in his clerical finery, through the grating of the convent.
19. Jeff Cramer, 'A Very Candid Conversation with Barry Sandler', *Stone Cold Crazy*, 1 July 2010, <http://jeffcramer.blogspot.com/2010/07/very-candid-conversation-with-barry.html> (last accessed 26 May 2022).
20. 'Ken Russell – Southern Visions', BBC, 12 May 2005, updated 3 April 2008, <https://www.bbc.co.uk/dorset/content/articles/2005/05/12/pictureofbritian_russell_feature.shtml> (last accessed 25 May 2022).
21. Ken Russell, *A British Picture: An Autobiography* (London: Heinemann, 1989), 7.
22. *Variety*, 3 October 1979, 6.
23. Russell, *A British Picture*, 7.
24. Matthew Melia, 'Altered States, Altered Spaces: Architecture, Space and Landscape in the Film and Television of Stanley Kubrick and Ken Russell', *Cinergie: Il Cinema e le Altre Arti*, vol. 6, no. 12, 2017, 139–52, <https://cinergie.unibo.it/article/view/7352> (last accessed 19 February 2022).
25. Charlotte Goodheart, 'Modernism at the Seaside', *Historic England Blog*, 24 August 2016, <https://heritagecalling.com/2016/08/24/modernism-at-the-seaside/> (last accessed 20 February 2022).
26. 'Chris Marker's *Junkopia*', *The Criterion Collection: Short Takes*, 2 August 2012, <https://www.criterion.com/current/posts/2400-chris-marker-s-junkopia> (last accessed 26 May 2022).
27. BBC Written Archives Centre, BBC WAC T32/1016.
28. Ibid.
29. Michael Brooke, 'The Lonely Shore (1962)', *BFI Screenonline*, <http://www.screenonline.org.uk/tv/id/1285002/index.html> (last accessed 26 May 2022).
30. Ken Hanke, *Ken Russell's Films* (Metuchen, NJ: Scarecrow Press, 1984), 116.
31. Haggerty.
32. BFI Archives Centre, Russell, Ken. 1976. *Elgar: Land of Hope and Glory*. Unrealised script. SCR-20506
33. BBC Written Archives Centre, *Debussy* File, T32/1, 095/1, Ken Russell, 1965. 'Why a film on a French composer was shot in Eastbourne'. Transcript of *Radio Times* article.
34. Joseph A. Gomez, *Ken Russell: The Adaptor as Creator* (London: New York: Pergamon, 1977), 34–5.

35. Ibid.
36. John C. Tibbetts, '"Il parait que c'était un musicien": Ken Russell's *The Debussy Film*', in Flanagan (ed.), 119.
37. BBC Written Archive, *The Debussy Film* File, Ref: T32/1, 095/1.
38. Michael Nolin, *Ken Russell and Other Madnesses*, Master's thesis, University of Southern California, 1985, 29.
39. BBC Written Archives Centre, *A House in Bayswater* file, T32/843/1.
40. BBC Written Archives Centre, *Bartók* file, T32/1072.
41. George Steiner, 'The Bluebeard Legend', *The Listener*, issue 233, 29 November 1973, 734.
42. Ibid.
43. Ibid.
44. The 1993 BBC Radio play *Scriabin* is a chaotic, darkly comic and carnivalesque rendering of the composer and occultist Aleister Crowley (Oliver Reed, in his last role for Russell), and constitutes Russell's own attempt to depict a Bluebeard-esque figure.
45. Michael Brooke, 'Béla Bartók (1964)', *BFI Screenonline*, <http://www.screenonline.org.uk/tv/id/907445/index.html> (last accessed 26 May 2022).
46. John Hill, ' Blurring the Lines between Fact and Fiction: Ken Russell, the BBC and the Television Biography', *Journal of British Cinema and Television*, vol. 12, no. 4, September 2015, 461.
47. *The Debussy Film* and *Isadora Duncan, the Biggest Dancer in the World* also begin at funerals and graveyards. Gothic imagery pervades *Dante's Inferno* too, in Rosetti's desecration of Elizabeth Siddal's (Judith Paris) grave, for instance.
48. BBC Written Archive Centre, *Bartók* file, T32/1072.
49. Bartók was a pre-eminent European modernist composer in exile much like many of the émigré film directors from central Europe who defined the Hollywood film noir style and who had fled the rise of Nazism in the 1930s.
50. Tibbetts, 129.
51. Nolin, 94.
52. Ibid.
53. Van Eecke, 137.
54. Interview between the author and Murray Melvin, 2018.
55. Phone interview between the author and Michael Nolin, 9 May 2020.
56. British Film Institute, Archive ref: SCR-7128. Russell, Ken, 1978, *Dracula*. Unrealised Script.
57. Ibid., 13.
58. Phone interview between the author and Michael Nolin, 9 May 2020.
59. Lanza, 323.
60. Ibid.
61. Including Russell's editor since his BBC days.
62. Van Eecke, 141.

PART 2

Ken Russell and Television

CHAPTER 4

Ken Russell and Television Advertising

Richard Farmer

INTRODUCTION

Given the detailed scrutiny to which Ken Russell's career has been subjected, the relative lack of attention paid to the television commercials that he directed is a curious oversight, and one that deserves correction. For although it would be hard to make a convincing case that television advertising forms as important an element of Russell's contribution to moving-image culture as the films he directed for the BBC or the cinema, it is nevertheless true that the commercials he made in the mid-1960s constitute a very important part of his oeuvre and contributed to his artistic development at a time in his career when he was making the move from television into feature films. This chapter will provide information on Russell's work in advertising whilst also seeking to tease out some of the influence that television advertising had on his work, both through his own direct experience and via his collaborators' involvement in this medium. The chapter will also suggest reasons as to why Russell stopped making commercials, moving beyond his own slightly hyperbolic recollections in order to more closely integrate his work in advertising with that in other areas.

Russell's tendency to dismiss the television commercials that he made, and his splenetic attacks on the industry that produced them, might in part explain why his adventures in advertising have so often been overlooked. It seems that scholars, critics and fans are often willing to take Russell at his word, because his word is frequently so entertaining. Take this diatribe, for example, which is reproduced in John Baxter's *An Appalling Talent*: 'The corrupted minds who produced [advertisements] are real enemies of the state. It's the ad men who are shaping society and they're shaping it to their own image, which is a rotting death's head.'¹ Such a passionate denunciation conforms to the idea of Russell as a visionary film-maker who momentarily compromised his integrity and virtuosity by prostituting his talent and becoming 'a media whore'.² Russell is often presented, not least by himself, as having attempted to atone for these lapses in his subsequent feature films, a number of which contain withering critiques of advertising and commercialism and their baleful influence on an artist's creativity. This thematic interest in advertising is perhaps best exemplified in an outrageous sequence in *Tommy* (Columbia, 1975) (based on material taken from unmade scripts for *The Angels* and *Music, Music, Music*)³ in which Nora (Ann-Margret) first watches commercials for Rex baked beans, Black Beauty chocolates and Hi washing powder before being covered in these products as they spray out of her television set in what Stephen Farber has described as both an 'obscene joke on the obsessions of the consumer culture' and 'a definitive mockery of TV advertising'.⁴ Critics have also explored the ways in which Russell made ironic use of slow-motion advertising aesthetics in *Women in Love* (United Artists, 1969),⁵ whilst Russell himself noted that aspects of *The Music Lovers* (United Artists, 1970) were a 'send up' of both the content and intent of television advertisements, claiming that some sequences in the film aped cigarette commercials (a product to which Russell refused to lend his talents) so as to communicate the 'destructive force of dreams, particularly daydreams, on reality' by satirising 'the ad-man's trick of passing off his dream world as an attainable and desirable reality'.⁶

Thus, although much of the literature exploring Russell's career mentions his forays into television advertising, critical discussions have tended to focus on his experiences in relation to (or as motivating) his subsequent hostility. Various filmographies carefully list Russell's amateur films, his television films and his feature films; my research did not uncover any that listed his television commercials.⁷ Indeed, constructive engagement with these films, or verifiable information concerning them, is infrequent at best; this might in part result from gaps in the historical record (including the fact that some of the commercials appear to be lost), or the fact that most television advertisements are shown essentially anonymously, meaning that in some cases it can be difficult to ascribe with any certainty a specific commercial to a particular director.

However, the willingness to marginalise Russell's television commercials (and we should remember that he also took photographs for print advertisements) speaks to a wider tendency to regard advertising as essentially banal, insincere and devoid of artistic merit.⁸ Such attitudes are, of course, not entirely inaccurate; all forms of popular culture are capable of churning out trite, mawkish, and poorly conceived and executed rubbish, but the ubiquity of television advertising means that we are more likely to encounter it.⁹ But such attitudes are also unhelpful, in that they tend to blind us to advertising's status as an inherently creative industry. As a consequence, although Joseph Lanza recognises that making television advertisements helped Russell 'cultivate a punchy, attention-grabbing style that would inspire some of his best films', few others appear willing to entertain the idea that Russell's commercials might have had any kind of constructive influence on his artistic development.[10] Indeed, Ken Hanke claims that those parts of *The Music Lovers* inspired by the aesthetics of television advertising did not succeed because Russell was 'too good' and too 'consummate' a film-maker to convincingly replicate 'the tackiness of the TV commercial'.[11] Rather, there is a tacit consensus that if Russell's commercials have any value, it lies exclusively in their having provided him with the training and material needed to skewer the aesthetics and pretensions of television advertisements later on in his career, in his 'proper' films; they are only ever regarded as a means to an end, never an end in itself.

KEN RUSSELL'S 1960S TELEVISION COMMERCIALS

In an interview published in the early 1970s, Russell noted that he had made 'a number of TV commercials in the early and mid-60s – about twenty, I suppose'.[12] Given that many of his contemporaries made scores of commercials, and some hundreds, the comparatively low number that Russell directed might be used to position him as something of a dilettante when it came to advertising. We might, though, want to be cautious when reaching such a conclusion. Some directors did not make any television commercials at all, although these refuseniks tended to be either very established figures such as David Lean, 'hot' directors such as Tony Richardson, or more experimental film-makers such as Peter Whitehead.[13] Furthermore, Russell's initial work in television advertising spanned *at least* the years 1964–6, and appears to have come to an end only shortly before his appointment to direct *Billion Dollar Brain* (United Artists, 1967): he might have become an enthusiastic critic of television advertising, but his initial forays into the medium were evidently not sufficiently morally or artistically compromising to prevent him from repeating them.

Of the twenty television commercials mentioned by Russell, I have found details of eight in the British advertising industry trade papers *Television Mail* and *Advertiser's Weekly*. Each entry in this list contains: name of product/brand; title of commercial, if known; length; production company and advertising agency; date of initial broadcast:

1. Cheese Wedges; 30 seconds; Augusta for Clifford Bloxham; July/August 1964.[14]
2. Ovaltine; 'You can't have too much of a good thing'; 30 seconds; James Garrett and Partners for Saward Baker; October 1964.[15]
3. Bri-Nylon; 'Photographer'; 45 seconds; James Garrett and Partners for Notley; April 1965.[16]

4. Delsey (toilet paper); 30 seconds; James Garrett and Partners for Foote, Cone and Belding; spring 1965.[17]
5. Butter Council; 'Building Site'; 45 seconds; James Garrett and Partners for J. Walter Thompson; May 1965.[18]
6. Birds Eye Cod Portions; 30 seconds; James Garrett and Partners for Lintas; March 1966.[19]
7. Rowntree's Black Magic; 'Castle'; 60 seconds; James Garrett and Partners for J. Walter Thompson; March 1966.[20]
8. TAB (soft drink); 'Swan'; 30 seconds; James Garrett and Partners for Erwin Wasey; July 1966.[21]

To these might be added a number of other advertisements, the details and possibly even existence of which remain uncertain as I have not found evidence to convincingly corroborate them. I make no claims that this list is exhaustive:

9–10. Butter Council. The March 1966 edition of *Round the Square*, the J. Walter Thompson agency's in-house magazine, notes that Russell directed 'several' commercials for the Butter Council (see 5, above).[22]
11. Unnamed soft drink, 1967. Mentioned in a 1989 *Times* article marking Russell's return to television advertising.[23] Possibly confused with 8, above.
12. Unnamed brand of baked beans. Mentioned by Russell in a 1972 interview with Guy Flatley in the *New York Times*, in which he claims that 'a little girl' whom he was directing had to eat so many beans that she threw up during filming.[24] Russell tells a similar story, albeit with a young male protagonist, in Baxter's *An Appalling Talent*.[25]
13. Horlicks. Again, mentioned by Russell in Baxter. Possible that Russell was confusing this commercial with the advertisement he directed for Ovaltine, a similar product (see 2, above).[26]
14–19. Galaxy chocolate. In Baxter, Russell claims to have directed 'half a dozen' commercials for this confectionery company, 'all slow motion things shot in Rome'.[27]
20. Unnamed brand of washing powder. Mentioned in Phillips:

> In order to make the soap suds appear to behave as advertised, Russell had to photograph the suds being pumped up through the drain and into the sink, and then run the film backwards to give the impression that they were disappearing down the drain just as quickly as the manufacturer boasted they would.[28]

According to Gene D. Phillips, this washing powder commercial was 'the last straw' for Russell and so might have been the final television advertisement that he directed until he returned to the field in the late 1980s. In this second coming, Russell directed films for Ross Foods (in which he also appeared as an irascible director) and the Lotus Elise sports car through his Sitting Duck production company, which was also responsible for making music videos for artists such as Elton John and Cliff Richard.

If Ken Russell was (or at least became) ambivalent about the advertising industry, the advertising industry appears to have entertained few such doubts about Ken Russell. On the back of his work at the BBC, Russell's reputation increased in the first half of the 1960s: his *Monitor* films were mentioned on several occasions in *Television Mail*'s time-buyers guide, which provided advance information about the broadcast of high-profile programmes so that advertising schedules could be planned accordingly. It is difficult to say whether the broadcast of a Russell film on the BBC helped or hindered advertisers on ITV, or altered the target demographic for products being promoted on the commercial network in the same timeslot, but it is clear that the quality and distinctive style of the films that Russell was making for the BBC made him an attractive figure to the advertising industry.[29] That Russell directed the majority of his commercials for the James Garrett and Partners production company serves to reiterate this point; JGP was a director-driven enterprise, noted for using the creativity of the film-makers it put under contract to connect products with consumers.[30]

Russell's distinct style had the potential to let any commercial he directed stand out from the competition. Russell's broader artistic hinterland was an additional point of appeal, and his previous work as a dancer and choreographer, for instance, was said by the J. Walter Thompson agency to inform his work 'with a wonderful sense of movement and design'.[31] Such traits were no doubt foregrounded in a commercial for Delsey toilet roll (see 4, above) where 'a ballet theme was featured to emphasise Delsey's main selling points "super softness-gentle strength"'.[32] Previous Delsey commercials had also incorporated elements of dance, so it is possible that Russell was engaged specifically to provide a balletic aesthetic to the advertisement. It was, however, Russell's willingness to blur the boundary between documentary and drama, particularly in his biographical films, that made him particularly attractive to advertisers;[33] these films did not rely simply on the recital of the facts of an artist's life, but instead sought to locate and express 'truth' through the emotions prompted by or expressed through specific pieces of music or art. This brought Russell into conflict with the BBC, which regarded such an approach with 'deep-seated anxiety' because of its potential to confuse or even mislead viewers.[34] The advertising industry, though, did not consider fact and fiction to be diametric opposites, as things that must be kept entirely separate in order to maintain the integrity of the whole, but rather as complementary, capable of advancing, commenting upon and accentuating each other. Television commercials thus offered Russell freedom from certain kinds of institutional constraints and expectations (whilst, obviously, imposing others), and so constituted an opportunity to make films dedicated to constructing mood or tone in order to stimulate particular feelings and attitudes in the viewer – ambitions that he would come to realise in many of his more effective feature films.

Russell's work in the advertising industry was part of a much wider trend. The introduction of the commercial ITV network in 1955 created an immediate demand for both television advertisements and people to make them. John Schlesinger – who himself made commercials for Joseph Janni prior to directing that producer's *A Kind of Loving* (Anglo-Amalgamated, 1962)[35] – noted that almost 'every major director'[36] then active in Britain made television advertisements. Numerous producers, art directors, cinematographers, composers and actors also got in on the act. There were several reasons for this widespread and productive cross-over of talent between the film and advertising industries. As well as the siren song of cold, hard cash, to which Russell at this stage of his career was clearly not immune – he was paid £200 to make the Black Magic commercial (7, above) – making commercials might also have interested creative practitioners for other reasons.[37] One of these was the chance to work with celluloid, something that might not have meant as much to Russell, who was employed by the BBC as a *film*-maker, as it did to, say, Richard Lester or Ridley Scott, much of whose early work involved directing for live television. For cinematographer Billy Williams, who had previously made documentaries on location for British Transport Films, advertising presented a chance to work with professional actors making fiction films in a studio, and taught him, by means of one particularly memorable jelly commercial, to develop the diffused lighting techniques that he would later use to such telling effect in films such as *Women in Love*.[38] The largesse often associated with the production of television commercials also afforded Williams, and others like him, access to the kinds of expensive lenses, stocks, lighting set-ups and processes of which documentarists, low-budget film-makers and those working in television could often only dream.

What's more, the brief shooting schedules and large number of commercials being produced each year (as many as 7,000–8,000 by the end of the 1960s) allowed innovation to take place quickly.[39] Russell noted of the music videos he shot in the 1980s that 'It's a week to shoot and a week to edit . . . And next week it will be shown all 'round the world and you're on to the next one.'[40] The same thing can be said of his television commercials. Compared with the 'endless battle'[41] of feature film production, or his run-ins at the BBC, where Russell's innovative decision to 'import elements of drama into documentary challenged generic boundaries and led to arguments',[42] moving-image advertising was more likely to actively encourage experimentation and a degree of risk-taking. In order to stand out from competitors hawking similar products, and the other advertisements appearing in the same commercial break, advertisers placed a premium on visual, tonal or narrative distinctiveness. This does not mean that every commercial was original or ground-breaking, or that Russell was afforded carte blanche when directing for the medium, but it should encourage us to remember that television advertising was not fundamentally uncreative.

Although seeking to compare the cost of film-making across different forms and media is difficult, the sizeable budgets associated with television advertising might also have appealed to Russell, whose work at the BBC had often been made on a relative shoestring. The 80-minute *Debussy Film* (BBC, 1965), for example, had cost somewhere in the region of £10,000, and was one of the more expensive films that Russell made for the Corporation.[43] Indeed, *Debussy*'s small budget meant that Russell and co-writer Melvyn Bragg had to structure the film so as to explain away the limited use of location shooting and period decor and costumes.[44] Even Russell's first foray into feature films, the 86-minute *French Dressing* (Associated British Picture Corporation, 1964), was made for just £179,467, and whilst this was a considerably larger sum than he was used to working with at the BBC, it constituted a pretty modest budget for a British feature at the time.[45] By comparison, Russell's minute-long Black Magic commercial had an initial production budget of approximately £6,500[46] and so cost, per foot, significantly more than both *French Dressing* and his television work. Even allowing for the likelihood that the Black Magic commercial was an outlier in terms of cost – the 'Building Site' commercial that he made for the Butter Council had a production budget of £2,076[47] – many of the other commercials that Russell directed were still likely to enjoy pro rata budgets that provided him with the chance to more fully indulge his creative and aesthetic visions. As such, they constituted important milestones on his journey towards the visual and narrative excess for which he was to become famous, not least because advertisers were often eager to ensure that the money ended up on the screen.

Television advertising also provided a chance to build professional relationships that could continue into subsequent work. For instance, Russell first worked with cinematographer Billy Williams when making commercials and Williams shot both the Ovaltine and Black Magic spots.[48] Their collaboration was maintained in both *Billion Dollar Brain* and, after that, *Women in Love*. Indeed, Williams notes that he was appointed to *Billion Dollar Brain* on Russell's recommendation, and only after showing producer Harry Saltzman his advertising show-reel.[49] Williams was not the only person who moved with Russell between advertising and film-making (or vice versa), and others include Ken Higgins, cinematographer on *French Dressing*, and actors Andrew Faulds and Jane Lumb.

However, even when Russell's cinematic collaborators had not worked with him in television advertising, their personal experiences of the medium could still inform Russell's work. The cinematographers with whom Russell worked provide a particularly striking example: all of the feature films directed by Russell during the 1960s and 1970s were photographed by cinematographers whose careers also took in television advertising: Higgins and Williams, as mentioned, and also Douglas Slocombe, David Watkin, Dick Bush and Peter Suschitzky. Although it is impossible to ascertain the extent to which the distinctive style that each of these cinematographers brought to Russell's films was the product of their experiences in advertising, many of the practitioners with whom Russell worked demonstrated a notable aptitude for television advertising, with commercials photographed by both Suschitzky and Watkin nominated for prizes in the prestigious annual *Design & Art Direction* awards in 1974, for example.[50] It seems likely that Williams was not unique in owing a debt to television commercials, even if he was unusual in acknowledging it in so effusive a manner. Advertising had, therefore, both a direct and indirect influence on the look and content of Russell's work, even if Russell's memories of his interactions with the industry rarely appear to have brought him any great pleasure.

A CASE STUDY: MAKING 'CASTLE' (ROWNTREE'S BLACK MAGIC)

Interesting light is thrown on Russell's work in television advertising by documents relating to the production of 'Castle', a commercial he made for Rowntree's Black Magic chocolates. Indeed, the materials relating to this advertisement held in the archive of the J. Walter Thompson (JWT) advertising agency, at the History of Advertising Trust, constitute the only contemporary documentation that I have been able to access on the production of Russell's television commercials, making this particular film particularly valuable. The majority of papers in the file relating to this commercial were produced by JWT and its client, Rowntree's; there is nothing written by Russell himself, nor much by the production company, James Garrett and Partners. However, the richness of the materials detailing the production of 'Castle', and the survival of the film itself, permit the discursive reconstruction of Russell's role and allow us an insight into some of the processes associated with the filming of television commercials.

JWT was adamant that it wanted to present 'more than an exotic setting for the product', and believed that the commercial's success would be heavily dependent on the creation of an on-screen 'atmosphere' capable of communicating 'interest, excitement, and magic'.[51] Although it is not clear if the commercial was written with Russell in mind, it is evident that Russell was encouraged to participate in planning and developing the shoot. During initial discussions with JWT representatives, the first of which took place on 2 July 1965 (more than two months before shooting started), Russell was said to be 'most enthusiastic about the script' and eager to turn his mind to solving 'the various problems relating to the film'.[52] For its part, JWT was certain that Russell was 'the right director' for the advertisement, considering him so 'essential' to the film's successful realisation that it offered him the chance to scout possible locations and have a casting session in Paris. So convinced was JWT that Russell was the right man for the job, that it developed the shooting schedule around his availability, even putting back location filming until 7–9 September 1965 – a delay of about three weeks – in order to accommodate his pressing commitments at the BBC.[53] Indeed, JWT was so sold on Russell's vision that it went so far as to advise cancelling production altogether rather than allow penny-pinching to reduce its effectiveness. The agency insisted that it would be better to 'begin again, from the beginning' with a different idea and a different director than undermine Russell's ability to deliver the film he had been engaged to make.[54]

Russell was asked to make an advertisement that did not seek to sell Black Magic 'on a strictly rational sense alone', but rather involved the viewer 'in the super-rational sequences of a dream'.[55] A note stating that Garrett's had 'agreed to supply a suitable panther' gives a sense of the commercial's aesthetic and tonal qualities.[56] In the film, a woman walks through a torch- and candle-lit 'fairy-tale castle of the Lichtenstein variety' until she finds her lover, who presents her with a box of Black Magic chocolates.[57] Via a series of dissolves, the same woman is then shown running through a meadow, lying languidly amongst wild flowers, and walking a cheetah, which had previously accompanied her through the castle. Elements of 'Castle' find striking visual echoes in *Women in Love*: Rupert and Ursula's picnic, for example, speaks to the commercial's anonymous model relaxing in a field of flowers, whilst both films feature carefully composed shots showing characters walking along the water's edge, and similar uses of candle-, torch- and fire-light to illuminate shots and sequences so as to permit the atmospheric deployment of shadow.

When an early cut of the commercial was tested, the majority of respondents felt that Russell and his crew had succeeded both in creating 'an impression of a high-quality, even luxury product' and 'communicating the desired mood of mystery, excitement and romance', with this feeling of intrigue registering 'as a not unpleasurable frisson'.[58] However, the oneiric tone of Russell's work was more pronounced than Rowntree's had anticipated or was comfortable with. The company was concerned that viewers might find 'Castle' bemusing or off-putting, not least because of the fragmented nature of the initial voice-over script (read by Jane Lumb): 'Why / does a man / Black Magic / to a woman / plain chocolates / bring / Black Magic.' The first version of the commercial was cut so that these words were 'matched to . . . changing images', mobilising Russell's ability to marry sound- and vision-tracks to create distinct and meaningful rhythms.[59] Indeed, *The Debussy Film*, shown on the BBC in May 1965 and so fresh in JWT minds as they mooted the idea of working with Russell, possesses 'a dreamlike flow in which change is suggested through imagery, form cutting, setting and the relationship of sound to image'.[60] Using such formal ingenuity to bind 'the hallucinatory state of [Debussy's] mind to the dreamlike quality of his music'[61] worked in an artist biography, but Rowntree's was hesitant to use it in one of its television commercials, convinced that the atmosphere of 'eeriness'[62] communicated by non-linear commentary and editing might alienate viewers or persuade them that the film's producers had 'mistakenly got some of the words transposed'.[63] Rowntree's rejected 'the "kinky" order of words', and a more conventional voice-over was recorded, reducing the radical nature of the commercial and changing its eventual impact.[64]

Rowntree's interventions shaped other aspects of the commercial, too. The non-conformist religious views of the Rowntree family still permeated the company, and so made it uncomfortable with the eroticised way in which the female protagonist was to be portrayed; 'sex', noted JWT, was 'a dirty word in York [where Rowntree's was based]'.[65] Such interference is unlikely to have pleased Russell, who had already demonstrated notable enthusiasm for shots of his actors in states of partial or complete undress: as the *Daily Mirror* noted approvingly of *The Debussy Film*, 'You don't often see a girl take her undies off on an arty programme.'[66] Although both Russell and JWT would have understood that they would not be permitted to include explicit sexual material in a television commercial, they were also aware that an overtly sensual approach could contribute to the advertisement's fantastical atmosphere, and so would most likely have been disappointed when Rowntree's objected both to 'the clothes which the girl is or is not wearing' and to her eroticised presentation.[67] As with the commentary, the client got their way; Russell was instructed to overshoot, so that Rowntree's could select footage 'that does not offend the Quaker ethic too much'.[68]

By the time that 'Castle' went out, in March 1966, Rowntree's had diluted the vision that Russell had developed in collaboration with JWT and James Garrett and Partners. Reviewing the week's new commercials, *Television Mail* observed that 'Castle' was 'all very nicely done but just a little confusing', noting that it was 'too full of bits and pieces': the dream-like flow and fantastical ambience of the project as initially conceived had become mundane and disjointed.[69] Concerned that 'Castle' was 'in danger of stretching the credulity of people to the limit of what they will accept', Rowntree's pushed for, and was provided with, a less expressive, less extravagant, less challenging commercial.[70] In short, a less 'Ken Russell' commercial.

CONCLUSION

As Ken Russell's reputation as a director grew, he stopped making television commercials and became openly critical of the industry that had only recently paid him to make them. He proclaimed that there was something fundamentally wrong with advertising per se, insisting that 'the minds and . . . values' of the ad men were 'depraved' and opining that working in the industry posed an existential threat to the artist's creative integrity:[71]

> I would say 'Tell me how you want this man to say these lines because frankly no human being would ever say that dialogue'. 'Oh' they'd say, quite brightly. 'They'd say it like this.' 'Fine.' And we'd do it their way, like that.[72]

Such claims about the ontological artificiality and cynicism of advertising have tended to colour subsequent explorations of Russell's work making television commercials, dismissing it as a creative dead end that served only to briefly distract him from his true calling directing television and feature films. But Russell's words also make clear the frustration he felt concerning the *practicalities* of working as a director in this medium, his frustration at having to yield control of a project to external forces. Here, the input of the agency, the client and the ITCA (the body responsible for regulating television advertising in the UK) are analogues of the constraints that, for example, the British Board of Film Censors and BBC managers placed on Russell, and against which he continually chafed: 'After one has poured his life blood into a project, it is difficult to accept the fact that someone else is really controlling [it].'[73]

We might, then, see Russell's decision to renounce advertising as part of a wider struggle for creative autonomy. When it comes to explaining his choice to turn his back on the industry, external interference in the production of his commercials should be considered alongside his ideological or ethical opposition to advertising; that, in part, he rejected the medium because he could not make the films as he wanted. And if, indeed, we understand that, in the mid-1960s at least, Russell recognised that television advertising offered him a means by which he might express his talent – whilst also offering the chance to develop his technique and style, build professional relationships, and enjoy the luxury of larger budgets – then we might recognise that Russell's television commercials constitute part of his corpus, contributing to both his identity as an artist and his status as a film-maker. We might note, too, that Russell was capable of making effective and successful advertisements: his Bri-Nylon film was nominated for a prize at the Cork International Film Festival and described as 'an exciting commercial with lots of good camera angles and skilled editing . . . convincing and memorable'.[74] Not all of his feature films received such praise.

ACKNOWLEDGEMENTS

This chapter was supported by the Arts and Humanities Research Council (grant number AH/L014793/1) and forms part of the 'Transformation and Tradition in Sixties British Cinema' project based at the Universities of York and East Anglia. I would also like to extend my thanks to the History of Advertising Trust.

NOTES

1. John Baxter, *An Appalling Talent: Ken Russell* (London: Michael Joseph, 1973), 131.
2. Joseph Lanza, *Phallic Frenzy: Ken Russell and His Films* (Chicago: Chicago Review Press, 2007), 45; Gene D. Phillips, *Ken Russell* (Boston: Twayne, 1979), 150.
3. Ken Russell, *Altered States: The Autobiography of Ken Russell* (New York: Bantam, 1991), 119; Phillips, *Ken Russell*, 149–50.
4. Stephen Farber, 'Russellmania', *Film Comment*, vol. 11, no. 6, 1975, 44. The sequence and its advertisements are discussed in Tom Wallis, 'Smashing Our Guitars, Deconstructing Our Idols: The Pop Art Aesthetic in *Tommy*', in Kevin M. Flanagan (ed.), *Ken Russell: Re-Viewing England's Last Mannerist* (Plymouth: Scarecrow Press, 2009), 95–7.
5. See, for example, Joseph A. Gomez, *Ken Russell: The Adaptor as Creator* (London: Frederick Muller, 1976), 91, 99; Phillips, *Ken Russell*, 98; and Ken Hanke, *Ken Russell's Films* (Metuchen, NJ: Scarecrow Press, 1984), 84.
6. *New York Times*, 15 October 1972, D15; Baxter, 131.
7. See, for example, the filmographies in such texts as Phillips, *Ken Russell*; Diane Rosenfeldt, *Ken Russell: A Guide to References and Resources* (Boston: G. K. Hall, 1978); Thomas R. Atkins (ed.), *Ken Russell* (New York: Monarch, 1976); Hanke, *Ken Russell's Films*; and Lanza, *Phallic Frenzy*. The filmographies in Baxter, *Appalling Talent*, and Gomez, *Ken Russell*, mention Russell's television commercials in passing, but neither provides any details.
8. Paul Sutton, *The Authorised Biography of Ken Russell. Volume One: Becoming Ken Russell* (Cambridge: Bear Claw, 2012), 93.
9. There were around 300,000 transmissions of commercials across the ITV network by 1959–60. Richard Farmer, 'Film and Television Advertising', in Richard Farmer, Laura Mayne, Duncan Petrie and Melanie Williams, *Transformation and Tradition in 1960s British Cinema* (Edinburgh: Edinburgh University Press, 2019), 303.
10. Lanza, 45.
11. Hanke, 84.
12. Baxter, 131. This is the most precise figure that I have been able to locate concerning the size of this particular element of Russell's corpus, although Russell's own hesitancy should counsel against understanding it as being a definitive total. As new evidence comes to light, we may find additional details of commercials of which we are already aware, or information concerning commercials about which we currently know nothing.
13. Jo Gable, *The Tuppenny Punch and Judy Show: 25 Years of TV Commercials* (London: Michael Joseph, 1980), 32. Richardson agreed to direct a commercial to pay for a new swimming pool, but quickly withdrew. David Watkin, *Why is There Only One Word for Thesaurus?* (Brighton: Trouser Press, 1998), 121–2. Whitehead signed a contract to direct commercials for Associated British-Pathe but does not appear to have made any. *Television Mail*, 15 March 1968, 9.
14. *Television Mail*, 31 July 1964, 19.
15. *Television Mail*, 16 October 1964, 16.
16. *Television Mail*, 9 April 1965, 20.
17. *Advertiser's Weekly*, 5 February 1965, 26.
18. *Television Mail*, 28 May 1965, 21.
19. *Television Mail*, 4 March 1966, 17.
20. *Television Mail*, 18 March 1966, 23.
21. *Television Mail*, 15 July 1966, 18.
22. 'A Sense of Direction', *Round the Square*, 30 March 1966, 6.
23. *Times*, 28 December 1989, 2.

24. *New York Times*, 15 October 1972, D15.
25. Baxter, 131.
26. Ibid.
27. Ibid.
28. Phillips, *Ken Russell*, 150. See also Farber, 44; Lanza, 48.
29. Sutton, *Authorised Biography*, 291. Sutton notes that Jonathan Benson '[h]awked Russell's BBC films to advertising agencies to try to get Russell work'. Ibid.
30. *Television Mail*, 24 April 1964, 29. Richard Lester was a founding partner of JGP; and directors such as Sydney J. Furie and Kevin Billington signed exclusive contracts.
31. 'A Sense of Direction', *Round the Square*, 30 March 1966, 6.
32. *Advertiser's Weekly*, 5 February 1965, 26.
33. John Hill, '"Blurring the lines between fact and fiction": Ken Russell, the BBC and "Television Biography"', *Journal of British Cinema and Television*, vol. 12, no. 4, 2015, 454.
34. Ibid.
35. William J. Mann, *Edge of Midnight: The Life of John Schlesinger* (London: Arrow, 2005), 175–6.
36. Gable, 32.
37. In another boost to the family finances, Russell appears to have cast his son, James, in one of his commercials. *Television Mail*, 16 October 1964, 16. On film-makers working in advertising, including the fees they commanded, see Farmer, 303–26.
38. John Gainsborough, 'Impeccable British Instincts', *American Cinematographer*, vol. 82, no. 3, 2001, 91; Billy Williams, interview with Neil Binney, recorded September 2003, <http://www.webofstories.com/play/billy.williams/24> (last accessed 26 May 2022).
39. Independent Television Authority, *ITV 1970: A Guide to Independent Television* (London: ITA, 1970), 127.
40. *Billboard*, 14 December 1985, 29.
41. Ibid.
42. Hill, 453.
43. Paul Sutton, *Talking about Ken Russell* (Cambridge: Buffalo Books, 2015), 84.
44. John C. Tibbetts, 'Ken Russell's *The Debussy Film* (1965)', *Historical Journal of Film, Radio and Television*, vol. 25, no. 1, 2005, 86.
45. Film Finances Archive, *French Dressing* – Film Finances to Kenwood Films, 25 April 1963.
46. JWT Advertising Agency, Television Production Estimate – Rowntree's Black Magic, 'Castle', 24 August 1965. Archive ref: HAT/JWT 50/1/158/2/2/3/2.
47. JWT Advertising Agency, George Waller to Jeremy Scott, 26 March 1965. Archive ref: HAT/JWT 50/1/30/2/2/2.
48. Williams also photographed Russell's Ross Foods commercial.
49. 'The Five Films Nominated for "Best Cinematography" of 1981', *American Cinematographer*, May 1982, 506. Williams would later photograph feature films for John Schlesinger, Jo McGrath and Ted Kotcheff, having first worked with them on television commercials.
50. See *D&AD 1974* (London: Design and Art Directors Association, 1974).
51. JWT Advertising Agency, Bob Judd to C. Thomas, 24 August 1965. Archive ref: HAT/JWT: 50/1/158/2/2/3/5.
52. JWT Advertising Agency, Ron Wiles to Donald Macmillan and Jeremy Bullmore, 7 July 1965. Archive ref: HAT/JWT: 50/1/158/2/2/3/5.
53. JWT Advertising Agency, Donald Macmillan to J. G. D. Shaw, 22 July 1965. Archive ref: HAT/JWT: 50/1/158/2/2/3/2.
54. JWT Advertising Agency, Bob Judd to Christopher Thomas, 24 August 1965. Archive ref: HAT/JWT: 50/1/158/2/2/3/5.
55. JWT Advertising Agency, untitled report on Black Magic 'Castle' television commercial (n.d.), 1. Archive ref: HAT/JWT: 50/1/158/2/2/3/6.

56. JWT Advertising Agency, 'Black Magic "Castle"' – Note on production and costs of 45-second commercial, n.d. (July 1965?). Archive ref: HAT/JWT: 50/1/158/2/2/3/5.
57. JWT Advertising Agency, John O'Keefe to Bob Judd, 15 July 1965. The commercial was eventually shot at Castello Odescalchi near Rome. Archive ref: HAT/JWT: 50/1/158/2/2/3/5.
58. JWT Advertising Agency, Adrian Cohen to Donald Macmillan, 15 December 1965. Archive ref: HAT/JWT: 50/1/158/2/2/3/5.
59. JWT Advertising Agency, untitled report on Black Magic 'Castle' television commercial (n.d.), 1. Archive ref: HAT/JWT: 50/1/158/2/2/3/6.
60. Joseph A. Gomez, '*Mahler* and the Methods of Ken Russell's Films on Composers', *Velvet Light Trap*, vol. 14, 1975, 46.
61. Ken Russell, 'Debussy', *Radio Times*, 13 May 1965, 31.
62. JWT Advertising Agency, Giles Shaw to Donald Macmillan, 2 January 1966. Archive ref: HAT/JWT: 50/1/158/2/2/3/2.
63. JWT Advertising Agency, Giles Shaw to Christopher Thomas, 2 September 1965. Archive ref: HAT/JWT: 50/1/158/2/2/3/2.
64. JWT Advertising Agency, Giles Shaw to Donald Macmillan, 5 January 1966. Archive ref: HAT/JWT: 50/1/158/2/2/3/2.
65. JWT Advertising Agency, Michael Cooper-Evans to John Ogden, 1 September 1965. Archive ref: HAT/JWT: 50/1/158/2/2/3/5.
66. *Daily Mirror*, 19 May 1965, 18.
67. JWT Advertising Agency, Giles Shaw to Christopher Thomas, 27 August 1965. Archive ref: HAT/JWT: 50/1/158/2/2/3/2.
68. JWT Advertising Agency, Michael Cooper-Evans to John Ogden, 1 September 1965. Archive ref: HAT/JWT: 50/1/158/2/2/3/5.
69. *Television Mail*, 18 March 1966, 2. Undermining the commercial's exoticism, an advertisement for hair conditioner featuring what appeared to be the same cheetah was also broadcast in the same week.
70. JWT Advertising Agency, Giles Shaw to Christopher Thomas, 13 December 1965. Archive ref: HAT/JWT: 50/1/158/2/2/3/2.
71. Quoted in Baxter, 131.
72. Quoted in ibid.
73. Quoted in Gene D. Phillips, 'An Interview with Ken Russell', *Film Comment*, vol. 6, no. 3, 1970, 17.
74. *Television Mail*, 9 April 1965, 22.

CHAPTER 5

Quartet: Ken Russell's Painter Biopics and How they Anticipate the Later Cinematic Work

Paul Davies

INTRODUCTION

In the DVD commentary to *Delius: Song of Summer* (BBC, 1968), Ken Russell describes Frederick Delius's French house, Grez-sur-Loing, as (according to the composer's amanuensis, Eric Fenby) 'absolutely packed with classic paintings' such as Edvard Munch's *Death of Marat I* (1907) and *The Kiss* (1897) and Paul Gauguin's *Nevermore (O Taïti)* (1897). In *The Lonely Shore*, a 16-minute, post-atomic era/post-apocalyptic sci-fi faux-documentary film made for the BBC's *Monitor* (1962), a team of alien archaeologists examines all that is left on a deserted beach to determine what life was like in that year. They find, among the cultural debris and detritus, Van Gogh's *Sunflowers* and eight Pablo Picasso paintings. These are two examples of how paintings and painters are incorporated into the cinematic/televisual space of Russell's BBC work. While he produced numerous painter biopics for the BBC, the films *Scottish Painters* (1959), *Pop Goes the Easel* (1962), *Always on Sunday* (1965) and *Dante's Inferno: The Private Life of Dante Gabriel Rossetti, Poet and Painter* (1967) will form the basis of this chapter's analysis. This quartet of films demonstrates how Russell's stylistic technique evolves from one film to the next, honing his skills, moving towards his ideal of the dramatised artist's biopic, especially regarding the interplay between image and sound(s)/music. In doing so, the chapter hopes to show how Russell frames and employs the painters' work within these four (somewhat neglected) films and also to show how they anticipate many of his later characteristic stylistic features and thematic concerns.

SCOTTISH PAINTERS

Scottish Painters focuses on Roberts MacBryde (1913–66) and Colquhoun (1914–62), who were both professional collaborators and lovers. It was one of Russell's first films for *Monitor* and the first of his films about visual artists/painters. The 'Two Roberts' (as they were collectively known) are also the first of Russell's gay artists, and he admitted that while *Scottish Painters* was 'a film about love', it 'couldn't be explicit at the time'.[1] Their relationship began when they met at Glasgow School of Art in 1933 and did not end until Colquhoun died in 1962. According to his autobiography, Russell first encountered their paintings and later the artists themselves at an exhibition of theirs when working in the Bond Street art gallery Lefevre in 1948, which was selling their work.[2]

While living and leading a bohemian lifestyle in the Soho of the 1940s, the Two Roberts simultaneously engaged with the contemporary London art scene through their friendships with Francis Bacon and Lucian Freud and came under the influence of the European modernist school (Picasso in particular). The Tate Gallery bought their paintings, Kenneth Clark championed them, and Vogue photographed them.[3] What drew Russell to them as subjects was their bohemianism. The first time he saw them he thought 'they resembled a couple of gypsies, both in their mode of life and appearance'.[4] Fifteen years later he met them again, looking exactly the same: 'My bohemian days were over, but I always looked back on them with nostalgia, so that it was inevitable that eventually I would pay them tribute.'[5]

Narrated by actor and writer Allan McClelland, the film opens with a shot of the artists atop their horse-drawn cart packed with paintings heading for their timber-cottage studio in Suffolk, 'close enough to London for them to be able to sell their paintings and cheap enough for them to do nothing but paint' (Figure 5.1). Russell's documentary 'consists purely of short interviews with each painter, followed by a montage of their work, with Russell's camera slowly tracking into fine details and pulling back to reveal the wider context',[6] and is accompanied by, for instance, Debussy's orchestral arrangement of the first of Erik Satie's *Gymnopédies*. This is an early example of how Russell made (particularly classical) music an integral part of his films and illustrates an early use of the *Gymnopédies* in film (to be used on many occasions afterwards). Early modernist and experimental composer Satie's music is also used to accompany shots of MacBryde painting and narrating. Debussy and Satie are an equally early example of an interest in French art which is sustained throughout Russell's career, and we are told MacBryde's 'interest is in form, shape and colour', something often attested to in Satie's compositions. Russell observes the underlying melancholy tone of the paintings and chooses this minimalist music because of the gentle, dreamlike drift from one moment (one painting) to the next. This gives the paintings time and space within the film (later, the same music plays over the opening credits of *Salome's Last Dance* [Vestron,

Figure 5.1 The Two Roberts.
Source: BBC, 1959.

1988]).⁷ *Scottish Painters* is, as Paul Sutton observes, 'an important milestone in the art of filming art' which 'shows the viewer how to read the paintings by deconstructing the compositions into interlinked component shapes, from the detail to the whole and back again using Eisenstein's matched dissolves'.⁸

A similar sequence with exactly the same film techniques of montage, tracking, incorporation of music and dissolves is dedicated to Colquhoun and what he admits is his 'endless concern with the human form'. In a style typical of Russell's later films, Colquhoun admits to an element of nostalgia in the creative wellspring for his work that 'came out of rather romantic memories' connected to where he lived. While he talks there is a dissolve from Colquhoun painting to a lone, wholebody, veiled figure walking away from the camera along a beach. This brief shot metaphorically evokes the everyday Scottish people who made such an impact on the painter during his childhood and whom he subsequently depicted in his paintings. The film illustrates the ways in which the Two Roberts engage both the local (the romance of everyday Scottish life) and the global (the attachment to a European modernist aesthetic; Satie, Debussy, and so on). A montage of his finished paintings is reminiscent of the one of Henri Gaudier-Brzeska's completed sculptures at the end of *Savage Messiah* [MGM-EMI, 1972]. Ultimately, all Colquhoun's paintings of human figures are 'an exercise in the use of paint and shapes'. This approach could well have appealed to Russell given his own interest in the way the human form moves through (filmic) space, motivated no doubt by his time as a (fully trained) ballet dancer.

Archived correspondence between Russell and the Two Roberts shows that the initial reaction of the painters was that while the film did make them look 'like a couple of bums', they still 'liked it, particularly the treatment of the paintings'. Russell, on the other hand, denied this was his intention and replied that the 'idea was to show that unlike the painters who compromise or make painting a part-time affair you two carry on painting whatever happens, through thick and thin'.⁹

POP GOES THE EASEL

In 1962 Russell completed *Pop Goes the Easel*, his first programme-length documentary portrait for *Monitor*. It depicts four contemporary English pop art pioneers: painter and illustrator Peter Blake (1932–); painter, graphic artist and film-maker Peter Phillips (1939–); painter, illustrator, collage artist, photographer, film-maker and sculptor Derek Boshier (1937–); and painter and collage artist Pauline Boty (1938–66). Aiming to capture and reflect their excitement and youthful energy, they are depicted in their studios and as active observers of various forms of popular entertainments and amusements (e.g. circuses and street markets), as well as in connection to pop art itself via vibrant collages/montages of dancing and playing pinball (anticipating the Russellian pop art of *Tommy* [Columbia, 1975]); flicking through the pages of illustrated magazines; movies, pop and jazz music, television and toys (Figure 5.2).

Figure 5.2 Pauline Boty and Peter Blake.
Source: BBC, 1962.

Russell's highly visual and musical approach to film-making (embryonic in *Scottish Painters*) is appropriately stylish, exuberant, freewheeling and playful, capturing the beginnings of the swinging sixties with the non-diegetic pop soundtrack. Russell 'constructs an elaborate, rapidly cut rhythmic kaleidoscope of images of film and pop stars (Brigitte Bardot, Buddy Holly), fashion magazines, fast cars, politicians, the space race, guns, girls, American culture in general' as he moves between fantasy and more realistic documentary-style sequences.[10] Kevin Flanagan maintains that Russell was concerned to present the arts in a constant symbiosis with what is popular and everyday. Russell abolishes the distinction between high and low culture, depicting artists of working- and lower-middle-class descent. Flanagan also refers to the director's '"doubling" of the pop aesthetic . . . his stylistic and formative use of pop modes to better showcase pop attitudes'.[11] The toys, magazines and comics of *Pop Goes the Easel* anticipate the constructed pop art style of *Tommy* (Marilyn Monroe masks and statues) and *Lisztomania* [Goodtimes Enterprises, 1975] (images of Elvis and Pete Townsend on a wall; the Pope's robe with stars).

Seated in front of a wall of pop art images, the patrician figure of Huw Wheldon introduces the film (reinforcing class distinctions and BBC cultural values). He asserts that while some may dismiss the world of pop artists as 'tawdry and second rate', it is a world all the same 'packed with its own mythology, its own heroes, its own heroines, its own laughter, its own poetry', one in which 'we all live whether we like it or not' and which the artists 'approach with the utmost relish'. Wheldon concludes with brief descriptions of the four artists after which there is a complete absence (or rejection) of patrician voice-over narration for the rest of the film.

Peter Blake's *On the Balcony* (1955–7) is a 'theme and variation' on *The Balcony* (1868) by Édouard Manet, collaging images of ordinary, everyday people (mostly youthful teenagers) with a newspaper photograph of the royal family, a photograph of his late tutor John Minton, a painting by fellow student Leon Kossoff, and products from the USA (a packet of Lucky Strike, an 'I love Elvis' badge and a copy of *Life* magazine). The painting reflects the conflicts and cultural changes of post-war Britain. In *Pop Goes the Easel* Blake's painting is 'dissected literally: the camera isolates sections and rhythmically cuts them to the gallop of James Darren's "Her Royal Majesty"'.[12] Here Russell has developed the technique of intercutting music with images, specifically paintings, established in *Scottish Painters*. This is a method employed elsewhere in *Pop Goes the Easel*: pans and tilts move in and out of Blake's walls onto which he has stuck cut-outs from magazines. *Pop Goes the Easel* is a point of evolution and it uses a more sophisticated approach compared with *Scottish Painters*, with extracts from other films inserted into the filmic text, a denser, more textured soundtrack, and more multi-layered editing and camera movement.

The sequence featuring Peter Phillips includes a musical accompaniment of some classics of late fifties jazz by Julian 'Cannonball' Adderley ('This Here', 1959), Charles Mingus ('Folk Forms Number One', 1960) and Ornette Coleman ('Embraceable You', 1960), establishing a connection between pop art and modern jazz. The funky soul sounds of 'This Here' can be heard while Phillips is being chauffeured in an American limousine by an African American driver through a London suburb. While Phillips is making himself breakfast in front of a(nother!) wall of pictures, the non-diegetic 'Folk Forms Number One' can be heard framed by the diegetic sounds from an adjoining flat of a woman at a pinball machine. In a montage sequence the camera lingers on some of the pinball machine's painted-on images as if they themselves were pop art. Lastly, the sad ballad 'Embraceable You' perfectly suits the gloomy, sombre portraits we see by Phillips of nude female dancers in a series of panning and tracking shots. The sequence, looking outwards to French artistic culture, is one of several in the film that homage the aesthetic and editing style of the French New Wave.[13]

Derek Boshier's career has taken him from London's Royal College of Art (studying with fellow students David Hockney and R. B. Kitaj) to Texas in the 1980s and his current home Los Angeles since the late 1990s. He voices his concerns with the 'whole set-up of the American influence in this country . . . the sort of infiltration of the American way of life', mainly through advertising as he sees it. This process, he believes, starts with the cornflakes on the breakfast table, continues with cut-outs of American characters like Yogi Bear and Walt Disney's characters, and ends with comics on the backs of cornflakes packets. Boshier admits that many of his paintings deal with the phenomenon of mass media saturation and the pervasive American cultural influence. Of the four pop artists, he is the one to go into the most detail about his art, which he does in a 4-minute sequence.

We see Boshier's painting of a Kellogg's cornflakes packet before turning to the painting *England's Glory* (1961) with its criticism of cultural imperialism. The American flag in the top left-hand corner is 'American influence creeping in' to the other more specifically English images such as the Union Jack. Boshier admits his interest in the space race is behind his next painting, *The Most Handsome Hero of the Cosmos and Mr Shepard* (1962). The images of the painting are intercut with a short animated sequence. One of its images is a comic one – a spaceman. Boshier often uses comic strip style conceptualisations, as he does in *Man Playing Snooker and Thinking of Other Things* (1961) where 'the images are split up into compartments as in a comic'. These are all linked to 'the general interest theme of England, television and the space probe'. More astronauts on their radios are the sound bridge to *I Wonder What My Heroes Think of the Space Race* (1962). The three heroes presented (all of whom died a hero's death and who are connected by their childhoods) are Lord Nelson (a half portrait in military dress and eye patch surveying the scene), Abraham Lincoln and Buddy Holly, whose 'Everyday' sets in non-diegetically to accompany the images. Boshier concludes that Buddy Holly personifies everything he likes about heroes in general. Russell again employs his familiar technique of montage, dissolves and pans, weaving in and out of the paintings.

Pauline Boty is the first of Russell's female artists, later to be followed by Isadora Duncan (*Isadora Duncan, the Biggest Dancer in the World* [BBC, 1966]), Elizabeth Siddal/Christina Rossetti (*Dante's Inferno*) and Mary Shelley (*Gothic* [Virgin Vision/Vestron, 1986]) with unfulfilled plans to make films about Maria Callas and Sarah Bernhardt as well. Whereas the previous male artists try to explain their work, Russell navigates Boty's female identity by having her place more emphasis on *showing* her work, for example her 'dense and disturbing collages', often in the form of spectacle/masquerade as in when she is in top hat and tails miming briefly to the song 'On the Good Ship Lollipop'. There is also the image of Boty vigorously brushing her hair and grooming to the strains of 'A Foggy Day in London Town', which dissolves into details from her paintings as the film (re)creates itself in her image as a collage of images just like Russell is attempting to create himself through the film as well. She is interested, Boty says, in the moments when 'something very extraordinary is happening, yet everyone around isn't taking any notice of it at all'. Then we have George Gershwin's 'They All Laughed' from the Astaire–Rogers musical *Shall We Dance* [Mark Sandrich, RKO, 1937] with Boty admitting her love of such 1930s musicals (a love shared by Russell, manifested in *The Boy Friend* [MGM/EMI, 1971]), which she says have influenced the various shapes and 'atmospheres' of her paintings. This is followed by a segue/match cut from the film into a twenty-one-shot montage of her collages.

Boty performs right at the start of *Pop Goes the Easel* in a short, dramatic, 2-minute nightmare sequence in which she is pursued by a sinister, sunglasses-wearing, wheelchair-bound villain and a stern German teacher accomplice treading on Boty's sketches through endless circling corridors: (in German) 'Pick up these drawings, they don't belong here, pull yourself together, you know it's not allowed, come on!' The electronic music is distorted, and a sound bridge links her desperately phoning for help to her waking up to her alarm clock. And while Russell can once more be seen to be creating himself again here, so can Boty, whom he allows equal creative space.

The film is bookended by an early sequence where our four protagonists visit a fairground together, and the wrestling match that they all enjoy is a dry run for the male nude wrestling sequence in *Women in Love* [United Artists, 1969]. In the 'Twist' party sequence to Clay Cole's 'Twist Around the Clock', David Hockney can be glimpsed briefly as can others like the African American driver and pinball player and all four pop artists (a collage of the film's characters?).

Right before the end credits we see them painting individually to the classical music of J. S. Bach's Concerto for Four Harpsichords in A Minor. Here Russell positions them in a wider context, in a longer tradition of artistic creation.

ALWAYS ON SUNDAY

Always on Sunday deals with the French post-impressionist (naïve) painter Henri Rousseau (1844–1910), 'the greatest Primitive painter the world has ever known'.[14] It was the first *Monitor* film in which the actors actually spoke lines and were allowed to use their own voices as characters (instead of actors playing characters, as in the film within a film of *The Debussy Film* [BBC, 1965]): previously everything had been narrated.[15] The film has a double voice-over and layers of self-reflexivity: James Lloyd – 'subject of the earlier documentary *The Dotty World of James Lloyd* [BBC, 1964] and whose own career as a misunderstood naïve painter had many similarities'[16] – as Rousseau speaks extracts from the painter's letters and critical reviews plus lines of dialogue in some of the film's dramatic sequences. Oliver Reed is the omniscient narrator of the script, written by Russell and his regular *Monitor* collaborator Melvyn Bragg. The film offers a series of vignettes detailing Rousseau's life which are presented as a hybrid of arts documentary and biopic, with actors dramatising and reimagining moments of the painter's life.

Annette Robertson is dubbed by the male actor Keith Smith to create an androgynous Alfred Jarry in an example of cross-gender casting.[17] Russell brings to life parts of the notorious *Ubu Roi* by Jarry. The play (which anticipated the Theatre of the Absurd) premiered in 1896 and was a deliberately provocative theatrical attack on the bourgeoisie. It prompted a riot and was subsequently banned. The famous opening line 'Merdre!', translated and spoken in English as 'Shitter!', caused the audience to scream, faint and boo, a reaction that anticipates some of the reactions to Russell's own later work. The ensuing riot is depicted with the audience literally turning into 'bourgeois pigs', class politics also anticipating the tensions between high and low culture in Russell's later films.

Rousseau had a job at the Paris city toll, the reason Jarry with a lack of precision called him Le Douanier or customs officer.[18] The title we see on the screen is 'Henri Rousseau: Sunday Painter', referring to the fact that his art had to be produced in his spare time, even after retirement. Henri Rousseau eventually retired from his position to paint full time instead of just on Sundays. The film is set after Rousseau's retirement, which coincided with the beginning of his career as a painter at the age of forty-nine. Though eccentric on one level, Rousseau was quite conventional and bureaucratic on another, professional one. Russell emphasises this contradiction in terms between the classic civil servant and the self-taught hobbyist, an autodidacticism with which Russell can quite clearly identify.[19]

Parallels may be drawn between Rousseau and Russell. Both were artists that challenged mainstream conventions. Rousseau and his paintings were greeted with neglect, ridicule and contempt; his work was constantly misunderstood by those who failed to recognise its originality. Here also is an early example of Russell's misunderstood artist. As Michael Brooke observes:

> Given Russell's own battles with both critics and producers it's tempting to assume that *Always on Sunday* is exorcising personal demons, as the film is both by and about artists who operate on instinct, frequently putting them at odds with the expectations of the mainstream establishment.[20]

Many of Russell's biopics explore the ostracised artist who manages eventual success in spite of a lifetime of frustration and criticism. *Always on Sunday* is one of the first to bear witness to 'Russell's trademark interest in the artist as a naïve outsider'.[21]

Rousseau took inspiration for his works not from actual first-hand experience and stays in exotic locales but from more local places he had visited, like zoos or the botanical gardens in Paris, or from illustrated books, print ads and magazines he had seen and read, connecting him thematically to Russell's pop artists in *Pop Goes the Easel*. The style and subject matter of popular print culture were reflected in his imagery and use of colour. Rousseau himself said of his inspiration the Parisian greenhouses and gardens, 'When I go into the glass houses and I see the strange plants of exotic lands, it seems to me that I enter into a dream.'[22] Likewise, dream sequences and nightmares recur across *Pop Goes the Easel*, and Pauline Boty notes the dream influence in her own work.

Ultimately, 'Rousseau's work defies classification; his paintings, like his artistic career, are highly individual.'[23] Rousseau's paintings went on to influence several generations of painters, including the early Surrealists, who were moved by his ability to evoke a dream state. And even though the Spanish painter patronised him at times, the only painting he sold throughout his entire life was to a young Pablo Picasso. Yet far from being completely alone, it was actually through other artists that Rousseau finally found some support and, just before his death, a proper audience. By capturing this aspect of his personality, Russell turns him into someone who believed anything was possible if only he could paint, summarised by part of the epitaph on his tombstone written by another admirer, Guillaume Apollinaire, who said, 'Let our luggage pass duty free through the gates of heaven. We will bring you brushes, paints, and canvas.'[24] Russell's biopic of Rousseau 'rejects naturalism and replaces it with an off-kilter aesthetic worthy of one of Rousseau's paintings. *Always on Sunday* is also one of the finest examples of a Russell film about a struggling, misunderstood artist.'[25]

Numerous paintings by Rousseau are featured in the film, and production secretary Anne James points out that as per Russell's instructions, designer Luciana Arrighi aimed to ensure they were all 'photographed and printed life-size onto canvas'.[26] Four have been chosen for brief discussion, taking into consideration whether Rousseau is depicted working on his painting, and the deployment of filmic techniques which by now can be identified as typically Russellian zooms and so on, in addition to a final montage sequence of several other works. All Rousseau's paintings have a dream-like quality, blending the familiar with the unknown as well as elements of fairy tales, adventure, the uncanny and the darkly sexual, which must have appealed to Russell.

We start with *Artillerymen* (1893–5). On two occasions we see Rousseau working on the details of the faces of the thirteen darkly dressed soldiers and their commander. It is the first one he lifts onto his cart to wheel to an exhibition, where it is commented on disparagingly.[27] We hear Russell's own voice as one of the critics, a deliberately ironic use from someone who had to endure more than his own fair share of criticism. Rousseau is also observed working on the composition *War* (1894), in the presence of Jarry, who is working on *Ubu Roi*. Though described in the voice-over as 'his most ambitious painting yet', the painting eventually (and ironically, given the critical reception of some of Russell's later work) met 'the scorn of an obese, philistine, uncomprehending bourgeois audience'. *The Sleeping Gypsy* (1897) has 'an effect of moonlight, very poetic'. In addition to the signature Russell zooms of, among others, *Scottish Painters*, the shot in which the painting's moon is paralleled by something spherical in the wall and another painting – *Portrait of Madame M* (1895–7) – is a highly successful attempt on the part of Russell at creating his own filmic painting. And *Old Junior's Cart* (1908) shows Rousseau 'working from a photograph as he often did but reorganizing the figures and adding new ones of his own . . . transforming the most haphazard snapshot into something personal and strange' – like a film-maker does when recreating paintings.

In a sequence towards the end of the film Rousseau shows his last love, Léonie, some of his paintings to 'entertain' her, as he puts it, but she proceeds to laugh the whole way through, laughter which then sound dissolves into the laughter of many imposing itself over Rousseau's narration. Yet while this laughter eventually drowns out Rousseau's words completely, the paintings assert themselves over it as the montage of his works increases in speed. They are the last things we see, again like the final montage of finished sculptures by Henri Gaudier-Brzeska in the final sequence of *Savage Messiah* which remain after he is killed in World War I.

As if to further validate the primacy of the paintings, we next see Rousseau painting 'one of his greatest canvasses', *The Dream* (1910), 'in which a dream lady is transported into a tropical paradise on Rousseau's faded plush settee'. The camera tilts up to him adding the final details to her outstretched left hand. While *Savage Messiah* ends with Gaudier-Brzeska's sculptures, the final words of *Always on Sunday* are 'His painting of *The Dream* is in the Museum of Modern Art in New York – valued at over a million dollars.' Yet even though we have just seen Rousseau die, the very final shot accompanied by triumphant non-diegetic music is of him wheeling his cart around as ever.[28]

DANTE'S INFERNO: THE PRIVATE LIFE OF DANTE GABRIEL ROSSETTI, POET AND PAINTER

Dante Gabriel Rossetti (1828–82) was a painter, illustrator, drawer, designer, etcher and sketcher. Russell had made an earlier film for television about the Pre-Raphaelites, *Old Battersea House* (BBC, 1961), the success of which had drawn attention to their then unfashionable art. *Dante's Inferno* is the only one of the quartet made for *Omnibus*, the successor to *Monitor*. Rossetti's art resembles that of his fellow Pre-Raphaelite painters in its sensuality, use of symbolism, and religious, mythological and literary themes. In addition, much like Caravaggio used people from the streets to model for him, *The Girlhood of Mary Virgin* (1848–9) portrays the likenesses of Rossetti's mother and sister as Mary and Saint Anne, while in *Ecce Ancilla Domini!* (*The Annunciation*, 1849–50) he used his sister as a model for the Virgin, an approach Russell would no doubt have thoroughly approved of inasmuch as he used his own family in his films.

Apart from Rossetti himself, *Dante's Inferno* features his sister, the poet Christina Rossetti; the painters John Everett Millais,[29] William Holman Hunt and Edward Burne-Jones; the decorative artist and founder of the English Arts and Crafts Movement William Morris; the poet Algernon Swinburne;[30] and the critic John Ruskin. The women at the centre are Rossetti's model and later wife, Elizabeth Siddal; Jane Burden, a model who later married William Morris before beginning an affair with Rossetti; and another model, Fanny Cornforth, with whom Rossetti lived off and on towards the end of his life. The film concentrates especially on Rossetti's relationship with Siddal, and while the film does stress her poor health and addiction to laudanum, it also makes it clear that she was an artist in her own right. In addition, Russell's film focuses on Rossetti as a poet with voice-over quotes from his work and the merging of verse and image in later sequences.

In *Dante's Inferno* 'the genesis of the director's favourite traits and themes' can be detected: 'artistic excess, madness, hallucinations and desire/eroticism'.[31] We may draw upon *Gothic* with its multiple, incestuous relationships and muses, hallucinatory visuals of breasts with eyes and mouths spewing cockroaches, and the all-round nightmarish atmosphere of drugs, sex and horror. In *Gothic* there is a similar use of *tableaux vivants*, specifically the recreation of Füssli's *Nachtmahr* (1781) in the dramatisation of Mary Shelley's waking dream. A sleeping woman bathed in white light stretches across a bed, her arms, neck and head hanging off the end of the mattress. An apelike incubus squats on her chest and stomach. On the far left a crazed horse with glowing eyes and flared nostrils protrudes from the background shadows, flash-lit, eyes burning, hair on end, out of nowhere, seemingly out of control. The painting is set on the border between dream and reality: maybe the woman is dreaming the whole thing. The dark, irrational forces mixed with eroticism and sexuality, the 'staging' and chiaroscuro are apposite for Russell's film style. His own film version of Mary Shelley's waking dream is lit by flashes of lightning as she first has a vision of the painting in the storm then sees the demon sitting on her chest, an image employed (controversially) in the marketing campaign for the film. She screams as it reaches for her throat.

A further similarity may also be ascertained between the actresses Gala Mitchell (Jane Morris) and Myriam Cyr (Claire Clairmont). *Dante's Inferno* presents Rossetti's vision of Morris bidding farewell to him in a boat on a lake with her arms outstretched, subsequently reflected in the water in the next shot. Similarly in *Gothic*, Claire Clairmont arrives in a boat on Lake Geneva at the Villa Diodati with Mary and Percy Shelley in a very similar gesture (and a self-aware visual quotation). *Dante's Inferno* is also the first of Russell's films to be shot partly or wholly in the Lake District along with *Delius: Song of Summer* [BBC, 1968], *Dance of the Seven Veils* [BBC, 1970], *The Boy Friend*, *Mahler* [Goodtimes Enterprises, 1974], *Tommy*, *The Rainbow* [Vestron, 1988] and, of course, *Clouds of Glory*, his dramatised interpretation of the lives of William and Dorothy Wordsworth and of Coleridge made for Granada Television, 1978.

The theme of the artist selling out (Tchaikovsky becoming a conductor for money in *The Music Lovers* [United Artists, 1970] or Mahler converting to Catholicism to please Cosima Wagner and further his career) is a persistent one in Russell's cinema. In *Dante's Inferno* it can be seen in the exhumation of Elizabeth Siddal's corpse to retrieve a volume of his poems he had buried with her to sell them later: a nightmare vision of his wife emerging from her coffin is what he gets for his pains in a sequence worthy of *The Devils* [Warner Bros., 1971] (its grotesque corpse imagery precedes that of the rotting corpses outside the walls of Loudun), not to mention German expressionist cinema. With music by Hans Werner Henze (his Fifth Symphony, 1962), the sequence is also in effect a reversal of the one in which Mahler has a vision of being buried alive.

Turning to the use of paintings in *Dante's Inferno*, numerous shots are consciously modelled on and quote actual Pre-Raphaelite paintings, for example *The Light of the World* (1851–3) by William Holman Hunt, who is shown painting and Annie Miller modelling for it. John C. Tibbetts writes of the film's 'sensitive blending of Dante Gabriel Rossetti's plangent lyrics to Russell's *tableaux vivants* re-creations of the paintings of the Pre-Raphaelites'.[32] In addition, the shot where Siddal and Dante Rossetti kiss is modelled after the embrace of the two protagonists of Rossetti's *The Wedding of St George and Princess Sabra* (1857).[33] Then Rossetti is shot in the process of painting both *Dante's Dream at the Time of the Death of Beatrice* (1869–71; the dream is of seeing Beatrice in death; Jane Morris modelled) and *Found* (1853), a work which depicts the social and moral problems of modern urban life in the form of an ailing woman collapsed in the road who has become a prostitute.

Furthermore, Elizabeth Siddal (Judith Paris) is acknowledged as an artist in her own right, working on her *Clerk Saunders* watercolour (1857) with Dante posing for it as he did in real life. In the image May Margaret meets the ghost of her murdered lover, Clerk Saunders, who materialises in order to renew his marriage vows. Kneeling on the bed, she kisses the wand to show her fidelity. While the theme of love and desire, the use of bright colours and medievalism all reflect Pre-Raphaelite characteristics, Siddal's painting is also a meditation on the contemporary issues of gender and class: this is a story about love between social unequals, a topic that interested Russell, particularly in his three D. H. Lawrence adaptations.

Russell films other sequences 'as if with the light employed in a Pre-Raphaelite painting: that is, the soft glow in dark Victorian interiors'.[34] The overall effect of such filmic reproductions or re-enactments is more of the 'movement' associated with Russell's later cinematic work along with more developed costume design, interior decoration and multiple paintings and sketches. The film's 'fantasy sequences greatly expand on the style and effect' of *The Debussy Film* made two years earlier.[35] The use in *Dante's Inferno* 'of fire, water, and mountain symbolism'[36] anticipates Russell's later cinematic style in *Mahler* and *Clouds of Glory*.

Two further sequences anticipate the later cinematic work. First of all, immediately after Siddal's exhumation and the brief intertitles, Rossetti leaps directly at the camera over a bonfire while paintings by Thomas Gainsborough and Joshua Reynolds are thrown in, declaiming, 'Down with the old masters!' to Prokofiev's Third Symphony. Rossetti's vision of a golden-clad Joan of Arc, sword in upraised left hand, recalls both Hel resurrected as a robot in *Metropolis* and Russell's own Cosima Wagner in fishnet stockings and helmet in *Mahler*, 'a combination Nazi Stormtrooper and Hell's Angel biker'.[37]

Turning to the lack of colour in the painter biopics, we should note that in the case of *Dante's Inferno* Russell lobbied for colour and, according to Brian Hoyle, 'even went so far as to suggest how he could colour-coordinate the palate of the film to match the personalities and work of the four protagonists'.[38] But the BBC 'had only recently begun investing in colour and due to the increased cost they were reluctant to take a risk on a feature-length project directed by someone as unpredictable as Russell'.[39] Shooting did actually start in colour and then switched to black and white for technical reasons.[40] In the end, however, this is more than amply compensated for by the overall look of the film, which references *Die Nibelungen* (Fritz Lang, 1924), *The Cabinet of Dr. Caligari* (Robert Wiene, 1920) and *Nosferatu* (F. W. Murnau, 1922). Russell 'brought out the look of a classic black and white horror film' to 'resemble a region of Transylvania'.[41]

Shooting in black and white has a further advantage. Steven Jacobs notes that there is the implication in the emphasis on 'visual correspondences between the artists' works and the world around them' that the painters 'represent the world as they are perceiving it'.[42] The art of the painter is thereby grounded in the way they perceive the world 'and is not presented as the result of an artificial construction'.[43] This, we may argue, is connected with the biopic's proclivity to present an artist's work 'as an aspect of the artist's personality and biography: a limited conception of art as subjective expression, diary or autobiography'.[44] Using black and white avoids both this and kitschy clichés of the *Bubbles* (1886) type, Millais's work known to generations by being used in Pears soap advertising.

CONCLUSION

As a concluding comment, Vito Adriaensens and Steven Jacobs argue that while in films like *Dante's Inferno* 'Russell's protagonists . . . conform to the romantic stereotype of the tormented and alienated artist', at the same time such films 'also demystify this cult of artistic genius by focusing on the mundane or laborious activities involved in the process of artistic creation, which is at odds with genre conventions that normally glorify this process'.[45] In *Dante's Inferno* we see Russell starting to approach the more critical attitude towards his artist subjects of his later feature film artist biopics.

Ken Russell's quartet of painter biopics sees him constantly in the process of refining his filmic art, an evolutionary and often self-reflexive process: from montages cut to classical music, tracking shots and dissolves of *Scottish Painters*, via the variegated images in *Pop Goes the Easel*, to the vignettes of Rousseau's life in *Always on Sunday* (featuring his paintings), to the *tableaux vivants* recreations of Pre-Raphaelite works of *Dante's Inferno*. The positioning, framing, editing and placement of the artist's work within the cinematic or televisual space is essential in drawing closer the relationship between art and artist (made clear in *Pop Goes the Easel* in the shot juxtaposing Peter Blake with his own self-portrait), film and film-maker. In his presentation of the relationship between painted image, sound/music and the film image, Russell was ahead of his time and anticipated later trends like the recent twenty-first-century mini renaissance of film painter biopics and their concern with the painted image, such as *Mr. Turner* (Mike Leigh, BFI and Canal+, 1014), *Big Eyes* (Tim Burton, SIlerwood FIlms, 2014), *Loving Vincent* (Dorota Kobiela and Hugh Welchman, Altitude Films, 2017), *At Eternity's Gate* (Julian Schnaelbel, Riverstone Pictures)[46] – and, from the German-speaking world, films about Paula Modersohn-Becker and Egon Schiele.

Ultimately, the quartet of films analysed here offers further evidence of Russell's vital contribution to twentieth-century TV and film culture.

NOTES

1. Paul Sutton, *Talking About Ken Russell* (Cambridge: Buffalo Books, 2016), 28.
2. Ken Russell, *A British Picture: An Autobiography* (London: Southbank Publishing, 2008), 79.
3. William Cook, 'The Two Roberts: Love, Paint and Poverty', BBC Arts Programmes, 2 February 2015, <https://www.bbc.co.uk/programmes/articles/2hscrfQSYK2BrFvHXbNhW5b/the-two-roberts-love-paint-and-poverty> (last accessed 6 November 2021).
4. Russell, 77–8.
5. Ibid.
6. Michael Brooke, 'Scottish Painters (1959)', *BFI Screenonline*, 2014, <http://www.screenonline.org.uk/tv/id/935980/index.html> (last accessed 27 May 2022).
7. According to numerous sources, Satie himself may even have been inspired for the atmosphere he wanted to evoke in his *Gymnopédies* by a painting, Pierre Puvis de Chavannes's languid portrait of three young girls by the seaside, *Jeunes Filles au bord de la mer* (1879).
8. Sutton, 28.
9. BBC Written Archives Centre, *Scottish Painters Monitor* file, T32/959/1.
10. Michael Brooke, 'Pop Goes the Easel (1962)', *BFI Screenonline*, 2014, <http://www.screenonline.org.uk/tv/id/1275788/index.html> (last accessed 27 May 2022).
11. Kevin M. Flanagan, 'Television, Contested Culture, and Social Control: Cultural Studies and *Pop Goes the Easel*', in Kevin M. Flanagan (ed.), *Ken Russell: Re-Viewing England's Last Mannerist* (Plymouth: Scarecrow Press, 2009), 75.
12. Ibid., 76.
13. The final 'Twist sequence' anticipates the dance sequence in Godard's *Bande à part* (1964) and the frequent framing of Pauline Boty surrounded by her male colleagues also recalls the character arrangements of Truffaut's *Jules et Jim*, released the same year.
14. Russell, 94.
15. Brian Hoyle, 'In Defense of the Amateur', in Flanagan (ed.), 46.
16. Michael Brooke, 'Always on Sunday (1965)', *BFI Screenonline*, 2014, <http://www.screenonline.org.uk/tv/id/1029244/index.html> (last accessed 27 May 2022).
17. See also Hetty Baynes as Long Jane Silver in *Treasure Island* [Ken Russell, Channel 4, 1995].
18. Richard Dumas and Juan Manuel Castro, 'The Dounier Rousseau: Archaic Candour', Musée d'Orsay, 27 July 2016, <https://www.musee-orsay.fr/en/exhibitions/presentation/douanier-rousseau-archaic-candour-196116> (last accessed 19 February 2022).
19. See, for example, how he explicitly mentions that Elgar and Ives were, as he terms it, 'self-taught' in Russell, 23 and 97, respectively.
20. Brooke, 'Always on Sunday'.
21. Ibid.
22. 'Biography of Henri Julien Rousseau', *Henri Julien Rousseau: The Complete Works*, <https://www.henrirousseau.org/biography.html> (last accessed 27 May 2022).
23. Dumas and Castro.
24. 'Biography', *Henri Julien Rousseau*.
25. Hoyle, 'In Defense of the Amateur', 47.
26. Sutton, 113.

27. This reminds us of MacBryde and Colquhoun riding their horse-drawn cart loaded up with canvases down a lane into the Suffolk village where their new studio is based.
28. Compare the final shot of *Elgar* (1962) with the needle stuck on a record on a turntable: the end of a record, the end of a life.
29. Played by pop artist Derek Boshier (see section on *Pop Goes the Easel*).
30. Played by the English poet Christopher Logue, part of the British Poetry Revival of the 1960s and 70s.
31. Robert Wilkes, 'Pre-Raphaelites on Film: Ken Russell's "Dante's Inferno" (1967)', *Pre-Raphaelite Reflections: A Blog Devoted to the PRB*, April 2016, <https://dantisamor.wordpress.com/?s=ken+Russell> (last accessed 6 January 2021).
32. John C. Tibbetts, '"Le Phoenix Terrible": A Ken Russell Season at the BFI, July 2007', in Flanagan (ed.), 241.
33. Wilkes.
34. Jeremy Mark Robinson, *Ken Russell: England's Visionary Film Director and Music Lover* (Maidstone: Crescent Moon, 2015), 199.
35. John C. Tibbetts, '"Il parait que c'etait un musicien": Ken Russell's *The Debussy Film*', in Flanagan (ed.), 116, n.23.
36. Ken Hanke, *Ken Russell's Films* (Metuchen, NJ: Scarecrow Press, 1984), 35.
37. Joseph Lanza, *Phallic Frenzy: Ken Russell and His Films* (Chicago: Chicago Review Press, 2007), 162.
38. Brian Hoyle, 'Dante's Inferno', in accompanying booklet to *Ken Russell: The Great Passions* (Blu-ray/DVD, BFI, 2017).
39. Wilkes.
40. Sutton, 146–7.
41. Lanza, 58.
42. Steven Jacobs, *Framing Pictures: Film and the Visual Arts* (Edinburgh: Edinburgh University Press, 2012), 53.
43. Ibid.
44. John Walker, *Art and Artists on Screen* (Manchester: Manchester University Press, 1993), 19.
45. Vito Adriaensens and Steven Jacobs, 'Celluloid Bohemia? Ken Russell's Biopics of Visual Artists', *Journal of British Cinema and Television*, vol. 12, no. 4, 2015, abstract.
46. BBC Written Archives Centre, Letter from Russell to Milligan, 1965, T32/1095/1. Russell was planning one with Spike Milligan as Van Gogh but it never materialised.

CHAPTER 6

'An Authentic Part of the History of European Painting': Ken Russell's Early Engagement with the Pre-Raphaelites

Jo George

INTRODUCTION

In the summer of 1965, a woman by the name of Mrs E. Crowder wrote to the BBC expressing her admiration for Ken Russell's *Monitor* documentaries. She also inquired as to how the film-maker chose his subjects. A representative from the programme wrote back to Mrs Crowder, stating that 'Mr. Russell's choice of subject for his films is purely personal. He makes films about people that interest him and that he feels would yield to film treatment.'[1] This letter suggests that Russell was given carte blanche, but (tactfully) neglects to mention that Huw Wheldon, Russell's producer and mentor at *Monitor*, vetoed the young film-maker's more outlandish ideas, such as the oft-mentioned pitch for 'a film about Albert Schweitzer playing Bach to lepers in the jungle',[2] or those he deemed potentially too expensive. Nevertheless, the letter is not wrong in its assertion that Russell was still afforded an enviable amount of freedom and was in the very privileged position of only having to make films about artists who interested him, and whose work he admired. In a letter from 1965 (a good three years before the broadcast of *Delius: Song of Summer*) to Dr Geoffrey Connell at the University of Nottingham, for example, Russell notes that he had 'thought of doing a film on Delius, whose music attracts me immensely. There are many pitfalls to the story, however, and as yet I have not seen my way around them all. Unless someone else beats me to it, I daresay I will film that story someday.'[3]

While the letter cited above illustrated that projects often gestated in Russell's mind for a long time, and his subjects were carefully selected, it is also worth noting that he writes that it is Delius's music, rather than any other aspect of the composer's life, that he is drawn to. In certain cases Russell's interest in an artist went beyond simple admiration for their work as he sometimes experienced a particularly personal connection with them. In *Elgar* (BBC, 1962), for instance, one can sense Russell's kinship with a fellow Catholic convert. Brian Hoyle also notes the film-maker's 'clear affection'[4] for both Henri Rousseau, the subject of *Always on Sunday* (BBC, 1965), and Isadora Duncan, both of whom Russell portrays as amateurs in the best sense of the word. These were artists who created out of love and a desire for community, rather than for commercial gain. For Russell, who never lost touch with his own roots as an amateur film-maker, this was the highest compliment he could pay to someone. With this in mind, this chapter will set out to show that the director felt a similar kinship with the members of the Pre-Raphaelite Brotherhood, whom he saw as his direct forebears.

Russell's most famous, though by no means his first, engagement with the Pre-Raphaelites is, of course, *Dante's Inferno: The Private Life of Dante Gabriel Rossetti, Poet and Painter* (BBC, 1967). Indeed, just as he mulled over the 'many pitfalls' of Frederick Delius's life for several years before he finally made a film about it, Russell built up to *Dante's Inferno* slowly and had already devoted a short *Monitor* documentary, *Old Battersea House* (BBC, 1961), and a pivotal scene in *The Debussy Film* (BBC, 1965) to the Pre-Raphaelites. As it has been discussed elsewhere, this chapter will forgo a detailed analysis of *Dante's Inferno* and instead examine Russell's earlier, less well-known encounters with this movement. I will argue that *Old Battersea House* did much to renew popular interest in the then very unfashionable group of Victorian artists, and the sequence in *The Debussy Film* subtly elucidates why Russell came to identify so keenly with them.

OLD BATTERSEA HOUSE

Old Battersea House takes its title from the London residence of the prolific writer Mrs Wilhelmina Stirling. Mrs Stirling was the sister of the Pre-Raphaelite painter Evelyn De Morgan, and the sister-in-law of William De Morgan, a potter, designer and close associate of William Morris's. Mrs Stirling's home was a shrine to the work of these artists and the Pre-Raphaelites in general. Huw Wheldon, in his commentary on the film, states that Old Battersea House was 'both a home and a museum in one', and Mrs Stirling, who was ninety-six at the time of filming, acted as an enthusiastic guide for the people who contacted her asking to view her extensive art collection. Wheldon also notes that a complete tour of the house with Mrs Stirling and her manservant, Mr Peters, lasted around five hours. Russell's documentary, however, in which Mrs Stirling takes five students from the Royal Academy Schools round her house, is just under 17 minutes' duration. Nevertheless, the combination of Wheldon's 'typically concise commentary',[5] and some intelligently assembled montages of the collection, give the viewer the sense that they have seen all there is to see, albeit in a slightly whirlwind fashion. In a sequence lasting just over 50 seconds, for example, Russell shows us four of De Morgan's most impressive paintings linked by slow dissolves: *Venus and Cupid* (1878), *Boreas and Oreithyia* (1896), *The Red Cross* (1914–16) and *Our Lady of Peace* (1907). Each canvas is filmed in a single take, with the camera either slowly craning up or down the length of the long, thin frames. By gliding his camera steadily and smoothly over these canvases, Russell gives the audience a private view of each work, and just enough time to appreciate it. Paul Sutton argues that:

> Television historians rightly praise Kenneth Clark's landmark serial *Civilisation* (1969), for the intelligence and insight of the commentary and for the grand visual style in which hallowed places were given three-dimensional space with a tracking camera. Russell got there first and did it equally well in *Old Battersea House*.[6]

It is not known whether Clark saw Russell's *Old Battersea House* before making *Civilisation* but Sutton is right to suggest that Clark's team came up with very similar solutions to the same problems. Making a filmed documentary about painting is a tricky enterprise. Even if one ignores the purely aural aspects of film after the late 1920s, the kinship the two share as visual media is superficial at best. On the most basic level, paintings are static objects and movies move through both space and time. Even the rules of framing and composition are different. As Peter Greenaway points out, 'if a painter wants to emphasise the narrowness of a giraffe's neck, he uses a long narrow frame',[7] but for a landscape they would most likely choose a frame which favoured the horizontal. The overwhelming majority of films, on the other hand, are locked into an unchanging aspect ratio, regardless of what is being filmed. As Angela Dalle Vacche states, the challenge for the film-maker is therefore to 'deal with the ontological differences of cinema and painting and [. . .] find some symbiotic ground between these two media'.[8] In order to prevent their films from becoming art history slide shows enlivened by some editing transitions, both Russell's and Clark's teams took advantage of the properties of cinema, most specifically editing, camera movement and the close-up, to create associations between sections of a canvas or entirely different works through montage. As a result, they were able to show with the camera lens details of paintings that achieve a far closer proximity, and greater clarity, than could ever be seen with the naked eye.

While this may seem a very effective strategy from a film-making point of view, Dalle Vacche argues that:

> For the art world, film recording and the disruptions of editing during postproduction are two disrespectful procedures. The first is mechanical, too passive, while the second is manual, manipulative, and too invasive. Combined, these two filmic interventions can shatter an artist's style.[9]

What both *Old Battersea House* and *Civilisation* do is employ the techniques of cinema to their best advantage while also trying not to distort the style of the original. This is mainly done by deconstructing each painting using the rules of classical continuity editing to give the audience a clear understanding of the full space of each canvas. Most commonly, this is achieved by treating each canvas as a short scene, with the full painting serving as a kind of master shot before zooming into or cutting to a detail. At other times the process is reversed, and the camera pulls back from a detail to reveal the whole picture.

Take, for example, the way that Russell presents De Morgan's *The Spear of Ithuriel* (1890) in his film. He begins by placing one of the art students near the camera framed in a close-up, then has them turn and walk out of the shot as the camera pulls focus on *The Spear of Ithuriel* at the back of the room. Russell lines up the top and bottom of the camera's frame with the top and bottom of the painting's very tall and ornately gilded frame (Figure 6.1). He also eschews the slightly off-centre compositions usually favoured in the cinema, and instead places the painting right in the centre of the shot. He lights the painting with what appears to be a spotlight, which leaves the wall to the right of it deliberately shrouded in darkness and the details of a second painting on the adjacent wall to the left impossible to make out. Nothing is allowed to distract the audience's attention from *The Spear of Ithuriel*. This shot, which lasts over 7 seconds, acts

Figure 6.1 *The Spear of Ithuriel*.
Source: BBC, 1961.

as an establishing shot which shows the position of this imposing canvas in the room. In a long shot like this one, however, it is difficult to appreciate much detail. Russell therefore cuts to the equivalent of a medium long shot. Ithuriel, the archangel depicted in the painting, is framed from the waist up. The objects that surround him are now clearly revealed to be flying cherubim, with their angelic faces and three-fold wings. Russell has his camera mounted on a jib arm, and in a shot lasting nearly 15 seconds he cranes the camera slowly downwards until it shows a naked Eve sleeping at the archangel's feet. This is followed by a medium shot of Eve lying in a bed of flowers, which is close enough to show the toad (an emblem of Satan) positioned close to her head, and a tight close-up of the toad. Russell here follows classical cutting conventions to a tee. He begins with an establishing shot and moves into an extended master shot, before finally inserting some coverage in the form of the medium shot and close-up. Russell may break up De Morgan's painting in the editing room, but he only does so after he has shown his audience exactly where the details recorded by the tighter framings exist in relation to the rest of the canvas.

Michael Brooke asserts that Russell's 'direction is uncharacteristically restrained, presumably because the house's collections are quite exotic enough to get by without any additional visual or conceptual flourishes'.[10] Indeed, a comparison between Russell's film and Alain Resnais's *Van Gogh* (1948), an earlier short documentary about painting by a fledgling iconoclast, more than bears Brooke out. Resnais's film tells the story of Van Gogh's early life and his time in Paris through 207 shots of various Van Gogh paintings and sketches. He rarely, however, shows us the full canvas, and never includes the frames that surround them. Rather, as Steven Jacobs notes, Resnais has 'rearranged dozens of paintings into a kind of [moving] storyboard or comic strip'.[11] He further argues that:

> rather than juxtaposing shots of paintings, [as Russell does], Resnais confronted parts of paintings to one another. Consequently, Resnais destroyed the integrity of the individual artwork in two ways: by focusing on isolated details on the one hand, and through jumping through an entire oeuvre on the other. In Resnais' film, Van Gogh's complete oeuvre is seen as a single vast painting.[12]

Russell is far less radical in his approach and does nothing to 'shatter' De Morgan's style, nor to 'destroy the integrity of [any] individual artwork'. It would take Russell time to grow so bold. Indeed, if one substituted painting for music, Jacobs's description of Resnais's treatment of Van Gogh's oeuvre could easily be applied to Russell's often audacious intercutting of different works by Tchaikovsky in scenes from *The Music Lovers* (United Artists, 1970) and Mahler in *Mahler* (Goodtimes Enterprises, 1974).

Brooke's assertion that Russell held back because the work of the Pre-Raphaelites was 'quite exotic enough [. . .] without any additional visual or conceptual flourishes' is an interesting one, but it is essential to point out here that the paintings shown in *Old Battersea House* are devoid of their most exotic feature: colour. Indeed, one cannot discuss Russell's engagement with the Pre-Raphaelites without touching upon this subject. Apart from his final film for the corporation, *Dance of the Seven Veils* (1970), about Richard Strauss, every film Russell made for the BBC was shot in black and white. This imposed clear limitations on his films, particularly those about painters. *Civilisation* was filmed and broadcast in colour, so when Clark turns his attention to the French impressionists in the final episode, entitled 'Heroic Materialism', not only is it possible for his camera to zoom in and out of details of Pierre August Renoir's *Le Déjeuner des canotiers* (1881) and *Bal du moulin de la Galette* (1876), but he is also able to display the splashes of red in the former and the intense blues of the latter. Working in 1961, long before the BBC's debut colour broadcast on 1 July 1967, Russell was not able to avail himself of these luxuries when shooting *Old Battersea House*.

What makes this particularly ironic is Russell's keen appreciation of the Pre-Raphaelites' vivid use of colour. Indeed, several documents in the BBC Written Archives show just how hard he lobbied for permission to shoot the film that would become *Dante's Inferno* (but was then provisionally called 'The Pre-Raphaelite Tragedy') in colour. In one extended memo to his bosses, Russell wrote that, given:

> the luminous and unique paintings, this film cries out for colour more than any subject I have yet come across. And pictorial values apart, colour would be invaluable in this film to evoke the atmosphere and state of mind associated with these men.[13]

Thankfully, his arguments convinced Stephen Hearst, the Executive Producer of Music and Arts Programming, who remarked that:

> When Ken Russell becomes really passionate about the use of colour, the end result of shooting in colour might be really out of this world. The period is so much within the range of Ken's interest that I can't help feeling that we might get an extraordinary piece of work that could be repeated several times when we start up our colour service.[14]

The controller of BBC 2, however, was not to be swayed, and the film was ultimately shot in black and white.

The experience of making *Old Battersea House* convinced Russell that black and white photography was unsuited to a film about Pre-Raphaelite paintings.

This perhaps explains why he lobbied so passionately to shoot *Dante's Inferno* in colour, even though he knew full well that there was little chance of this happening. By 1967 and the production of *Dante's Inferno*, however, Russell was an expert at compensating for the limitations that black and white stock imposed on his films about painters. For instance, in *Always on Sunday*, another work about an artist with a penchant for vivid hues, Russell made up for the lack of colour by finding a filmic equivalent to Henri Rousseau's primitive style, with its idiosyncratic approach to perspective and space, through eccentric, and sometimes deliberately grotesque framing choices. In *Dante's Inferno* he rose to the challenge by focusing on Rossetti, rather than the entire Brotherhood, and emphasising the more macabre aspects of the artist's story. The film begins with the unsettling image of Lizzie Siddal's coffin being exhumed in order that Rossetti can retrieve the unpublished poems that he buried with her. This unforgettable opening becomes the film's visual keynote. To quote Joseph Lanza, Russell adopted 'the look of a classic black and white horror film and made his heavenly Lake District resemble a region of Transylvania'.[15] While Lanza and others, including Hoyle, have seen Russell's unusual choices in dictating the look of *Dante's Inferno* as being particularly inspired,[16] this this Gothic-horror aesthetic is already present in the opening minutes of *Old Battersea House*.

Indeed, despite being a relatively restrained and conventional work, *Old Battersea House* is not without directorial flourishes. Russell begins the film with a complicated 180-degree pan which starts with an extreme long shot of the four distinctive smokestacks of Battersea Power Station before moving left to follow a train. He then shows the coils of barbed wire that top Mrs Stirling's back wall, before alighting on her slightly overgrown garden and the back of Old Battersea House itself on a windswept afternoon. If the combination of a power station, barbed wire, and the sight of the old mansion were not enough to create a particularly unsettling atmosphere, Russell's use of excerpts from Roger Sessions's *The Black Maskers* Suite (1923; revised 1928) on the soundtrack cements it. The first interior shots, still accompanied by Sessions's eerie, discordant music, emphasise the house's many dark corners. They are also illuminated with a spotlight before receding back into the shadows. As the camera follows some of the young art students around the house, Huw Wheldon's voice-over begins by drawing attention to Russell's rather Gothic images. Weldon then declares that 'Old Battersea House, at first glance, seems a ghostly, spooky place. And, indeed, there is a current legend that the place is haunted.' It is an arresting opening to a documentary, and one which attests to Russell's vivid imagination. At the same time, however, it also demonstrates that the director was a pragmatic problem solver. As the building's name suggests, Old Battersea House is indeed old. It was most likely built in 1699 and by the early 1960s was still only partly wired for electricity. Therefore, about 6.5 minutes into the film Wheldon, almost as an aside, explains that Mrs

Stirling's manservant, Mr Peters, 'carries a lamp to illuminate [the house's] darker corners' for visitors. Russell therefore turned the far from optimal filming conditions to his advantage and used these dark, mysterious corners (as well as Mr Peters's lamp) to create the unsettling atmosphere with which the film opens.

It is worth noting that both the reference to Mr Peters's lamp, and the first section of the voice-over, which begins with the legend that the house is haunted and ends with Wheldon introducing Mrs Stirling and her 'crisp attitude towards life in general and ghosts in particular', are two of several additions made in pen to the original typed script held in the BBC archives. The handwriting is not Russell's, and so is presumably Wheldon's. The additions nevertheless show a real sensitivity towards what Russell is trying to do visually and they make an impassioned case for the then unfashionable Pre-Raphaelites as 'an authentic part of the history of European painting'. It is therefore tempting to posit that the director may have co-written them. One of the original typed speeches for the voice-over also seems to speak for Russell. In it, Wheldon challenges some of the accusations levelled against the Pre-Raphaelites by saying that:

> While it's easy enough to condescend to them, the fact remains that the Pre-Raphaelites were not simply fatuous aesthetes. Their energy was tremendous. And their work extended to sculpture, and furniture, and architecture, and design, and fabrics, as well as the whole world of craftsmanship, as well as painting and pottery.

If ever a film-maker has celebrated tireless creative energy, it is Russell. Indeed, one (rather uncomplimentary) review of *Savage Messiah* (MGM-EMI, 1972) made the astute observation that 'the director's overriding credo [is] that art and films are a matter of how much energy you exert'.[17] If their tireless energy is yet another thing Russell admires about the Pre-Raphaelites, it is worth remembering how critical he could be of artists he believed had squandered their genius by either failing to produce (as Debussy often did) or producing sub-standard work (the '1812 Overture' sequence in *The Music Lovers* is, amongst other things, a brilliant and scathing depiction of an artist selling out). As a consequence, it becomes clear that the portrait of Rossetti in *Dante's Inferno* is perhaps the most ambivalent depiction of an artist in the Russell canon. Russell certainly admired Rossetti's work, but the director also presents the artist as a dilettante who lazily 'drifts between being a poet and being a painter, whatever impresses most, is least effort and pays best', and is the first to suggest a drink or some 'stunner hunting' when the work does not come easily.

By contrast, Mrs Stirling, who is as much the subject of *Old Battersea House* as the Pre-Raphaelites or her titular home, is anything but the dilettante. Rather, the film presents her as the last vestige of 'the terrific energy of her generation', who works with the enthusiasm of someone a third of her age. Russell clearly took a liking to Mrs Stirling and expanded her role in the final programme (several of the handwritten additions to the voice-over include details about her). Russell even devotes almost a third of the film to talking head shots of Mrs Stirling. In these she reminisces about her sister, the many ghosts that reside in the house, and the toad that lived in the garden and visited De Morgan after posing for *The Spear of Ithuriel*. These anecdotes are delightful in their eccentricity. So much so, in fact, that Russell clearly felt they needed no visual augmentation.

Towards the end of the film, one of the art students asks Mrs Stirling if she thinks that 'the Pre-Raphaelites will come back into fashion'. Mrs Stirling answers in the affirmative, arguing that 'people will get sane again'. She further remarks that modern paintings are 'only fit to hang in the lunatic asylum'. Given her age and her close relationship with the Pre-Raphaelites, Mrs Stirling's response is not surprising. Indeed, her quip about hanging modern art in a lunatic asylum is remarkably similar to Rossetti's initial estimate of Édouard Manet voiced in a letter to Janey Morris in 1865. One also wonders how the art students (who appear to be in their twenties) took Mrs Stirling's withering dismissal of modern art. As the film is trying to make a case for the Pre-Raphaelites, though, the voice-over does its best to challenge her opinion by arguing that she 'couldn't be described as living in the past'. This, despite her obvious lust for life, seems rather disingenuous and is perhaps the film's one minor misstep. Luckily, however, Russell was rather more eclectic in his tastes. Less than a year after finishing *Old Battersea House*, and almost four months before Andy Warhol would debut his *32 Campbell's Soup Cans* in New York, Russell directed *Pop Goes the Easel* (BBC, 1962) for *Monitor*.

If *Pop Goes the Easel*, which is both a documentary about pop art and a work of pop art in its own right, can be described as being 'as cutting-edge in both content and form as anything the BBC had ever considered for broadcast',[18] it could also be argued that *Old Battersea House* was ahead of its time in a different way. In an obituary of the influential art historian and gallery owner Jeremy Maas, Nicholas Barker writes that 'Interest in Victorian art never wholly died in the 60 years after Queen Victoria's death, but if its revival can be dated it must be to 1961, the year that Jeremy Maas held his first Pre-Raphaelite exhibition.'[19] Maas's exhibition, 'The Pre-Raphaelites and their Contemporaries', which contained 126 drawings and thirteen paintings, was held at the Maas Gallery between 13 November and 8 December of that year. It was the first ever commercial showing of their work in the twentieth century and, according to Barker, the 'impact of this exhibition is, to all who saw it, as vivid now as it was 35 years ago'.[20] He further notes that:

> At that time it was not so much difficult to sell Victorian art as impossible: there was no demand and no supply. The major Victorian paintings

hung in public collections, where most visitors hurried past them. The market centred on 1800; only a few long-lived figures, [Hercules] Brabazon, [George Bryant] Campion, [William] Callow, went on well into the 19th century. It was a landscape market too: genre, moral or religious pictures, let alone fantasy, were unknown.[21]

On the back of this exhibition, prestigious international institutions such as the Pierpont Morgan Library in New York bought Pre-Raphaelite paintings and drawings from Maas for their permanent collections. The revival of interest in the Pre-Raphaelites continued to gain momentum as the 1960s wore on and, as Tim Barringer, Jason Rosenfeld and Alison Smith point out:

> The modern exhibition history of the movement began with a revelatory reassessment of Brown by Mary Bennett in Manchester in 1964, followed by full-scale retrospectives of Millais (1967), Hunt (1969), Rossetti (1973) and Burne-Jones (1975). These exhibitions won popular and critical acclaim in the 'Swinging '60s' and psychedelic early 1970s: audiences found resonances with the Rossettian avant-garde, with even the clothing and hair in works by Rossetti and Burne-Jones seeming to mirror Carnaby Street.[22]

The first broadcast of a major work dedicated to the Pre-Raphaelites like *Dante's Inferno* in 1967 clearly reflects the growth in interest in the artistic movement in the last years of the decade. *Old Battersea House*, however, is truly *avant l'heure*. Indeed, Russell's film, which was initially broadcast on BBC 2 on 4 June 1961, pre-dated Maas's gallery exhibition by nearly six months. Moreover, a television programme would, no doubt, have reached a far wider audience than a gallery showing in London. Brooke and many others have noted how Russell's *Elgar* 'significantly raised the public profile of its then-neglected subject'.[23] It can also be argued that *Old Battersea House* helped do the same, and evidence of this can partly be found in the BBC archives. In a letter dated 7 June, just three days after the broadcast, Mrs Stirling wrote to Russell care of the BBC and took him to task for not making it clear in the film that the house was only open to visitors on Saturdays from October to May. 'The result is', she writes, 'I am being rung up all day long and [have] over a hundred letters to answer, all [from] would be visitors.'[24] She does admit, however, that 'the broadcast seems to have been a great success judging from all the letters I am receiving!!' (her punctuation).[25] At the same time, the BBC were also being sent letters from members of the public asking how they could arrange a visit. The corporation therefore offered to assign someone to answer the correspondence sent to Old Battersea House as well. On 20 June, however, Mrs Stirling replied, politely declining the proposal:

I think the worst is over! I answered a hundred letters personally and engaged a secretary to cope with the rest! And though still they come, it is in quantities which it is possible for me to deal with more at my leisure . . . Moreover the telephone and doorbell were ringing all day long, and I yearned to escape to a desert island and get a little peace.[26]

These letters attest to the fact that Russell's film made a considerable impression on its original audience and helped to challenge the view that the Pre-Raphaelites were unfashionable. Moreover, it is worth remembering that films, even short ones, can have a long gestation period. In a letter from Russell to Mrs Stirling in the BBC archives from late April 1961, for example, the director writes that it has been 'over a year since my wife and I had the pleasure of calling on you and seeing your lovely house and collection [. . .] in connection with a proposed programme for [. . .] Monitor'.[27] He was therefore planning to do the film a good year-and-a-half before the ground-breaking exhibition at the Maas gallery. On the basis of this, Russell deserves to be counted alongside the likes of Maas and the painter L. S. Lowry as one of the earliest public figures to advocate for a reappraisal of the Pre-Raphaelites.

KEN RUSSELL AND THE BROTHERHOOD

Russell felt a kinship with the Pre-Raphaelites for a number of reasons. As noted above, he was drawn to the Brotherhood's visionary use of colour and would often replicate it in his own colour films. He also clearly shared their fascination with the landscape of Britain and would have responded positively to their (seemingly contradictory) commitment to realism in technique combined with often mythical, mystical and religious subject matter. But more than this, it could be argued that he saw the Pre-Raphaelites as being his direct artistic forebears. Indeed, if the place of the Pre-Raphaelites in British art is now firmly established, it is worth recalling that they were once *enfants terribles*. Take, for instance, the vehement criticism of their earliest public exhibitions by a figure as influential as Charles Dickens. The novelist's excoriating review of John Everett Millais's *Christ in the House of His Parents* (1849–50) posits that the painting depicts 'the lowest depths of what is mean, odious, repulsive, and revolting' and goes on to claim that Millais's Virgin Mary 'would stand out from the rest of the company as a Monster, in the vilest cabaret in France, or the lowest ginshop in England'.[28] How could the director of *Dance of the Seven Veils* and *The Devils* (Warner Bros., 1971) not empathise with such earnest (and in hindsight hyperbolic) accusations of obscenity and blasphemy? Similarly, passages from 'The Fleshly School of Poetry', Robert Buchanan's scathing 1871 attack on the writings of Rossetti and his circle, in which he speaks of

Pre-Raphaelite women who 'bite, scratch, scream, bubble, munch, sweat, writhe, twist, wriggle, foam, and in a general way slaver over their lovers',[29] could have been written a century later by any one of the prudish critics who were shocked by the impious behaviour of the nuns in *The Devils*.

To compare only the most prurient facets of their work is, however, to do both Russell and the Pre-Raphaelites a disservice. Closer examination shows that Russell and the Pre-Raphaelites were first and foremost *aesthetic* rebels. A painting like Millais's *The Knight Errant* (1870), which was the artist's one and only female nude, depicts a woman being rescued by a knight in full armour. She is naked and tied to a tree after a presumed sexual assault (in the top right of the canvas her attackers can be observed fleeing the scene). This painting, was, like Millais's earlier *Christ in the House of His Parents*, viewed by some as obscene, and it was not merely the presence of an almost life-size, unclothed woman that upset the Victorians. Contemporaries of Millais, such as Albert Moore and the future President of the Royal Academy Frederic Leighton, painted their share of female nudes. Rather, as Alison Smith notes, 'by 1870, questions of style were becoming as important, if not more important, than subject matter in critical evaluation'.[30] Leighton and Moore were thoroughgoing academic neo-classicists. Their nudes were often depicted as mythological subjects, like Venus or Actaea, or anonymous figures in an unmistakably classical setting. Keren Rosa Hammerschlag has even claimed that for Leighton, 'beauty was achieved through a process of academic generalization and idealization that involved the transformation of the imperfect flesh of the life model into the smooth perfection of classical statuary', and that this could lead to accusations of an 'apparent lack of liveliness' in his nudes.[31] No such accusation could be levelled against the unclothed figure in *The Knight Errant*, not even in the revised version of the painting in which Millais, in an act of self-censorship, repainted the woman to show her averting her gaze, rather than meeting that of her rescuer. Her skin may seem pale in comparison to her flowing red hair and the dimly moonlit, rather Gothic forest behind her, but it nevertheless bears no comparison to the smooth, marble-like skin in a work like Leighton's *Venus Disrobing for the Bath* (1867), which was first shown three years earlier. The allegorical nude has been replaced by the matter-of-factly naked one. To paraphrase the title of Robert Buchanan's attack on Rossetti, Millais's canvas belongs to 'The Fleshly School of Painting'. In *The Knight Errant*, Millais abandoned classical perfection for something far more red-blooded and naturalistic, with contours (and even cellulite) seen on the figure's buttocks and upper thighs.

In the opening minutes of *Dante's Inferno*, Russell depicts Rossetti and the other founding members of the Brotherhood burning canvases and repeatedly shouting, 'down with the pretty ladies'. Although no works by Leighton or Moore are shown being tossed onto the fire, one is tempted to see this attack on 'pretty ladies' being at least partly directed at these painters' rather bloodless nudes. During this rather powerful scene the voice-over, read by Christopher Logue, states: 'Arson, raping, riots, civil insurrection are terrifying Europe. The date is 1848. In England rebels conspire to overthrow the Royal Academy of Arts. The rebels are students and idealists. They are against industry, state religions and official art.' By introducing the Pre-Raphaelites in the same breath as the more violent revolutionary acts of 1848, Russell is immediately both drawing attention to the movement's anti-establishment credentials as well as forging a link between the Pre-Raphaelite Brotherhood and the artistic revolution which accompanied the political turmoil on the Continent and would give rise to Édouard Manet and the French impressionists. Indeed, despite the trappings of neo-medievalism and the Gothic, a painting like *The Knight Errant*, with its earthy female nude, has more in common with those in Édouard Manet's *Le Déjeuner sur l'herbe* (1863) and *Olympia* (1865) (paintings which shocked the Paris art world a few years earlier with their modernity) than it does with anything by the likes of Leighton or Moore.

It is also telling that the voice-over states that the Brotherhood was 'against [. . .] official art'. While it may seem strange to make a direct connection between the deeply conservative Royal Academy, which dictated the taste of the art world in Victorian England, and the often left-leaning tradition of social realism in British cinema, it could be argued that the latter had been long established as the 'official', critically favoured mode of film-making in Britain by the time Russell began his career at the BBC. From John Grierson, to Michael Balcon, through to Free Cinema, the British New Wave, the films of Ken Loach and much of the work for influential programmes like *Play for Today*, realism has come to dominate the landscape of British cinema and television. Russell, perhaps more than any other British film-maker, set out to challenge that dominance head on. Indeed, in an otherwise dismissive review of *Tommy* (Columbia, 1975), which described the film as a 'wearisome experience', Geoff Andrew nevertheless conceded that Russell was 'virtually the first film-maker to escape the strictures of realism and telestyle that have dogged British cinema since the heyday of Powell and Pressburger'.[32] It can be argued that it was his deep-rooted desire to counter the official artistic style and trends of his day that led Russell to identify so closely with the Pre-Raphaelites.

If Russell's most public battles with Mary Whitehouse, the censors and the arbiters of public taste were still ahead of him when he was making *The Debussy Film*, he was already beginning to develop a reputation for challenging what was deemed artistically permissible to be seen on British television. The most basic comparison between Loach's *Cathy Come Home* (BBC, 1966) and Russell's *Elgar*, two of the BBC's most watched programmes of that decade, makes this clear. *Cathy Come Home*, which was ironically made for the drama series *The Wednesday Play*, feels far more like a documentary than Russell's film, which is actually a documentary. Everything from Loach's use of handheld cameras to the use of both professional and non-professional actors is designed to make his film seem more realistic and nothing is allowed to challenge that illusion. Russell's film, on the other hand, is keen to reveal itself as a work of *cinema* from the outset. The celebrated opening sequence of the young Elgar riding a pony over the Malvern Hills features elaborate zooms and fast dolly shots that follow the horse and rider as they gallop along. In a guide to making educational films for the television industry that was published while Russell was still working for the BBC, Lewis Herman advises aspiring filmmakers to deploy zooms with caution, claiming that 'zooms are tricks. Too many of them call attention to themselves.'[33] Russell, however, who in one shot zooms out of an image of the young composer before tilting the camera upwards and zooming into the peak of the tallest hill on the horizon, clearly wants the camera to call attention to itself, and the same attitude applies to the sweeping tracking shots. Moreover, the music he places over these images, Elgar's Introduction and Allegro for Strings, op. 47 (1905), seems to have partly dictated the pacing and the placing of cuts within the sequence. This once again makes the audience aware that they are watching a film. This level of self-reflexivity is not sustained throughout *Elgar*, but it is certainly present in the film's most celebrated and bravura sequences, such as the montage of Great War newsreel footage accompanied by 'Land of Hope and Glory'. Russell, was, however, only getting warmed up at this early stage of his career, and *The Debussy Film*, finished four years later, is so thoroughly self-reflexive that Russell's friend and champion, Brian Forbes, compared it favourably with Federico Fellini's *8½*.[34]

The comparison with Fellini is indeed an apt one. Writing about the 'Martyrdom of St Sebastian' sequence towards the start of *The Debussy Film*, John C. Tibbetts argues with great insight that Russell, through the figure of the director (played by Vladek Sheybal), is alluding to his own increasingly problematic place in British television and cinema in the mid-1960s. Tibbetts believes that at this juncture in his career, Russell was moving away from conventional documentary and realism towards more idiosyncratic and 'imaginatively interpretive work' which bore the hallmarks of Continental art cinema as typified by directors like Fellini.[35] And as Tibbetts further observes:

> Despite the fact that at the time of the film's release, Russell was gaining some positive critical notice and popularity, he was also aware that as a television-trained Englishman making 'art' films he was not taken as seriously in some quarters as if he were a continental film director – a source of insecurity that would never entirely leave him.[36]

Russell's own feelings are revealed in a letter to a Miss Ann Beach, quoted by Tibbetts, in which the director writes:

Most English people seem to resent a native making the sort of film I do (good or bad); what's O.K. for a continental film director certainly won't do for an English one and one born and bred in television at that.[37]

The Pre-Raphaelite room in the Tate Gallery seems to allude to this sentiment by drawing attention to the relationship between the Pre-Raphaelites and the French impressionists, a relationship that is only implied at the start of *Dante's Inferno*. Around 10 minutes into the film, the director and Russell-surrogate takes the actor playing Debussy (Oliver Reed), and a rather bored Gaby (Annette Robertson), around the Pre-Raphaelite room in the Tate Gallery and explains that:

Most of the young students and artist in France in the [18]80s were impressed by the Pre-Raphaelites. Especially Debussy. They seemed to choose the subjects that he himself wanted to do. Indeed, one of the things he wrote while he was in the Prix de Rome was based on a poem by Rossetti, 'The Blessed Damozel'. You see Rossetti's situation was similar to that of Debussy [. . .] Art Nouveau, aestheticism, it was all going on in Paris and in London in the 1890s.

On the most basic level, Russell and his writer, Melvyn Bragg, are establishing a connection between this Debussy and the Pre-Raphaelites that will help a documentary about a French composer seem relevant to British audiences. Russell is also, however, making the point that Debussy, a forward-thinking French composer whom Pierre Boulez credited with having 'awakened' modern music with the first bars of Prélude à l'après-midi d'un faune (1894), was instantly drawn to Rossetti and the Pre-Raphaelites, while native critics were at first dismissive of the Brotherhood and its work. Russell, the film-maker who once quipped that he would 'fare better in the hands of British critics if I was called *Russellini*',[38] could not but sympathise with fellow British artists who felt marginalised in their own country but found great critical appreciation on the Continent.

CONCLUSION

Opinions change, of course. In 2012, the Tate Britain curated the lavish exhibition *The Pre-Raphaelites: Victorian Avant-Garde*. Writing in the *Guardian*, Laura Cummings observed that 'though this is the first Tate survey in almost 30 years, it never feels that way. The pre-Raphaelites are always with us.'[39] A statement like this would have been unthinkable in the early 1960s when Russell, Maas and Mrs Stirling were arguing for a reappraisal of this then unfashionable group of artists. In the early 1970s, Russell was one of the most, prolific and notorious film-makers In the world. By the early 1990s, however, he too had become marginalised, unfashionable and, by his own admission, 'unfundable'. With the appearance of this book, the second collection devoted to Russell this century; conferences dedicated solely to his work and legacy; the long overdue restorations of some of his finest BBC films; and younger British film-makers such as Ben Wheatley calling Russell one of his 'holy trinity' (alongside John Boorman and Nicolas Roeg),[40] one suspects that the tide is starting to turn. If it is, we can only hope that Russell will be the subject of a reappraisal comparable to the one he himself was instrumental in bringing about for the Pre-Raphaelites, and to paraphrase a line from Wheldon's commentary to *Old Battersea House*, perhaps he will soon be viewed as an authentic part of the history of British and European cinema.

NOTES

1. BBC Written Archives Centre, Letter to Mrs E. Crowder from *Monitor*, 8 July 1965, T32/1095/1.
2. Ken Russell, *Directing Film: From Pitch to Premiere* (London: Pavilion Books, 2014).
3. BBC Written Archives Centre, Letter from Russell to Dr. Geoffrey Connell, 22 June 1965, T32/1095/1.
4. Brian Hoyle, 'In Defence of the Amateur', in Kevin M. Flanagan (ed.), *Ken Russell: Re-Viewing Britain's Last Mannerist* (Plymouth: Scarecrow Press, 2009), 49.
5. Michael Brooke, 'Old Battersea House (1961)', *BFI Screenonline*, 2014, <http://www.screenonline.org.uk/tv/id/1284993/index.html> (last accessed 12 May 2021).
6. Paul Sutton, 'Ken Russell at the BBC, 1959–70', in Flanagan (ed.), 15.
7. John Petrakis, 'Blasphemy in Cinema: An Interview with Peter Greenaway', in Vernon Gras and Marguerite Gras (eds), *Peter Greenaway: Interviews* (Jackson: University Press of Mississippi, 2000), 175.
8. Angela Dalle Vacche, *André Bazin's Film Theory: Art, Science, Religion* (Oxford: Oxford University Press, 2020), 30.
9. Ibid.
10. Brooke, 'Old Battersea House'.
11. Steven Jacobs, *Framing Pictures: Film and the Visual Arts* (Edinburgh: Edinburgh University Press, 2012), 24.
12. Ibid., 25.
13. BBC Written Archives Centre, Memo dated 28 March 1966, T53/99/2.
14. BBC Written Archives Centre, Memo from Stephen Hearst to Controller BBC2, 28 July 1966, T53/99/2.
15. Joseph Lanza, *Phallic Frenzy: Ken Russell and His Films* (Chicago: Chicago Review Press, 2009), 58.
16. Brian Hoyle, 'Dante's Inferno', in accompanying booklet to *Ken Russell: The Great Passions* (DVD/Blu-ray, BFI, 2017), 19–21.
17. Anonymous, 'Savage Messiah', in Tom Milne (ed.), *The Time Out Film Guide* (Harlow: Longman, 1989), 522.
18. Michael Brooke, 'Pop Goes the Easel (1962)', *BFI Screenonline*, 2014, <http://www.screenonline.org.uk/tv/id/1275788/index.html> (last accessed 27 May 2022).

19. Nicholas Barker, 'Obituary: Jeremy Maas', *Independent*, 23 October 2011, <https://www.independent.co.uk/news/people/obituary-jeremy-maas-1286047.html> (last accessed 12 May 2021).
20. Ibid.
21. Ibid.
22. Tim Barringer, Jason Rosenfeld and Alison Smith, *Pre-Raphaelites: Victorian Avant-Garde* (London: Tate Publishing, 2013), 16.
23. Michael Brooke, 'Elgar (1962)', *BFI Screenonline*, 2014, <http://www.screenonline.org.uk/tv/id/482790/index.html> (last accessed 12 May 2021).
24. BBC Written Archives Centre, Letter from Mrs Stirling to Ken Russell, 7 June 1961, T32/1000/1.
25. Ibid.
26. Ibid.
27. Ibid.
28. Charles Dickens, 'From Old Lamps for New Ones: in *Household Worlds* (15 June 1850)', in Victor Shea and William Whitla (eds), *Victorian Literature: An Anthology* (London: Wiley, 2014), 101.
29. Thomas Maitland (Robert Buchanan), 'The Fleshly School of Poetry: Mr D.G. Rossetti', *The Contemporary Review*, vol. 18, October 1871, 343, *The Victorian Web*, <https://victorianweb.org/authors/buchanan/fleshy.html> (last accessed 22 February 2022).
30. Alison Smith, *The Victorian Nude: Sexuality, Morality, Art* (Manchester: Manchester University Press, 1996), 157.
31. Keren Rosa Hammerschlag, 'Frederic Leighton's Paintings of the Female Nude', *Victorian Studies*, vol. 56, no. 3, Spring 2014, 447, 442.
32. Geoff Andrew, 'Tommy', in Milne (ed.), 609.
33. Lewis Herman, *Educational Films: Writing, Directing and Producing for the Classroom, Television and Industry* (London: Crown Publishers, 1965), 62.
34. BBC Written Archives, Memo from Ken Russell, 20 June 1966, T32/1095/3.
35. John C. Tibbetts, 'The Debussy Film', in Flanagan (ed.), 114.
36. Ibid., 115.
37. Ibid., 125.
38. Ken Russell, *Fire Over England: British Cinema Comes Under Friendly Fire* (London: Hutchinson, 1993), 82.
39. Laura Cumming, 'Pre-Raphaelites: Victorian Avant-Garde – Review', *Guardian*, 16 September 2012, <https://www.theguardian.com/artanddesign/2012/sep/16/pre-raphaelites-victorian-avant-review> (last accessed 13 October 2021).
40. Josh Slater-Williams, 'Ben Wheatley on High Rise', *The Skinny*, 8 February 2016, <https://www.theskinny.co.uk/film/interviews/ben-wheatley-high-rise> (last accessed 27 May 2022).

PART 3

Design, Staging and Stardom

CHAPTER 7

Shirley Russell and the Role of *The Boy Friend* in 1970s Retro

NJ Stevenson

INTRODUCTION

> Once there was a happy time that everyone remembers but no one ever really knew. How do you capture the look, the sound, the style of a time that has remained so vividly alive in our imagination? It isn't easy but it can be a lot of fun.[1]

In the short documentary *All Talking, All Singing, All Dancing*, by Kaleidoscope films, made to promote the release of *The Boy Friend* (MGM-EMI, 1971), the voice-over explains director Ken Russell's approach to adapting composer Sandy Wilson's 1950s Broadway hit, originally written as a pastiche of 1920s musicals: 'Russell decided it would have to be three things: a typical stage musical of the twenties; an affectionate salute to the cinematic musical fantasies of the 1930s; and a take-off of all the backstage Hollywood musicals of all time.'[2] The documentary adds another layer to the conflation of time in Russell's adaptation. Set in the 1920s, *The Boy Friend* blends the story of a down-at-heel English theatre company who are performing the musical 'The Boy Friend' on stage. When they hear that the Hollywood director Tony De Thrill (Vladek Sheybal) is in the audience, the vigour of their presentation is increasingly brought into contrast with the lacklustre backstage atmosphere and amateur production values and aesthetics. De Thrill reimagines the stage scenes in 1930s-style Technicolor, as cinematic fantasies implying the possibilities of Hollywood to come.

All Talking, All Singing, All Dancing shows the cast rehearsing and filming in 1971: learning the choreography in a dance studio in leotards, then being filmed doing the Charleston in their flapper dresses while Ken Russell, in wraparound shades, presides over the crew who are in jeans and T-shirts. Twiggy, interviewed in the back of a cab, switches from the innocence of her role as Polly Browne, to the insouciance of a famous fashion model. It also reveals how *The Boy Friend* is a testament to the 'nostalgia mode' of the early 1970s as identified by cultural historian Elizabeth Wilson.[3] It is a quotation of the past which cannot be viewed without the context of the present. Ken Russell's film is a defining moment in the historical dialogue between nostalgia, film and fashion that contributed to the emergence of 'retro' after pop-inspired modernity had become ubiquitous by the mid-1960s: a style which looked backwards to move forwards. This 'nostalgia mode' began as an anti-fashion in the 1960s, becoming prevalent in popular culture by the mid-1970s.

The collaboration between Ken Russell and his first wife, the costume designer Shirley Russell, produced a cogent example of a reimagining of earlier historic periods in popular culture that came to inform and construct retro, a visual style in its own right. Furthermore, the Russells' particular practice of historical revisionism, honed through numerous collaborations including *Delius: Song of Summer* (BBC, 1968), the biopic of composer Frederick Delius set in the 1930s, and the seventeenth century based *The Devils* (Warner Bros., 1971), facilitated the construction of a visual style of their own, making an important contribution to the retro movement of this period.

Historian Raphael Samuel defines his concept of 'retrochic' as a revision of a fairly recent past, albeit a fantasised version which embraces a camp performative glamour.[4] Russell's *The Boy Friend* looks back fifty years to present a reimagined Art Deco style which could be simultaneously identified in contemporary fashion garments in the early 1970s. As film theorist Pam Cook points out, rather than being an 'authentic history', each time a new film set in the past captures the imagination of a contemporary audience, our 'relationship to the past' shifts perspective and develops, revealing 'the connections between past and present'.[5]

While this chapter aims to broadly discuss the presence of nostalgia within the popular culture of the early 1970s, its central focus will be on Ken Russell's film version of *The Boy Friend* and its position at the crux of this tendency towards retrochic. It will consider how the vital creative collaboration between Ken and Shirley Russell (an aspect of Russell's work which has gone largely unnoticed in critical writing), as well as their individual relationships with the past, contributed to the construction of a retro style and the practice of retrochic. Film-making was a driving force in their partnership since the making of the experimental, amateur *Peepshow* (1956). As Shirley Russell described,

> We're always discussing ideas for films, deciding what we're going to do and how we're going to do it. It's not so much him as us, really. But when we start shooting a film, my role as costume designer is enough.[6]

SHIRLEY RUSSELL AND THE PORTOBELLO STYLE

Born in 1935, Shirley Ann Kingdon met Ken Russell while studying fashion at Walthamstow College of Art, where he was studying photography. After Kingdon progressed to the Royal College of Art (RCA), they married in 1957. The Russells honeymooned in Haworth in Yorkshire where Ken photographed Shirley in a series of pictures emulating the Brontë sisters, wearing original Victorian dresses bought in their local Portobello market, 'with her meagre savings as a Dickens and Jones shop assistant'.[7] Shirley began to amass a collection of period costume found in market barrows and jumble sales. It was this collection, Shirley's dedication to research and her design training that formed the bedrock for the look of Russell's early productions, as Ken Russell remembered in his autobiography:

> Undoubtedly one of her greatest talents was the ability to sort through mountains of old clothes and unearth a Fortuny dress – the equivalent of coming across a Stradivarius in a junk shop. One only has to look at *Savage Messiah*, *The Music Lovers* and *The Boy Friend* to see that it all paid off. But the Second Hand Rose, as Shirley is affectionately known by some members of the industry, was equally at home at the drawing board, designing weird and wonderful creations for my more stylised efforts.[8]

Victoria Russell, the Russells' fourth child, who like her brothers featured in her father's films, 'as a form of childcare',[9] remembers pre-production development as a constant conversation around the kitchen table. Ken and Shirley Russell had both grown up in the south of England and had collaborated and learnt their crafts together since college days. Their shared references, together with Shirley's understanding and experience of her husband's processes, became a form of communication between them. However, even the most dramatic fantasies, for Shirley, were grounded in research and she actively attempted to avoid anachronism, as she discussed in 1976:

> With *Women in Love*, my idea was to get everything as genuinely 1919 as possible . . . I think it helps actors get into the part. But on *The Devils*, where you can't possibly find any 17th century costumes, I tried to be very accurate in detail . . . When you have to make the costumes yourself, you start to stylise, it's very tempting.[10]

For a costume designer, *The Boy Friend* offered the scope to create three different worlds and draw on a set of talents that pooled historical knowledge and creativity. The dowdy backstage scenes called for a sense of realism, the onstage costumes were a representation of 1920s society glamour, and the Busby Berkeley-style musical fantasies afforded Shirley Russell free rein (Figures 7.1 and 7.2).

148 NJ STEVENSON

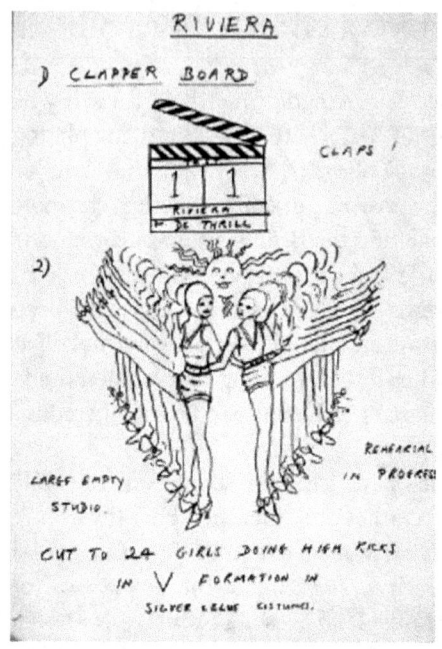

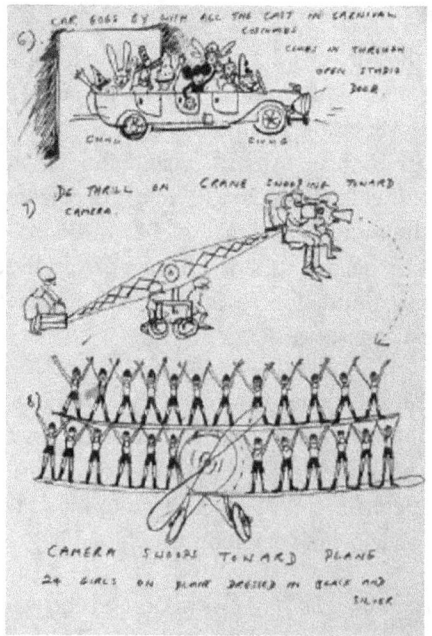

Figures 7.1 and 7.2 Shirley Russell's storyboards for *The Boy Friend*.
Source: Victoria Russell, 1971.

The role of the costume designer is to work with the director to create the on-screen narrative and to build character. Developing character through costume, especially when dressing a star with their own identity and recognisable appearance, can leave designers open to criticism of period inauthenticity when the look of a historical film seems to favour its production era. The notion of authenticity is further complicated when contemporary fashion design echoes a current on-screen representation of an earlier time.

According to Pam Cook, the gap between past and present, which she calls 'slippage', is an essential component in making a film relevant to a contemporary audience, allowing the imagination of the director and the audience to meet, facilitated by the costume designer.[11] Shirley Russell's designs for *The Devils*, where she was tempted to 'stylise', for instance, Louis XIII dressed as a golden Venus, often communicate this 'slippage' or the way that Russell plays with temporalities.

Authenticity was a primary concern for Shirley Russell. In the *Sunday Times Magazine*, Shirley, interviewed to accompany a colour spread of stills from *The Boy Friend*, discusses her costuming practices, including shopping with Twiggy:

> We would go round to second-hand stalls and junk shops looking for old clothes. I always like to use genuine things as much as possible; even if you pay a lot for things, it is still cheaper and more authentic than copying. Twiggy's golfing sweater cost 37p and would have been impossible to copy.[12]

When designing for *The Boy Friend*, Shirley Russell used a mixture of original vintage pieces from her collection and costumes specifically made for the film, often from patterns created from original pieces of clothing that were too small or delicate to be used. She stated,

> On location the genuine old stuff would be falling to pieces as fast as we were filming; I would work out the patterns of a dress on the train with someone from Nathan's (London costumiers) who would go back and make it for the next day.[13]

While continuing her fashion studies at the Royal College, Shirley Russell worked for the costume historian Doris Langley Moore on Saturdays. Langley Moore is a prominent figure in the development of dress museology in Britain, and it was from her that Shirley Russell learned to identify and date period clothing and gained valuable cut, construction and fabric knowledge: 'I roamed free among her priceless 18th and 19th century costumes and got to know them inside out.'[14]

Langley Moore was an influence on both Shirley Russell's collecting practices and those of another fashion student, John Bright. Russell and Bright became friends and important figures in the London costume industry when Bright opened his own costume house, Cosprop, in 1965. Shirley's market hunting was to become an all-consuming occupation, with Portobello a primary source. At a time when second-hand goods were still very much tainted with the stigma of poverty, a small number of radicals instigated new systems of exchange of original clothing in the 1960s. In London, these numbered among them Jane Ormsby Gore, who worked with the antiques dealer Christopher Gibbs and also at *Vogue*, and opened the Chelsea boutique Hung on You with her husband, Michael Rainey, and Michael English; Sheila Cohen, who layered her finds with the psychedelia at the Kings Road boutique Granny Takes a Trip; and Cleo Butterfield, now the owner of the C20 Vintage fashion archive, who opened her second-hand clothing shop, Sunset Boulevard, on Portobello Road in 1971.

Samuel calls this phenomenon 'retrochic', an 'anti-fashion' originating in the Portobello area in London, although the term was imported from Parisian flea markets. Inspired in part by exhibitions of decorative art of the late nineteenth century, 1960s counterculture appropriated and modified into retrochic, a 'self-consciously minority taste'[15] where ephemera from past times are collected and used as everyday objects to the point where contemporary life borrows from history. Samuel defines his concept of retrochic as 'tongue-in-cheek . . . when it borrows, it puts its loans, metaphorically speaking, in quotation marks'.[16]

In 1971, Shirley Russell opened the Last Picture Frock round the corner from Portobello market on Pembridge Road. The Last Picture Frock sold second-hand clothing but doubled as a costume and fancy dress hire company. Victoria Russell, who later worked there as a Saturday girl, described the shop as decorated in an interwar period style with original fittings. Costumes that had been worn in films were available to buy, although her mother soon came to regret selling the vintage garments that had been so painstakingly sourced from markets and it became a hire-only organisation.[17] Shirley Russell's predilection for finding antique clothing and goods blurred the lines between her costuming work in Ken's period films and her family life, as she furnished the house and dressed herself, her husband and her children in second-hand finds and involved them in the hunt. Ken Russell said, 'Some of our happiest moments together were spent in junk shops with me as her willing assistant.'[18] This retrochic way of life, which historian Elizabeth Wilson determines as an 'anti-consumerist' alternative practice,[19] identified the Russells as bohemian West Londoners – even the family car was a 1947 Rolls-Royce.[20] It is speculative to conclude that this unconventional 'second-hand' lifestyle correlates with Ken Russell's non-conformist approach to constructing film narrative, but the partnership of Ken and Shirley Russell did produce an alternative representation of contemporaneity, both at home and in their work.

During this period, RCA students under Madge Garland, and subsequently Janey Ironside and Bernard Nevill, were sent to carry out research at the Victoria and Albert Museum (V&A) archives. Fashion historian Judith Watt notes how fashion students at the RCA had become interested in the 'retro glamour of Art Deco' by 1967.[21] Professor Nevill introduced 'the fashion illustration of the interwar period . . . and Hollywood's silver screen . . . the aesthetic filtering through the imaginations of designers in the late 1960s was above all *cinematic*'.[22] By the start of production on *The Boy Friend* in 1971, fashion designs by RCA graduates – including Ossie Clark, Antony Price and Bill Gibb – were incorporating the bias cut, the draped satin, moss crepe and silk jersey, and the sweetheart necklines and padded shoulders of the 1920s, 30s and 40s. Bevis Hillier discusses the renewed interest in the Deco period:

> It was inevitable that the nostalgics and revivalists would fasten on to the 1920s and 1930s as the next period to resurrect. This revival began in earnest with a commemorative exhibition staged at the Musée des Arts Décoratifs, Paris in 1966, titled, 'Les Années 25'. It was the sub-title of the show – 'Les Arts Deco' – which gave the style its modern name of Art Deco.[23]

An expert on the modernist decorative style, which became more prominent after World War I, Hillier had written *Art Deco of the 20s and 30s* in 1968 and the catalogue to the 1973 exhibition 'The World of Art Deco' at the Minneapolis Institute of Arts. He details the proliferation of interest in 1920s and 1930s style by 1967, and cites Ken Russell's biopic *Isadora Duncan, The Biggest Dancer in the World* (BBC, 1966) as a precursor to Arthur Penn's *Bonnie and Clyde* (Warner Bros., 1967) '[i]n bringing the Art Deco era to the screen'.[24] As a collector, Shirley Russell had a fondness for the 1920s and 30s period, and although unable to work on set because she was due to give birth,[25] has a shared costume credit for *Isadora*, presumably for providing costume and historical knowledge.

In explaining retrochic, Samuel states that, 'Janus-faced, it looks both backwards and forwards in time.'[26] 'Retro' here implies looking backwards to move forwards, a stylistic mode that plunders the past. Retro absorbs the ephemera of popular culture from previous times as its raw material with a playfulness and sense of irony and humour. Contemporary fashion and film in the 1960s and 70s were particularly involved in the retro movement, cross-referencing fashion and cinema from earlier eras. *The Boy Friend*, with its homages to golden era Hollywood musical and 1920s fashion, embodies the ideology of retro.

Portobello, the area of London where Ken Russell had roamed in the 1950s photographing Teddy Girls when it was a post-war wasteland, gradually became a breeding ground for a new culture. In 1968 a group of film enthusiasts started a cinema club in the dilapidated Electric cinema on Portobello Road, which showed a mix of underground films and Hollywood classics. The Electric was frequented by 'The Ladbroke Grove in-crowd',[27] which included the fashion designer Ossie Clark, his wife, the textile designer Celia Birtwell, and the artist David Hockney. Many of this circle were involved in the creative arts, and the prevailing attitude was one of performative flamboyance. Shared influences and ideas coursed through a creative vein that connected the disciplines of film, fashion, art and music, resulting in a common language of style which music writer Simon Reynolds identified as 'conscious camp' after Susan Sontag's 1965 definition of camp.[28] This conscious camp play-acting was particularly concerned with retrochic's referencing past styles with a knowing wink.

Habitués of the Electric recall it as a centre of this camp subversion. Cosey Fanni Tutti, of the Leeds-based experimental group Throbbing Gristle, remembers staying in Colville Terrace in 1972, round the corner from

> The incredible Electric Cinema ... we went with friends from the Gay Lib Street Theatre to see the film *The Boy Friend*. As the Busby Berkeley-type dance sequences came on screen, the Gay Lib crowd all shot to the gangway and joined in. It was a glorious sight.[29]

In 1972 both the UK Gay Liberation Front and Genesis P. Orridge and Cosey Fanni Tutti's COUM Transmissions (the confrontational performance group that spawned Throbbing Gristle) were at the forefront of radicalism. The reception of *The Boy Friend* in Fanni Tutti's memory places both Ken Russell's work and retro within the framework of contemporary avant-garde experimentalism, clearly following a precedent set by his earlier work, notably *The Devils*.

Although MGM billed *The Boy Friend* as a 'nostalgic musical', Russell harnesses retro's subversive element and camp way of playing with the notion of glamour.[30] The cinematic representation in the fantasy scenes of *The Boy Friend* epitomises a nostalgia for the 1920s and 30s that is particularly concerned with glamour, and it is this that makes the film relevant to the wider dissemination of retro in 1971. Much of the iconography that Ken Russell uses to denote Art Deco is cinematic, taken from *Flying Down to Rio* (Thornton Freeland, RKO, 1933), *Footlight Parade* (Busby Berkeley, Warner Bros., 1933) and *42nd Street* (Lloyd Bacon, Warner Bros., 1933). The conflation of period dress and of cinematic styles; the camp knowingness of Max Adrian hissing, 'Do a Ruby Keeler'; the playful and knowing irony of a famous fashion model playing an ingénue and the *Carry On* actress Barbara Windsor playing an actress playing a French maid; Russell's happy-ever-after ending for the Portsmouth Players which pastiches that of Wilson's musical, all contribute to sense of postmodernist alternative interpretation that Alistair O'Neill considers to be a defining feature of retro:

> A prominent facet of postmodernism is how it offered alternative histories that could represent minority cultures; much of this was informed by the material culture trawled through the practice of retrochic that offered and afforded the trappings of alternative strategies.[31]

The Portobello area housed a community of like-minded people, many of whom became part of a social scene around the Electric. Shop owner Cleo Butterfield asserts that their proclivity for wearing second-hand clothing and their fascination for black and white Hollywood films segued, resulting in a lifestyle that infused reality with nostalgia, albeit an imagined nostalgia, expressing a longing to escape conformity:

> It was wonderful, very sociable and everybody looked at all the Fred Astaire films. I think that is part of the dressing up thing, it's about reinventing yourself and being who you want. We thought we were in a film, dressing up and play-acting was very important.[32]

Rediscovering old cinema was part of the lexicon of retro. This group of fashionable people in London, many of them RCA graduates, came to be part of the movement identified as 'Them' in an essay by journalist Peter York, published in *Harpers & Queen* in 1976. 'Them' were consummate Art Deco collectors, and references to Hollywood's golden age during this period were manifold. Watt concurs that 'The camp of it all, the artifice and exaggeration, translated from film costume onto the street ... The trend for glamour became a story with Russell's *The Boy Friend* in the cinemas.'[33] York saw 'Them' behaviour as inherently insincere: 'The thing about camp is that it is a very confusing, over-under-sideways-down way of looking at the world, which takes as basic the notion that nothing is quite what it seems.'[34] Adrian Garvey sees *The Boy Friend* as an 'anti-musical', quoting Barry Keith Grant: the film 'employs camp as a double-edged sword that simultaneously mocks and celebrates the classic Hollywood musical'.[35]

The nostalgic pastiche found in *The Boy Friend* is certainly multi-layered, no doubt a result of the depth of meaning that cinematic reference had for Ken Russell. This wealth of references originated from his own childhood cinema visits. From the 1930s to the 1950s, film attendance was an important leisure activity for many, and as a child in the 1930s Ken Russell frequented the cinema more than most, going every day with his mother.[36] To be born in the early to mid-twentieth century is to have a distinct relationship with the moving image, and for the Russells' generation, watching films was an immersive experience which had an effect on the way they saw and imagined visual culture.

THE BOY FRIEND: NOSTALGIA AND RETRO

Elizabeth Wilson sees retrochic as a marker of the beginning of a new order in the fashion system. She states:

> this obsession with pastiche, this 'nostalgia mode' is related to the way in which the dictatorship of haute couture broke down in the 1960s and 1970s. A single style can no longer dominate in the post-modern period. Instead, there is a constant attempt to recreate atmosphere.[37]

In 1971 the exhibition 'Fashion: An Anthology' opened at the V&A in London. Although the 1963 Mucha and 1966 Beardsley exhibitions at the V&A had generated huge interest and have been identified as early influences of retrochic,[38] the 1971 exhibition, curated by Cecil Beaton, was the first exhibition of clothing to explore the twentieth century. Beaton's idea was to use his society contacts of women whom he had photographed since start of his career in the 1920s, to amass a collection of the finest examples of haute couture. This was diametrically opposed to Shirley Russell's market rag-picking technique, but Beaton's involvement in fashion and museology also brought layers to the narrative of retro in the early 1970s. Then in his seventies, Beaton continued to be as fascinated with young society as he had been with the 'Bright Young Things' of the 1920s. Photographed with Mick Jagger on the set of *Performance* (Donald Cammell and Nicolas Roeg, Goodtimes Enterprises, 1970) filmed near Portobello Road, and with David Hockney at his home, Reddish House, Beaton commanded respect as a link between the past times that he had known and those that his younger acquaintances imagined. He had been celebrated for his fancy dress parties, and his V&A exhibition referenced the popularity of the costume ball in the 1920s section with an original fancy dress costume made for the theatrical designer Erté.[39]

In his introduction to the exhibition catalogue, Beaton describes 1971 fashion as 'no need for fancy dress parties anymore when every day can be used for dressing up'.[40] 'Dressing up' and 'costume' are central motifs in *The Boy Friend*: Twiggy, already dressed in character as the onstage Polly Browne, is delivered her costume for the ball by Tony (Christopher Gable) disguised as a bell boy. Twiggy's outfit for the 'Poor Little Pierrette' costume ball scene was an original 1920s fancy dress costume remade in the model's size.[41] The reprise of Wilson's scene allowed Shirley Russell to reference the fancy dress balls of Cecil Beaton's Bright Young Things. Production designer Tony Walton's backdrop referenced Erté's signature silhouetted style, backlit by the moon, made from 'a collage of fabrics, acetate, silver paper and tinsel . . . from things we picked up in the Portobello Road'.[42]

The gallery installations for the 1920s and 1930s sections of the 'Fashion: An Anthology' exhibition contained many of the visual references to Art Deco (the sunray motif; mirrored surfaces) which Shirley Russell and Tony Walton reprised in costumes and sets for the 'I Could Be Happy with You' fantasy sequence in *The Boy Friend*. However, it was Erté, whom Beaton referenced as an important contributor to 1920s visual style in his exhibition, who was the catalyst for the development of *The Boy Friend* as a 'retro' piece. Erté's 1922 fancy dress costume 'Claire de Lune' was not completely obscure to a 1971 exhibition audience. The fashionable Grosvenor Gallery, run by Eric Estorick, had mounted the first retrospective of the designer's original 1920s illustrations in 1967. Capturing the vanguard of a burgeoning taste, the exhibition had been a great success. Louche echoes of a Deco-esque glamour began appearing in fashion magazines, identified by Simon Reynolds as 'the first area of popular culture to succumb to retro's auto-cannibalistic archive-raiding logic'.[43]

Lesley Hornby, or Twiggy, was then, at eighteen, at the height of her fame as a model. Already interested in the style of the interwar period, she had requested to meet Erté, then seventy-five. Estorick arranged a dinner to follow a show: *The Boy Friend*, which had been reprised for the first time in 1967 on a London stage since Wilson's original production in the 1950s. At dinner Erté suggested that Twiggy should play the film part of Polly Browne. As Twiggy wrote six years later

> The most important thing at that time was meeting Erté . . . My clothes had become more and more twenties. I wore lots of pale colours like oyster and beige. One fashion writer who saw me in Biba's one day said I looked, 'like Erté's sketchbook come to life.' Which was just how I wanted to look.[44]

Twiggy was already friends with Ken and Shirley Russell, to whom she had been introduced by Paul McCartney in 1967 when discussing an earlier shelved film deal – an adaptation of William Faulkner's 1927 fairy story *The Wishing Tree* – and had mischievously been an extra in a scene in *The Devils*, disguised by Shirley as a male courtier.[45] She visited the family regularly for cinema nights that rivalled those at the Electric, to watch 'Busby Berkeley movies and films by Mamoulian and Fred and Ginger films'.[46] The Russells also introduced Twiggy to Philip Jenkinson, the journalist and film archivist who supplied Twiggy with 'all twenties and thirties film ever made', from his Filmfinders collection to help her prepare to play Polly Browne.[47]

Contemporaneous film magazines evidence frequent mention of nostalgia, and the practice of alternative exhibition had become popular.[48] A 1971 edition of *Films and Filming*, which features an interview with Russell on *The Boy Friend*, holds advertisements for the Starlight Club at the Mayfair Hotel, 'one of the few cinema clubs showing films from the golden age of the cinema. And the only one to recreate the atmosphere of those bygone days', and for 'classics on 8mm . . . for the comfort of your own home!'[49]

By December 1967 Twiggy had tired of her gamine look: 'I started wanting to look like my heroine, Greta Garbo. I'd always been into thirties things.'[50] Twiggy did her own make-up for a photoshoot and transformed herself into Greta Garbo, Marilyn Monroe, Rita Hayworth and Theda Bara, using film stills from the BFI as reference material in an attempt to change her image and have more control over her career. The photographs were sold to *Queen* magazine and syndicated globally, influencing fashion photography and placing a household name in the context of revival. The copy reads, 'What is the face of Sixty-Eight! It's a face from the past, face from the history-books of movies, a face from Garbo and Harlow – The face of The Great Days of Hollywood.'[51] Her screen debut in the 1969 'Jazz Age spectacular' commercial for Diet-Rite cola by photographer Mel Sokolsky, dancing in a tailcoat and top hat which echoed Marlene Dietrich in *The Blue Angel* (Josef Von Stern Berg, UFA, 193),[52] encouraged Twiggy's wish to give up modelling for film. After the meeting with Erté, *The Boy Friend* was the subject of a champagne-fuelled evening with Ken Russell, who became resolute in his pursuit of the project.[53] His desire to recreate the exuberance of Wilson's creation was discussed in a *Films and Filming* interview: 'I never want to do a violent, disturbing film like *The Devils* again. That's why I did *The Boy Friend*. It's pure escapism and fun. And Twiggy became a kind of rejuvenating force for me.'[54]

The friendship between Twiggy and Shirley Russell was also instrumental in making the project satisfying. Shirley mentored the model's amateur interest in the costume history of a period for which they had a shared love. Twiggy had started buying second-hand Deco era clothing after discovering a shop selling ex-Hollywood costumes on a first visit to Los Angeles. Shirley, who storyboarded *The Boy Friend* in entirety, found Twiggy's enthusiasm 'a joy'.[55] Victoria Russell, who had played a child in a fantasy scene, remembered her mother 'practically directing it, she was so involved. We went to Walthamstow and saw a little production of it before the film was even funded and Twiggy came with us and caused a bit of a stir.'[56]

On a visit to the set of *Savage Messiah*, which followed *The Boy Friend* in 1972, John Baxter, Ken Russell's biographer, witnessed the dynamic of the Russells at work: 'Shirley Russell's influence is critical, and quite separate from either her role as his wife or that of his regular costume designer. She sits on and makes comments about every step of a production and her views are obviously respected.'[57] However, Shirley remembered the filming of *The Boy Friend* as overly demanding, having to deal with the challenges of the scale of the piece, an inadequate budget and the dissent of the chorus: 'I call *The Boy Friend* the last of the mammoth horrors . . . you had to be thinking on three different levels all the time – realistic, stagey and fantastic.'[58]

Conversely, Twiggy adored the process, and the mixed reviews that *The Boy Friend* received were unanimous in their praise of her performance. Twiggy credits Shirley in educating her in authenticity, but her taste for period styling had been stimulated when she was a schoolgirl, saving her Saturday job earnings to shop in Biba: 'I met Barbara when I was sixteen, she was a huge influence on me because she took a lot from the twenties and thirties.'[59] Biba, conceived by Barbara Hulanicki and her husband Stephen Fitz-Simon, had grown from a tiny shop in Kensington in 1964. Hulanicki's design borrowed from numerous historical periods, refashioning for the 'dolly bird' in her signature 'auntie' muted colours. Less expensive than Mary Quant, Biba was the first label to make youth fashion widely accessible in the United Kingdom through mail order. A year after *The Boy Friend*, its fourth incarnation was a seven-storey department store, Big Biba, in the Derry and Toms store on Kensington High Street, which had been designed by Marcel Hennequet in 1933. The decor concentrated the Biba ethos into fun Deco exoticism. Hulanicki, who had retreated from a difficult childhood by spending long days in the cinema, had developed an auteur vision and translated her nostalgic imagination into a lifestyle achievable for the consumer.[60] Biba was a series of sets and scenes where fantasies were encouraged.

During the planning stage for Big Biba, Hulanicki had copied production designer Tony Walton's oversized furniture from *The Boy Friend*'s 'Room in Bloomsbury' scene for the pregnant mothers' department, the toadstools from the fairy sequence for the children's department, and the oversized record player for the record department. Shirley Russell returned the kudos when she persuaded the ten-year-old Victoria to appear in *Tommy* by buying her costume from Biba.[61] The retro nostalgia that Biba promoted was above all filmic, calling to mind the camp mania of *Cabaret* (Bob Fosse, 20th Century Fox, 1972) entwined with the soft-focus romance of *The Great Gatsby* (Jack Clayton, Paramount, 1974), for which Hulanicki had to pass on the role of costume designer as she was too consumed in her magnum opus of the Derry and Toms store.[62] But material evidence connects Biba to *The Boy Friend* via the glamour of retro. An image in the December 1973 issue of British *Vogue* shows Twiggy modelling a satin negligee in the Mistress Room of Big Biba. The negligee is intended for the bedroom but, removed from that context, could just as easily be evening wear, and was bought for that purpose, as Hulanicki remembers: 'We used to sell millions of them. It was sort of negligee stuff because if you had it in one area, the taxes were much lower so you could get the prices down, and people wore them in the evening.'[63]

The 'nightie' is almost identical to the white, bias-cut, satin slip dress that Twiggy wears in the 'Room in Bloomsbury' sequence in *The Boy Friend*. This original 1930s gown is Shirley Russell's quotation of the 1930s Hollywood vamp Jean Harlow in *Dinner at Eight* (George Cukor, MGM, 1933).[64] The evening dress that costume designer Adrian produced for Harlow for the final scenes barely differs from the negligees in which she is costumed for most of the film's running time. The pre-code fluid movement of satin on skin became shorthand for 1930s glamour – it was this that was used as a signifier by Shirley Russell and in the dissemination of retro by Barbara Hulanicki.

CONCLUSION

As the *All Talking* promotional documentary reveals, the layered temporalities of *The Boy Friend* correlate with those of the retro movement. The retro of the late 1960s and early 1970s is an imagined nostalgia seen in the context of its period of production. That it featured Art Deco styling is the result of a combination of influences: a new appreciation of the decorative art of the interwar period by arts institutions, and a pursuit of a more exclusive style by antiques collectors after earlier periods became too popular. However, as Elizabeth Guffey asserts, 'The Art Deco style was not born in the 1930s but in the 1960s.'[65] As an appropriation of an amalgamation of stylistic references,

> Art Deco was discovered not by historians, but rather by a diverse group of retro popularizers who included writers and curators and especially Pop artists, defining and memorializing the styles and icons of their formative years, namely popular Modernism and the mass culture of the inter-war period.[66]

Consequently, it could be concluded that Art Deco is a product and a commodity of retro.

The Art Deco style sets used by production designer Tony Walton for *The Boy Friend* and installation designer Michael Haynes for Beaton's 1971 exhibition complemented Shirley Russell's original 1920s and 30s costumes and Erté's original 1920s costume with elements that signified the glamorised Hollywood musical extravaganzas. The refit by design studio Whitmore Thomas for the Derry and Toms Biba store contextualised Barbara Hulanicki's period-inspired fashion for a contemporary consumer. Interestingly, the Deco Biba store borrowed not only visually from film but also in its use of lighting, Egyptomania, carpeted stairways and cigarette girls, from the interiors of 1930s cinemas – which were conceived to bring luxury to ordinary people.[67] Retro lifestyle did not emulate the Great Depression. Retro communicates a recognisable representation of the 1920s and 1930s which is a phenomenon of the 1960s and 1970s. It is the representation of De Thrill's Hollywood-ised fantasy of 1930s modernity in *The Boy Friend* rather than the shabby 1920s provincial theatre dressing room. Ken Russell uses Shirley Russell's period costuming skill, conveying backstage drabness, pastiched onstage 1920s society, and 1930s filmic glamour, to expose and satirise the difference. Rather than the period costuming practices of Shirley Russell, it is Ken Russell's communication with enthusiasts of camp which provides the 'slippage' of retro which 'tells us more about (their) relationship with the past'.[68]

As a film on three levels, *The Boy Friend* was problematic for Shirley Russell: the scale of ambition proved challenging. Although the fantasy scenes fed into the idealised camp retro enjoyed by 'Them', her research processes ensured that they remained true to her dress history training that prized authenticity.

Retro has been criticised as having a glossy ambivalence to the past.[69] Garvey sees Ken Russell's approach as 're-present[ing] the past in a complex way which both foregrounds its construction and ironises ideas of nostalgia and period styling'.[70] It could be argued that Shirley's meticulousness which, Garvey appreciates, 'lends a weight and authenticity to the characters', strengthening retro style with substance.[71]

The montage of styles and decades is echoed in Barbara Hulanicki's construction of experiential retro in Biba. Costume designer Sandy Powell remembers wearing original 1930s dresses from Oxfam to the Rainbow Room as a fourteen-year-old in a bid to fit in with the aesthetic because her pocket money did not stretch to a Biba version.[72]

Hulanicki and Twiggy were both prominent figures in the dissemination of the retro Art Deco glamour of the 1970s, but the work of Shirley Russell, which was embedded in a grounding in museology and dedicated research, was influential to both. This was valued by Twiggy, who at twenty-two had found the experience not only 'fun' but 'life-changing';[73] she maintained that 'Shirley has a lot to do with why Ken's so wonderful. She and Barbara Hulanicki are the two women I admire more than anyone in the world.'[74]

Ken Russell's relationship to the past is evidenced in a response to his immersion in cinema. Shirley shared this but, in addition, her material engagement with history was the foundation of the visual representation, combined with her experience as their collaboration grew over time: 'because I know him so well, I know exactly what he wants'.[75]

The interaction of the three women, Shirley Russell, Lesley Hornby and Barbara Hulanicki, encapsulates the cause-and-effect narrative of film, fashion and nostalgia which led to the stylistics of 1970s retro moving from 'minority taste'[76] to influence fashion and visual culture much more widely. Ken and Shirley Russell's quotation of early Hollywood production in *The Boy Friend* is not just synonymous with a prevalent style in popular culture in the early 1970s, but a significant contribution to it. The synthesis of film, fashion and historical reference is a marker of time in its own right.

ACKNOWLEDGEMENTS

With thanks to Victoria Russell, Pamela Church-Gibson and Stewart Williams, and to Victoria and Amelia Russell for permission to use the images.

NOTES

1. *All Talking, All Singing, All Dancing*, documentary, Kaleidoscope Films, UK, 1971.
2. Ibid.
3. Elizabeth Wilson, *Adorned in Dreams: Fashion and Modernity* (London: Virago, 1985), 172.
4. Raphael Samuel, *Theatres of Memory: Past and Present in Contemporary Culture* (New York and London: Verso, 1994), 91.
5. Pam Cook, *Screening the Past: Memory and Nostalgia in Cinema* (London: Routledge, 2004), 2.
6. Maureen McAndrew, 'Shirley Russell. Filmmaking: A Family Affair', Women and Film issue, *Cinema*, no. 35, 1976, 36.
7. John Baxter, *An Appalling Talent: Ken Russell* (London: Michael Joseph, 1973), 92.
8. Ken Russell, *Altered States: The Autobiography of Ken Russell* (New York: Bantam, 1991), 104–5.
9. Victoria Russell, interviewed by the author, 2016.
10. McAndrew, 36.
11. Cook, 2.
12. Valerie Wade, 'The Girlfriend', *Sunday Times Magazine*, 2 January 1972, 22.
13. Ibid.
14. McAndrew, 36.
15. Samuel, 91.
16. Ibid., 95.
17. Victoria Russell, interview.
18. Ken Russell, 105.
19. Wilson, 172.
20. Ken Russell, 105.
21. Judith Watt, 'For Your Pleasure: The Quest for Glamour in British Fashion 1969–1972', in Darren Phi (ed.), *Glam: The Performance of Style* (London: Tate Publishing, 2013), 46.
22. Ibid.
23. Bevis Hillier, *Art Deco* (London: Studio Vista, 1968), 161.
24. Ibid.
25. Gordon Gow, 'Them and Us. Shirley Russell', *Films and Filming*, October 1977, 14.
26. Samuel, 91.
27. Watt, 46.
28. Simon Reynolds, 'The Rift of Retro: 1962? Or Twenty Years On?', in Phi (ed.), 66.
29. Cosey Fanni Tutti, *Art, Sex, Music* (London: Faber and Faber, 2017), 94–9.
30. *All Talking, All Singing, All Dancing*.
31. Alistair O'Neill, *London: After a Fashion* (London: Reaktion, 2007), 169.
32. Cleo Butterfield, interviewed by the author, 2017.
33. Watt, 46.
34. Peter York, 'Them', *Harpers & Queen*, October 1976, reprinted in *Them: Duggie Fields, Derek Jarman, Andrew Logan, Luciana Martinez, Kevin Whitney* (London: Redfern Gallery, 2020).
35. Adrian Garvey, 'The Boyfriend: Ken Russell's "Anti-musical"', in Laurel Forster and Sue Harper (eds), *British Culture and Society in the 1970s: The Lost Decade* (Newcastle upon Tyne: Cambridge Scholars Publishing, 2010), 229.
36. Baxter, 59.
37. Wilson, 193.
38. Samuel.

39. Judith Clark and Amy de la Haye with J. Horsley, *Exhibiting Fashion: Before and After 1971* (New Haven, CT and London: Yale University Press, 2014), 69.
40. *Fashion: An Anthology by Cecil Beaton* (London: V&A Publishing, 1971).
41. Twiggy Lawson, interviewed by the author, 2019.
42. *All Talking, All Singing, All Dancing*.
43. Reynolds, 73.
44. Twiggy, *Twiggy By Twiggy* (St Albans: Mayflower Books, 1975), 114.
45. Ibid., 81, 123.
46. Twiggy Lawson, interview.
47. Twiggy, 10.
48. Vincent Porter, 'Alternative Film Exhibition in the English Regions During the 1970s', in Paul Newland (ed.), *Don't Look Now: British Cinema in the 1970s* (Bristol: Intellect, 2010), 57–70.
49. *Films and Filming*, vol. 18, 1 October 1971.
50. Twiggy, 93.
51. *Queen*, 8 May 1968.
52. Twiggy, 104.
53. Baxter, 213.
54. 'Ken Russell Films *The Boy Friend*', *Films and Filming*, vol. 18, 1 October 1971, 34–5.
55. McAndrew, 36.
56. Victoria Russell, interview.
57. Baxter, 56.
58. Gow, 14.
59. Twiggy Lawson, interview.
60. Bevis Hillier, *The Style of the Century* (London: Herbert Press, 1998), 214.
61. Victoria Russell, interview.
62. Barbara Hulanicki, interview with the author, 2016.
63. Ibid.
64. Twiggy Lawson, interview.
65. Elizabeth Guffey, *Retro: The Culture of Revival* (London: Reaktion, 2006), 86.
66. Ibid., 73.
67. *Odeon Cavalcade*, documentary, directed by Barry Clayton, Greendow Film Productions, UK, 1973.
68. Cook, 9.
69. Fredric Jameson, *Postmodernism, or the Cultural Logic of Late Capitalism* (Durham, NC: Duke University Press, 1991); Guffey.
70. Garvey, 233.
71. Ibid.
72. Sandy Powell, interviewed by the author, 2016.
73. Twiggy Lawson, interview.
74. Twiggy, 117.
75. Gow, 14.
76. Samuel, 91.

CHAPTER 8

'No Better Director to Learn From': The Collaboration and Parallel Careers of Ken Russell and Derek Jarman

Brian Hoyle

INTRODUCTION

Looking back at his nearly six years at the BBC's flagship arts programme *Monitor*, Ken Russell argued that it was 'the only experimental film school that Britain ever produced'.[1] This may at first seem hyperbolic, but on closer inspection, one can see his point. The National Film School would not be founded until 1971, a year after Russell left the BBC; and the only official film school in Britain at the time, the London School of Film Technique (now the London Film School), was perhaps not all that experimental. Several of Britain's most idiosyncratic film-makers, however, received their film education working for *Monitor*, or were mentored by its managing editor, Huw Wheldon. Indeed, under Wheldon's guidance young directors at the BBC including Russell, John Boorman and Tony Palmer (Russell's one-time assistant) were given a rare amount of freedom to innovate and experiment.

It is worth remembering, however, that in 1959, when *Monitor* was less than a year old and Russell was just about to replace John Schlesinger in its ranks, William Coldstream, who was then Principal of the Slade School of Fine Art, was on the brink of winning his three-year battle to hire its first lecturer in Film Studies. The job was given to Thorold Dickinson, who had previously directed two extremely atmospheric British films, the original *Gaslight* (Anglo-American, 1940) and *Queen of Spades* (Associated British Pictures, 1949). Dickinson gave his inaugural lecture in January 1961 and went on to make a lasting (if unheralded) impression on British film culture. As Henry K. Miller argues, 'Dickinson's programmes, which were open to students from all over London, would set out the historical background for what was everywhere felt to be an exceptionally exciting moment in European cinema – one in which his students eventually played a part.'² Among these students were budding film scholars Raymond Durgnat and Charles Barr; aspiring film-makers Marco Bellocchio, the director of *Fists in the Pocket* (Doria, 1965); and Don Levy and Peter Whitehead, two British film-makers whose work merits the label 'experimental'.

One other student who attended Dickinson's courses was Derek Jarman, Russell's future friend and set designer, who studied fine art at the Slade between 1963 and 1967. According to Tony Peake, the young art student did not miss 'a single screening on the film course'.³ Under Dickinson's tutelage, Jarman developed his growing interest in the European art cinema of Federico Fellini, Pier Paolo Pasolini, Michelangelo Antonioni and Ingmar Bergman, amongst others. Peake notes that Jarman was also 'introduced to the work of Sergei Eisenstein, Carl Dreyer, Jean Renoir, Max Ophuls, and [. . .] Humphrey Jennings'.⁴ Perhaps more importantly, he was able to immerse himself in the work of key figures of the European avant-garde, like Jean Cocteau and Jean Genet, and their American counterparts such as Kenneth Anger, Maya Deren, Stan Brakhage and Andy Warhol, who showed him how an artist could use a camera like a paintbrush to create small, personal works. The Slade was therefore Jarman's first film school and even if, as Peake argues, Jarman still 'had no inkling he might one day pick up a camera, he [received] an invaluable theoretical training' there.⁵

This chapter will, therefore, argue that Jarman's tenure working for Russell as the set designer on *The Devils* (Warner Bros., 1971) and *Savage Messiah* (MGM-EMI, 1972) was the second and even more vital half of Jarman's film education. It was, in fact, his equivalent of working for *Monitor*, and Russell was his somewhat improbable Huw Wheldon. It will also be demonstrated here how this training inspired Jarman to abandon his original ambitions in painting and design, for film-making, and instilled in him a very personal sense of how to (and how not to) make movies.

THE DEVILS

More attention has been given to *The Devils* than any other of Russell's films. While a great deal of it is dedicated to the controversy the film generated, Jarman's sets have also been widely discussed. The recreation of the city of Loudon on the back lot of Pinewood Studios was an impressive achievement, to be sure, and even the most scathing reviews of the film, like the one in London's *Time Out*, nevertheless singled the sets out for praise:

> no matter how thickly Russell piles on the masturbating nuns, tortured priests and dissolute dauphins, there's no getting round the fact that it's all more redolent of a camp revue than a cathartic vision. Derek Jarman's sets, however, still look terrific.⁶

Film-maker Alex Cox went further, recalling that he could not 'think of any other British film [of the period] that has had such massive, purpose-built sets, such awesome visual ambition'.[7] In his first volume of memoirs, *Dancing Ledge* (1984), Jarman himself muses on the role of set design in the cinema:

> The key to a film *can* be the design – too often left to designers who dress the film in a kind of wrapping, like a doily on a birthday cake. Audiences see nothing but the surface [. . .] but when design is integrated into the intentional structure, and forms part of the dialectic, the work begins to sing.[8]

For Jarman, two of the finest examples of this kind of integrated film design were Sergei Eisenstein's *Ivan the Terrible* (Central United Studio/Mosfilm, 1944–6) and Victor Fleming's *The Wizard of Oz* (Warner Bros., 1939). *The Devils* should also be on that list.

Although Cox is not wrong to stress the 'awesome visual ambition' of the sets, which according to Jarman, were 'apparently [. . .] the largest since the ill-fated *Cleopatra*',[9] what is equally striking about them is their simplicity. Indeed, for a film with such a reputation for baroque excess, *The Devils* is remarkably uncluttered visually. Though the scale of the sets recalls Fritz Lang's *Metropolis* (UFA, 1927), the plain white brick walls that dominate the Loudon scenes nevertheless pre-empt the stripped-down aesthetic of Jarman's subsequent feature films, most notably *Caravaggio* (BFI/Channel 4, 1986) and *Edward II* (British Screen Productions/BBC/Working Title, 1991), with their bare walls and sparse set dressings.

While the white walls contribute enormously to the aesthetic and meaning of the film, the decision to use brick was initially a pragmatic one. Jarman recalled that in his original sketches the walls of Loudon were made from stone, and the decision to change to brick was made 'in the plaster room' at Pinewood, 'where they have brick and stone moulds of every description'.[10] Russell elaborated:

> We experimented at Pinewood with all their moulds, including those for old stone, but obviously when you use the same cast time after time you end up with an absolutely uniform pattern, so we thought; let's accept the limitations imposed on us by a machine-made product and use the *most* machine-made thing, the ordinary household brick. The whole town is made out of Pinewood standard brick mould. But having decided on this basic material, we had to make it distinctive and put over the ideas we ourselves had about the town.[11]

For Russell, the decision to make the bricks white, rather than the 'more usual brick colours – yellows and reds' that they initially tested,[12] was 'inspired by one particular line in Huxley's book [*The Devils of Loudon* (1952)], "The exorcism of sister Jeanne [. . .] was equivalent to rape in a public lavatory.'"[13] The white walls do more than just lend a clinical atmosphere to the exorcism sequence, however. In an earlier scene in which Madeleine (Gemma Jones) visits Sister Jeanne (Vanessa Redgrave) at the convent to enquire about joining the order, Sister Jeanne's cell seems especially claustrophobic due to the low ceilings. In addition, the arch-shaped bed and the quadrant-shaped door evoke the nun's hunchback. The white bricks here conjure up images of a hospital or insane asylum, a fact which serves to remind the audience of all the young women, like Sister Jeanne, with physical and mental impairments who were sent to convents by their families. As the camera pulls back and repositions over Madeleine's shoulder, the black bars on Sister Jeanne's cell become visible and make her quarters look like a prison. In this new framing, green creepers can be seen to Madeleine's left running up the white walls. This simple design choice places Madeleine next to the only vivid colour in the scene and separates her from the austere, black and white world of the nuns. This is later echoed when she is shown walking through a green field, reading a letter from Grandier. This is intercut with the priest stopping on his journey to take Communion. By placing the couple outside of the sterile walls of Loudon and moving through nature and surrounded by colour, Russell and Jarman show that they are natural and decent people in a world that is otherwise unnatural and decadent.

The white brick walls of Loudon are also deliberately anachronistic. Much has been made of how the anachronisms in the film serve the double purpose of demonstrating that the residents of Loudon would have viewed their town as modern and as reminders of contemporary political situations where fear and hysteria are used to control the people. Anachronisms of this kind were not uncommon in Russell's previous work. As Rowland Wymer argues, Russell was in fact drawn to

> the use of authentic period details (such as the green lipstick that was fashionable for a time in seventeenth-century France), which would seem anachronistically 'modern' to the uninitiated and which would clash disconcertingly with more familiar and conventional images of the past.[14]

Earlier examples include Jane Morris playing with a yo-yo while posing for the Pre-Raphaelite mural in the Oxford Union in *Dante's Inferno: The Private Life of Dante Gabriel Rossetti, Poet and Painter* (BBC, 1967). It is a brilliantly timed gag, which shows the model's boredom and her indifference to the pompous rhetoric of the male artists. To an audience in the 1960s a yo-yo would seem quite modern, as the toy was extremely popular at the time. In truth, however, bandalores (as they were previously called) had been known in Britain since the seventeenth century. Similarly, the scene in *The Debussy Film* (BBC, 1965) in which the composer and Gaby play with toy balloons causes the director (Vladek Sheybal) to comment that 'they did play with balloons. I checked.' These are just two examples of many, and they offer further proof that decisions that critics often thought were either random or designed to provoke on Russell's part were actually often the result of careful research.

After *The Devils*, Russell's use of anachronisms became even more overt. For instance, Gustav Mahler died in 1911, but Russell's film about him is full of swastikas and references to Fritz Lang, the Marx Brothers and Al Jolson. This was taken to the extreme in *Lisztomania* (Goodtimes Enterprises, 1975), the design of which cannot be situated in any specific historical period. Although we cannot say for certain how much Jarman inspired this shift, he was even more suspicious than Russell of 'authentic' period films, referring to British costume dramas as 'lurex for an Oscar'.[15] The costumes in Jarman's adaptation of *The Tempest* (Boyd's Company, 1979) offered, in his own words, 'a chronology of the 350 years of the play's existence',[16] ranging from Elizabethan ruffs to modern-day boiler suits. *Caravaggio* features a wide historical variety of costumes and props, from 1940s motorbikes to pocket calculators, as a way of evoking the artist's own anachronistic use of contemporary dress in his paintings of biblical subjects. *Edward II* similarly employs modern costumes and props to hammer home the contemporary relevance of Marlowe's play by exposing the homophobia of Thatcher era Britain.

Though designing *The Devils* was an enormous opportunity for Jarman, it was not always a happy experience. He and Russell clashed on occasion, most notably over the scene where Louis XIII shoots Huguenots dressed as blackbirds, which Jarman felt the director reduced to 'a flip joke'.[17] Additionally, there was an incident that unquestionably affected Jarman. At the climax of the film, following Grandier's burning at the stake, the city walls Jarman had built were meant to be blown up. When the explosives were accidently set off before the cameras began rolling, the young designer had to rebuild the walls only to see them demolished for a second time on film. Jarman was devastated. Even before the reconstruction, the sets cost an estimated £97,000. This would be more than the budgets of his first two features combined. Upon completion of the filming, Jarman wrote that

> Almost every waking moment of 1970 was spent working on *The Devils*. When I began in January I had no idea that a film of this size usurps your life. By the time I emerged from Pinewood in December, the easy life of the 1960s – designing and painting – had gone forever.[18]

Looking back on his time spent working on *The Devils*, Jarman felt that he 'had discovered (imperceptibly) how a feature film ran'.[19] But it had also convinced him that he 'had no desire to become permanently part of the industrial system of production which characterises commercial cinema'.[20] Jarman's diary entries make it clear that he found film-making on this grand scale exhausting as well as wasteful. At the same time, he was strangely energised by the experience, which, he argued, had 'without realising it, relocated my work'.[21] Jarman subsequently acquired a Super-8 camera and began making short films. At first these were more like home movies, but soon they began to draw on the avant-garde work of film-makers like Deren, Anger and Warhol that he had first seen at the Slade; works that were 'close to something one could actually do oneself [and which demonstrated] that it didn't matter if you didn't adhere to all the technicalities and rules'.[22] In short, Jarman, like Russell before him, chose to align himself with the amateurs; the film-makers who made films for love, rather than profit. Though Russell had, at least temporarily, lost touch with his amateur roots, Jarman was ultimately very complimentary about his teacher, noting that there 'was no better director to learn from, as he would always take the adventurous path even at the expense of coherence'.[23] This is arguably one of the most perceptive descriptions of Russell's virtues, and occasional vices, as a film-maker. The fact that one could also apply these words to Jarman as a film-maker shows just how like-minded the two could be.

SAVAGE MESSIAH

Wymer argues that '*The Devils* continued to haunt Jarman's imagination for the rest of his life.'[24] Few, if any, critics have made similar claims about *Savage Messiah*, the second and final feature film Jarman designed for Russell. A biopic of the French sculptor Henri Gaudier-Brzeska, *Savage Messiah* was in many ways the flip side of *The Devils*, both as a film and as a film-making experience. It is one of Russell's more restrained works and was also made on a shoestring. Expensive, purpose-built studio sets of the kind that made *The Devils* so impressive were a luxury that this far smaller production could not afford. A great deal of the film was therefore shot on location. As Peake states, 'the design was largely a matter of choosing, and sometimes dressing, the locations needed to suggest early twentieth-century Paris and London', so there was far less for Jarman to do here.[25] Jarman scholars have tended to gloss over the film, pausing only to mention the impressive Wyndham Lewis inspired sets used for the fictitious Vortex club. Linda Ruth Williams describes these as 'extravaganzas of kinetic design', and they bring a welcome blast of colour and abstract shapes to what is otherwise Russell's most naturalistic-looking film.[26]

Savage Messiah and the experience of making it are more present as influences in Jarman's subsequent work than has previously been believed. The scene in *Caravaggio*, for instance, where the artist (Nigel Terry) first paints

Ranuccio (Sean Bean), who is posing as the executioner in *The Martyrdom of St Matthew* (1599–1600), harks back to what Ken Hanke calls 'the most famous set piece' in Russell's film.[27] In this scene we find Gaudier-Brzeska (Scott Antony), in a frantic burst of creativity, working through the night on a sculpture of a woman's torso. To emphasise the sculptor's energy and spontaneity, Russell condenses over six hours of chiselling and sanding down to a mere five minutes of screen time. He still takes care, however, to show what a laborious, physical process sculpting is. Throughout the sequence Gaudier-Brzeska speaks to his art dealer friend, Corky (Lindsay Kemp), in order to stay awake. Hanke describes this monologue as a 'subconscious flow of words and thoughts'.[28] A discussion of Cézanne, for instance, ends with an allusion to W. B. Yeats's poem 'When You Are Old and Grey and Full of Sleep', the significance of which will later become apparent. The poem was one of many by Yeats to Maud Gonne, the poet's unrequited love. This situation mirrors that of Gaudier-Brzeska, whose relationship with his wife Sophie was unconsummated. The main thrust of the monologue, however, provides Gaudier-Brzeska's (and by extension Russell's) views about art and artists. For Hanke, the assertion that an artist 'needs an audience' is 'purest Russell'.[29] Indeed, for all that his work is perceived as difficult, and his taste in subjects such as composers, painters and poets deemed highbrow, Russell was no elitist; he always tried to speak to a popular audience. Gaudier-Brzeska's statement in the scene under discussion, 'Of course I do it because it pleases me. If I don't get a lot from doing it, how the hell is it going to give anything to anyone else?', could well be Russell's credo too.

The equivalent scene in *Caravaggio* has many superficial similarities. Both set out to demonstrate that artistic creation is 'usually five percent inspiration and ninety-five percent perspiration and hard slog'.[30] In both films we have an artist working through the night, and Jarman has Caravaggio's assistant, Jerusaleme (Spencer Leigh), and Ranuccio's lover, Lena (Tilda Swinton), yawning and struggling to stay awake, just as Sophie does in the earlier film. If Russell used this scene to expound his theories about artists and their audiences, Jarman does something similar by interrogating the relationship between painting and cinema. Jerusaleme is seen angling a large gold light reflector to illuminate the posing Ranuccio. Light reflectors of this kind are still commonly used on film sets today. In this way, Jarman illustrates how similar the two art forms can be, and suggests that Caravaggio helped invent cinematic lighting long before cinema was invented. The presence of the light reflector, and the way Caravaggio physically shifts Ranuccio into the position and posture he wants, also draws comparisons between painter and director, model and actor.

Aside from its meta-cinematic subtext, Jarman also comments upon the relationship between art and commerce. Caravaggio has been commissioned by a patron, Cardinal Del Monte (Michael Gough), who pays the artist with gold coins. From time to time, Caravaggio tosses one of these coins to his model, who stuffs each one in his mouth. The audience literally sees the money trickle down from the top. These exchanges also speak to the desire that artists often feel for their models, and, in this instance, the love triangle that will develop. The final coin is given directly from Caravaggio's mouth to Ranuccio, who is next seen laughing with Lena and playing with the coins. The scene is a complex one, full of meaning and a great deal of narrative information. It also plays out without a single word being spoken. This is in direct contrast to the scene in *Savage Messiah* discussed above. As Hanke notes, the heavy use of dialogue in the sculpting scene is 'rather unusual for Russell who generally prefers to make his points on a more visual level'.[31] In a clear example of the pupil outdoing the master, Jarman relies on nothing more here than careful framing and editing, slight but meaningful looks and gestures, and a discreet sound design.

The Devils was a baptism of fire for its young designer, and it made Jarman realise that he did not want to make films the same way. *Savage Messiah* showed Jarman that there was a viable alternative as it saw Russell moving away from the large budgets of *The Devils* and *The Boy Friend* (MGM-EMI, 1971), putting up most of the film's budget himself. While it might seem that self-funding put more pressure on Russell, it ironically had the opposite effect. No longer beholden to a big studio or other outside financiers, Russell became liberated. He was working on a scale far closer to his final BBC films and enjoying a level of creative freedom he had arguably not experienced since his days filming *Amelia and the Angel* (BFI Experimental Film Fund, 1958). *Savage Messiah* gave Jarman his first experience of making the kind of low-budget independent feature film that he would become known for. At the same time, the crew, many of whom had been employed on *The Devils*, were also noticeably happier working together on this smaller project. As Peake notes, there was a 'cosy sense of family' on *Savage Messiah*.[32] Indeed, Jarman would later remark that it was the closest 'Russell would ever come to making a home movie',[33] and it shaped his own desire to make films primarily 'for the camaraderie'.[34]

SEBASTIANE AND RELIGIOUS THEMES

Although the pair would discuss further collaborations, including an adaptation of François Rabelais's *Gargantua*, *Savage Messiah* marked the end of Jarman's role as Russell's designer. He turned down the chance to design *Tommy* (Columbia, 1975),[35] preferring instead to make his own ultra-low-budget feature debut, *Sebastiane* (Cinegate/Disctat/Meglovision, 1976), which chronicles the last days and martyrdom of Saint Sebastian. Made independently for around £20,000, *Sebastiane* is like *Savage Messiah* in its pragmatic use of locations to offset budgetary limitations; and like Russell's film, it is arguably Jarman's most naturalistic work. The key difference between the two, however, is Jarman's preference for minimalism. Russell filmed *Savage Messiah* in and around the grounds of various houses, cottages, museums and a railway station to evoke the early twentieth century and lend the film higher production values. Jarman, however, apart from the opening sequence in the court of Emperor Diocletian, uses nothing more in *Sebastiane* than a 'Sardinian landscape of sea, sand, sky, a ruined cottage, and one ancient watchtower'.[36]

Like the minimalist mise en scène, the decision to film *Sebastiane* in Latin is pure Jarman. Other aspects, however, show further overlaps between Jarman's aesthetics and Russell's. Most superficially, *Sebastiane* featured possibly the most censor-baiting full-frontal male nudity in any film since *Women in Love* (Ken Russell, United Artists, 1969). For all the bare flesh on display, however, Edward Norman views *Sebastiane* as 'not a film about sex [. . .] but about exile, and the desolation of the soul; it is about spirit, not flesh'.[37] Indeed, Jarman's debut offers a serious treatment of a religious theme, which is something of a rarity in British cinema. Norman, the former Chancellor of York Minster, elaborates on this in his published lecture 'Religious Symbolism in British Film':

> There are, in this country, few filmmakers in whose work the presentation of a religious conflict of ideas, or the seriousness of religious imagery, or the pursuit of a religious theme, seem persistent – or even present at all in any sustained manner. There is no British Pasolini, or Visconti, or Buñuel, or Scorsese: the director of films in which modernity confronts religious belief in stark sequences of sceptical visual explanation, but where, nevertheless, religious understandings of human life are accorded considered significance.[38]

He then qualifies this statement by adding, 'except, that is, for Jarman, and he called himself "an atheist"'.[39]

Even British film-makers with an interest in the mystical and the metaphysical, like Michael Powell and John Boorman, feature conspicuously little religious imagery in their films. Jarman, on the other hand, made his first film about a saint, and won an award from the International Catholic Organization for Cinema and Audiovisual (OCIC) for *The Garden* (Basilisk/Channel 4/British Screen Productions, 1990), which reimagines Christ as a pair of gay lovers. Jarman believed this to be his equivalent of Pasolini's *The Gospel According to St Matthew* (Arco Film, 1963). *Caravaggio*, by virtue of its subject, recreates, in tableaux, numerous paintings of religious subjects, culminating in *The Entombment of Christ* (1604). *War Requiem* (Anglo International/BBC/Liberty Film Sales, 1989), a film of Benjamin Britten's oratorio, which itself contains the text of the Latin Mass, is littered with crosses, crowns of thorns, and images of entombment and resurrection, and recreates the story of Abraham and Isaac. Norman sees something inherently Christian in Jarman's recurring treatment of exile and 'love itself as a redemptive force', and even argues that the unchanging monochromatic screen of his final film, *Blue* (Channel 4/Arts Council of Great Britain/Opal Records, 1993), offers a 'hint of transcendent realities'.[40] He further believes that the spoken text of the film is a 'memorial to the pathetic resourcefulness of human hope and even the dignity of human life', in which 'we come to recognise the tenacity of a sort of faith'.[41] Norman's contention that Jarman is 'the most important representative of religious themes in modern British cinema' is difficult to dispute.[42]

Jarman's only competition is Russell. At the Edinburgh International Festival in 2002, Tilda Swinton read out an open letter to Jarman in which she said that he 'should have been a Catholic'.[43] Russell, who converted at twenty-eight, *was* a Catholic. Indeed, in the mid-1970s he claimed that 'except *The Boyfriend*, my films have been Catholic in outlook: films about love, faith, sin, guilt, forgiveness and redemption – films that could only have been made by a Catholic'.[44] This is apparent from his very first films. His unfinished amateur documentary *Lourdes*, for example, is about the pilgrimage site, whereas *Amelia and the Angel* was produced by a Catholic priest and ends with a miracle. Issues of faith also permeate several of his BBC films, especially *Elgar* (BBC, 1962), about a fellow Catholic convert, and *Delius: Song of Summer* (BBC, 1968), in which the devout Eric Fenby attempts to reconcile his love of Delius's music with his disapproval of the composer's personal immorality. Even the grotesque parody of the conversion scene in *Mahler* (Goodtimes Enterprises, 1974) can be read as an assertion of Russell's Catholicism. The Nazi imagery, references to the Siegfried myth, and Wagner's music clearly represent the shameful anti-Semitism that forced Jews like Mahler to convert to Christianity. But as ever with Russell, the sword is double edged, and for a genuine convert such as himself, Mahler's insincere conversion *is* a grotesque parody of what should be a solemn act.

Then there are *The Devils* and *Tommy*, arguably Russell's two most overtly religious films. Unpacking the theological implications of a work like *The Devils* would take far more space than is available here. On the one hand, it was condemned by the Catholic Church in America as well as by the Vatican. On the other, it found two of its most vocal champions in the Jesuit critic Gene D. Phillips and Jay Cocks, who would go on to co-write Martin Scorsese's own masterpiece about Jesuit priests, *Silence* (Paramount, 2016). Contemporary Catholic critics have built on Phillips's and Cock's example and continue to re-evaluate the film as a testament of faith, with Deal Hudson in *The Catholic Herald* writing that those 'who in the name of God and decency, have condemned *The Devils*, have been ill-served by their preoccupation with nakedness and sex [and] missed the meaning of Russell's masterpiece'.[45] He then goes on to compare *The Devils* to Robert Bresson's *The Trial of Joan of Arc*

(Agnes Delahaie Productions, 1962), arguing that Grandier 'dies a true martyr with a nobility similar to St Joan'.[46] Hudson's references to Bresson's film, and Russell's and Jarman's direct allusions to Dreyer's earlier *The Passion of Joan of Arc* (Société Générale des Films, 1929) make it clear that Russell views Grandier's death as a Christ-like Passion. This makes Joseph A. Gomez's comment that 'Anyone familiar with the work of Ken Russell must have registered mild surprise when it was announced that [. . .] Russell would make a film version of The Who's *Tommy*'[47] rather hard to believe. In 1976 Russell was the only logical choice amongst British film-makers to take on a rock opera about, to use Russell's own words, 'a modern messiah [who] was totally exploited and commercialised'.[48] Indeed, Pete Townsend's libretto was, to quote Hanke, so similar to Russell's 'personal thematic overview that he almost might have written it himself'.[49]

Even if it got harder to call Russell a Catholic film-maker in the 1980s, films like *The Lair of the White Worm* (Vestron, 1988) and *Gothic* (Virgin Vision/ Vestron, 1986) have more than their share of crucifixes and ecstatic religious visions. Similarly, *Salome's Last Dance* (Vestron, 1988) draws a (somewhat misleading) parallel between Oscar Wilde's battle with the censors over dramatising religious material (the Lord Chamberlain's Office banned all plays with biblical subjects until as recently as 1968) and Russell's own issues with the British Board of Film Censors over *The Devils*. That decade also saw him make *Crimes of Passion* (New World Pictures, 1984), where the antagonist is a priest. Additionally, he directed two operas based on the Faust myth: Charles Gounod's *Faust* (Vienna State Opera, 1985) and Arrigo Boito's *Mefistofele* (Opera di Genova, 1987), and one film which drew heavily upon it, *Altered States* (Warner Bros., 1980), all of which feature a preponderance of religious imagery.

Norman admits that Jarman, the avowed atheist, 'is an eccentric – even a perverse' choice to name as British cinema's leading religious film-maker.[50] Russell is clearly one too, but Norman neglects even to mention him in his lecture. Perhaps the controversy surrounding *The Devils* still looms too large, or possibly stunts like casting Ringo Starr as the Pope in *Lisztomania* overshadow the many serious statements he made about religion. Whatever the reasons, more thought needs to be given to this aspect of both film-makers' work, if for no other reason than it helps demonstrate why the two artists felt such an instant kinship. It also offers further proof of their position as outsiders in the British film industry.

CARAVAGGIO AND THE BIOPIC

Gomez is not exaggerating when he argues that Russell 'revolutionised the nature of the bio-pic',[51] described by Dennis Bingham as a 'respectable genre of low repute'.⁵² Russell absorbed some of the conventions of the genre into his biopics, including the use of flashbacks and, in some cases, birth to death narratives, but he turned most of them on their head. Apart, perhaps, from *Elgar*, none of Russell's biopics could be called hagiographies.⁵³ Nor could they be seen as being objective. Russell instead brought a clear sense of subjectivity to the genre; his biopics never pretend to be definitive or official versions of a life. By bringing his own viewpoint into his biopics, alongside what Gomez sees as 'the protagonist's own romantic self-image, [and] a more objective view revealed by the perspective of time',⁵⁴ Russell made it possible for the voice of the film-maker to be heard just as clearly as that of their subjects. In short, Russell created the auteurist biopic.

Caravaggio is also an artist's biopic made in the subjective, auteurist tradition pioneered by Russell. Some aspects of *Caravaggio* are reasonably conventional. The film begins with the painter on his death bed and flashes back and forth between this moment and scenes from his past. Jarman does not include the painter's entire life, but he does show him as a teenager (played by Dexter Fletcher) as well as an adult (played by Nigel Terry); however, Jarman surrenders any pretence of objectivity. Little was known about the painter, and the film was released prior to the publication of several important biographies and critical studies which filled large gaps in the existing knowledge about the painter's life. Jarman therefore took some generally agreed upon biographical details – including the painter's relationship with prostitutes and use of them as models; his ambivalent sexuality; his implication in the murder of a man named Ranuccio, and subsequent flight from Rome; and the circumstance of his death – and combined these with his own personal and subjective analysis of a selection of Caravaggio's paintings. For instance, he pays close attention to the self-portraits and sees Caravaggio's signature, 'f. Michelangelo' ('I, Michelangelo did this'), emerging from the saint's blood in *The Beheading of John the Baptist* (1610) as a confession to Ranuccio's murder. If this is not an entirely unconventional reading, Jarman's interpretation of *The Entombment of Christ* certainly is. Although it is not one of the agreed upon self-portraits, Jarman nevertheless places Terry's Caravaggio as the central figure in a tableau recreation, and therefore equates the painter's impending death and subsequent artistic immortality with Christ's Passion and Resurrection. In an even bolder move, Jarman includes a voice-over over the *Entombment* scene that presents his own memories of his first love as those of the painter, once again blurring the line between film-maker and subject.

The idea of structuring a biopic around an explicitly subjective reading of an artist's work, rather than conventional biographical sources, and including elements of autobiography, would have been almost unthinkable before Russell. Indeed, Jarman's treatment of Caravaggio's painting is directly comparable to the way Russell uses the music of Tchaikovsky, or Mahler, or almost any other composer he made a film about. When the critic for *Time* magazine accused Russell of making 'every bar of music programmatic' in *The Music Lovers* (United Artists, 1970), they were not far wrong.[55] Like Jarman's selective use of Caravaggio's paintings, Russell's choice of works is also highly selective. For example, one hears very little of Tchaikovsky's lighter side after the first five minutes of *The Music Lovers*. Moreover, like Jarman's decision consciously to misprepresent *The Entombment of Christ* as a Caravaggio self-portrait, Russell sometimes goes as far as to rearrange a work or works of a composer to suit his own vision. Therefore, he amalgamates sections of the Pathétique and Manfred Symphonies in the train sequence of *The Music Lovers* and edits together a seamless montage of musical allusions to nature from four different symphonies towards the beginning of *Mahler*.

WAR REQUIEM AND THE COMPOSED FILM

In 1987, soon after *Caravaggio*, Russell and Jarman contributed segments to Don Boyd's *Aria*, a multi-director anthology of short films based on popular operas. It was enough of a success for Boyd to pitch to record companies like Decca several equally ambitious projects which, in the producer's words, 'involve[d] the combination of music and film'.[56] Only one of these was eventually made, Jarman's *War Requiem* (1989). A feature-length visualisation of Benjamin Britten's 1962 oratorio, the film marks the one occasion in Jarman's career on which the constraints placed on him were not simply budgetary. By this time, he was well known as a controversialist, a queer rights activist, and a director suspicious of conventional narrative cinema. The Britten-Pears Foundation and Decca therefore added numerous clauses to Jarman's contract designed to rein him in. For example, it stipulated that he had to use the recording of the oratorio that Britten himself conducted for Decca in 'its entirety [. . .] with no cuts, pauses or other alterations'.[57] *War Requiem* is, however, one of those rare films for which the limitations imposed on the production proved to be beneficial.

Jarman was no doubt aware that he was following in the footsteps of his (and Russell's) British film idol, Michael Powell. Powell directed opera films like *Tales of Hoffmann* (The Archers, 1951, with Emeric Pressburger) and *Bluebeard's Castle* (Norman Foster Productions, 1963). Jarman would also have been mindful of his erstwhile mentor's subsequent innovations matching images to orchestral music. At the same time, Jarman advocated what Powell called 'the composed film', a work shot entirely to a pre-existing score with a new, more contemporary direction.

Like Powell, Russell's preferred method of filming musical sequences, whether in a studio or on location, was to use 'playback'. This involves playing music, which could either be a 'temp track' (as when he shot the honeymoon train ride in *The Music Lovers* to Shostakovich rather than Tchaikovsky) or the music intended for that scene (Russell's more common practice), while filming is taking place. Filming to playback is, however, time-consuming. The BBC archives, for example, show that the filming of *Dance of the Seven Veils* (BBC, 1970) was prolonged, and associated costs increased, due to 'the difficulties of filming to playback'.[58] Nevertheless, for Russell, this method was preferable for several reasons. First, the lack of direct sound allowed him to direct his actors and crew while the camera was running. This made for both greater spontaneity while shooting and more complex choreography of the action and the camera movement guided by the rhythms of the music. More importantly, however, shooting without direct sound enabled the director to use what is referred to as a 'MOS camera', like the Arri Arriflex IIC or the Arri 35II. These are cameras without sound inputs that are far smaller, lighter and more manoeuvrable than equivalent cameras that did record sound and therefore had to be muffled by a soundproofing 'blimp' that could more than triple their weight. These smaller cameras enabled Russell to move more freely as he does in the musical sequences in his films (like the opening minutes of *The Music Lovers*).

Jarman, by contrast, used playback very sparingly on *War Requiem*. He instead chose to shoot his 35 mm footage without on-set music and began the process of matching images to the score later in the cutting room. Boyd writes:

> We have an editing machine on location. Between Derek and I we have worked out a way to get a sense of what his film is like by synchronising some of the images he has shot with the music now transferred to 35mm film. Tonight we will be looking a 29 mins on a big screen in this way.[59]

The most notable exception to this is the 'Sanctus' sequence, which was shot to playback. It is comprised of a single medium close-up, lasting just over 6 minutes, of Tilda Swinton's character reacting to Britten's music. It is a daringly sustained shot, the length and lack of movement of which would be almost unimaginable in a Russell film. Its restraint is, however, characteristic of the 35 mm footage in *War Requiem* and is part of the aesthetic strategy of the film. Jarman saw Britten's oratorio, with its interweaving of Owen's poems and the Mass, as 'a collage. A cut up', and he sought to create its visual equivalent. Jarman included montages of notably graphic found footage of wars in the film, which John Maybury edited on video, as well as some scenes depicting Owen's childhood shot on Super-8. For the director, 'part of the plan [was] that the classical restraint of the 35mm film would be disrupted by the Super-8 and, particularly, the video material'.[60] The most notable of these 'disruptions' occurs during the final third of the film. The first, which plays over Britten's setting of Owen's poem 'The End', features grainy black and white footage mainly derived from the two world wars. It is slowly obscured by superimposed images of fire. The second, a 7-minute assemblage accompanying the 'Libera Me' section of the Mass, is effectively the climax of the film, and as Jarman describes it in his script,

> It is at this moment that we bring our documentary footage right up to the present – a montage of footage from the Sahel, Cambodia; all the wars that have erupted since Britten composed this music [. . .] The final image is of the atom bomb exploding on Hiroshima.[61]

The pervasive mood of these sequences, especially the second one, is violence. Violence in terms of content, certainly, as brutal images of combat injuries, suffering and mass destruction accompany some of Britten's most challenging music. Beyond this, however, Jarman and Maybury's montage is also aesthetically violent.

If these deliberately disruptive sequences have a direct antecedent in British film, it is the 'Land of Hope and Glory' montage in Russell's *Elgar*, which shows an abrupt and bitterly ironic switch from jingoistic footage of soldiers marching in parades to footage shot in the trenches. Jarman takes things even further, however. The juxtaposition of different film stocks, colours and grains is deliberately jarring and clashes with the carefully lit chiaroscuro of the 35 mm footage that bookends the sequence. By electing to cut these montages using the latest video-editing technology, rather than on celluloid like the rest of the film, Jarman and Maybury were able to edit with incredible precision and rapidity, with two sections employing near-subliminal cuts. In these moments Jarman gives the composed film a contemporary feel by bringing to the genre the vocabulary of the music video (a form which Jarman helped to establish through his collaborations with Marianne Faithfull, The Smiths and Pet Shop Boys, among others). Jarman's montage of atrocities makes Russell's segue into war footage in *Elgar* seem subtle and restrained. Rather, he comes closer to the deliberate shock tactics that Russell employs in *The Devils*, or his most overtly Brechtian work, *Dance of the Seven Veils*. Russell once said that he, like Brecht, wanted 'to shock people into awareness'.[62] Jarman does just this. By being confronted with real footage of violence and death, the audience are no longer able passively to consume the work and view it as 'only a movie'.

With *War Requiem*, Jarman created something that Russell was sadly never able to: a through-composed feature film. Russell's knowledge of classical music and opera was arguably unparalleled in British cinema. Jarman recalled that the conductor Riccardo Chailly, when collaborating with Russell on a 1982 production of Igor Stravinsky's *The Rake's Progress* in Florence (which Jarman designed), 'often stop[ped] orchestral rehearsals to ask Ken's opinion and act[] on it'.[63] Moreover, as Norman Lebrecht recalls,

Klaus Tennstedt, the most instinctual Mahler conductor I have known, called [Russell's *Mahler*] the best film he had ever seen about music and watched it over and over again. When opera houses asked him to conduct Strauss, he named Ken as his preferred director. When they refused – on grounds of Ken's turbulence and notoriety – so did Klaus. They never worked together, but they met several times and enjoyed each other's company.[64]

Indeed, the closest Russell ever got to making a full-length opera film was *Tommy*. And the nearest he came to creating a complete orchestral work was the 1983 ITV television film of Holst's *The Planets* (made for *The Southbank Show* and a relatively minor work which contained no original footage shot by Russell). An examination of Boyd's archives in the Bill Douglas Centre demonstrates that Russell was, however, keen to make a feature-length composed film.[65] In fact, among the projects Boyd touted to Decca were potential collaborations with Russell on a film of Richard Wagner's *Tristan und Isolde* and a full-length visualisation of Hector Berlioz's Symphonie Fantastique.

Letters in the archive indicate that executives at Decca were reluctant to work with Russell, and this is quite telling. Jarman, after all, was hardly uncontroversial. Even with prominent conductors like Chailly and Tennstedt complimenting Russell's films and his knowledge of classical music, it seems that Russell's reputation as a 'difficult' film-maker was by this point so great as to be insurmountable for many potential backers. Both *The Debussy Film* and *Dance of the Seven Veils* incurred the wrath of the Debussy and Strauss estates, a fact that did not make a collaboration with Russell an attractive proposition for a record company like Decca. While the prospect of a Ken Russell film of *Tristan und Isolde* is tantalising to say the least, one can understand why the executives at Decca would be wary of any association with such a project. Russell's notoriety certainly deprived him of the chance to make more than a few films, but it is worth noting that it is this same reputation that enticed a fellow iconoclast like Jarman to work with him. Russell created a space in British cinema for film-makers like Peter Greenaway, Alex Cox, Sally Potter, Simon Rumley and Ben Wheatley, directors who also take the more challenging route. But it is with Jarman that Russell shares the closest kinship, for Jarman initially learnt the art of film-making from Russell. As has been seen, in his subsequent career Jarman often built on his early mentor's unique approach. The pair were more than just mentor and pupil or collaborators, however. They were idiosyncratic, singular artists whose oeuvres, despite some notable differences in the approach and scale of their work, are mutually illuminating. It also goes without saying that Russell and Jarman shared a stubborn determination to cock a snook at the established conventions of British cinema. And in this they both succeeded brilliantly.

NOTES

1. Michael Brooke, 'Ken Russell on Television', *BFI Screenonline*, 2014, <http://www.screenonline.org.uk/tv/id/1030140/index.html> (last accessed 30 July 2021).
2. Henry K. Miller, 'Slade Film School: The Department That Was Nearly a Movement', *Guardian*, 28 January 2011, <https://www.theguardian.com/film/filmblog/2011/jan/28/slade-film-school-studies-ucl> (last accessed 30 July 2021).
3. Tony Peake, *Derek Jarman* (London: Little, Brown, 1999), 113.
4. Ibid.
5. Ibid.
6. Tony Rayns, 'The Devils', in Tom Milne (ed.), *The Time Out Film Guide* (Harlow: Longman, 1989), 522.
7. Alex Cox, 'This is Indecent', *Guardian*, 19 February 2004, <https://www.theguardian.com/film/2004/feb/19/2> (last accessed 30 July 2021).
8. Derek Jarman, *Dancing Ledge* (London: Quartet Books, 1984), 186.
9. Ibid., 100.
10. Ibid.
11. John Baxter, *Ken Russell: An Appalling Talent* (London: Michael Joseph, 1973), 206–7.
12. Jarman, *Dancing Ledge*, 100.
13. Stuart Jeffries, 'Ken Russell: The Last Fires of Film's Old Devil', *Guardian*, 28 April 2011, <https://www.theguardian.com/film/2011/apr/28/ken-russell-the-devils> (last accessed 30 July 2021).
14. Rowland Wymer, 'Derek Jarman's Renaissance and *The Devils*', *Shakespeare Quarterly*, vol. 32, no. 3, Fall 2014, 342.
15. Derek Jarman, *Queer Edward II* (London: BFI Publishing, 1992), 86.
16. Ibid., 196.
17. Jarman, *Dancing Ledge*, 104.
18. Ibid., 105.
19. Ibid.
20. Rowland Wymer, *Derek Jarman* (Manchester: Manchester University Press, 2005), 25.
21. Jarman, *Dancing Ledge*, 105.
22. Jonathan Hacker and David Price, *Take Ten: Contemporary British Filmmakers* (London: Clarendon Press, 1991), 249.
23. Jarman, *Dancing Ledge*, 105.
24. Wymer, 'Derek Jarman's Renaissance and *The Devils*', 340.
25. Peake, 175.
26. Linda Ruth Williams, 'Sweet Smell of Excess', *Sight and Sound*, July 2007, <http://old.bfi.org.uk/sightandsound/feature/49385> (last accessed 27 February 2022).
27. Ken Hanke, *Ken Russell's Films* (Metuchen, NJ: Scarecrow Press, 1984), 199.
28. Ibid., 200.
29. Ibid.
30. Joseph A. Gomez, *Ken Russell: The Adaptor as Creator* (London: Frederick Muller, 1976), 175.
31. Hanke, 200.
32. Peake, 174.
33. Ibid.
34. Derek Jarman, *The Last of England* (London: Constable, 1987), 163.
35. Peake, 208.
36. Wymer, *Derek Jarman*, 40.
37. Edward Norman, *Religious Symbolism in British Film: Derek Jarman* (York: York Minster, 2004), unpaginated.

38. Ibid.
39. Ibid.
40. Ibid.
41. Ibid.
42. Ibid.
43. Tilda Swinton, 'In the Spirit of Derek Jarman', *Vertigo*, vol. 2, no. 4, Spring 2003, <https://www.closeupfilmcentre.com/vertigo_magazine/volume-2-issue-4-spring-2003/tilda-swinton-in-the-spirit-of-derek-jarman/> (last accessed 30 July 2021).
44. Gene D. Phillips, *Ken Russell* (Boston: Twayne, 1979).
45. Deal Hudson, 'Ken Russell's *The Devils* is Badly Misunderstood', *Catholic Herald*, 7 February 2019, <https://catholicherald.co.uk/ken-russells-the-devils-is-badly-misunderstood/> (last accessed 30 July 2021).
46. Ibid.
47. Gomez, 194.
48. Ibid.
49. Hanke, 253.
50. Norman, n.p.
51. Gomez, 89.
52. Dennis Bingham, *Whose Lives Are They Anyway? The Biopic as Contemporary Film Genre* (New Brunswick, NJ: Rutgers University Press), 3.
53. Ibid.
54. Gomez, 35.
55. Stefan Kanfer, 'Cinema: False Notes', *Time*, 8 February 1971, para. 6, <http://content.time.com/time/subscriber/article/0,33009,909849,00.html> (last accessed 15 October 2021).
56. Bill Douglas Centre, Don Boyd, 'Letter to Michael Kustow of Channel Four', 4 January 1988, box DB093.
57. Bill Douglas Centre, Draft Clause 9, Contract with Boosey and Hawks, 30 September 1988, box DB082.
58. BBC Written Archives Centre, 'Programme Budget Estimate, Omnibus: Richard Strauss', T53/159/1.
59. Bill Douglas Centre, Don Boyd, 'On Set Diary for *War Requiem*', 20 October 1988, box DB084.
60. Quoted in Wymer, *Derek Jarman*, 126.
61. Derek Jarman, *War Requiem* (London: Faber and Faber, 1989), 41.
62. Briton Hadden, 'Director in a Kaftan', *Time*, vol. 98, nos. 10–17, 53.
63. Jarman, *Dancing Ledge*, 224.
64. Norman Lebrecht, 'Ken Russell and Mahler: Fragments of a Conversation', *Slipped Disc*, 28 November 2011, <https://slippedisc.com/2011/11/ken-and-mahler-fragments-of-conversation/> (last accessed 15 October 2021).
65. Bill Douglas Centre, box DB093.

CHAPTER 9

The Hermeneutics of Noise: The Sounds of Salvation in Ken Russell's *Tommy*

K. A. Laity

INTRODUCTION: A STRANGE VIBRATION LAND

Ken Russell's 1975 film of The Who's rock opera *Tommy* (Columbia, 1975) is among the best known of his films, celebrated both for its music as well as for its daring phantasmagoric spectacle. While the former has been entirely attributed to the band (especially guitarist and writer Pete Townshend), the symbiosis between the film-maker and the music-makers is much richer than may be apparent at first viewing. Far too much of film criticism still focuses on narrative, acting and visuals whilst neglecting the importance of sound, and as Rick Altman has argued, the theoreticians who overlook sound usually do so quite self-consciously, proposing what they consider strong arguments in favour of an 'image-based notion of cinema'.[1] With Russell's visual pyrotechnics this is perhaps an excusable point of view, but a careful examination of the narrative and extra-narrative sound will demonstrate how Russell's film not only presents the story of *Tommy* as Townshend and The Who did musically, but also adds an additional rhetorical flourish to the aural aspects of this tale of enlightenment gained through the unlikely medium of pinball.

The initial impact of the film on most viewers is of an ecstatic and overpowering visual stimulus. In reviewing the film, thirty-five years after it was released, the late critic Ken Hanke argued that 'No one had seen anything like it. Remember this is pre-MTV. In fact, for good or ill, Ken Russell and *Tommy* may be viewed as having largely spawned MTV.'[2] The fast cuts and technological sound innovation were enough to prompt the young critic to pursue all of Russell's films and eventually write one of the key studies of the oeuvre. Even in 1984 Hanke could see that the spectacle of *Tommy* (as well as Russell's other films) would prove inspirational, and that the world of popular music was the first to grasp its visual immediacy, causing him to note, 'There are more pirated images from *Tommy* than can be comfortably counted, all drenched in pseudo-Russell symbols that, in this usage, are devoid of all meaning.'[3] The intoxicating mix of rock music's power and opera's larger-than-life theatrics could be seen as inspiring similar works, from Pink Floyd's dystopic *The Wall* (1982) right up to the recent smash, the irresistible rap-fuelled musical *Hamilton* (Lin-Manuel Miranda, 2015).

The hallucinatory visuals of the rock opera, of course, intend to provide the viewer with a transcendent experience, mimicking the drug-fuelled catharsis associated with the era's rock music. For example, Alan Parker's 1982 film adaptation of Pink Floyd's *The Wall* (Goldcrest International/MGM/Tinblue) would adapt this practice to evoke the mental disintegration of the burnt-out protagonist. However, the sound design (from a team headed by Iain Bruce, who also worked on Russell's *Mahler* [Goodtimes Enterprises, 1974] and *Lisztomania* [Goodtimes Enterprises, 1975]) gives a tangible grounding in reality that for the viewer, who is able to survive the ecstatic experience and to incorporate it in the literal sense, becomes a part of them in the 'strange vibration land' of their surroundings – the movie (or home) theatre. It also offers the chance of individual transcendence, via the holistic relationship of sound, music and image (in key sequences such as the 'Acid Queen' sequence, or as this chapter will examine, the 'Amazing Journey' sequence), that becomes replayable with the music even without the visual assault.

Nina Sun Eidsheim argues that 'We have come to the formulation that music is the practice of vibration', and that since music is formed from vibrations, there are multitudes of material circumstances and variables that contribute to each of its articulations, each unrepeatable and unique.[4] While the casual filmgoer may not intend to scale Russell and Townshend's intended heights of awareness ('My name is Tommy and I became aware this year'), affected only by what Anahid Kassabian calls 'ubiquitous listening',[5] it is still true that this 'kind of diffuse and unintentional hearing nonetheless structures the acoustic unconscious', as Deborah Kapchan argues (drawing comparisons with the effect of shopping mall 'muzak').[6] In other words, we are affected by sounds we don't consciously notice.

In *Tommy* this effect is intentional. As Rick Altman reminds us, 'recordings do not reproduce sound, they represent sound', that is, a repetition of the original performance is reproduced via the playback technology (be it on vinyl, CD, streaming or cassette).[7] While the complicated and innovative technical side of the recording aimed to reproduce The Who's live experience, the soundtrack accompanying the film represented the broader sound of the immersive transformation central to the film's narrative. 'Your senses will never be the same': not just a tagline but a promise. While Russell has long been acknowledged as an innovator of arresting visual power, he also pushed at the boundaries of sound in both the technical and sensory arenas, in recognition of which the Cannes Film Festival gave *Mahler* the award for Best Technical Achievement.[8] *Tommy*'s sensory surround-sound assault of pioneering Quintaphonic sound also broke new ground and provided the prototype for the now ubiquitous Dolby sound in cinemas, as Robert Heiber notes:

> The wizardry of *Tommy* extends beyond director Ken Russell's imaginative visuals and The Who's rock opera score for the distinction of introducing Quintaphonic Sound theatrically . . . Quintaphonic sound, however, was extremely short-lived because of the simultaneous development of Dolby® stereo. Unlike Dolby® stereo tracks, which could be recorded optically on motion picture prints, the Quintaphonic soundtrack was recorded on expensive 35mm magnetic-striped prints. Thus TOMMY was the only film to be exhibited theatrically in 5-channel Quintaphonic sound.[9]

'HE PLAYS BY INTUITION . . . HE PLAYS BY SENSE OF SMELL'

To properly convey the subjective experience of the deaf, dumb and blind boy Tommy (Barry Winch), Russell immerses the audience within a disorienting soundscape. In her article 'Re-orienting Sound Studies' Aural Fixation', Sarah Mayberry Scott notes that 'Julian Henriques coined the term *sonic dominance* to refer to sound that is not just heard but that "pervades, or even invades the body".'[10] This experience renders sound experience as tactile and felt within the body itself. Anne Cranny-Francis describes the intimate relationship between hearing and sound, believing that 'sound literally touches us'.[11] This process of listening is described as an embodied experience that is 'intimate' and 'visceral', which Steph Ceraso calls 'multi-modal listening'.[12] The audience of *Tommy* is thrust into a multi-modal listening experience that uses all the senses. They may not process the input in traditional ways, but they are immersed within its onslaught. This finds parallel in Tommy's pinball fixation: the sound and visuals of the pinball machines that are accessible to the viewer are denied to Tommy; instead, the sensory experience of pinball, one must assume, enters his physical body in the form of vibrations. Deaf, dumb and blind he may be, but his heightened tactile senses remain.

In his writing on acoustic palimpsests, J. Martin Daughtry notes that 'in all but the most clinical of circumstances, we are confronted by sound that emanates from multiple sources'.[13] Though we might wish to drown out the sounds of our morning commute with headphones, the sounds are still there. Conscious or not, we experience this multi-modal listening in layers. We may focus on the music, though part of us listens for the train, too, or the possibility of escalation in a conversation or argument nearby. As Daughtry argues, 'these moments of layered listening are easy to disregard because they are ubiquitous, ephemeral, largely unconscious, and relatively benign'.[14] However, as Russell demonstrates in the sound design of this film, they can be organized to enhance that unconscious experience to a significant degree.

Tommy offers opportunities for 'layered listening'; it's not required but the experience is there and inviting to the filmgoer. For the teenage fan of The Who listening anew to the experience that had previously been just an ever-changing kaleidoscope of images in their own brain, the film offers a fixed sequence of images with a new, more fully orchestrated sound that, while stable in terms of being a consistent soundtrack, offers a new palimpsest with each viewing (as Daughtry argues). The sonic context is ever changing. Hearing it for the first time is different from hearing it the second; hearing it in a crowded theatre is different from hearing it in an empty one. Hearing it on videotape in the 1980s is different from the full home theatre experience in the twenty-first century.

A firm believer in the magic powers of music himself, Ken Russell makes clear in the interview included in the bonus disc of the limited-edition DVD that he's aware of the potentiality of this rich symbiosis: 'I find with the right music and the right image; I realise the power that cinema could become . . . finding an amazing image and putting it with some amazing music.'[15] That power offers a transcendent experience for the filmgoer who may be there only to glimpse the rock opera brought to life with no intention of having a spiritual or emotional transformation. However, the powerful experience of the spectacle will dazzle all but the most obtuse viewer, who may be unable to comprehend the experience without some prior knowledge or understanding of hermeneutics.

HERMENEUTICS: *TOMMY* AND THE 'AMAZING JOURNEY'

In the deftest terms we can define hermeneutics, as the Stanford Encyclopedia of Philosophy does, as 'a toolbox for efficiently treating problems of the interpretation of human actions, texts and other meaningful material'.[16] Intertwined for millennia with the practice of biblical exegesis, we most often think of it in terms of religious discourse, interpreting texts or actions as analogies of biblical stories or lessons. In a broader sense, as applied here, it is a way of unpacking the plethora of signifiers in the rich multi-modal experience of an extraordinary film like *Tommy*, particularly in terms of its sound design (as argued in this chapter).

Sound has long been a method for transcending mundane experience. In one of the oldest texts in existence, *The Descent of Inanna* (5,500 years old), the goddess asks her confidant Ninshubur to have the women beat the drums to help her return from the underworld.[17] Religious chanting is well known for its mental effects, as sober scientific investigations have demonstrated.[18] The power of sound across space and time has proved much more than the entertainment or irritant we often reduce it to, though we seldom think about the impact it has, nor about how to interpret the performances or accidents we experience. We are used to interpreting *the word*, but we are often less sure on interpreting *the sound*. And yet sound is so powerful and pervasive, on a physical level as well as a cognitive level, and its impact can be profound. As the late Pauline Oliveros, a true hermeneutical music pioneer, put it, 'I am also interested in music expanding consciousness. By expanding consciousness, I mean that old patterns can be replaced with new ones', a practice she started on her own body:[19] 'I noticed that I could change my emotional state by concentrating my attention on a tone.'[20] Whether you look at the possibility of transformative sound from a mystical side or a practical one, the opportunity is there for real change as vibrations invade the physical body.

I wish here to offer an analysis of *Tommy*, in order to present a hermeneutic study of the alchemy of sound, focusing particularly on the 'Amazing Journey', which I argue is the first moment of true transcendence in the film; the moment the movie separates from the mimetic to the allegorical and even (if you are of that kind of mind) the mystical. Although hints of the mystical appear prior to that point, the film's central narrative is rather straightforward, though of course with all the dazzling visual brilliance you'd expect from a Ken Russell film. While reality may be heightened and occasionally slightly bizarre, counterintuitive and cognitively dissonant (e.g. sequined dancers cavorting through the bombed-out city in dull green gas masks), it is nonetheless recognisably 'real' (as far as movie reality goes).

The 'Amazing Journey', as the title suggests, takes Tommy and the audience beyond the realm of the 'real', that is, the shared material world, into a dimension that reflects the boy's interior experience. This sequence reflects the expansion of the boy's (cultural) consciousness through shared imagery which he interprets to make sense of his own psychic trauma after the violent and bloody death of his father (and its equally impassioned cover-up by his mother and new stepfather). As the lyrics make clear ('Come on the amazing journey / and learn all you should know'), it's a learning experience for the boy, of course, but also for the audience, too. They need to grasp how the words and the sound work with the visuals to transform Tommy's psychic break into an experience the audience can vicariously share with all the verisimilitude the sound effects.

In her ground-breaking work *The Skin of the Film*, Laura U. Marks argues (building on the work of Benjamin and Deleuze) that 'cinema can be the site of new configurations of sense knowledge, produced in (or in spite of) the encounter between different cultures', particularly when dealing with loss and the memories (often beyond words or images) that films can provoke by awakening that lost knowledge.[21] Haptic film experience invites the audience to evoke those sense memories (and few bodies of film could match Russell's own for immersing the audience into a fantastic feast of sensual pleasures and horrors – one need only look to *The Devils* [Warner Bros., 1971] or even *The Music Lovers* [United Artists, 1970] for other examples of this). Current film-makers like Nicolas Winding Refn (see Adam Powell's chapter in this volume) and Anna Biller have followed in his vivid visual tradition, while the exquisite sound design of film-makers like Peter Strickland and Bong Joon-Ho demonstrates how powerful that sense remains.

The one dimension of film-making that Marks doesn't much dwell on, however, is sound, though she pauses to imagine what haptic sound might be. One might call 'haptic hearing' that usually brief moment when all sounds present themselves to us undifferentiated before we make the (unconscious or conscious) choice of which sounds are most important to attend to. In some environments the experience of haptic hearing can be sustained for longer, before the specific sounds focus our attention: quiet environments like walking the woods and lying in bed in the morning, or overwhelmingly loud ones in a nightclub dance floor or a construction site. In these settings the aural boundaries between body and world may feel indistinct.[22]

This is the experience of *Tommy*. It is an overwhelmingly *loud* experience (like The Band's *The Last Waltz* [Martin Scorsese, FM Productions, 1978], which opens on a title card stating, 'This film should be played loud!'), but it is also an immersive and almost undifferentiated experience where music, lyrics and images all assault the senses at once, claiming equal prominence. While this might be said of all of Russell's films, the difference with *Tommy* is the familiarity of the rock idiom. Classical music retains, for many, a sense of awe, which is reflected across Russell's composer films. Rock music is the people's music, and a form of music of which Russell was, at least publicly, sceptical. Certainly, it can lose that sense of being demotic with the ambitiousness of progressive rock or the empty capitalistic nihilism of arena shows, but it's a form of music meant to hit at a visceral level. As Townshend says in a 1960s interview captured in The Who's retrospective *The Kids Are Alright* (Jeff Stein, The Who Films, 1979),

> You have to resign yourself to the fact that a large part of the audience is sort of thick, you know, and don't appreciate quality however much you put it over. The fact that our group hasn't got any quality. It's just musical sensationalism. You do something big on the stage and a thousand geezers sort of go, 'Ah!' It's just basic Shepherds Bush enjoyment.

Townshend clearly developed higher ambitions than just 'musical sensationalism' but that doesn't mean he ever abandoned that quality in the work, especially the rock operas, not only *Tommy* but the difficult to realise *Lifehouse* and 1973's *Quadrophenia*. That sensationalism won Russell over to the 'dark side' of rock music away from his classical loves. Kit Power sums up the meeting of Russell and Townshend, which happened while the band was recording 'Drowned' from *Quadrophenia* during a storm that managed to fill the studio piano booth: '*The composer's arts*, Ken thinks. *The dark and the divine.*'[23]

The dark and the divine are just what *Tommy* offers, achieved through a combination of technical expertise and extraordinary vision: the technical side includes the team of sound designers headed by Iain Bruce, and the vision encompasses both Pete Townshend's narrative tale of transcendence and Russell's visual mastery. It is easy to imagine that the technicians were interested primarily in the problems of conveying the new Quintaphonic surround sound. 'We believed in sprockets', music editor Terry Rawlings says on *The Story of the Sound* documentary on the bonus disc. The process involved a lot of unexpected problems and technical challenges. Rawlings describes the complex set up: 'Main desk where Bill [Rowe] and Ray were, desk in the middle . . . desk in front of that Pete . . .' Not only were there many inputs, but the recording levels were incredibly loud. Ray Merrin, dubbing mixer, shares a story about Lindsay Anderson in the dubbing studio next door complaining, causing them to work at night. After three months mixing the Quintaphonic soundtrack, Rawlings says, 'You had to leave it for two weeks until your ears unwound so that you could do the scaled down versions' necessary for theatres not capable of playing the complicated original soundtrack.[24]

Central to that extraordinary experience is the song that embodies the emotional lynchpin of the film. The 'Amazing Journey' sequence begins immediately after the murder, and the assault on the boy's consciousness ensures that 'he didn't hear it, didn't see it, won't say nothing to nobody ever in his life what he knows is the truth'. It establishes not only the postlapsarian sequence of his young life but the birth of a self-consciousness that was not previously apparent, even as his parents attempt to control that sense of self and make him (even visually) one part of a 'whole' family. The family, of course, is too fractured to be whole.

In an almost literal embodiment of the Lacanian mirror stage, Tommy becomes aware of the past as well as the present as something in which he exists and existed, as well as choosing which elements to savour as a balm to his wounded psyche (the kindly father sharing his cockpit), dissociating from the sensory input around him as needed (and indeed as demanded by his mother and father surrogate). The film expands upon this notion by showing Tommy's mirror stage as also a moment of traumatic splintering, later literalised into the disparate, colour-coded self-images. Conflicting impulses respond to the trauma: his reflection when isolated is quickly distorted, but it is more often splintered into many possible selves, all little dancing Tommies. As Lacan has written,

> The mirror stage is a drama whose internal pressure pushes precipitously from insufficiency to anticipation – and for the subject caught up in the lure of spatial identification, turns out fantasies that proceed from a fragmented image of the body to what I will call an 'orthopedic' form of its totality.[25]

Tommy, however, remains for some time within that fragmented image in the mirror (Figure 9.1).

If you compare the soundtrack version of the song with the original LP, the difference is plain. The original is subdued, almost demo-like, and there are almost no drums or bass until a minute in, drummer Keith Moon playing at first with great restraint, unlike his usual style. Townshend argues that the pop song was 'designed' to deliver spiritual messages: 'Good pop at its best frees the spirit.'[26] But there were changes: as Moon later said, 'It was, at the time, very un-Wholike. A lot of the songs were soft. We never played like that.'[27] On the original recording Moon's drums end up being the most emphatic part of the track, which is mostly acoustic guitar enhanced by flourishes of synthesised embellishments. Roger Daltrey's double-tracked vocals are likewise restrained and must negotiate a somewhat awkward transition from third person narration to the first person experience of the messiah figure who leads the boy to his awakening. John Entwistle's usual bass flourishes are noticeably absent.

Figure 9.1 Young Tommy in the mirror.
Source: Columbia, 1975.

The spiritual guide described is much more like a kind of Gandalf figure than a uniformed Captain Walker or even Townshend's own spiritual guru, Meher Baba. Given the popularity of *The Lord of the Rings* after its publication in paperbacks in 1965 (even the Beatles were rumoured to have been exploring plans to make a film of the books), this is not too surprising: the lyrics refer to the glitter and sparkle of the robes he wears, that his beard shines as gold, flowing nearly the length of his body. However, such an image would have matched poorly with the largely mimetic world of the film. While fantastic things may happen, they all happen within the realm of the real.

The soundtrack took three months to record prior to filming. Russell was there every day, adding to the ambience in direct and indirect ways. Gone are the restrained vocals, charged by the phantasmagoria of images accompanying the 'Amazing Journey', which is, as The Amboy Dukes would put it, a journey to the centre of your mind (or rather Tommy's mind). Visually the sequence begins with Tommy and then the family emerging from the darkness of a brick tunnel, all dressed in matching clothes, an ironic counterpoint to the family now irretrievably ripped apart (Figure 9.2). As much as the exhortations not to see, hear or speak about what has happened, Tommy's parents impose their will upon the silent child even through the very clothes they wear, cut from the same cloth.

As Kit Power argues in his volume on the film, on the face of it, for this 'brutalized' kid, 'injury is shown to be the catalyst, the key, to Tommy's spiritual enlightenment. And that is, if you'll pardon the expression, pretty fucking gross.'[28] However, that's not how it works out. Power is right to point to how

Figure 9.2 The family.
Source: Columbia, 1975.

much Russell changes the song and how his film embodies the changes to make sure that this is *not* the conclusion we draw. The changed lyrics become an accusation: 'The guilty are safe, but always accused by his empty eyes . . .' For Power, this sequence and Tommy's delirium capture 'a kind of mass PTSD'.[29] The use of a funfair is not to demonstrate the exhilaration of spiritual enlightenment but 'Delirium masquerading as Delight', and it turns out to be 'fundamentally disorienting, nauseating, terrifying place'.[30] Like many spiritual breakthroughs, it's awful and completely harrowing, something he has to get through, and only the first of his breakthroughs.

In tracing the history of labyrinths, Penelope Reed Doob follows the roots of 'amazing' back to Old and Middle English where *mase* had meant a 'difficult process, annoyance, confusion',[31] though by the thirteenth century 'amased' had gathered a clearer sense of disorientation, being 'out of one's mind, irrational, foolish', according to the *Middle English Dictionary*.[32] The song and this sequence fit much more clearly into this historical sense of 'amazement' than the more modern way of using it as acclaim. For those who enter a labyrinth, it is easy to get lost, to become disoriented, and even terrified.

The soundtrack music offers a rich pageant of synthesiser sounds in counterpoint to the grim determination showed by the doggedly walking family. Power likens the parents to prison guards marching the child along, suggesting a parallel to the unenlightened seeker who needs to break free of the material world. Townshend's vocals assert the truths of the narrative: 'Now he is deaf, now he is dumb, now he is blind.' While the audience may focus on what has been lost, as a journey of transcendence, it is the first step to recognise that spiritual state. Simple vocals over a sustained organ chord evoke a memory of churches (usually considered the locus of spiritual experience), then some light percussion and the presence of the horns punctuate the music. The narrative voice keeps to the third person narration while the visuals allow us to experience Tommy's new isolation, echoed by the horn line soaring above the layer of synth. The sensory deprivation the lyrics suggest is at first amplified by the tunnel in which they walk, though as their colourful matching attire hints, we are about to be overwhelmed by sensory input that Tommy can no longer access. The seeming mise en abyme of the tunnel behind them, punctuated by a regular sequence of lights in the darkness, presages the later scene in which the mirror's infinite regressions will bring together all the fractured images of Tommy, colour-coded by the traumas he has endured. Indeed, both visuals and audio at this moment take on a carnivalesque flight into the baroque. Just as the opening scenes of the film rewind Russell's own traumatic experiences during the Blitz, the surreal is linked to a strange but real experience. Likewise, Townshend has spoken of recycling his own childhood sexual abuse memories in the experiences Tommy later undergoes as one of the splintered, colour-coded aspects of his character.

The synthesiser soars into wild churning swoops of sound, mirroring the funfair imagery that next fills the screen. The energy reflects the bright lights, mirror ball and swift movements of the funfair rides, swirling before our eyes, matching the movement of the sound in ironic counterpoint to the empty eyes and unhearing ears of Tommy. Mechanical fun endured with a mechanical expression.

The images cut between the family at the fair and the wide-open universe in which we get a hint of the opening worlds of Tommy's imagination. His physical senses have shut down, but his psychological vistas have blasted open. Whilst he remains outwardly unchanging, all the sensory input births a new, dream-like universe. The mirror ball repeats in images like planets hurtling through the galaxies, blending with the flashing lights of the carnival rides against a background of stars. The original lyrics present the messiah-like figure appearing to lead the boy to enlightenment through a hazy delirium that flows upon him until he is confronted by a strange, tall figure without warning.

The film, however, offers a much more familiar solution: not the bearded sage but the dead father returning to lead the boy on his 'Amazing Journey', both of them in the cockpit of his fighter plane. Tommy's face (immobile in the funfair shots) shows animation and emotion as he rides the aeroplane with his father. The overdubbed vocals on the repeated refrain 'Sickness will surely take the mind / where minds don't usually go' parallel this opening up of space, as if a choir now sings (Townshend's own vocals reverberating). The image and the sound together suggest a multiplicity of experiences even though we focus only on the boy Tommy. The path to enlightenment is one that is shared even if we cannot see others from our occluded perspective. Tommy, now seeing beyond the fallible physical senses, glimpses a transcendent guide who can lead him through amazing experiences to an eventual return to psychological or psychic wholeness.

The music continues to soar and swirl as the vocals parallel it with the lyrics 'soaring and flying images spin' (as does the camera around the Ferris wheel), reiterating 'he is your leader, he is your guide' for this amazing journey and, most importantly, 'together you'll ride': the isolated boy is no longer alone. His lost senses may remain lost, but the lost father is returned to him and to him alone. The privileged position of the silenced, blinded boy is now assured. Visually the mimetic scene (albeit realistic yet disorienting as 'soaring and flying images spin') gives way as the camera cuts to the arcade game graphics. Continuity comes through the thematic elements: the father's cockpit gives way to the phalanx of drawn and animated fighter plane images, repeated as they are shot at and sometimes shot down, as well as, of course, the music.

For the first time since the sequence began, we have the presence of potentially diegetic sound, as the music mimics the sound of the arcade machine gun that Uncle Frank helps Tommy shoot, even though the boy continues to stare

THE HERMENEUTICS OF NOISE 191

blankly ahead. As the scene continues, however, the certainty of the noise being diegetic fades as there appears to be a rupture in the synchronisation of action and sound. This mirrors the rupture between the couple as Ann-Margret's Nora stalks away and Oliver Reed's Frank continues to mouth the rat-a-tat-tat sounds of the machine gun even though it no longer appears to be shooting. There's a powerful collision of visual and aural cues. Things being not what they seem becomes the norm for this amazing journey.

The power of the overlaid sound of the artillery gun mirrors the aesthetic mix of the military, father, saviour and sacrifice that provides the heady whirling centre of the psychological drama. Just as the planes become crosses and later the crosses become the iconic pinball-topped Ts, the acoustic mix overlies the disparate layers of reality and fantasy: the reality of the fantasy carnival rides; the fantasy of the father's return after the tragic reality of the father's unexpected return; the reality of the aeroplanes as engines of his supposed death; the gun as a fantasy representation of the very real death; the fantasy of the arcade machine gun and its very real sound. It is striking that the real sound of Captain Walker's death comes from a lamp, a metaphor for enlightenment.

When both adults abandon Tommy at the arcade pinball game, Nora to sullenly contemplate her own wretched position, Frank to play a one-armed bandit, the synthesiser swirls continue, and though we can immediately imagine the sound to be coming from the fruit machine, there is no diegetic sound to accompany it. Tommy wanders off, lost, and the scene cuts from the realistic fantasy park to the metaphoric representation of the boy in the black box as the swooping synthesiser is augmented by the grounding sound of the acoustic guitar strumming. We cut back to the sightless boy staring (initially upside down, once again disorienting) at his reflection in the comic arcade mirror, his head suddenly enlarged beyond the size of the sensory-deprivation box in the previous shot (as if to suggest the growing size of the thoughts within), and Townshend's solo vocal soars as he holds the note on 'know' just as the camera turns to regard Tommy in a close-up that quickly moves to extreme and in through his eye, which in turn gives way to his father holding the sun disc standing atop a peak in the Lake District. Round mirror, round pupil, round camera iris, round sun.[33]

Townshend's vocals are once more overdubbed to give emphasis to the truth he conveys: 'his eyes are the eyes that transmit all they know'. This truth gets overlooked because only the mirror (and the audience) looks into his eyes. The urgency of the vocals rises as the shot tracks into the disc of light, and the overlay of drums pounds home the realisation before the light fills our eyes and the screen with its truth, 'a white sun burning the earth and the sky', as the lyrics tell us. While the image of the father with the sun disc is clearly metaphoric, it is rendered as mimetic, so the flash at the end of the sequence allows us to make the transition with the end of the vocal sequence and a break in the drumming, before it picks up again with the images of the cross-like aeroplanes that seem to have escaped from the arcade game into the universe in Tommy's mind to fly against a background of stars.

As the bouncing pinball turns the planes into the familiar Remembrance Day, red poppy-bedecked crosses (Figure 9.3), there's an illusion of diegetic sound as cymbal crashes often match up with the impact and transition.

But once the pattern is established, it gets abandoned. Russell expects our minds to follow the patterns quickly, to learn, remember and be enlightened as the music makes the circuits connect. A hail of drum blows signals the link: Captain Walker as a Christ figure laid out on the bomber plane, before the pinball strikes him too, and completes the final transformation into the pinball-topped T complete with unnerving, potentially seizure-inducing, flashing. Father becomes son as the synthesiser returns to a top note like a pageant blare against the flashing lights that assault the eyes. As the camera moves in, the pinball splits like a zygote, cleaved to reveal in duplicate the happy face of Tommy, first regarding himself, then the audience as the half-spheres open. The synthesiser swoops up and down, mirroring the buoyant mood as the two Tommies become one, and we zoom in yet again on the eye that 'transmits all it knows' and which we are receiving: the pupil full of multiple images of Tommy dancing joyfully at the recognition of finding his place in the universe. The music's crescendo is reached, and the pace finally slows as we pull back out to see the actual Tommy dancing before the mirrors. When he stops, the music stops too. The ecstasy arises from the vision granted, but it is, as always, fleeting.

The discordant sounds that start up as he confronts his mother's tears and Frank's scepticism reflect that his eyes may transmit this psychological and

Figure 9.3 Fighter planes.
Source: Columbia, 1975.

spiritual epiphany but at this point Tommy appears to be the only one who looks in that mirror. The grumbling voices in the background mix turn to outright laughter as the boy turns away from reality and back to the mirror. He has had the first amazing journey towards enlightenment, but he cannot share the experience yet. It's striking that the only spoken word in the film occurs here, as Nora seeks to reach Tommy beyond both the reality of the scene and the fictional musical world established. The ache in Ann-Margret's voice as she says his name offers a resounding echo from the rift between mother and child. The mother is both victim and conspirator and finds it much more difficult to recover from the psychic trauma.

CONCLUSION

The hypnotic visuals of this haptic film offer a peak experience in multi-modal listening. The sonic dominance impressed upon the audience by the experience of 'Amazing Journey' in particular, but of course *Tommy* as a whole, rewards a layered listening opportunity that combines psychedelic visuals with a grounding, pounding aural assault that assures indeed that 'your senses will never be the same'.

NOTES

1. Rick Altman, 'Four and a Half Film Fallacies', in Jonathan Stern (ed.), *The Sound Studies Reader* (New York: Routledge, 2012), 225.
2. Ken Hanke, 'Cranky Hanke's Screening Room: Tommy: the Movie – an Appreciation', *Mountain Express*, 21 August 2010, <https://mountainx.com/movies/movie-news-previews/cranky_hankes_screening_room_itommy_i_the_movie_-_an_appreciation/> (last accessed 4 November 2021).
3. Ken Hanke, *Ken Russell's Films* (Metuchen, NJ: Scarecrow Press, 1984), 428.
4. Nina Sun Eidsheim, *Sensing Sound: Singing and Listening as Vibrational Practice* (Durham, NC: Duke University Press, 2015), 155.
5. Anahid Kassabian, *Ubiquitous Listening: Affect, Attention, and Distributed Subjectivity* (Berkeley: University of California Press, 2013), 5.
6. Deborah Kapchan, *Theorizing Sound Writing* (Middletown, CT: Wesleyan University Press, 2017), 4.
7. Altman, 229.
8. Ken Hanke, 'Mahler', *Mountain Express*, 21 April 2015, <https://mountainx.com/movies/reviews/mahler-2/> (last accessed 18 January 2021).
9. Robert Heiber, 'Tommy, Can You Hear Me? – The Quintaphonic Restoration of a "One Hit Wonder"', *AMIA Tech Review*, October 2010, <https://amianet.org/wp-content/uploads/Publication-AMIA-Tech-Review-V2-2010.pdf> (last accessed 31 May 2022).
10. Sarah Mayberry Scott, 'Re-orienting Sound Studies' Aural Fixation: Christine Sun Kim's "Subjective Loudness"', *Sounding Out*, June 2017, <https://soundstudiesblog.com/2017/06/05/re-orienting-sound-studies-aural-fixation-christine-sun-kims/> (last accessed 31 May 2022).

11. Quoted in ibid.
12. Steph Ceraso, 'The Plasticity of Listening: Deafness and Sound Studies', *Sounding Out!*, 27 February 2012, <https://soundstudiesblog.com/2012/02/27/the-plasticity-of-listening-deafness-and-sound-studies/> (last accessed 31 May 2022).
13. J. Martin Daughtry, 'Acoustic Palimpsests and the Politics of Listening', Music & Politics, vol. 7, no. 1, 2014, 54.
14. Ibid., 55.
15. Ken Russell interview, *Tommy* (2-disc special edition DVD, Prism, 2004).
16. C. Mantzavinos, 'Hermeneutics', Spring 2020, in Edward N. Zalta (ed.), *The Stanford Encyclopedia of Philosophy*, <https://plato.stanford.edu/archives/spr2020/entries/hermeneutics/> (last accessed 28 February 2022).
17. Diane Wolkstein, Samuel Noah Kramer and Elizabeth Williams-Fort, *Inanna, Queen of Heaven and Earth* (New York: Harper & Row, 2004), 61.
18. Junling Gao, Jicong Fan, Bonnie W. Wu, Georgios T. Halkias, Maggie Chau, Peter C. Fung, Chunqi Chang, Zhiguo Zhang, Yeung-Sam Hung and Hinhung Sik, 'Repetitive Religious Chanting Modulates the Late-Stage Brain Response to Fear- and Stress-Provoking Pictures', *Frontiers in Psychology*, vol. 7, 10 January 2017, doi:10.3389/fpsyg.2016.02055.
19. Kerry O'Brien, 'Listening as Activism: The "Sonic Meditations" of Pauline Oliveros', *New Yorker*, 9 December 2016, <https://www.newyorker.com/culture/culture-desk/listening-as-activism-the-sonic-meditations-of-pauline-oliveros> (last accessed 28 February 2022).
20. Pauline Oliveros, *Deep Listening: A Composer's Sound Practice* (New York: iUniverse, 2005), xvii.
21. Laura U. Marks, *The Skin of the Film: Intercultural Cinema, Embodiment, and the Senses* (Durham, NC: Duke University Press, 2000), 195.
22. Ibid., 183.
23. Kit Power, *Midnight Movie Monographs: Tommy* (London: Electric Dreamhouse/PS Publishing, 2019), 18.
24. *The Story of the Sound* documentary, *Tommy* (2-disc special edition DVD, Odyssey, 1975).
25. Jacques Lacan, 'The Mirror Stage as Formative of the *I* Function', in Jacques Lacan, *Écrits*, trans. Bruce Fink (New York: W.W. Norton, 2007), 78.
26. *The Story of the Sound* documentary, *Tommy* (2-disc special edition DVD, Odyssey, 1975).
27. Andy Neill and Matt Kent, *Anywhere Anyhow Anywhere: The Complete Chronicle of The Who 1958–1978* (London: Virgin, 2007), 152.
28. Power, 33.
29. Ibid., 35.
30. Ibid., 36.
31. Penelope Reed Doob, *The Idea of the Labyrinth from Classical Antiquity through the Middle Ages* (New York: Cornell University Press, 2019), 98.
32. Robert E. Lewis et al. (eds), *Middle English Dictionary* (Ann Arbor: University of Michigan Press, 1952–2001); online edition available at Frances McSparran et al. (eds), *Middle English Compendium* (Ann Arbor: University of Michigan Library, 2000–18), <https://quod.lib.umich.edu/m/middle-english-dictionary> (last accessed 22 June 2022).
33. Hanke's chapter on *Tommy* in *Ken Russell's Films* covers the pervasive images of circularity in the film.

CHAPTER 10

Mythologising Valentino: Stardom, Biography and Performance in Ken Russell's *Valentino*

Jade Evans

INTRODUCTION

Ken Russell's biopic *Valentino* (United Artists, 1977) was released fifty-one years after the premature death of its subject, Rudolph 'Rudy' Valentino, in 1926 at the age of thirty-one. The film is rooted in both Russell's preoccupation with early silent cinema, as a form of pure cinema as well as in his aborted *Nijinsky* project from 1967.[1] Nicknamed the 'World's Greatest Lover', Valentino was one of the silent film era's most prominent stars. He was idolised by audiences for his charming on-screen persona and Italian good looks that set him apart from many other early male leads, who were largely Anglo-American in appearance. Valentino's unexpected death shocked fans around the world, and his funeral prompted hysteria as mourners flocked to the surrounding streets: women reportedly fainted and rumours emerged that, in their grief, two women killed themselves 'in front of the hospital where Valentino died'.[2] It is this culture of hysteria that Russell mines for the opening of his film. Beginning with the star's funeral, it proceeds to track back through the life of Valentino, portrayed here by Russian ballet dancer Rudolf Nureyev, in a series of flashbacks triggered by those who knew him, who in turn recount their time spent with the star. It is through these oral histories that Russell's film examines Valentino's star image. The non-linear nature of the narrative's timeline maintains focus on his legacy, building an account of Valentino's life that concomitantly explores his legend as well as his identity and significance as a star.

Brian Faucette observes that 'Russell's treatment of Valentino as a character in a novel rather than a historical figure allows him to explore the myths, facts and mediated knowledge of the actor.'[3] In Russell's film, Valentino is presented as a 'man of contradictions' that are in many ways born out of the complexity of his multifaceted star image; these 'contradictions' are explored in sub-narratives that contort the figure, each rendering different aspects of Valentino's myth.[4] As each of these components of Valentino's stardom is explored, the film constantly changes style, which for Russell was employed 'because it's about the divergence of a man from his image. The real man is not known and he is never seen ... Nureyev isn't just playing Valentino, he is playing Valentino playing someone else.'[5] In casting Nureyev in the lead role, Russell states that the decision was a

> Case of a myth playing a myth ... [Nureyev] is a myth. People don't know a great deal about him. He's before the public every day of his life and no one has heard him speak – and so, he's a living legend whom nobody knows.[6]

Through this casting, Russell utilises the mythic qualities of Nureyev's stardom to express the myth of Valentino explored in this film by merging the image of both. The film maintains a distance to Valentino himself, incorporating both documentary style footage and recreations of moments from his life to remain vague in whether this film is intended to be a historically accurate depiction of Valentino's life or a fictional account rooted in exaggeration. The shifting definition of the biopic is referred to by Deborah Cartmell, who notes that 'An obligatory feature of the promotion of films which purport to reproduce a "real life" is the insistence on historical accuracy.'[7] In this way, Russell's film is less of a biopic and more of an anti-biopic, with a depiction of Valentino's life that is built on contradictory and inconsistent perceptions of him. The film does, however, feature and comment upon a selection of biographical elements and events that are based in truth, many of which fans of Valentino will already be familiar with, but it does so through an exaggeration of those events, constructing the myths surrounding him.

A selection of the biographical material is explored in Russell's film, including the accusations of bigamy that Valentino faced after he married Natacha Rambova whilst not yet divorced from his first wife, Jean Acker, after they reportedly failed to consummate their marriage. This led to references in the narrative of the public condemnation that Valentino faced for his apparent lack of masculinity, as well as the gossip surrounding his sexuality. Russell's biopic is itself based on a salacious biography of Valentino and interweaves fact with details that are subject to debate on the private and public aspects of the star's life.[8] As Russell explained in an interview during filming, Valentino had 'an action-packed life, and one always has a problem of condensing such a man's life into two-and-a-quarter hours', and so he had 'to sacrifice a bit of warmth and domesticity ... which shows his background [in order to focus on] the key changes in his life', resulting in a reduced focus on his personal life, with more attention given to Valentino's public life as a film star.⁹

If Russell's film implies a 'real' Valentino, it is one that comes with its own set of contradictions, embodied in the somewhat comedic performance of Nureyev that is difficult to associate with the smouldering intensity of the screen star Valentino. The sexual appeal of Valentino stirred jealousy in men, who feared that the infamous sheik would steal their wives. This prompted attacks on his masculinity,¹⁰ as in an infamous *Chicago Tribune* article in which the author, offended by the appearance of a powder puff dispenser in a men's bathroom, blames Valentino for the downfall of the all-American male.¹¹ This reception of the star in turn inspired a scene towards the end of *Valentino*, in which he is subject to ridicule as he watches dancers, who, dressed up as pink powder puffs, perform a song which provocatively asks, 'Oh Rudy, what have you done to the U.S. male? We liked him better when his cheeks were pale.' This scene is one of many within the film to address the breadth of rumours, gossip and contradictions surrounding Valentino. Decades after Valentino's death, Russell's film revived interest in the star, and contributed to a discursive resurgence on the subject of Valentino that reframed the way in which audiences thought about him and, more broadly, the silent film era and its stars.

In this chapter, I will explore how Russell's film constructs (and deconstructs) Valentino's star image. I will consider how it both incorporates and reconstructs archival footage relating to Valentino with the intention of complicating biographical accounts, presenting a star image that remains intentionally unclear in its depiction of Valentino's life. Furthermore, I will examine how *Valentino* explores the idolisation and popularity of its subject through references to classical mythology. In doing this, comparisons are drawn in the film between Valentino and figures of antiquity, thus positioning him as a figure of idolatry and exaggerating the myths surrounding his stardom. Finally, I will investigate the ways in which exaggeration and excess are utilised to explore Valentino's stardom alongside the emergence of fan culture during the silent film era.

RECEPTION

In the broader context of Russell's filmography, *Valentino* is a lesser-known entry (and one that Russell himself publicly disowned¹²), having not been screened on terrestrial television in the UK for some decades.¹³ A remastered edition of the film was made available by the BFI on DVD and Blu-ray in 2016, which introduced the film to new audiences.¹⁴ For viewers new to *Valentino*, and established fans, this release provided the opportunity to view it with an array of bonus features, including an audio commentary, with information on how Russell's film constructed its account of Valentino's life, as well as a montage of the actual footage of Valentino's funeral. This enabled viewers to witness for themselves the hysteria that the film attempts to recreate, somewhat authenticating and justifying the popularity of Valentino presented within the film. *Valentino* received negative reviews on its original release, in part, according to Brian Faucette, for its 'distortion of the facts of Valentino's life' and the belief that 'the film was anti-American'.[15] However, the film does not present itself as an authentic biopic (in the same way as other Russell biopics do not); it is instead 'about the divergence of the real man from his image. The primary action takes place after he is dead. The film is about flickering shadows. The "real" man is never seen and nothing is known about him.'[16] Whilst Russell's film remains an examination of the image and myth of Valentino which the star himself is unable to contradict, he is permitted some form of agency within the narrative in his attempts to defend himself against the onslaught of rumours and gossip directed at him, reacting to the ridicule to which he was subjected.

Discussions of Valentino's stardom found their way into a series of reviews, which only contribute to the contradictory perceptions not only of Valentino but likewise of Russell's film. Janet Maslin, in her *New York Times* review of the film, writes that 'For all of his glamour, [Valentino] was a bland figure, more of a star than he was an actor.'[17] Nureyev's performance as Valentino, meanwhile, was commented on in a *Sight and Sound* review for bringing a 'masculine beauty and sheer mystique to the proceedings', contradicting the apparent lack of masculinity in the star he was portraying.[18] However, Nureyev's performance was deemed to be a somewhat forced depiction of Valentino, with 'Russian-accented line readings [which] lack[ed] emotional credibility'.[19] Even in the press surrounding Russell's film, the reception of *Valentino* continues to be fuelled by contradiction, speculation and anecdotal observations. Jeanine Basinger commented that what Valentino 'wasn't, certainly, was a great actor. Valentino is at his worst when he tries to act. When he goes over the top, nostrils flaring and eyes popping, he becomes the caricature people think he always was.'[20] Basinger nevertheless concedes that Valentino 'has focus and intensity, and he never looks awkward or uncomfortable'.[21] Despite contesting Valentino's acting abilities, it is agreed that he had an otherworldly quality on-screen which contributed to the continuing allure and fascination with him. His manager, George Ullman, observed that 'There really was something extraordinary that happened when Rudy was photographed in any role. He had magnetism in person, of course, but the camera revealed something deep and mysterious . . . It might have been the reflection of his soul.'[22]

Following Valentino's death, he remained a subject of interest, and the coinciding of his premature death with the peak of his career resulted in a poignant remembrance of Valentino and the preservation of his image as a young matinee idol who would never age. As Michael Williams states, 'the image of stars who have died young is inevitably enshrined in pathos and a particular discourse of lost promise and glowing beauty that somehow connotes a poetic "living on" in the imaginations of those who remember them'.[23] Russell's film articulates the ways in which Valentino's stardom was shaped by subjective representations of the star following his death by building a narrative of his life based on the flashback accounts of others. It reveals the contradictory and multifaceted nature of Valentino's stardom, which, according to Alexander Walker, lies at the root of his appeal because Valentino remains 'an object of abiding contemporary speculation . . . Valentino is the personality who keeps us guessing.'[24] The film pays tribute to the enigmatic Valentino and, in constructing the narrative through flashback, explores the construction of his stardom, portraying for new audiences the phenomenon, myth and idolisation of Valentino.

THE PHENOMENON OF VALENTINO

Valentino became an overnight star following his successful performance in *The Four Horsemen of the Apocalypse* (Rex Ingram, Metro Pictures Corporation, 1921). In a *Photoplay* article of 1923 entitled 'My Life Story', Valentino commented on his discovery, telling readers:

> I was utterly unknown in Hollywood. I was just a beginner like thousands of others. Don't think that people exclaimed upon meeting me, 'Here is a wonderful find!' No one hailed me for photographic qualities, for personality or for anything else.[25]

This statement suggests that Valentino did not regard himself as particularly special or believe that he embodied any innate star qualities. The discovery of Valentino by screenwriter June Mathis (Felicity Kendal) in Ken Russell's film, however, results from her recognition of a star quality rooted in the appeal of his exotic Italian looks. In one flashback scene, June attempts to convince Richard Rowland (Alfred Marks) that Valentino would provide the perfect leading man for the *The Four Horsemen of the Apocalypse*, but Richard dismisses Valentino and notes that the boy-next-door Wally Reid would make a more suitable choice for the role. As Richard remains reluctant to offer Valentino a chance, June reminds him that the hero of the film is from South America, and she therefore believes that Valentino's looks would offer a more convincing portrayal of a Latin American man. June tells him, 'I know the women of America and they wanna vamoose from the boy next door. Valentino's their ticket to a faraway land of romance.' June indicates that the tastes of women in the 1920s have shifted, and it is Valentino's exoticness interwoven into his appeal as the romantic lead which proves him to be the ideal casting. When she initially speaks to Valentino in consideration for the part, Valentino comments that there is only one sort of hero – 'the clean-cut American boy' – and that he is 'as Yankee as they come', believing himself to be the best choice for the role. Valentino's statement here is contradicted by Nureyev's delivery of the line in a pronounced Russian accent, reminding the spectator that Valentino is an immigrant and revealing his eagerness to conform to the archetype of the American boy-next-door in order to be cast in the part. Whilst his reasoning for venturing into acting is to earn enough money to bring his ill mother over to America from Italy, he is willing to sacrifice his Italian identity in order to do so, a point at odds with Nureyev, who retains his Russian identity in his performance of Valentino.

Mathis rejects Valentino's proposed performance as the boy-next-door, explaining that the role is that of a Latin American man. From the inception of Valentino's discovery, his casting is rooted in the utilisation of his Italian looks to perform a number of non-Anglo-American roles; many of his castings, according to Amy Lawrence, 'attempted to transform the actor's origins into a nonspecific pan-ethnicity where he was likely to be anything but Italian',[26] with Valentino performing characters whose ethnicity ranged from English to Russian to part-Indian and Arabian. She states that only twice did he play an American (the lost *Uncharted Seas* [Wesley Ruggles, Metro Pictures Corporation, 1921] and *Moran of the Lady Letty* [George Melford, Famous Players-Lasky Corporation, 1922]), and only once an Italian (*Cobra* [Joseph Henabery, Ritz-Carlton Pictures, 1925]), despite their being 'the two nationalities the actor could claim'.[27] The casting of Valentino in these roles therefore assimilates his Italian heritage with a variety of other national identities in order to reinforce his immigrant status. The decision to cast Nureyev in the role of Valentino in Russell's film then works to reinforce the enigma of Valentino's identity, omitting any clear or substantial reference to Valentino's Italian background.

It is in Valentino's role in *The Sheik* (George Melford, Paramount, 1921) where the promotion of his exotic appeal is most evident. In Russell's recreation of the rape scene from the original film, Valentino as Sheik Ahmed drags a woman (played in the original film by Agnes Ayres and performed by Jennie Linden in Russell's film) into his tent as she kicks her legs in an attempt to resist his advances. He throws her onto the bed before demanding that she 'lie still you little fool', forcing himself on her. The scene, which exhibits more intimacy than in the original film, cuts to a shot of a cinema in which a crowded audience, notably made up entirely of women, sits watching it. Here Russell exaggerates the appeal of Valentino to a predominantly female audience.

In intercutting the recreation of the rape scene in *The Sheik* with shots of the women watching it, Russell's film positions Valentino as the object of the female gaze, focusing on the reactions of female audiences to his performance, illustrating Lawrence's statement that 'The compounding of Valentino's foreignness with the "otherness" of Sheik Ahmed magnifies the sense of romantic and sexual transgression, paradoxically intensifying the response from female audiences rather than repelling them.'[28] One such woman in the audience is June. The camera tracks in to focus on her reaction as she sits crying. The shot then cuts to a brief fantasy of hers, in which Valentino rides with her on a horse in the desert setting of *The Sheik*, grabbing her hair and kissing her passionately. *The Sheik* for June, as it is implied for the other women watching, becomes an opportunity for them to vicariously live out their sexual fantasies, with the film emerging at a time when women were 'asserting the right to their own enjoyment of life', with the implication that it is Valentino's casting in roles of the exotic, romantic lead which are responsible for the phenomenon of his popularity.[29] Valentino was, according to Gaylyn Studlar, 'the greatest evidenciary support of women's challenge to traditional sexual relations and American ideals of masculinity', and in opting to depict Valentino's performance of Sheik Ahmed, Russell's film promotes the masculine and sexual appeal of Valentino that contradicts the ongoing attacks (predominantly from men) against his masculinity throughout the rest of the narrative.[30] Russell's film therefore polarises the responses of women and men to exaggerate the gendered reception of Valentino, suggesting that his popularity is largely a result of his role in re-forming the performance of gender and sexuality.

Following the filming of a scene for *Monsieur Beaucaire* (Sidney Olcott, Paramount, 1924) alongside Lorna Sinclair (Penelope Milford), the stagehands drop a pink powder puff into Valentino's lap with the intention of insulting his masculinity. In response, Natacha instructs Valentino to 'screw that little whore Lorna, and make sure the whole crew knows about it' in order to reclaim an apparent degree of respect through the public demonstration of heterosexuality. In the scene which follows, Valentino seizes his opportunity when both he and Lorna strip off their costumes, and Lorna mounts Valentino on the bed. Valentino remains uninterested by the situation as Lorna proceeds to insist to Valentino, 'Imagine you're the Sheik on your big white stallion, crushing life out of me in your arms', swiftly losing herself in a monologue of fantasy as she imagines herself and Valentino's Sheik Ahmed lost in the throes of passion. As Joseph Lanza points out, looks are 'everything, [and following this scene] they return to the set to redo the love scene [and] everyone presupposes that "nature" took its course',[31] with Valentino feeling that his dignity is intact, having reaffirmed his masculinity and (hetero)sexuality. This is only for show, however, with the implication that Lorna's pleasure resulted from her own fantasy rather than as a result of any actual sex with Valentino.

The emphasis in Russell's film on the merging of Valentino with his performance of characters such as Sheik Ahmed reveals the extent to which the qualities of those characters are embedded into Valentino's star image. The appeal of Valentino in these performances, and perhaps through an audience identification with the women he lusted after in the films, resulted in an intense adoration of him through an affection for his characters, which made the death of Valentino all the more potent, resulting in an exaggerated recreation in *Valentino* of the public response of hysteria during his funeral sequence.

THE FUNERAL SEQUENCE

Before navigating Valentino's life through flashback, Russell's film opens with a montage of his funeral, combining archival documentary footage with Russell's recreations of the scene. The black and white footage, both real and constructed, depicts the monumental scale of Valentino's funeral, incorporating shots of police officers on horses trying to control the large number of people who are pushing against each other in the crowded street, attempting to break into Valentino's resting place. The sequence interweaves the archival footage seamlessly with additional, staged shots. The false recreations only become obvious when the scene cuts to close-up shots of Richard Rowland (Alfred Marks) emerging from his car. The incorporation of documentary footage of the funeral into the reconstructed sequence in Russell's film suggests an attempt at authenticating the representation of this historic event. This is the first instance of many in Russell's *Valentino* of sequences where it is unclear if they can be deemed an accurate portrayal of Valentino, sequences that explore the myths of his stardom by commenting on the inability to distinguish these from the factual details of Valentino's life.

Figure 10.1 Rudolph Valentino's funeral.
Source: United Artists, 1977.

The funeral montage progresses, and throughout the sequence, images of newspapers announcing Valentino's death zooms into the foreground. The first newspaper's headline proclaims, 'World shocked! Rudy dead! Dead! Dead!'; the second newspaper declares, 'Sheik lies in state! New York fans riot!'; and the third newspaper's headline reads, 'Valentino dead; Millions mourn' (Figure 10.1). The accompanying images in the newspapers depict Nureyev as Valentino in Russell's restaging of Valentino's film performances in *The Four Horsemen of the Apocalypse*, *Camille* (Ray C. Smallwood, Metro Pictures Corporation, 1921) and *The Sheik*, respectively. The latter image depicts a naked (except for his headdress) Nureyev as Valentino, embracing the similarly naked Michelle Phillips as Natacha Rambova. Pausing on a close-up shot of the image on this newspaper, there appears a credit reading, 'Rudolf Nureyev as Valentino'. The credit for Nureyev appearing over the reconstructed image of Valentino in his most iconic role makes clear that Russell's film is reinterpreting the star through Nureyev's performance, merging the image of both whilst simultaneously maintaining a distance from the real Valentino himself. The newspapers depict (reconstructed) images of Valentino's film performances, commenting on the dominance of Valentino's stardom over his personal life, demonstrating that (at least in Russell's film) it was the images of Valentino in character that were circulated in the press surrounding his death, omitting any reference to his personal life.

Following the funeral crowd shots, the scene cuts to an interior close-up shot of Valentino's face as he lies in an open casket. The shot is black and white and the credit 'directed by Ken Russell' appears over Valentino's face, reminding viewers that the film is Russell's interpretation of Valentino's life. In a similar way, both the titles for *The Music Lovers* (United Artists, 1970) and *The Devils* (Warner Bros., 1971) begin with the prefix 'Ken Russell's film of . . .' This credit appearance triggers the shot's slow transitioning into colour (disregarding any previous suggestion that the black and white shot of Valentino could have been taken from documentary footage, similar to that of the crowd scenes), and the camera tracks back from Valentino, forming a physical distance from the star indicative of the distance from Valentino's personal life that Russell's film seeks to create. At the start of the opening scene the only audible sound is the song 'There's a New Star in Heaven Tonight', written in tribute to Valentino following his death, which plays throughout the sequence. As the close-up shot of Valentino's face tracks away, however, we start to hear the sound of the hysterical crowds outside. This becomes increasingly audible until it dominates the soundtrack while the scene becomes overpowered by the ferocity of his fans as they try to break inside the building and invade Valentino's resting place. This scene distances itself from Valentino in favour of focusing on the overwhelming public response to his death, commenting on Valentino's stardom more broadly, and establishing the phenomenon of Valentino that Russell goes on to examine throughout the narrative.

MYTHOLOGISING VALENTINO

Mythological references are drawn throughout Russell's film in order to express and explore Valentino's stardom. In one key sequence, Valentino participates in a photoshoot, based on an actual photoshoot of Valentino that was staged by Natacha Rambova whilst he was filming *Moran of the Lady Letty*. Through the incorporation of references to Greek mythology, the scene draws comparisons between Valentino's star image and that of Pan, a mythological faun and the god of the wilderness, commenting on the relationship between the idolisation of stars, and specifically that of Valentino, and the worshipping of a god. The ancient Romans assimilated the figure of Pan with their god Faunus, who was likewise pictured as half-man and half-goat. Like Pan, Faunus was a god of the wilderness and woodland, and so, whilst Valentino embodies the faun from Nijinsky's ballet *The Afternoon of a Faun*, his image is reminiscent of Faunus, suggesting a reference to his Italian roots and a positioning of Valentino's image as an Italian god, further mythologising any references to his identity and emphasising, perhaps unintentionally, the appeal of his Italian looks which led to the promotion of Valentino as a figure of idolatry (Figure 10.2).

According to Emily W. Leider in her biography of Valentino, the photos from the shoot were partly Rambova's 'celebration of Rudy's beautiful Greek

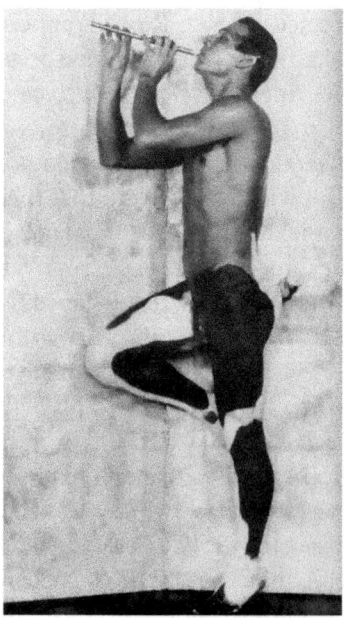

Figure 10.2 Rudolph Valentino as a faun.
Source: out of copyright.

god's body, and partly [taken] as an homage to [Vaslav] Nijinsky' after Rambova had been mesmerised by Nijinsky's erotic performance in *The Afternoon of a Faun*.[32] During Rambova's photoshoot, Valentino's legs and feet were painted with black patches to resemble goat skin, with Valentino wearing only a painted G-string and a small tail. A photograph of Valentino from this shoot appeared in an issue of *Life* magazine in 1950, with a caption stating that 'the old movies are revived from time to time; and young people get a chance to see the flash of savage charm and beauty that made him seem to a whole generation of women like an incarnation of the Greek god Pan: a symbol of everything wild and wonderful and illicit in nature'.[33]

Russell's film reconstructs this photoshoot in a montage sequence which incorporates detailed references to *The Afternoon of a Faun*. During the scene, Natacha and Alla direct and photograph Valentino as he poses in a variety of positions from the ballet, celebrating his talent as a dancer through the associations made between Valentino and Nijinsky in these shots, notably allowing Nureyev to demonstrate his love for Nijinsky and reference his background in ballet. Valentino's full body is painted, and he sports only a leaf-covered G-string and crown, much like in the original photoshoot, decorated to resemble the faun of Nijinsky's ballet, perpetuating the mythic associations of Valentino's image through the visual references made to Pan. Alla and Natacha contribute to the construction of his myth in this scene by directing the photoshoot whilst dressed as nymphs as they pose alongside Valentino in some of the more recognisable dance positions from the ballet. However, the sequence ends with Valentino intertwined with Natacha on the floor as they kiss passionately, Natacha's scarf underneath them. This moment is a reference by Russell to the ending of Nijinsky's ballet when, as *The Afternoon of the Faun* 'reaches its climax, so does the faun. A final orgasmic shudder ends the ballet. It was this closing gesture that created such wild controversy . . . The 1912 premiere created an absolute scandal that was kept alive for days.'[34] The controversy of the ballet is echoed in this scene as Alla secretly photographs them in their moment of passion, with a cut to the next shot revealing the photograph of the pair on the front page of a newspaper, partly covered by a 'CENSORED' banner.

Throughout the photoshoot sequence, 'The Sheik of Araby' – a song written by Francis Wheeler and Harry B. Smith inspired by Valentino's popularity in *The Sheik* – plays, emphasising Valentino's role as commodity within the film industry and the sellability of his star image in its associations with his performance in *The Sheik*. In referencing Valentino's performance in that film, Russell associates Valentino's lustful, wild and exotic role in *The Sheik* with his performance of Pan, who is similarly emblematic of those traits, reinforcing these qualities within Valentino's star image. Despite the promotion of Valentino's masculinity through his performance of Pan, the song is, according to Faucette, 'used to clearly question Valentino's masculinity and will appear later to punctuate the struggles in Valentino's life', demonstrating the contradictions of representation in Valentino's stardom being explored in this scene.[35] Furthermore, Valentino is positioned through the female gaze in this shoot but, despite that, exhibits a performance of masculinity and heterosexuality that manifests itself through his embodiment of Pan. In Michael Morris and Evelyn Zumaya's examination of Rambova, they state that 'Here we have a female artist (Natacha Rambova) focusing upon the nudity of her husband (Valentino) and disseminating it for the pleasure of other female gazers.'[36] The decision to incorporate this scene into Russell's film works to explore the ways in which the myth of Valentino was constructed and promoted, continuing to position him in character as opposed to focusing on the man behind the myth, and finally, it comments on the shaping and exploitation of Valentino's star image throughout his career. Decades after his death, the comparison between Valentino's image and that of a god perpetuates the enduring myth of his stardom.

THE IDOLISATION OF VALENTINO

Valentino's popularity is examined in Russell's film via the ways in which the public responded to him through acts of obsession and idolisation. As the narrative progresses, it increasingly darkens in its depiction of fan obsession at its most extreme, commenting on the emergence of a fan culture and its impact on Valentino's personal life. For instance, in one scene, Valentino's personal space is breached as a fan attempts to break into his private bungalow. As the fan sneaks through the garden fence, she is swiftly caught by a security guard who restrains her as she desperately calls out, 'Rudy!', kicking the guard and attempting to justify her actions by explaining that she is the president of the Santa Monica fan club, angrily yelling that Valentino is expecting her. The scene cuts to a shot of Valentino in profile, dressed in his *Monsieur Beaucaire* costume, silent in response to this fan's invasion of his property. This brief shot of a pensive Valentino allows him a moment in which to react to the intense emotion shown towards him by a fan who believes herself entitled to encroach on his space. Later in the film, Russell employs the use of exaggeration to contort and intensify the representation of fan idolisation and the fans' worship of Valentino. In the scene, Natacha and Valentino sit either side of a crystal ball in their home as Natacha consults Meselope, her Ancient Egyptian spirit guide, asking what their destiny is to be. Their session is cut short, however, when they are interrupted by a hoard of fans outside who recite a variation of Valentino's published poem 'YOU'. The scene intercuts between shots of Valentino and Rambova at their table and shots of the fans outside in a number of unified chants of worship, calling out to Valentino that he is 'the spirit that moves the universe', 'the song that makes the day' and 'the waves that soothe the sand', embodying Valentino with the qualities of a deity that illustrate the extremity of the fans' idolisation of him.

In her attempts to ignore the ongoing mass of Valentino worshipers outside, Natacha keeps trying to contact Meselope, asking if she and Valentino will continue working together. The apparent lack of a response she receives, however, implies a premonition of Valentino's death and the soon to come ending of their personal and working relationship. This is perhaps the darkest and most macabre scene within Russell's film, and becomes tenser through the rapid use of editing, leading Natacha in her distress to cry out, 'Listen to them! They think you're God!', a statement that is somewhat ironic perhaps, considering that Natacha contributed to the construction of Valentino's image as a god in her staging of him as Pan. However, her statement nevertheless echoes Valentino's earlier comment:

> I tell you what is ridiculous, George! That I should be born into such a time when a machine is invented that can turn a man who wants only to be a farmer into some kind of a god! That people can stand in line for hours to sit in some dark room, to see me flickering past their eyes. They fall in love, they destroy your marriage, they tear you to shreds.

Russell's film both celebrates Valentino, the man who immigrated to America with the intention of owning an orange grove, in all of his on-screen magnetism, and vilifies the star, witnessing him at his lowest moments.

CONCLUSION

Ken Russell's examination of Valentino may not offer audiences a historically accurate account of the star's life, but it provides an insight into the complicated, contradictory and multifaceted nature of his stardom, celebrating the star who, decades after his death, still retains the 'capacity to stir in women and men the most intimate erotic and spiritual fantasies, and to pique the possessive feelings that are usually reserved for living lovers, [which] hasn't dimmed'.[37] Furthermore, it suggests the dominance of his star identity over his personal life. Valentino is still referred to as the Sheik, or the Great Latin Lover, associating him with his film roles (which largely ignore his Italian background and make little room for his personal ambitions to own an orange grove). The obsession with Valentino has continued, with his image becoming 'a benchmark for masculine sex appeal against which all new leading male stars were measured. A parade of dark-haired and charismatic leading men . . . were declared "the new Valentino".[38] However, despite any attempt to recreate or embody his star appeal, Natacha's comment early in Russell's film that 'I only know there will never be another Valentino. There will never be one even remotely like him' illustrates the impossibility of that task.

Valentino remains a source of interest. Russell's film examines his substantial impact on 1920s stardom, considering the ways in which the stardom of Valentino has been shaped over time by the ongoing myths, speculation and contradictions in the discourse surrounding him. In this way, the film similarly contributes to the discourse around Valentino by perpetuating those myths and exaggerating his biographical accounts, only fuelling the contradictions and speculations further. A biopic it may at first appear, but Russell's account of Valentino provides little opportunity to settle any of the contradicting accounts of his life.

NOTES

1. Matthew Melia, 'Ken Russell's Unfinished Projects and Unmade Films, 1956–68: The BBC Years', in James Fenwick, Kieran Foster and David Eldridge (eds), *Shadow Cinema: The Historical and Production Contexts of Unmade Films* (New York: Bloomsbury Academic, 2021), 102.
2. Edgar Morin, *The Stars* (London: Evergreen Books, 1961), 16.
3. Brian Faucette, 'Defending Rudy: Alternative Masculinities in Ken Russell's *Valentino*', in Kevin M. Flanagan (ed.), *Ken Russell: Re-Viewing England's Last Mannerist* (Plymouth: Scarecrow Press, 2009), 158.
4. Ibid.
5. Paul Sutton, 'Valentino: A Film by Ken Russell', in accompanying booklet to *Valentino*, directed by Ken Russell, 1977 (DVD/Blu-ray, BFI, 2016), 2.
6. Herb A. Lightman, 'With Ken Russell on the Set of Valentino', *American Cinematographer*, vol. 58, no. 11, November 1977, 1210.
7. Deborah Cartmell, 'The Hollywood Biopic of the Twentieth Century', in Deborah Cartmell and Ashley D. Polasek (eds), *A Companion to the Biopic* (Hoboken, NJ: John Wiley & Sons, 2020), 91.
8. In the audio commentary by Tim Lucas included on the 2016 BFI DVD/Blu-ray release of Valentino, Lucas states that the Ken Russell and Mardik Martin script of Valentino has a 'basis' in the biography *Valentino: An Intimate Exposé of the Sheik* by Brad Steiger and Chaw Mank (1975), but observes that the film has more in common with Irving Shulman's earlier book *Valentino* (1967), which also utilises the funeral as a framing device.
9. Lightman, 1206.
10. Faucette, 155–78.
11. 'Pink Powder Puffs', *Chicago Daily Tribune*, 18 July 1926.
12. Russell's relationship with his film was complicated by his negative experience of working with Nureyev. He disowned the film during his appearance on BBC Radio 4's *Desert Island Discs*.
13. Thank you to Sheldon Hall for providing this information. The last terrestrial TV screening in the UK that I am aware of is 20 February 1988 on Channel 4.
14. *Valentino*, directed by Ken Russell, 1977 (DVD/Blu-ray, BFI, 2016).
15. Faucette, 155.
16. Lightman, 1165.
17. Janet Maslin, 'Film: Vital Nureyev Upstages "Valentino"', *New York Times*, 6 October 1977, <https://www.nytimes.com/1977/10/06/archives/film-vital-nureyev-upstages-valentino.html> (last accessed 31 May 2022).
18. Trevor Johnston, 'Valentino', *Sight and Sound*, vol. 26, no. 4, April 2016, 103.

19. Ibid.
20. Jeanine Basinger, *Silent Stars* (New York: Alfred A. Knopf, 1999), 267.
21. Ibid., 268.
22. George Ullman, *The S. George Ullman Memoir* (Turin: Viale Industria Pubblicazioni, 2014), 95.
23. Michael Williams, *Film Stardom, Myth and Classicism: The Rise of Hollywood's Gods* (Basingstoke: Palgrave Macmillan, 2013), 176–7.
24. Alexander Walker, *Rudolph Valentino* (London: Elm Tree Books/Hamish Hamilton, 1976), 8.
25. Rudolph Valentino, 'My Life Story', *Photoplay*, April 1923, 49–53.
26. Amy Lawrence, 'Rudolph Valentino: Italian American', in Patrice Petro (ed.), *Idols of Modernity: Movie Stars of the 1920s* (New Brunswick, NJ: Rutgers University Press, 2010), 91.
27. Ibid.
28. Ibid., 97.
29. Walker, 7.
30. Gaylyn Studlar, '"The Perfect Lover"? Valentino and Ethnic Masculinity in the 1920s', in Lee Grieveson and Peter Kramer (eds), *The Silent Cinema Reader* (London: Routledge, 2004), 290.
31. Joseph Lanza, *Phallic Frenzy: Ken Russell and His Films* (Chicago: Chicago Review Press, 2007), 205.
32. Emily W. Leider, *Dark Lover: The Life and Death of Rudolph Valentino* (London: Faber and Faber, 2003), 185.
33. 'The Great Lover', *Life*, 2 January 1950, 36.
34. Jon Teeuwissen, 'A Controversial Masterpiece: Prelude to the Afternoon of a Fawn', *Michigan Opera Theatre*, 15 June 2020, <https://michiganopera.org/a-controversial-masterpiece-prelude-to-the-afternoon-of-a-fawn/> (last accessed 13 March 2021).
35. Faucette, 168.
36. Michael Morris and Evelyn Zumaya, *Beyond Valentino: A Madam Valentino Addendum* (Turin: Viale Industria Pubblicazioni, 2017), 45.
37. Leider, 5.
38. Lisa Bode, 'The Afterlives of Rudolph Valentino and Wallace Reid in the 1920s and 1930s', in Lucy Bolton and Julie Lobalzo Wright (eds), *Lasting Screen Stars: Images That Pervade and Personas That Endure* (London: Macmillan, 2016), 167.

PART 4

Transgression and the Russell Legacy

CHAPTER II

An Extraordinary Parallel: Ken Russell and Dennis Potter Side by Side

Mateja Đedović

INTRODUCTION

Looking back on the golden age of British television, it seems that most historians and critics have focused predominantly on grittier, political works such as those by Ken Loach or Jack Rosenthal, leaving by the wayside the truly incredible variety of programming available in the 1960s. Comparatively little has been written about the many sitcoms of the age, the variety shows, and the growing trend of non-naturalism in television plays. Even the original television works of such writers as Harold Pinter or Tom Stoppard are most frequently relegated to mere footnotes in their biographies. Such is also the case with two of the most notable proponents of non-naturalism in television, Ken Russell and Dennis Potter. And while Russell's television work has received some increased attention in recent years, most of Potter's work, though nominally admired, languishes in relative obscurity.

What is more surprising, however, is that even in the little that has been written about their work, no one has pointed out the clear parallels between them: their preoccupation with the themes of sex, religion and death; their use of musical non sequiturs, which became a trademark of Potter's and a defining feature of Russell's work in the 1970s; as well as their layered structures, which combine fantasy and reality in the broken psyches of their leading characters. Of course, it may seem counterintuitive to compare the work of a director and a writer, but it bears mentioning that both Potter and Russell were clear authors of their work. Russell wrote most of the screenplays for the films he directed but even when he didn't he was either heavily collaboratively involved in the writing process (for instance, underlining the passages from the novel he wanted in the film of *Women in Love* [United Artists, 1969] from a script written by American playwright Larry Kramer,[1] or in his work with Stephen Volk or Barry Sandler on *Gothic* [Virgin Vision/Vestron, 1986] and *Crimes of Passion* [New World Pictures, 1984], respectively) or would end up imposing his own style and ideas over a screenplay originally intended to play out completely differently (Paddy Chayefsky, the writer of *Altered States* [Warner Bros., 1980] removed his name from the film due to what he perceived as Russell's unwelcome intrusions). Potter, on the other hand, wrote mainly for television, where the writer is seen as the auteur. His scripts were noted for their detailed stage directions including even suggestions for camera angles, movement and instructions on musical selections. Even the few times when Potter did yield under directors' demands – such as Jon Amiel's requests for rewrites on *The Singing Detective* (BBC, 1986), his most renowned work – Potter would handle the changes himself, without allowing anyone else to reshape his script.[2] Furthermore, Potter was not one to hold back on his opinions, and his views on the broadcast versions of his plays are well noted through his columns and personal recollections of his colleagues, such as his distaste for the way his play *The Bonegrinder* (ITV, 1968) came across.[3] In other words, when making this comparison we can safely claim that everything that made it to screen was either conceived or approved by Potter and Russell, and the several examples in which this is not the case are well enough documented.

NON-NATURALISM

Both Potter and Russell began their television careers at the BBC. Huw Wheldon, the producer of the arts program *Monitor*, had seen Russell's 1958 short film *Amelia and the Angel* (BFI Experimental Film Fund, 1958) and offered him a job.[4] Despite Russell crediting Wheldon as a mentor, they still disagreed vehemently as Russell veered more and more towards non-naturalism. The most contentious aspect of Russell's work was his desire to feature re-enactments in what were supposed to be documentaries. They first clashed on the issue over Russell's debut *Monitor* film on John Betjeman, *A Poet in London* (BBC, 1959), in which he proposed to use actors to portray the poet's relatives. Wheldon won and the scene was cut.[5] Russell was eventually allowed to portray the hands of Prokofiev in *Prokofiev* (BBC, 1961) and his reflection in a pond, 'so long as it's a murky pond and the water is rippling',[6] and Elgar but only as a figure, 'no acting'.[7] It would take until *The Debussy Film* (BBC, 1965) for Russell's actors to be allowed to speak on-screen and fully embody the artists they played, but again not without controversy. The Soviet Embassy complained about the portrayal of Prokofiev,[8] and in 1968 Russell's proposed film on Lytton Strachey was cancelled due to similar objections from the writer's family.[9]

Dennis Potter began his BBC contract in 1959, straight out of Oxford, and as a general trainee got the chance to work with famed documentarian Denis Mitchell, which inspired the young Potter to make his only documentary, the 1960 BBC film on the Forest of Dean, *Between Two Rivers*.[10] This intriguing though somewhat condescending film would eventually be released on DVD by the BFI in 2013 as part of the box set *Visions of Change*, which also included Ken Russell's 1962 *Monitor* documentary *Pop Goes the Easel*. Just as Russell's early career is rooted in his work on *Monitor*, Potter's was similarly associated with the BBC's literary programme *Bookstand*, which was innovative in that it featured acted excerpts from newly published books. Most of these segments were dramatised by Dennis Potter. Like Russell's re-enactments, Potter's dramatisations found a predominantly negative reception at the BBC. A 1961 memo from the then Controller of programmes Kenneth Adam criticises *Bookstand*'s dramatisation of an excerpt from Camus's *The Stranger* as 'quite unworthy of the book' and in it, he reinforces his dislike of this method of treatment.[11] Here it is hard not to think of the response to Ken Russell's film *Elgar* (BBC, 1962), which dramatised the composer's life using actors and was met with little enthusiasm within the BBC because it was thought impossible to impersonate a composer and his family in 'a realistic or convincing way'.[12] The BBC management was also concerned that the boundaries between documentary and drama – and 'fact' and 'fiction' – should be maintained.

What both Russell and Potter were experimenting with in their BBC work was the concept of non-naturalism as opposed to the prevalent style of the time, which Potter referred to as 'the simple, naturalistic, tediously "authentic" drama'.[13] Potter would later suggest the main distinction between the two styles lies in the relationship between the word and the world. A naturalist author trusts that relationship, and his art seeks to describe or represent or understand and perhaps change the world out there by using the strict patterns endemic to television; while a non-naturalist author, in the very structure of his work seeks to disorient the viewer, disrupt the pattern, and upset or expose that narrative style.[14] In 1962, the year Ken Russell's *Elgar* was first broadcast, Potter more harshly divided the naturalist writers from the non-naturalist:

> On one side there are those who want to be cautious and take plays and ideas direct from the theatre. On the other are the revolutionaries who want to shake things up a bit. They are eager to inject new forms, fresh techniques, bolder themes into the TV play.[15]

Although no record exists of Potter's opinions on any of Russell's *Monitor* films, it is not hard to imagine that he would certainly have admired the young director for his undeniable boldness. Around the same time that Potter bemoaned 'the essentially trivial preoccupation with styles of production and modes of technique rather than with . . . what you *do* with these techniques',[16] Russell was making what were, in his words, 'mould-breaking biographical studies, told in a cinematic style which mirrored the nature of the subject under review'.[17] Russell's idea to have the style of the biopic mimic the style of the artist depicted ('*Isadora Duncan* [BBC, 1966] was exuberant, choreographic, humanistic and celebratory; *The Debussy Film* was dreamy, impressionistic and ambiguous"[18]) was exactly the kind of non-naturalistic technique which would have thrilled Potter. As further proof of this, we may contrast Potter's remark about non-naturalist drama showing 'the frame in the picture when most television is busy showing the picture in the frame"[19] with the conclusion Joseph A. Gomez draws in his book on Russell's films, *Ken Russell: The Adaptor as Creator*, that 'his films are complex experiments involving form and structure which force the viewer to reconsider the very nature of the biopic genre'.[20]

Despite the BBC's misgivings, its audiences were also growing tired of strait-laced seriousness on television. Their appetites for something new and exciting were growing, and Potter would soon prove to be the man for the job, becoming, in the words of Graham Fuller, 'not only dauntingly prolific but the most important creative figure in the history of British television'.[21] After briefly leaving the BBC in 1961 and a failed attempt at a political career, Potter reinvented himself as a television playwright, first gaining attention with his two TV plays about Nigel Barton, a miner's son from a small village who goes to Oxford and runs for Parliament. After the Barton plays, Potter went on to shock and awe with his powerfully non-realistic plays such as *Double Dare* (BBC, 1976), *Angels Are So Few* (BBC *Play for Today*, 1970), and the controversial and (for a time) banned *Brimstone and Treacle* (BBC, 1976); his religious plays such as *Son of Man* (BBC, 1969), *Joe's Ark* (BBC, 1974) and *Where Adam Stood* (BBC, 1976); and, what is by most considered the absolute peak of his writing career, his three 'musical serials': *Pennies from Heaven* (BBC, 1978), *The Singing Detective* and *Lipstick on Your Collar* (BBC, 1993). Even though these serials brought him attention from Hollywood, Potter never gave up on television. His attachment to the medium was more than a simple caprice, however. 'Television is the only medium that really counts for me. It's the only one that all people watch in all sorts of situations. Television is the biggest platform, and you should fight and kick and bite your way on to it',[22] he said in 1970, concluding nine years later, 'I regard TV drama as *the* National Theatre.'[23]

Russell, meanwhile, who had come to the BBC as a film-maker, used television as a stepping stone to cinema. Unlike Potter, his approach to television was thoroughly cinematic in style. Whereas Potter found his niche in writing studio-bound TV plays, Russell's television work more frequently resembled mini-movies shot on film and on location and relying on expressionistic visuals to move the narrative along instead of dialogue. Unlike Potter, he found more freedom and the means to express himself in cinema, which allowed him to make certain projects that would not be feasible on television due to limited budgets and stricter censorship. However, his cinematic work continued from his television work almost seamlessly with a series of films based on artists' lives. In the 1970s, like Potter, he began experimenting with blending fantasy and reality and utilising musical non sequiturs as a kind of bridge between the two in such films as *Mahler* (Goodtimes Enterprises, 1974), *Tommy* (Columbia, 1975) and *Lisztomania* (Goodtimes Enterprises, 1975).

STRUCTURE AND MUSIC

Potter's and Russell's mutual commitment to non-realism is, perhaps, best reflected in their use of structure. Dennis Potter's 1971 BBC serial *Casanova* takes place on three separate narrative levels. The first, which we shall call 'present day', begins with Casanova being arrested and imprisoned in a tiny, rat-infested jail cell. Bored, miserable and sick, Casanova amuses himself by recalling his former adventures. This narrative level, which we shall call 'the retrospective level', proceeds in a regular, almost linear fashion detailing Casanova's various love conquests. However, Casanova's illness begins blending the present-day reality with his fantasies and hallucination, giving the serial its third narrative level, which we shall name 'the fantasy level'. His past conquests begin haunting his jail cell, and elements from them start cropping up in his memories of the past, as sexy nuns look on.

Ken Russell employs an almost identical three-level structure in *Mahler*. The present-day level is set during a train journey that Mahler takes with his wife Alma. Even though his physical imprisonment is less drastic than that of Casanova, Mahler is still stuck in a single, confined space without anyone to keep him company (his mercurial wife is hardly the ideal travelling companion). He is also, unbeknownst to him, deathly ill. Like Casanova, Mahler is pushed into the world of memories due to his confinement and illness. This is where the second, retrospective narrative level comes into play: Mahler recounts his childhood, his early life with Alma, and his struggles to be accepted into the world of music. As in *Casanova*, the retrospective level of *Mahler* proceeds in a linear fashion, parallel to the present-day level. It is only the third, fantasy level which exhibits clear surrealist imagery. Motivated by his increasing fever, Mahler's troubled life and his creative work mix in a series of musical sequences, such as the one in which he imagines his funeral set to his own first symphony and the one in which his conversion from Judaism to Christianity is turned into a silent spoof of Fritz Lang's *Die Nibelungen* (UFA, 1924). When one examines the structures of *Casanova* and *Mahler* closely, one sees that this quote from Potter could easily refer to either of the works: 'I wanted to do a portrait, if you like, that accumulated, that sifted through layers of various incidents and how they changed perspective [because] we're walking compendiums in a way of memory.'[24]

Russell's one major addition to the three-layer structure is the way in which he connects and moves between the three layers with the use of music. For instance, Nick, Mahler's childhood friend, is incorporated into Mahler's funeral scene by having him play an accordion to the first symphony, which underscores the sequence. Russell also uses music as ironic commentary, for example in the conversion sequence when Mahler is forced to convert from Judaism to Christianity to appease the intensely anti-Semitic Cosima Wagner, the widow of Richard. Thus, the sequence is underscored with Wagner's *Ride of the Valkyries*.

Potter's use of music in *The Singing Detective* resembles its use in Russell's *Mahler*. The structure of the serial is a built-up version of the structure of *Casanova*, but with a new, added level. First, there's the present-day level focusing on Philip Marlow, a writer bedbound in a hospital ward. Unable to move, he reflects on the memories of his childhood which form the second, retrospective level. The new level is formed by Marlow's memories of a novella he wrote years ago, *The Singing Detective*. To amuse himself, Marlow imagines himself as the novella's lead, a private detective/cabaret singer. Finally, there's the fourth level, the fantasy level, in which the previous levels combine due to Marlow's fever-induced hallucinations. According to director Jon Amiel, the four levels were imagined like storeys in a building, and the elevator that shuttled you between the different floors was the music.[25] For instance, a scene in the first episode begins firmly on the present-day level. A group of doctors comes to examine Marlow. Suddenly, they begin lip-syncing and dancing along to the song 'Dem Bones'. They then open the curtain around Marlow's bed to reveal the cabaret dancers from *The Singing Detective* novella. We have been shuttled to the fantasy level, where reality and fantasy mix freely.

Potter's use of music developed throughout his career. In his early works, it is present mainly either in the play's titles, which are taken from song lyrics (*Moonlight on the Highway*, *Lay Down Your Arms*, *Paper Roses*), or as plot elements. For instance, *Moonlight on the Highway* (ITV, 1969) is about a man who finds solace in the songs of Al Bowlly. An early instance of a commentary use of music occurs in the very first Nigel Barton play, *Stand Up, Nigel Barton* (BBC, 1965), which ends with Nigel and his father in their poor village walking away from the camera to the 1965 song by The Animals, 'We Gotta Get Out of This Place'. Similarly, his 1970 ITV play *Lay Down Your Arms* begins with footage of an army parade and the War Office underscored by the song 'Lay Down Your Arms', a satirical move comparable to Ken Russell's underscoring of harrowing World War I footage with the bombastic 'Land of Hope and Glory' in *Elgar*. Ironic use of music is commonplace in Russell's work, as noted by Gomez: '[Music] supplies means for ironic commentary and disorientation of the audience as well as a rich context for allusion.'[26]

Potter and Russell both used music as a catalyst for fantasy. Russell's Tchaikovsky biopic *The Music Lovers* (United Artists, 1970) features an extended sequence in which Tchaikovsky premieres his First Piano Concerto. As he plays, Russell lets us into the minds of several audience members, showing us the fantasies evoked in them by the music. Similarly, in his 1978 serial *Pennies from Heaven*, Potter also deals with a peculiar music lover in whom the songs he listens to evoke fantasy. The serial's lead, Arthur Parker, is a profoundly unhappy sheet-music salesman who suffers from an inability to express himself. Whenever he tries to, he makes a fool of himself. Potter then shows us what he meant to say by taking us into his mind where he allows Arthur to express himself by singing and dancing along to his favourite songs in an expressive move which W. Stephen Gilbert describes as 'characters calling down a common culture to articulate universal feeling'.[27]

GENRE, SEX AND DEATH

Like music, genre was also used by Potter and Russell for expressionistic, ironic or commentative means. Russell's *The Lair of the White Worm* (Vestron, 1988) and Potter's *Midnight Movie* (Renny Rye, BBC/Whistling Gypsy, 1994), for example, are both homages and parodies of British horror films of the 1960s. Both Potter and Russell make use of the same tropes in their respective films: a mysterious, sexy woman arriving in a small English village and moving into a manor house. Both films contain a sequence in which the female antagonist seduces a sexually innocent man and then causes his demise. This idea of a killer maiden is certainly taken wholesale from the horror films of old when Peter Cushing battled *The Brides of Dracula* (Terence Fisher, Hammer, 1960) and Edward Woodward was drawn into *The Wicker Man* (Robin Hardy, British Lion, 1973) by Britt Ekland. However, the connection between sex and death, Eros and Thanatos, is a motive present in almost all the works by both Potter and Russell.

Examples in Potter's works include the sexually motivated murder which begins his play *A Beast with Two Backs* (BBC, 1968); Arthur's sexual urge towards an unnamed blind girl which leads him to the gallows in *Pennies from Heaven*; a montage sequence in *The Singing Detective* which counterpoints young Marlow seeing his mother have sex with Marlow witnessing the death of a fellow patient; and finally and most explicitly, the entirety of his play *Double Dare*, which follows two pairs in the same restaurant, a writer and an actress discussing a new script and a prostitute and her customer haggling over the price. In both cases, the man kills the woman he's with and in the end it is revealed they were, in fact, both the same couple. Potter draws a clear line connecting sex as a catalyst with its natural outcome: death.

In Russell's work examples include the memorable match cut between a couple having sex and a pair of corpses in a deathly embrace in *Women in Love*; sexual repression which leads to mayhem and the demise of the male lead in *The Devils* (Warner Bros., 1971); the concealed sexual urges which lead both Tchaikovsky and Nina into respectively death and madness in *The Music Lovers*; and the ending of *Whore* (Cheap Date/Trimark, 1991) which features a man dying precisely at the moment of sexual climax. Memorably, both *The Lair of the White Worm* and *Midnight Movie* end with the female antagonist revealing her true nature whilst chasing the protagonist topless with the intent of killing them.

It is also worth noting that both films are adaptations. Russell's film is based on Bram Stoker's *The Lair of the White Worm*, which Russell found disappointing. He took only the basic plot of the novel, making up the rest himself.[28] Potter's film, in turn, is based on *Moths*, a potboiler by Rosalind Ashe. No record exists of Potter's opinion on the novel, but it can't have been very high as no credit is given to Ashe in the opening, and in the closing scroll her name is relegated to an 'inspired by' credit. Furthermore, like Russell, he takes only the basic storyline of the novel. He then dutifully changes almost every other aspect of the plot and the characters. The romantic Oxford don and desirable bachelor becomes a repressed small village solicitor, the sexy American vixen becomes the pathetic Cockney wannabe model, and her husband James, utterly forgettable in the novel, is inundated by Potter with characteristics all his American characters share: boisterousness, brashness and bad manners.

ADAPTATION AND BIOGRAPHY

These transformative adaptations are very unusual coming from Russell and Potter, whose other adaptive work tended to be quite faithful to the source material. While working on *Women in Love*, adapted from a novel by D. H. Lawrence, Russell was appalled to find that the screenwriter Larry Kramer had changed much of the original novel's plot.[29] He rewrote the screenplay with Kramer so that it stayed true to the novel, even copying vast amounts of dialogue straight from the page. In *The Lion Roars*, he explains that he was 'only putting on the screen what D.H. Lawrence had written half a century before',[30] and yet, as Gomez notes in his book, 'It is the manner in which Russell visually captures Lawrence's characters and themes while also reflecting his own responses, however, that makes the film a significant adaptation.'[31] His forte as an adaptor became finding cinematic ways of translating the emotions and situations from the page to the screen. Most effectively, he utilised grotesque imagery, atonal music, and disorienting camera and editing techniques (repeated zoom-ins and zoom-outs, a fast-editing tempo) to portray the anarchy that occurs in *The Devils*, his adaptation of Aldous Huxley's 1952 book *The Devils of Loudon*.

Potter was also a noted and respected adaptor who exhibited in his adaptations a restraint not present in the rest of his oeuvre. His work adapting Thomas Hardy's short story *A Tragedy of Two Ambitions* for the BBC was seen as 'a highly restrained, enabling job',[32] and he was soon given the task of adapting Hardy's *The Mayor of Casterbridge* into a serial in 1978. The result was immediately seen as a masterpiece of television adaptation. What Potter did with his adaptations was not refashioning but, like Russell, translating, finding ways to make the story work as a TV drama while staying entirely true to the authorial intention and storyline. Potter continued to apply the same careful style of adaptation with varying degrees of success on such TV serials as *Late Call* (BBC, 1975), *Tender is the Night* (BBC, 1985) and *Christabel* (BBC, 1988).

More than adaptation, Russell is known for his biographical films of composers and artists; Potter attempted to write several biopics. Both were attracted to similar kinds of characters: outsiders who continue to practise what they believe in despite the misgivings of their more respected peers. For Potter these outsiders were Franz Anton Mesmer, a self-proclaimed hypnotist despised by the medical professionals (and reminiscent of Uri Geller, the self-proclaimed psychic and the subject of Russell's *Mindbender* [Major Motion Pictures, 1994]); the misunderstood Lewis Carroll, the nature of whose attraction to children is left ambiguous; and Christabel Bielenberg, a good British girl who married a German in 1934. For Russell, they were his embattled artists: Tchaikovsky mocked by Rubinstein, Mahler dismissed by Cosima Wagner, and Henri Gaudier-Brzeska and Henri Rousseau pretty much ignored by everyone.

Potter's approach to the biopic was very similar to Russell's: 'You get a starting point from what people talk about or from the newspapers, but they become, one hopes, people. You want to know them as people.'[33] He complained that modern biographies dealt more with trivial events or quirks of characters rather than examine the artist through their work.[34] Ken Russell, in his book *The Lion Roars*, agrees: 'My intention was never to produce a factual, day-by-day account of the composer's life . . . What I've always been after is the spirit of the composer as manifest in his music.'[35] Thus, Russell and Potter both tried to portray their subjects as real, tangible people, and they strived to explain their work through them and to have their work explain them.

RELIGION

For Potter and Russell, religion was a major factor in both work and life. In Russell's films, religious imagery and themes recur from the earliest works. *Amelia and the Angel*, his 1958 short, is about a little girl starring as an angel in a school play who loses her wings and goes looking for a replacement. Less obliquely, his 1959 documentary *Lourdes* is all about the faithful making a desperate pilgrimage to a holy site. Religious imagery would then continue to crop up in his *Monitor* films, for instance in the form of the spectacular crucifixion vision in *Elgar* or the re-enactment of Saint Sebastian's martyrdom in *The Debussy Film*. After Russell left television for cinema, religious imagery and themes in his work would only continue to increase throughout the 1970s, most notably in *The Devils*, which examines the dichotomy between religion and the Church. Religion also crops up as a theme in *Tommy*, which satirically examines false prophets and messiahs in a world in which pop culture has become a religion and Marilyn Monroe has replaced the Virgin Mary. Corrupt and perverted religious figures also continue making sporadic appearances, most memorably in the form of Reverend Peter Shayne in *Crimes of Passion*, and religious imagery (most often crucifixes) figures in almost all of Russell's films, most prominently in the hallucinations in *Altered States* and for the snake woman to spit on in *The Lair of the White Worm*.

Dennis Potter, on the other hand, openly claimed that most of his plays were religious in essence, such as *Joe's Ark*, a play about the question of God's cruelty, or *Brimstone and Treacle*, which is about the relationship between good and evil. He also claimed that *The Singing Detective* was a religious work, the story of seeing a man pick up his bed and walk; Glen Creeber agrees: 'The framework upon which this all hangs is essentially a Christian one, one man's progress from Eden to fall and from crucifixion to resurrection.'[36] In his 1976 TV play *Where Adam Stood*, Potter most openly makes his case for a practical, non-dogmatic approach to religion. The play concentrates on the dynamic between Philip, a widower who wears his religion like blinkers, and his son Edmund, who slowly realises that his teachings don't stand up in the real world. By the end of the play, Edmund has found a way to reconcile his beliefs with the real world out there, something his father is unable to do. His approach to religion is very similar to the practical and passionate approach advocated by Urbain Grandier in *The Devils*: a red-blooded enjoyment of all of God's creation and an ardent fight against dogmatism and manipulation with religion.

THE CRITICS

Of course, by tackling religion and sex in such a frank manner, Potter and Russell both attracted the wrath of the guardians of public morals, becoming the targets of the puritanical Mary Whitehouse. Potter became 'one of her most reliable targets',[37] while Russell found himself on the roster after the airing of his controversial Richard Strauss biopic *Dance of the Seven Veils* (BBC, 1970).[38] Furthermore, Ken Russell frequently found himself in the crosshairs of film critics. The *Evening Standard*'s Alexander Walker accused *The Devils* of being nothing more than a 'garish glossary of sadomasochism [resembling] the masturbatory fantasies of a Roman Catholic boyhood'.[39] Walker's scathing review led to a televised debate which culminated with Russell hitting Walker over the head with a rolled-up copy of his own review.[40]

The American film critic Pauline Kael also profoundly and continuously misunderstood Russell's work. In her savage 1976 beatdown of *The Devils* in the *New Yorker*, she mused that 'Ken Russell doesn't report hysteria, he markets it',[41] adding in her review of *Savage Messiah* (MGM-EMI, 1972) that 'one can't just dismiss Russell's movies, because they have an influence. They cheapen everything they touch.'[42] Her dislike for Russell's movies went as far as her stating that *The Music Lovers* made her feel as if she should 'drive a stake through the heart of the man who made it',[43] while Walker threatened to come hunting for the director with an elephant gun.[44]

Potter, in turn, had always had a good relationship with critics until his controversial and confusing 1989 BBC serial *Blackeyes*, which is when the critics turned on him. He was nicknamed 'Dirty Den' and became a favourite target for vicious mockery and abuse by every tabloid in the country. Both Potter and Russell suffered the most at the hands of censors, however. Potter had two of his plays banned. The first of them, 1966's *Almost Cinderella*, never even made it to recording. Potter was commissioned by the BBC to write a modern version of the fairy tale. The script he turned in, however, proved too modern for the very conservative BBC, with its sexual degenerate Prince Charming raping Cinderella on the stroke of midnight.[45] Potter defended his intentions by explaining that he wanted to bring out the impact of the story on adults rather than retell it as they saw it when they were children.[46] A similar fate befell Potter's 1976 TV play *Brimstone and Treacle*, which culminates with the Devil curing a comatose girl by raping her. It made it to recording but was banned before broadcast.

Ken Russell had a similar experience with *Dance of the Seven Veils*, which was aired but then banned from ever being repeated. The film mercilessly lampooned Richard Strauss by portraying his life in a series of vignettes, each culminating by exposing his connection with the Nazi Party. According to Russell, it portrayed the composer as an amalgam of the characters portrayed in his music, which he then stripped away one by one to reveal the Nazi underneath.[47]

Russell's battles with the censors would continue well into his cinema career, most notably in the case of *The Devils*, which had its striking sequence of a group of hysterical nuns raping the statue of Jesus cut at the insistence of the British Board of Film Censors.[48] The footage was considered lost until it was rediscovered in the Warner Bros. vault and reinserted into the film.[49] Nevertheless, this director's cut of *The Devils* is to this day conspicuous by its absence on home media and remains unavailable to the public.

UNMADE SCRIPTS

Having examined Potter's and Russell's extant oeuvre it will also be interesting to take a look at two of Potter's unfilmed scripts. The first is *Phantom of the Opera*, commissioned by Lorimar in 1987.[50] Potter moved the well-known story from the 1880s to the 1940s. The mixture of opera, Gothic horror and Nazis is pure Russell. The film follows the basic plot of the novel faithfully but adds one of Russell's favourite topics, the one which had got him in such trouble with the Strauss family: collaborationism. Potter examines the issue through the character of Christine, who finds herself torn between her hatred for the Nazis and her budding romance with an SS lieutenant. As everyone around her either refuses to collaborate and is swiftly eliminated or collaborates out of fear for their lives, she must make her decision between love and principles.

Besides this thematic connection, the script abounds with Russellisms such as the use of classical music to comment on the plot. In one of the scenes, Caspar, a Jewish singer about to be sent to the camp, sings onstage, 'No, nought can save you from fate's dark abyss!'[51] During a bar brawl, just as one of the fighters lands a punch, the villagers onstage in the opera sing, 'Hooray! Long live the champion!'[52] Another moment that brings Russell to mind is the scene in which the Gestapo investigator Milch is introduced. The whole scene plays out like a counterpoint to the scene in *Savage Messiah* in which Henri comments on the statues in the park. In bleak contrast to Henri's enthusiasm, Milch sits glumly in a garden observing a nude statue. 'We should obscure her nakedness,' he says. 'We should put knickers on her. And those things ladies use to hold up and hide their breasts.'[53] This conflating of sexual repression and art criticism is both pure Potter and pure Russell.

However, the script could have certainly benefited from Russell's gift of translating the written word to the screen. He could have freed it up from the overabundance of dialogue characteristic for Potter much as he did with Paddy Chayefsky's script for *Altered States*. He also would have doubtlessly been able to bring to life the visual set-pieces and tableaux only briefly sketched out by Potter, such as the film's climax, reminiscent of *Tommy*, in which the Phantom is killed and is then seen flying off into the sky in a fighter plane as 'This Love of Mine' plays. It is also worth noting that Ken Russell was no stranger to *Phantom*, having directed the 1986 music video for the Andrew Lloyd Webber song of the same name.

Commissioned the same year as *Phantom* was a biopic on Alexander Pushkin.[54] The film begins with a sequence in which Pushkin writes *Eugene Onegin* and imagines himself as the young hero engaged in a duel to the death. We are treated to such scenes throughout *Pushkin* which connect the author to the work so that we understand the work through the author and the author through the work, much like Russell's own artist biopics did. Potter portrays Pushkin himself as a Russellian character, exuberant to the point of exhaustion. In a scene in which he returns to Moscow after a long trip, he, boyishly excited, runs through the city shouting, 'Streets! Crowds! Theatres! Ballrooms! Friends!'[55] In that regard he is reminiscent of Russell's Henri Gaudier-Brzeska; however, he is also massively popular, followed by fans wherever he goes and inciting mass hysteria whenever he appears, and in this respect he resembles Russell's Liszt from *Lisztomania*. In several scenes throughout the script Potter attempts to emulate the same kind of hysteria which occurs whenever Liszt makes a public appearance in Russell's film. In one scene, he is spotted by an elderly man in the street, causing everyone within earshot to congregate before the bemused poet, chanting his name.

The script is also full of moments of levity and slapstick, such as the scene of Pushkin engaging in a comical sword duel reminiscent of a similar scene in *Lisztomania* in which Liszt engages in a sabre duel with the husband of his mistress. With its mixture of comedy and Gothic imagery, fantasy and reality, this biopic is both stylistically and thematically reminiscent of Russell's films. It examines not only the artist at hand through his work but also his relationship with the women in his life, which is a recurring theme in all of Russell's biopics.

CONCLUSION

This parallel look at the careers of Ken Russell and Dennis Potter was never meant to absolutely demonstrate that the two men ploughed the same creative furrow; however, it is hard not to be struck by the similarities and parallels between their styles and recurring themes when seeing them listed. Stylistically, both men fought for the right to express themselves through non-conventional forms, which they both enjoyed using to evoke in the viewer the emotional states their protagonists were going through. Both employed complex narrative structures combining fantasy and reality, using music as connective tissue between the layers. In that sense, Potter was not just Russell's contemporary but also his comrade in the seemingly unending battle against the suffocating norms of British television and cinema and in defence of what Potter called non-naturalism. Consequently, they both faced the ire of their benefactors (in Potter's case the BBC, in Russell's case also the various film studios he worked for) and their critics, giving them undeservedly bad reputations as British *enfants terribles* at best and perverted old men at worst. Of course, as ever, these bad reputations stemmed mainly from their frank and observant explorations into the taboo subjects of sex and religion, both of which permeate every facet of their creative output, be it as the main subject or merely as symbolic imagery or brief references. Furthermore, both men earned their reputations as excellent adaptors and frequently took inspiration from great literary works of art, experimenting with their genres and exploring or outright spoofing the tropes inherent within them.

There is an interesting moment of synchronicity which occurs in *Pennies from Heaven* when Arthur and Eileen imagine themselves dancing on a spinning phonograph record just like Polly and Tony in Russell's *The Boy Friend* (MGM-EMI, 1971). And in the end, it is just such little synchronicities and similarities which convince me that Potter and Russell separately reached the same subversive and form-busting ideas about where cinema and television should be heading: away from the boring conventions of the TV play and the stodgy 'British picture' and towards a more open, non-naturalistic approach which would allow the author to show the frame within the frame and use it to bring the viewer closer to the story. What is undeniable, however, is that both men were well ahead of their time and paid the price of being disregarded, disrespected and discarded by their peers.

NOTES

1. Joseph A. Gomez, *Ken Russell: The Adaptor as Creator* (London: Frederick Muller, 1976), 80.
2. Humphrey Carpenter, *Dennis Potter: A Biography* (London: Faber and Faber, 1998), 447–50.
3. W. Stephen Gilbert, *Fight and Kick and Bite: The Life and Work of Dennis Potter* (London: Sceptre, 1995), 158.
4. Ken Russell, *A British Picture: An Autobiography* (London: Southbank Publishing, 2008), 15.
5. Ibid., 22.
6. Ibid., 23.
7. Ibid., 25.
8. Ibid., 23.
9. Matthew Melia, 'Ken Russell's Unfinished Projects and Unmade Films, 1956–68: The BBC Years', in James Fenwick, Kieran Foster and David Eldridge (eds), *Shadow Cinema: The Historical and Production Contexts of Unmade Films* (New York: Bloomsbury Academic, 2021), 103.
10. Carpenter, 98–9.
11. BBC Written Archives Centre, Memo from Adam to Miall, 17 February 1961, T32/1, 579/1, quoted in Gilbert, 88.
12. John Hill, 'Elgar', in accompanying booklet to *Ken Russell: The Great Composers* (DVD/Blu-ray, BFI, 2016), 6.
13. Dennis Potter, 'This Was a Glorious Wallop', 'In My View' column, *Daily Herald*, 30 March 1963; reprinted in Dennis Potter, *The Art of Invective: Selected Non-Fiction 1953–94*, ed. Ian Greaves, David Rolinson and John Williams (London: Oberon, 2015), 49–50.
14. Dennis Potter, 'Realism and Non-Naturalism', Edinburgh International Television Festival, 1 September 1977, in *The Art of Invective*, 208–12.
15. Dennis Potter, 'Praise Be for a Bold Experiment', 'In My View' column, *Daily Herald*, 8 September 1962.
16. Potter, 'Realism and Non-Naturalism', 204.
17. Ken Russell, *The Lion Roars: Ken Russell on Film* (London: Faber and Faber, 1994), 100.
18. Ibid.
19. Potter, 'Realism and Non-Naturalism', 212.

20. Gomez, 17.
21. Graham Fuller, *Potter on Potter* (London: Faber and Faber, 1993), xiv.
22. Quoted in Gordon Burn, 'Television is the Only Medium That Counts', *Radio Times*, 8 October 1970.
23. Quoted in Richard Grant, 'For 17 Years I've Been Fantasising about How to Improve TV', *Evening News*, 21 May 1979.
24. Carpenter, 265.
25. Glen Creeber, *The Singing Detective* (London: BFI, 2007), 22.
26. Gomez, 30.
27. Gilbert, 241.
28. Philip Nutman, 'A Descent into the Lair of the White Worm', *Fangoria*, December 1988.
29. John Baxter, *Ken Russell: An Appalling Talent* (London: Michael Joseph, 1973), 167.
30. Ibid., 73.
31. Gomez, 87.
32. Gilbert, 228.
33. Fuller, 45.
34. Dennis Potter, 'The Face at the Window', Unread Classics series, *Times*, 3 August 1968.
35. Russell, *The Lion Roars*, 75.
36. Creeber, 67.
37. Ben Thompson (ed.), *Ban This Filth! Letters from the Mary Whitehouse Archive 1963–2001* (London: Faber and Faber, 2012), 172–3.
38. Peter Waymark, 'Russell's *Seven Veils* Shocks Critics', *Times*, 17 February 2001.
39. Alexander Walker, 'Review of *The Devils*', *Evening Standard*, 22 July 1971, Press archive, British Film Institute.
40. Geoffrey McNabb, 'Farewell to the Wild Man of Cinema', *Independent*, 29 November 2011, <https://www.independent.co.uk/arts-entertainment/films/features/farewell-wild-man-cinema-6269271.html> (last accessed 5 November 2021).
41. Pauline Kael, quoted in Richard Crouse, *Raising Hell: Ken Russell and the Unmaking of The Devils* (Toronto: ECW Press, 2012), 157.
42. Pauline Kael, *Reeling* (Boston: Little, Brown, 1976), 52.
43. Will Brantley (ed.), *Conversations with Pauline Kael* (Jackson: University Press of Mississippi, 1996), 28.
44. Crouse.
45. Hunter Davies, 'Trials of a TV Man', Atticus Column, *Sunday Times*, 30 October 1966.
46. *Daily Mail*, 7 December 1966.
47. Russell, *The Lion Roars*, 100.
48. Crouse.
49. Michael Brooke, 'Censoring the Devils', *BFI Screenonline*, <http://www.screenonline.org.uk/film/id/1050759/index.html> (last accessed 5 November 2021).
50. Carpenter, 472.
51. Dennis Potter Archive, The Dean Heritage Centre, 'Phantom of the Opera', Ref: DP2012.22.571.
52. Ibid.
53. Ibid.
54. Carpenter, 469.
55. Dennis Potter Archive, The Dean Heritage Centre, 'Pushkin', Ref: DP2012.22.573=574.

CHAPTER 12

Ken Russell and the Sexual Dimension of the Outsider Artist: An Exploration of *Elgar: The Erotic Variations* and *Delius: A Moment with Venus*

Kevin Fullerton

INTRODUCTION: KEN RUSSELL, OUTSIDER ARTIST

'Here you see the typical Englishman,' says Percy Grainger in Ken Russell's 2007 novel *Delius: A Moment with Venus*, 'one mention of the word sex and he disappears behind a smoke-screen.'[1] This comment from the Australian-born composer is aimed at Eric Fenby, the youthful amanuensis to the acid-tongued Frederick Delius. Yet it could just as easily be read as a barbed response to Russell's critics. In his home country and in the United States, Russell's films came under constant scrutiny for their portrayals of sex, with the director's flamboyant and baroque sensibility mistaken for a voyeuristic leer. While one could quote any number of negative reviews he received over the course of his career, Roger Ebert's withering opinions of *Salome's Last Dance* (Vestron, 1988) typify the attitude of many of the film-maker's critics:

> Russell demonstrates again that he is most interested in literary figures when their trousers are unbuttoned. And even then, he isn't interested in why, or how, they carry on their sex lives; like the de-frockers of the scandal sheets, he wants only to breathlessly shock us with the news that his heroes possessed and employed genitals.[2]

Attacks of this kind were levelled at Russell with the release of almost every new film. He was vilified by critics who thought his depictions of sex were one-dimensional and superfluous and, more often than not, the attitudes expressed by contemporaneous reviewers betrayed a puritanical streak in the world of film criticism. This is especially true during the 1960s and 1970s when the full pantheon of human sexuality was restrained by a social conservatism that wrapped its tendrils around the views of many commentators on the arts. Such sexual myopia was coupled with an understanding of arts criticism which relied heavily upon nineteenth-century attitudes towards taste, class and decorum, and a circle of critics with prudish values comparable to those of the Lord Chamberlain's office, which censored the theatre until 1968. As Melvyn Bragg remarked of Russell, 'He was at the start an outsider and in a country such as ours which had in the sixties an exclusive hierarchy of taste, Ken's erudite eclecticism, self-taught and self-thought, again marked him as a gypsy, not one of "them".'[3]

Russell's progressive themes, although stemming from an era of social reform, must have seemed like wishful liberal utopianism to those living outside of swinging Central London, as evidenced by the many times his films were banned in provincial towns and cities across the UK. The 1960s, while sexually progressive in terms of legislation for hitherto marginalised groups, remained socially conservative; the Pill, forever viewed as a symbolic catalyst for the swinging sixties, was largely limited to married women for most of the decade, as was receiving any information about it.[4] The seventies saw a similar wellspring of change, with the passing of the Equal Pay Act and more explicit portrayals of sex in cinema from directors like Russell, Bernardo Bertolucci, Pier Paolo Pasolini and Nicolas Roeg.[5] Yet these supposed freedoms saw many films banned and, as a result of this, the British Board of Film Censors underwent an existential crisis regarding how it classified sexually charged or violent cinema, one which almost led to its closure.[6] The eighties saw gay rights activist, artist, film-maker and erstwhile set designer for Russell, Derek Jarman, edge his way into the broader cultural conversation with *Caravaggio* (BFI/Channel 4, 1986) but also saw section 28 of the Local Government Act passed in 1988, which forbade the 'promotion' of homosexuality as an 'acceptable' lifestyle.[7] These three decades of increased sexual liberation, tempered by intense sexual conservatism, also mark Russell's heyday. His baroque style and liberal slant towards sexual permissiveness mirrored the prevailing attitudes of the London bohemia he was ostensibly a part of, but that the conservative majority could never embrace. That sexuality was a primary focus of the vitriol aimed at Russell is telling, especially from a critical circle which adhered to the attitudes of taste and propriety favoured by the ruling classes.[8]

It should be noted at this point that Russell did have a few supporters in the media, most notably the *Guardian*'s film critic Derek Malcolm. Some critics who were usually against his work were also occasionally known to enjoy some of his films – Ebert, for instance, wrote reluctantly positive reviews for *Lisztomania* (Goodtimes Enterprises, 1975) and *Altered States* (Warner Bros., 1980). Yet these examples were the minority. Russell's valorisation of sexuality, within his artist biopics in particular, was anathema to an establishment mentality which believed that the probing of an artist's personal life from a fictive perspective was nothing better than, to quote Nina Hibbin's review of *The Music Lovers* (United Artists, 1970), 'gross irresponsibility'.[9] Yet his 'irresponsibility' is to portray artists as human beings, with all their supposed virtues and vices. Moreover, the subjects of sex and creativity are inextricably linked in Russell's work. Sex is a means of exploring the most intimate aspects of his subjects' creative psyche, not a tawdry exhibitionism (Malcolm was correct when he said that Russell viewed sex as a 'mainspring of most things'[10]). Its centrality within Russell's films and novels is emphasised by Jack Fisher, who quipped that if sexual content was removed from *The Music Lovers*, what would remain is a 'fifteen minute entertainment starring Max Adrian'.[11] The most infamous sequence of *The Music Lovers*, in which Tchaikovsky is sexually tormented by his new bride within the confines of a violently rocking train, is the perfect example of this, emphasising in both content and form that Tchaikovsky's homosexuality was what Joseph Lanza calls the 'centrepiece in an internal and external war'.[12]

NOVELS

Nonetheless, the condemnation Russell received throughout his career cast him as a serial outsider in the industry and rendered each new escalation of sexuality or kitsch humour an act of defiance in the face of traditional notions of British taste. While this particular aesthetic was initially profitable, it resulted in him becoming, by his own admission, 'unbankable' by the early 1990s.[13] Unable to secure funding for a significant feature, he tackled a number of non-film based creative ventures, including the publication of several novels from 1999 to 2007. The content of these novels is as varied as his films. *Mike & Gaby's Space Gospel* (1999) is a satirical take on the story of Jesus and is reminiscent of Douglas Adams's *Hitchhikers' Guide . . .* series; *Violation* (2005) is a Rabelaisian story imagining a world in which football has become a state religion, so much so that all adherents to other faiths have been deported to a National Penal Colony; while *Elgar: The Erotic Variations*, *Delius: A Moment with Venus*, *Beethoven: Confidential* and *Brahms Gets Laid* (2007) are written equivalents of Russell's composer biopics, the sub-genre he is arguably best known for. Moreover, as their respective titles imply, these novels reinforce his recurring stance that sex is as intrinsically linked to the act of creation as nature, politics or love. Conversely, the state attempts to curtail the free expression of these four composers and their associates, primarily for the benefit of the status quo. The sexual impulse behaves as an act of defiance in Russell's composer novels, allowing creativity to flourish and fostering bohemian environments in miniature. The composer novels were sold in two volumes, one of which contained *Elgar: The Erotic Variations* and *Delius: A Moment with Venus*, the other *Beethoven: Confidential* and *Brahms Gets Laid*. In part this was due to their relative brevity, but the pairings also provided Russell the opportunity to explore his central themes more fully with a variety of composers. The rest of this chapter will focus on the two novels devoted to British composers about whom Russell had made his two most acclaimed films for the BBC, *Elgar: The Erotic Variations* and *Delius: A Moment with Venus*. This will allow for comparisons to be made between the novels and the films that preceded them, but also to look at how Russell utilises sexuality to reflect his wider project to examine artists and bohemians who, directly or indirectly, stand in opposition to state control.

Russell is not the only film-maker to have dabbled in prose fiction. Elia Kazan wrote several bestsellers and, more recently, directors such as David Cronenberg and Gus Van Sant have taken time away from their successful careers as directors to experiment with the novel. Russell's literary forays, however, belong in the same category as Michael Powell's *A Waiting Game* (1975), Mike Hodge's *Watching the Wheels Come Off* (2010) and John Boorman's *Crime of Passion* (2016), in that they are works written in his dotage, when funding for his films was almost non-existent. Like the novels listed above, Russell's late-career interest in prose also grew out of a need to see long-standing unfunded film projects realised in some form, even if not within his preferred medium. Yet the transition from film-maker and screenwriter to novelist is not always an easy one. Cronenberg offers an invaluable insight into the differences between writing films and novels, stating, 'When you're reading a screenplay, you're not really interested in the prose, you're interested in the imagery it conjures up in your head.'[14]

It must be said, the quality of Russell's prose is rarely equal to his prodigiousness behind the camera. He falls into the trap Cronenberg clearly tries to avoid, and his novels often read like reformatted screenplays. In his review of Russell's collection of composer novels, Lloyd Evans was largely complimentary about their narrative and characterisation, but he noted how the writing regularly bears the hallmarks of a recycled film script, claiming, 'Instead of intimacy and fluency there's a stilted fussiness as Russell gets all the details of his shot just right.'[15] Such criticisms, while justified, do nothing to diminish the importance of these novels within Russell's oeuvre, not least because they provide readers the opportunity to experience his creative vision unmediated by the cuts of censors or financial backers. As most of Russell's papers were lost in a house fire in 2006, his six novels also point to potential ideas for screenplays that would otherwise be lost (*Mike & Gaby's Space Gospel*, for instance, started life as a script written with Jarman, while *Beethoven: Confidential* was originally a film project set to star Anthony Hopkins that had to be abandoned after funding fell through).[16]

The composers covered by Russell's novels are invariably 'outsiders' in some form or another, a term which is, by necessity, nebulous in its definition, not least because artists and writers can become outsiders for any number of reasons. Throughout the twentieth century, some (like Ngũgĩ wa Thiong'o) were exiled for their non-conformist political views, others (like D. H. Lawrence) for the extremity of their art, and some (like James Joyce) declared their own exile to break from the communal myth created in their homeland. Andrew Gurr says of the artist in exile, 'He marks the still point between two straining forces ... By reacting against [his] community the artist knows his individuality. By exiling himself he loses it.'[17] Similarly, Colin Wilson, who was a friend of Russell's and a prominent champion of his work, argues, 'The Outsider ... prefers to consider the man who sets out to be very good or very wicked rather than the good citizen who advocates moderation in all things.'[18] For Russell, the profound individual is an outsider who lives in an extreme state of unrest while standing in opposition to a normative mode of living and thought. In both his films and his novels, Russell has regularly conveyed these extremes via the use of physical functions, whether that means filming the excrement-eating sequence from Alfred Jarry's *King Ubu* in *Always on Sunday* (BBC, 1965), Joanna Crane wiping semen from her mouth as she satirises American values in *Crimes of Passion* (New World Pictures, 1984), or the cacophony of vomit, plague pustules and mass nun orgies in *The Devils* (Warner Bros., 1971).[19] Sex, however, is his primary concern. For both Russell and his subjects, the outsider instinct is firmly intertwined with sexuality, especially in any non-heteronormative or non-monogamous capacity, and is synonymous with rebellion and satire, from the works of François Rabelais onwards.

ELGAR: THE EROTIC VARIATIONS

In *Elgar: The Erotic Variations*, the sexual impulse is presented as a direct form of inspiration. Elgar's position as an outsider, though more tenuous than that of many of Russell's other subjects, exists both because of his working-class upbringing (which renders him forever a 'shopkeeper's son'[20] to the tabloid media) and because of the many extramarital love trysts he engaged in throughout his life. The novel itself looks at the life of Elgar from the moment of his honeymoon with wife Alice Elgar, and follows him until after his death, where he receives a punishment laced with dramatic irony in heaven. This gives Russell the opportunity to focus on many of Elgar's compositions, while exploring their meaning more fully than he was able to in his two television films on the composer, *Elgar: Portrait of a Composer* (BBC, 1962) and *Elgar: Fantasy of a Composer on a Bicycle* (ITV, 2002). Some of the material within *The Erotic Variations* may also stem from his unmade film on the composer from 1976, entitled *Elgar's Land of Hope and Glory*, which centres around an unknown woman, who may or may not be one of Elgar's mistresses, as she tours the Malvern Hills.[21] It is worth noting that *Portrait of a Composer* was Russell's most enduringly popular film, possibly because, as a result of the squeamishness of BBC arts programming at the time, he avoided any discussion of Elgar's sex life. Russell states in the preface to the novel, 'these films were highly pictorial, and there was little opportunity to delve below the surface of this complex man with the persona of Colonel Blimp and the passion of a Don Juan'.[22] As the novel's title implies, Russell's prose depiction of Elgar is also his most sexually explicit, acting as a direct and deliberate rebuttal to the restraint of previous biopics, and as such presents the carnal dimension of Elgar's personality more thoroughly. Russell's rags-to-riches version of Elgar's life in *Elgar: The Erotic Variations* illustrates the intertwining nature of sexual appeal, artistic success and wealth. Elgar is an outsider from the first page of the novel, having married a wife who is of a higher social class than him, and is treated as an opportunist aiming to raise his socioeconomic status. Even porters at the train station he visits with his wife in the novel's first chapter appear to see through Elgar's position in Britain's rigid class system:

> The bloke spoke like a country bumpkin and wore a Sunday-best suit that would have been the laughing stock of Saville Row. The lady, on the other hand, was definitely top drawer, even if she was a bit hoity-toity . . . The things some men will do for money, the porter thought as he touted for his next customer.[23]

The first chapter of the novel emphasises the socially precarious nature of the marriage between Edward and Alice, painting them as outsiders in a class-conscious society. She has been rejected by her family for marrying Elgar, in part because of his working-class background but also because of his Catholicism. Alice retains her social aspirations and is convinced that the world will discover the genius of Elgar and that, in time, her social standing will be repaired. At this point, both Elgar and Alice are economic and social outcasts, and their sex life suffers as a result. Instead of having sex on their honeymoon, Alice frets over Elgar's uncouth command of language, speculating 'on how long she would have to work on him before he was sufficiently groomed to be accepted into polite society'.[24] While Elgar's genius stems in part from his background and, in turn, his position as an outsider from both his class and Alice's, she wants to regain her foothold in society and, inadvertently, corrupt Elgar's innate talent by forcing him to conform to the fashionable composition styles of the day. Paradoxically, it is Elgar's unique talent that Alice is attracted to, as Russell shows when Elgar composes a song inspired by one of his wife's poems

> She was soon to find out, as in a fine tenor voice Elgar started to broadcast their voice to the world. Whereupon Alice's despair immediately gave way to a cry of joy, as the realisation of their extraordinary achievement finally hit home. That night their marriage was consummated.[25]

Alice's passions for Elgar run concurrent with his mounting success, and Russell intensifies his sexualised language as she grows more comfortable with her erotic impulses, as shown when she witnesses a full symphony orchestra perform one of his compositions: 'The event was a real turn-on. Alice could hardly wait to get back to their bedroom and get down on her hands and knees.'[26] As sexuality and creativity go hand in hand in Elgar's life, Russell shows Elgar courting many more lovers in order to broaden his horizons and diversify his body of work. In turn, he lives within a sexual bohemia that aids his art but alienates his wife. Elgar, newly anointed with success, lives a more straightforwardly conventional life than many of Russell's subjects; his casual disregard for sexual mores is his only extreme, and even the consequences of these actions are deliberately underplayed. Russell spends much of the novel showing these trysts from the perspective of innocents, including Elgar's bulldog Dan and his daughter Carice. In one passage, Carice describes her father's 'friends' for a school essay, and in doing so shows Edward as having male friends who can help his career and female friends with whom, it can be inferred, he is having sex. Tellingly, Carice writes, 'Then there's Mama, though I don't know if a wife counts as a friend, does she?', implying a fractious relationship between Edward and Alice.[27] Alice remains on the outskirts of the narrative as the novel progresses, regaining the social status she craves but gradually finding herself excluded from Elgar's creative process in favour of new women. These trysts provide Elgar with fresh points of reference (his friend Rosa, for instance, has a passion for Aubrey Beardsley) and regularly act as a buffer from outside forces aiming to destroy the world Elgar has created for himself. These negative influences can most easily be characterised by the umbrella term of the 'establishment'.

The hand of the establishment features heavily in the works of Russell, usually serving the function of attempting to destroy the non-conformist world of the fictions' protagonists. Elgar presents a unique problem in Russell's oeuvre, operating within the establishment by composing many works which directly served the need for patriotic unity within Britain at the time, while still remaining ambivalent about his place within it. If there was anything which made Elgar a non-conformist outsider, in Russell's view, it was his many relationships with women. He illustrates this with the character of Miles Spooner, a snooping journalist prepared to discredit Elgar by exposing his many affairs. While Carice and Dan show how natural Elgar's actions seem to insiders, Spooner shows how readily the press, and by extension the establishment, will exploit his eccentricities to send his name into disrepute, serving much the same plot function as the morally bankrupt journalists in Russell's film *Mahler* (Goodtimes Enterprises, 1974). Much like the women who come to the rescue in the denouement of Russell's *Lisztomania*, the women around Elgar keep his secrets and protect his reputation. Despite this, the damage control by those closest to him never completely negates the impact of his actions. The outsider creates casualties, and Elgar is no exception. His casual dismissal of his wife becomes egregious for his daughter Carice as she grows older. Russell writes, 'The piece reminded her of her father's unalloyed pleasures at the expense of her mother's stoic pain . . . he had never fully outgrown the guilt over his treatment of Alice, even if he had eventually come to live with it.'[28]

Russell makes the punishments for his outsiders much more obvious in his novels than in the ambiguous endings to his films. The final chapter of *Elgar: The Erotic Variations* takes place after the composer's death, at the point when he reaches heaven. Here his myriad flaws are pointed out to him, and he is sentenced to live two extra lives, one in the body of his wife, the other in the body of his daughter. His hell, as he discovers, is to live through the pain of the two people most impacted by his actions.

DELIUS: *A MOMENT WITH VENUS*

Delius: A Moment with Venus continues the theme of sexual profligacy with a profile of the composer Frederick Delius, about whom Russell had previously made the BBC film *Delius: Song of Summer* (1968). The film was based on Eric Fenby's book *Delius as I Knew Him*,[29] published in 1936, and is widely regarded as Russell's most complete interpretation of a composer.[30] While the film focuses on the companionship between the ageing and syphilitic Delius and his amanuensis Eric Fenby, the novel divides itself into two sections: the first is a recounting of Delius's sexually hyperactive youth and the second, a precis of his old age and the toll that promiscuity has taken on his body. The title itself, *A Moment with Venus*, is a variation of the saying, 'One night with Venus, a lifetime with Mercury', a reference to the debilitating treatment that kept syphilis at bay during the era.[31]

In much the same way that Alice remained alongside Elgar in *The Erotic Variations*, Delius's wife Jelka remains dutifully by his side in spite of his near constant philandering, showing a devotion that is as much due to his genius as his disposition. Delius is a more extreme variation of the outsider than Elgar, having exiled himself from England, his country of origin, for much of his life. The novel shows the hardships that temperamental artists inflict on those around them in a more tangible and melodramatic form. The actions of Delius also allow Russell to explore two of the central questions of his entire body of work: what does a genius have to do before he is exiled even from his small group of admirers, and to what extent does an artist's personal life impact their work? Fenby himself, writing in 1936, was ambivalent about how biographical details could affect art, believing that biography facilitated 'a natural and healthy curiosity so long as a true sense of values is maintained'.[32] His reluctance to wholeheartedly endorse the inherently probing nature of biography most likely stemmed from his close working relationship with Delius, which resulted in several nervous breakdowns both during his time at their French retreat and after the composer's death. Russell, who became an acquaintance of Fenby's during the production of *Song of Summer*,[33] is sensitive to the dilemma presented by Fenby. His definition of 'a natural and healthy curiosity' is, however, no doubt more flexible than that of the amanuensis, as Fenby's seeming lack of interest in Delius's sexuality indicates. *A Moment with Venus*, by comparison, views Delius's sexual dimension as central to his character, to his music and to his fraught relationship with his wife (whom, it is pointed out, he may have also infected with the then-fatal disease of syphilis).

In the first half of the novel, Russell explores the carefree sexual exploits of Delius's youth in the manner of *Tom Jones* or *Don Juan*, painting a rambunctious portrait of a man whose sexual urges could never be satisfied. Throughout the first half of the picaresque narrative, Delius's undisciplined mind floods with regular sexual digressions, all of which emphasise his insider status as the son of a wealthy landowner, and his outsider status as a serial philanderer, libertine and atheist. The first sexual encounter he reminisces on concerns Lindy, an African American woman he slept with on his father's plantation:

> and the little half-caste picaninny, rumour had it, was the fruit of their labours. Sex under the mosquito nets that invariably enveloped them had always been a sweaty business. In fact it was her sweat that first excited him when the Negro workers on his plantation had thrown a party to welcome their new master on the night of his arrival.[34]

The description is wrought with ambiguity and raises questions about the extent to which the plantation worker consented, or could consent, to have sex with Delius. The composer's overtly racist language implies a self-perceived superiority over Lindy, typical of the era Russell is depicting. In short, this is a plantation owner raping his worker. Moreover, his sense of arousal at the idea of her 'sweat' implies a tacit connection between the physical labour undertaken at the plantation and the sexual act. It connects Delius's background as a plantation owner's son and the primalism that connects his art with nature and the earth. The exploitation in this brief paragraph is difficult to miss, and illustrates Delius's ability to use others as raw material for his own gratification or his art. In the two-novel cycle of *The Erotic Variations* and *A Moment with Venus*, this is the first instance in which the outsider instinct for sexual gratification and extremity bleeds into an instance of rape.

Delius's trek across the globe allows Russell a broader canvas in comparison with Elgar's travels from Yorkshire to London. In doing so, he shows that Delius is not an artist in isolation. Instead, the artist in exile is almost an archetypal figure, necessarily so because the defiance of conventional social mores can only inhabit a limited number of forms, especially when sexuality is restricted to a heterosexual paradigm. According to Wilson, the outsider realises that 'chaos must be faced'.[35] Delius, like many artists of his time, crafted his own chaos via a panoply of sexual encounters and bacchanalian orgies. These encounters point to a desire for individualism which typify the outsider artist of the early twentieth century, a time when separating one's self from the masses was viewed as a necessity (and when an increasing number of people were growing literate and engaging with culture).[36] In many cases the artistic community aimed to deliberately alienate society at large, proclaiming a dislike of children, a love of obscurantism, a strong belief in the superiority of the intelligentsia, and the seemingly genuine belief that the working classes lacked souls.[37] This also created strong artist communities across the globe, not least in Paris, where many of the leading lights of art, literature and music lived together from the end of the nineteenth century to the early twentieth century, spawning movements such as the 'lost generation' of expatriate writers who resided in France's capital during the 1920s.[38]

Russell uses this era of alienated artists banding together to continue his depiction of Delius's sexual indiscretions, describing a threesome between the composer, Henri de Toulouse-Lautrec and the Moulin Rouge dancer Valentin le Désossé in the Moulin Rouge:

> The little Frenchman, who was none other than Henri de Toulouse-Lautrec, had sacrificed his usual 'salon de lux' in honour of visiting Victorian royalty. For this he was rewarded by the madam of the establishment with a freebie in the form of one Valentin le Desosse (Valentin the Double-jointed) who lay snoring between the two men who had spent an active night sharing her favours. The second lucky man, almost double the size of the midget painter, was Fritz Delius, a virtually unknown English composer.[39]

The combination of sex and artists implies fertility not only in the bedrooms of the Moulin Rouge but also in the act of creativity at the turn of the twentieth century. A *ménage à trois* solidifies the bond between the artists, all exiled from society and all using sex as a signifier for their freedom from mass conceptions of decorum. Despite their equal genius as artists, it is notable that Lautrec, whose diminutive stature is mentioned several times in this brief passage, is at a severe physical disadvantage to Delius, who, it is suggested, is living on the finances of Lautrec at this time. Like Delius with Lindy, Lautrec is being exploited. The homoerotic overtones of this passage are also evident, not least because Valentin le Désossé is, in fact, a man. Whether this is a deliberate mistake, or a confusion on Russell's part between Désossé and his dance partner Louise Weber, is unclear.

The second half of the novel shifts from the psychological perspective of Delius to a number of the characters closest to him in his later life as syphilis robs him of his sight and the ability to walk. The depiction of the autumn years of the composer's life in the novel bears a perhaps unavoidable similarity to *Song of Summer*, particularly regarding the vampiric impact of Delius on the mental well-being of others. He has continued to exploit anyone he comes into contact with, now out of necessity rather than greed. Fenby is given particular precedence in the narrative, his comfortable Catholic upbringing contrasting with Delius's atheistic non-conformity.

In this sense, Fenby represents what Ferdinand Tönnies describes as *Gemeinschaft*, a common term in sociology denoting a small society,[40] which in artistic terms is conformist, traditional and conservative.[41] Delius, conversely, has lived within a state of *Gesellschaft*, or cosmopolitanism, which has untethered his art from the conformities of any traditional notions of community. He is a man without a country, and while the first half of *A Moment with Venus* looks upon this as the carefree development of the artist as a young man, the second utilises Fenby as a counterpoint on which to reflect how alienated Delius has become. Fenby's virginity, referred to throughout the novel, underscores the contrast in *Gemeinschaft* and *Gesellschaft* between them. As the effects of syphilis wither Delius, he is as much an outsider in his own body as he is in society. This, to Fenby and to Russell, means that Delius's only respite from his constant pain lies in music, as well as its being the only way he can transport himself into transcendental sexual bliss. Fenby becomes aware of this as he listens to 'A Poem of Life and Love' at the Albert Hall: 'Then, as the music became more sensual and grew towards a climax, he visualized a couple lying in the heather making love – which had him blushing and wondering whether Delius had ever consciously set the sex act to music.'[42] This brief musing shows Fenby awakening to the sexual world, and to the notion that art and sex may be linked, implying that this impressionable young man is moving from the confines of *Gemeinschaft* into Delius's world of *Gesellschaft*. Fenby's newfound sexual awareness also attunes him to the imperfectness of the artist compared with their work, and of the necessary disconnect between Delius's outsider state of living and the music he gives to the world. As Fenby's innocence is lost, so too does he develop an increasing disillusionment with art. The conflict inhabiting Fenby culminates in a debate with Delius's friend and fellow composer Percy Grainger, who sums up Fenby's dilemma by asking, 'How can such godawful shits write such heavenly music . . . so far as the value of the music and the music alone is concerned, does it really matter?'[43] The question acts as a rhetorical device for Russell, partly a direct address to the reader as well as a contributing factor to Fenby's torment as he learns more about the victims of Delius's carnal desires.

The dutiful nature of Fenby, despite his growing ambivalence towards his collaborator's personality, points to the driving force within *The Erotic Variations* and

A Moment with Venus: the outsider artist can only sustain themselves via the help of individuals who are willing to sacrifice their personal ambitions in favour of a perceived genius. As in *The Debussy Film* (BBC, 1965), *Dante's Inferno: The Private Life of Dante Gabriel Rossetti, Poet and Painter* (BBC, 1967), *The Music Lovers* and the majority of Russell's other artist and composer biopics, the sexual liberalism which defines the outsider artist creates reluctant co-conspirators, most of whom live their lives obfuscating the truth about a creative virtuoso's private affairs.

Russell's initial desire to extinguish the mystique of the artist coincided with the romanticisation of the outsider figure as seen in Colin Wilson's *Outsider* cycle of books, the Angry Young Men of the theatre, and the archetype of the lone spy in the James Bond and Harry Palmer series, the latter of which Russell contributed to with the film *Billion Dollar Brain* (United Artists, 1967). Russell's interest differs from many of these works in that it focuses on the support network which both impedes the artist and protects them from the castigation of a conservative society. The novels reconfigure the pattern of the artist and the artist's victims to make the penalty paid by those closest to Elgar and Delius clearer, while also emphasising the mental strain that these victims are under in order to protect the legacy of the work they hold dearly. Russell utilises the indefinable connection created by sex, and the complications of a monogamous relationship, to add the sense of an inescapable desire that is both linked to and repelled by the genius of the artist in question, whether that means Fenby's constant contemplations about Delius's philandering, or Alice's subtle side-lining in favour of younger women and new bursts of inspiration. Written in the twenty-first century, fifty years after their television incarnations, it is perhaps telling that the valorisation of the exiled artist in the novels is far less evident than in the BBC biopics. As Wilson claims, 'the Outsider is a social problem', and Russell's defining project in *The Erotic Variations* and *A Moment with Venus* is to show both the benefits and the disadvantages of the outsider artist allowed to thrive in a largely traditionalist society.[44] Their publication in the twenty-first century also indicates a self-reflexive attitude towards Russell's past work as he implicitly surveys his own history as an outsider artist, incorporating an 'openly subjective' autobiographical element into his work as he has with the majority of his biopic films in the past.[45]

In one of the final chapters of *A Moment with Venus*, Fenby, looking after the dead body of Delius before a funeral service, is confronted with the syphilitic penis of the famous composer:

> Fenby had never seen a body in the advanced stages of syphilis before, especially with the diseased member triumphantly rampant in its state of rigor mortis and attired in royal purple . . . What to do? Jelka would be putting in an appearance soon, causing Fenby frantically to search for a way to spare her blushes . . . Jelka seemed quite oblivious.[46]

Jelka's wilful blindness towards Delius's misdeeds characterises the people who shield the outsider artist from the world at large, foregoing monogamy or stability in service of genius. In *Elgar: The Erotic Variations*, sex as an enjoyable pastime is a quiet rebellion, something that defines the lives of bohemians and outsiders, but it is not without victims. The lines between unfettered freedom and abject cruelty are more ambiguous in *Delius: A Moment with Venus*. By the novel's end, Delius is portrayed as a philanderer, statutory rapist, psychological abuser of his wife, and a racist. Elgar's cultural status as a romantic hero, one which Russell himself helped to create with his first film on the composer, is interrogated yet not quite diminished by his extramarital trysts, painting him as a complex and contradictory figure like Urbain Grandier in *The Devils*, one who is given the opportunity to realise the error of his ways by the narrative's denouement. Delius is given no such reprieve. Society attempts to derail any transgressive behaviour of both composers, leaving these characters in a state of constant exile, never directly punished for their actions, nor ever sated by them. Death, as is shown at the end of both stories, is the sole respite from Elgar's and Delius's sexual appetites, leaving only the genius of their legacy behind. It is left to the reader to decide whether that legacy is tempered by their personal lives.

NOTES

1. Ken Russell, *Elgar: The Erotic Variations and Delius: A Moment with Venus* (London: Peter Owen, 2007), 174.
2. Roger Ebert, 'Salome's Last Dance', 17 June 1988, *RogerEbert.com*, <https://www.rogerebert.com/reviews/salomes-last-dance-1988> (last accessed 9 January 2018).
3. Melvyn Bragg, 'Foreword', in Ken Russell, *A British Picture: An Autobiography* (London: Southbank Publishing, 2008), i.
4. Yvonne Tasker, 'Permissive British Cinema?', in accompanying booklet to *Deep End*, directed by Jerzy Skolimowski, 1970 (DVD/Blu-ray, BFI, 2011), 8.
5. Ibid.
6. John Trevelyan, *What the Censor Saw* (London: Michael Joseph, 1973), 225.
7. Local Government Act 1988, <http://www.legislation.gov.uk/ukpga/1988/9/contents> (last accessed 22 January 2020).
8. Alexander Walker, 'Preface', in Trevelyan, 15.
9. Nina Hibbin, 'The Music Lovers', *Morning Star*, 26 February 1974.
10. Derek Malcolm, 'Ken Russell Obituary', *Guardian*, 28 November 2011, <https://www.theguardian.com/film/2011/nov/28/ken-russell> (last accessed 4 October 2020).
11. Jack Fisher, quoted in Thomas R. Atkins, *Ken Russell* (London: Monarch Press, 1976), 49.
12. Joseph Lanza, *Phallic Frenzy: Ken Russell and His Films* (Chicago: Chicago Review Press, 2007), 92.
13. Ibid., 211.
14. Candice Carty-Williams, 'An Interview with Writer and Director David Cronenberg', 1 October 2014, <https://www.4thestate.co.uk/2014/10/an-interview-with-david-cronenberg/> (last accessed 1 June 2022).

15. Lloyd Evans, 'The Food of Love', *The Spectator*, 23 June 2007, <https://www.spectator.co.uk/article/the-food-of-love> (last accessed 1 June 2022).
16. Bernard Rose, 'Hi Ken, Sorry I Stole Your Movie', *Guardian*, 15 September 2008, <https://www.theguardian.com/film/2008/sep/15/biography> (last accessed 6 October 2021).
17. Andrew Gurr, *Writers in Exile: The Identity of Home in Modern Literature* (Brighton: Harvester Press, 1981), 33.
18. Colin Wilson, *The Outsider* (London: Picador, 1978), 210.
19. John Baxter, *Ken Russell: An Appalling Talent* (London: Michael Joseph, 1973), 31.
20. Russell, *Elgar*, 34.
21. BFI catalogue, SCR-20506.
22. Russell, *Elgar*, 8.
23. Ibid., 16.
24. Ibid., 23.
25. Ibid., 29.
26. Ibid., 31.
27. Ibid., 54.
28. Ibid., 122.
29. Ken Russell, Audio Commentary for *Song of Summer* (2002), directed by Ken Russell, 1968 (DVD/Blu-ray, BFI, 2016).
30. Michael Brooke, 'Song of Summer (1968)', *BFI Screenonline*, 2014, <http://www.screenonline.org.uk/tv/id/482807/index.html> (last accessed 23 April 2020).
31. Lindsey Fitzharris, '"One night with Venus, a lifetime with Mercury": Syphilis and "Syphilophobes" in Early Modern England', *Wonders and Marvels*, <https://www.wondersandmarvels.com/2012/03/one-night-with-venus-a-lifetime-with-mercury-syphilis-and-syphilophobes-in-early-modern-england.html> (last accessed 4 October 2020).
32. Eric Fenby, *Delius as I Knew Him* (London: Charles Birchall and Sons, 1948), 161.
33. Russell, Audio Commentary for *Song of Summer* (2002).
34. Russell, *Elgar*, 143.
35. Wilson, 25.
36. John Carey, *The Intellectuals and the Masses: Pride and Prejudice Among the Literary Intelligentsia, 1880–1939* (London: Faber and Faber), 8.
37. Ibid., 10.
38. Craig Monk, *Writing the Lost Generation: Expatriate Autobiography and American Modernism* (Iowa: University of Iowa Press, 2008), 1.
39. Russell, *Elgar*, 149.
40. Ferdinand Tönnies, *Community and Society (Gemeinschaft und Gesellschaft)* (London: Transaction Publishers, 1996), 1.
41. Gurr, 7.
42. Russell, *Elgar*, 172.
43. Ibid., 175–6.
44. Wilson, 21.
45. Ken Hanke, *Ken Russell's Film's* (Metuchen, NJ: Scarecrow Press, 1984), 9.
46. Russell, *Elgar*, 183.

CHAPTER 13

A Short History of Ken Russell's Films in Japan

Sawako Omori

INTRODUCTION

The arrival of Ken Russell's films in Japan in the early 1970s impacted greatly on Japanese cinema and film culture and on the lives of younger moviegoers in particular. *Women in Love* (United Artists, 1969), *The Music Lovers* (United Artists, 1970) and *The Devils* (Warner Bros., 1971) heralded the arrival of a major new talent from the UK, whose work (admittedly not to everyone's taste) fascinated a cult of younger film enthusiasts through its use of a unique and visual film language. Although his films had been ignored by a wider audience accustomed to old-fashioned, more traditional modes of storytelling style at the time (the work of David Lean, for example, another British director who had gained popularity among Japanese moviegoers), the most prominent and significant advocate for Russell's work was the film critic Yuji Konno, a prominent film and (rock) music critic then emerging out of this new generation of younger Japanese film enthusiasts, and a former culture and fashion magazine editor.

Konno was an enthusiastic supporter and wrote many influential essays on Russell, especially for *Kinema Junpo* (founded in 1919), Japan's most established and revered film publication. He labelled Russell a 'monster of imagination' in a review of *The Music Lovers* in 1972.[1] His reviews and talks on TV and radio shows had a strong influence over young filmgoers interested in new and expressive modes of cinema – the free style of Robert Altman, for instance, or the surrealistic visuals of Federico Fellini. Some of these enthusiasts, mostly in their twenties, established the Ken Russell Film Club in 1975, which published booklets dealing with his work and further consolidating Russell's cult reputation; these and other younger fans would later organise film events, including a significant and successful Ken Russell Retrospective in 1987. Russell therefore found a unique place in the hearts and minds of Japanese film enthusiasts across the 1970s and 1980s, despite never being regarded as a 'master' director like Stanley Kubrick.

The aim of this chapter is to consider the influence Ken Russell within the Japanese film industry and offer a short history of how his films were received by fans and critics alike. Russell's influence and presence in Japanese film culture has, until now, evaded critical examination, and this chapter aims to consider, for the first time, Russell's influence in a non-Western context.

RUSSELL-MANIA IN 1970S JAPAN

The first Ken Russell film to gain a large degree of media attention in Japan was *Women in Love*, an adaptation of the 1920 D. H. Lawrence novel, which was released in the country on 9 May 1970. The film's narrative and its erotic scenes of sensuality, sex and nudity caused a furore in the more conservative national press, and its depiction of sex was unlike anything that had, or up until that point, been seen in (mainstream) Japanese cinema.[2] One of those upon whom the film had an immediate impact was the critic Yoshio Shirai, legendary editor-in-chief of *Kinema Junpo* since 1968. In a recent interview with this author, he recalled the impact of the film when he saw it for the first time at the press review: 'I was overwhelmed by the power of the film. It was made by a new director named Ken Russell and his overpowering style was different from other directors at the time.'[3] According to Shirai, there was a secret press screening before the film was reviewed for censorship. Haruo Mizuno, the general manager of the publicity department for distribution company United Artists Japan (who would later become a nationally famous critic, writing the first landmark interview article on Russell and Glenda Jackson entitled 'The Directors of the World: Ken Russell and his Actress' for *Kinema Junpo* in June 1971), anticipated that the film would fall foul of the notoriously strict and conservative Japanese censorship laws which prevented the showing of pubic hair, and feared that by cutting the film it would lose its power and immediacy. He responded by organising secret preview screenings for the press using an original print. Shirai said in an interview with this author that the screening was a pivotal moment, providing a platform for Russell's film to take hold in Japan. Off the back of it he edited a special issue of *Kinema Junpo*, '*Women in Love* and Sexuality'.[4] He was also one of five writers to write critical essays around the film in the special issue; his short review was entitled 'Pushing the Boundaries of Expression?', and focused on the depiction of sex in the film:

> The film has created one of the most shocking and wild scenes of sexual intercourse in the history of cinema. Their explicit lovemaking scenes recur several times across the course of the film, which includes the wrestling match of two naked men near a fire.[5]

Furthermore, he felt that the younger, British director, producer and screenwriter had provided a palpable sense of balance in the film, stating, 'These bold sexual acts take place within the beautiful, pastoral surrounds of Nottinghamshire, as a result, these acts feel like a part of the surrounding nature.'[6]

Shirai was not the only writer to be moved by the language and expression of the film. Hiroshi Minami, another Japanese critic (also a famous psychologist) writing in the same issue, discussed the film's depiction of sexuality in the essay entitled 'Refreshing the Ideas of Lawrence', stating that D. H. Lawrence had 'regarded it as the life force of a human being, a religious and sacred act', and that Russell had understood the world Lawrence had created entirely, transposing these ideas, faithfully, to the screen.[7] However, the film was destined for the cutting room and was damaged by the censor.

The Oliver Reed–Alan Bates nude wrestling scene was shown with the images blurred, censored for its display of genitalia and pubic hair, and was regarded as obscene in the eyes of the law. Criticising these blurred images, Minami stated that 'Those censors denied the author's ideas and damaged his perspective on humanity.'[8] His article on the film suggested the blurred images confused Japanese audiences, who were interested in but unable to identify the style of wrestling presented on-screen – especially as the scene features 'Japanese style wrestling' (the scene struck a chord with Japanese viewers, speaking to the national and cultural interest in the sport): all that was visible were the faces of the actors and the upper parts of their bodies.

The display of pubic hair and genitalia had long been forbidden in Japanese cinema and was deemed culturally transgressive and taboo. It was, however, lucky for Russell that the film was distributed by a major company, United Artists Japan, which had the power to appeal to and influence the media. As a result, other publications followed *Kinema Junpo* in their defence of the film and of Russell's work more broadly. *Screen*, for instance, selected *Women in Love* as one of the must-see films of the month in July 1970, and Kyoko Yamamoto, one of the few female film critics at the time, wrote the following favourable review: 'Many recent love stories have included lovemaking scenes; however, most are not inspiring. You will be moved by the sexual acts of men and women in *Women in Love* because they are natural and beautiful.'[9] Nei Kawarabata, a renowned critic for one of the largest daily newspapers, *Yomiuri Shinbun*, also positively reviewed the film on 11 May 1970, stating, 'Ken Russell has directed a wonderful film mixing reality with poetry.'[10]

However, despite the good reviews appearing in the press, *Women in Love* was not successful at the box office. The tragedy for Russell was that there were so few arthouses in 1970s Japan. Norio Nishijima, Professor Emeritus (Film Study) of Tama Art University and a specialist in a range of film directors including Russell, recalled the situation of cinemas in the 1970s in a recent interview with this author:

The situation of arthouse had dramatically changed in the 1980s. Many arthouses were built in Tokyo and became significant places for viewing the work of European directors. That was one of the reasons why there was a renaissance of interest in Russell films in the late eighties in Japan. But the circumstances were not good enough for his seventies films because most films were released at cinemas with large capacities and where many popular Hollywood movies were shown. As a result, his films were not successful at these cinemas because moviegoers who were used to old-style film-making did not understand his revolutionary cinematic language. I stayed in Paris for about a year in the mid-1970s and Russell had gathered attention as one of the most controversial directors at the time. I was personally impressed by *The Music Lovers* being shown at the Cinémathèque Française, Paris. There were many small cinemas for art films at the time in the city. But the situation was very different in Tokyo and you could not find the right cinema for a director like Russell in the early 1970s.[11]

Women in Love was released at the Miyuki Cinema in Tokyo, a sophisticated cinema in the centre of the city with large-capacity seating. The film was not a success at the box office despite the Miyuki's reputation for showing European arthouse films by the likes of Pier Paolo Pasolini and Jean-Luc Godard. The release of the film, however, paved the way for Russell to emerge as a new talent from Britain to look out for (this was certainly helped by Glenda Jackson's Academy Award for Best Actress in 1971). The film also opened the door for other sexually daring and transgressive films from Europe to find their way into the Japanese film market. Three years later *Last Tango in Paris* (Bernardo Bertolucci, United Artists, 1972) opened to a sensation, as did Liliana Cavani's *The Night Porter* (Lotar Film Productions, 1974) and Nagisa Oshima's *Ai No Corrida/In the Realm of the Senses* (Argos Films/Oshima Productions, 1976) which had been produced as a French co-production to get around Japanese censorship laws.

Shirai was willing to offer space for younger writers, such as Konno, to engage with the work of these directors and their films. He believed the times were changing and in the importance of giving a platform to younger writers who could catch and respond to a new wave of cinema around the world from the late 1960s to the 1970s. Konno wrote a favourable review of *The Devils*, released in Japan on 30 October 1971, and given a restricted (three-year) release by Warner Brothers Japan, and *The Music Lovers* (released on 1 April 1972) for the magazine. In his review of *The Devils*, he wrote:

> If *Women in Love* was released without heavy censorship, I would have selected it as the film of the year in 1970 because it was one of the most sensual films I ever saw in my life. Ken Russell and Oliver Reed became

kind of Gods of eroticism to me . . . The acting of Reed again was powerful and sensual, and Russell captured the nature of politics and the essence of madness in a crazy world.[12]

Elsewhere he stated:

Madness vs Lyricism; Violence vs Intelligence – You can find many different fierce conflicts in his film and he tried to express complicated feelings and emotions on screen as a 'monster of imagination' . . . He made a great success of adapting *Women in Love* by D. H. Lawrence with his rich imagination and again used his amazing power to depict the private life of Tchaikovsky. Some parts were a fiction that Russell had created for his film and it was very thrilling for viewers to experience this overpowering and unique visual explosion.[13]

Kinema Junpo provided a new platform for the critical exploration of Russell's work, and an offshoot publication, a book entitled *Three Ground-breaking Directors of Sexually Themed Films*, was published in 1973. It was volume 21 of a series focusing on world film directors and included editions dedicated not only to Bertolucci but also to Yugoslav director Dušan Makavejev, director of *W.R.: Mysteries of the Organism* (Neoplanta Film/Telepool, 1971). The book included a detailed biography, 'The Biography of Ken Russell and His Work', translations of his interviews entitled 'Russell's Comments', as well as essays by two essential critics in the study of Russell in the 1970s.

Konno wrote a long essay entitled 'The World of Ken Russell' for the book in which he predicted the future of the director: 'As a famous photographer in New York, Francesco Scavullo predicted, it would need more than a decade for Russell to be accepted as an extraordinary director because his work is far ahead of the time.'[14] Another important contributing critic was Mitsutoshi Ishigami, who wrote a long essay for the book entitled 'Unique Viewpoints of Ken Russell'. He was a writer of the new generation, like Konno, and had a specialist knowledge of genre cinema, especially mystery, horror and science fiction. He regarded *The Ipcress File* (Sidney J. Furie, Rank, 1965), the first Harry Palmer film, as one of the best spy films and was astounded by the third in the series directed by Ken Russell, *Billion Dollar Brain* (United Artists, 1967; released in Japan on 6 July 1968). He wrote:

I did not have many expectations for the film because it was the third Palmer film and I was shocked to see the climax. The most striking images appeared in this scene: big tanks with many armed soldiers were sinking into the ice lake. You watched moments of cruel death . . . borrowing ideas from *Alexander Nevsky* by Sergei Mikhailovich Eisenstein . . . it was too powerful, and it haunted you like a nightmare. The film presented an image of hell during its climax and you came to a conclusion that the fierce battles between America, Britain and Russia were essentially meaningless. One of the most important themes of the film must be the cruelty of death and it was unlike a typical mystery adventure film.[15]

Ishigami wrote that he regarded the film as one of the ten best of the year's (ranking it in seventh place in a list of foreign films) for the magazine *Film Critic* in 1969. He was one of the first critics to rate *Billion Dollar Brain* highly in Japan. He also expressed his impressions of *Women in Love* in the book, stating:

The director must be more interested in death than in life. The death of young lovers in the lake and the one of Gerald in the snowy mountain had more impact than the life force of the other young couple, Birkin and Ursula.[16]

Ishigami was also a producer of commercial films and of the legendary Japanese film director, Seijun Suzuki. He had been a long-time fan of Suzuki and had provided ideas for some of his films, including *Branded to Kill* (Nikkatsu, 1967) released in Japan the year before *Billion Dollar Brain*. He offered television commercial work to Suzuki after the director was fired from his major film studio, Nikkatsu, and their first TV commercial for baby's underwear received an ACC silver award. It was no wonder that Ishigami also championed Russell, who had also made TV commercials.[17] Both directors shared an exuberant visual cinematic style and presented visually idiosyncratic and surrealistic film worlds in both *Branded to Kill* and *Billion Dollar Brain*. Although he never wrote an essay explicitly comparing Suzuki to Russell, we may imagine how he would have been drawn to Russell through Suzuki.

THE KEN RUSSELL FILM CLUB

If enthusiastic critics like Konno and Ishigami opened the way for a younger generation of critics to engage with Ken Russell's work, Shirai had given pages of *Kinema Junpo* over not only to younger critics but also to a highly motivated amateur writer, nineteen-year-old Russell fan Masao Fujita (who later became an editor of an entertainment magazine in Japan). He penned a three-page essay on *The Devils* for the magazine in 1972, which became a landmark article, in which he wrote:

Yuji Konno called Ken Russell a kind of god in his review and to me Russell also become one of the most impressive contemporary directors after seeing *Women in Love* . . . Russell must have grown up with an uncontrollable child within himself . . . He wielded his own sword as a director and with all his power in *The Devils*.[18]

The cult of Ken Russell among younger film fans in Japan saw the founding of the Ken Russell Film Club in 1975. The president of the club was Kazuo Takahashi, who had been deeply moved by *The Devils* when he happened to see it at a double bill cinema in Tokyo. He decided to form the club in order to support Russell's films. Takahashi felt Russell's work had been ignored by general film audiences and made two modest booklets, including a detailed biography and a collection of essays written by fans, which sold at double bill cinemas. He said in a recent interview with this author:

> I was a part-timer at the movie company and met many younger film fans. Some of the people joined my club and helped me to make the booklet. We had fun just chatting about new films and directors like Russell at the time. It was a small circle of friends.[19]

I also joined the club after seeing *Tommy* (Columbia, 1975), which appealed to younger rock fans despite its failure at the box office. The club held a small Ken Russell exhibition with posters, books and soundtrack records at the old cinema. Members also worked for the owner of an underground cinema when he showed Russell's amateur films at the hall, like the 16 mm *Amelia and the Angel* (BFI Experimental Film Fund, 1958). One of the most memorable events which took place was Takahashi's trip to the UK to meet Russell himself. He decided to visit the studio of United Artists UK, where Russell had planned to shoot *Valentino* (United Artists, 1977, released on 29 April 1978 in Japan). Although Takahashi missed the chance to see him, his trip was a catalyst to his becoming a commercial film director. Another member became the promoter of *Crimes of Passion* (New World Pictures, 1984) in the 1980s, and I became a freelance writer after translating articles on Russell in English at the club. The activities of the club influenced and impacted on the lives of its members.

Although Russell's films were never huge successes at the Japanese box office during the 1970s, ATG (Art Theatre Guild), the most famous independent company known for releasing auteurist art films (including ambitious Japanese films like the work of Nagisa Oshima and the films of Ingmar Bergman), announced the release of *Savage Messiah* (MGM-EMI, 1972) in 1973 or 1974, but cancelled its plans to do so for contractual and economic reasons. *Mahler* (Goodtimes Enterprises, 1974) never even made it to a theatrical release – Russell being regarded as a director with little *commercial* value in the Japanese market in 1970s. Nevertheless, some enthusiastic critics and fans had influenced younger audiences and there would be an unexpected resurgence of interest in Russell's work during the 1980s.

THE RESURGENCE OF KEN RUSSELL IN THE 1980S: THE KEN RUSSELL RETROSPECTIVE

Before this renaissance, two of Russell's films made in America (rather than within the British film industry) were released in the early part of the decade. The first was *Altered States* (Warner Bros., 1980), released on 25 April 1981 in Japan and shown at cinemas with large-capacity seating. The film was not a failure at the Japanese box office, and it attracted the attention of science fiction fans. The powerful trip that the leading character, Dr Eddie Jessup (William Hurt), experiences appealed to renowned contemporary pop artist Tadanori Yokoo, who earned his reputation with an exhibition at MOMA in New York and was known for designing album covers for both Miles Davis and Santana. He wrote the first review of Russell's film for a special issue of *Kinema Junpo*:

> What happened in the film was very real to me because I had, in the past, also experienced a similar unconscious trip to another world in my mind . . . I saw the moment of my birth and death at the same time . . . I had to get back to my real life for the love for my family . . . The film depicted the rules of a universe where love made everything possible. It was a rare film that analysed the mechanism of love from a universal point of view. I think Ken Russell has a unique sense that is ahead of the time.[20]

The next American film, *Crimes of Passion*, was released four years later in Japan on 7 September 1985. Although it failed to find a wider audience, there was nevertheless a body of fans who adopted it and turned it into a cult film. This author was one of them and had my first chance to write about Russell as a professional writer for *Kinema Junpo*:

> The acting of Kathleen Turner, dressed to kill and with dangerous poison, was absolutely fascinating in the new Ken Russell film. She played a complex role: a woman with two faces. She is a capable fashion designer by day and a street whore by night. Russell depicts a loneliness and a fear of love in modern life through her own dual life . . . He also created the seductive image of a woman through the referencing of the work of Aubrey Beardsley and Gustav Klimt. Her image reminded me of the poisonous portraits of other women in film: Glenda Jackson in *Women in Love* and Theresa Russell in *Bad Timing* (Nicolas Roeg, Rank, 1980) – which also used the pictures of Klimt.[21]

Though the interest film enthusiasts had in Russell's work in the 1970s had passed, there were still favourable reviews of his American films. Ishigami, once an important advocate for Russell, was not moved by *Altered States*, however. He admitted being confused by the film in his review in *Kinema Junpo*:

> The content of the film reminded me of sleazy old SF films like *The Neanderthal Man* [E. A. Dupont, United Artists] in 1953 and *Man-Made Monster* [George Waggner, Universal] in 1941. Audiences, who did not see these SF films or other Russell work, might think the story original and meaningful. I am not one of them.[22]

Konno, another Russell cultist, also confessed his dissatisfaction with *Crimes of Passion* in an essay in the booklet on Russell published in 1987:

> I was disappointed with *Crimes of Passion* when I first saw it in 1985 because the story was so flat and lacked imagination. I came to understand the director's view through *Blue Velvet* in 1987, a masterpiece of David Lynch, which had a similar structure to *Crimes of Passion*.[23]

Norio Nishijima commented on the situation in which the director found himself in the 1980s following a major film retrospective of his work: 'An old maverick director from Britain, Ken Russell, who was almost forgotten in this country . . . resurged suddenly with his *Pia* Retrospective in 1987.'[24] The popular magazine *Pia* announced a retrospective of twenty of Russell's films. It was well known for its film competition for younger film-makers which began in 1977, and for launching new talents like Shinya Tsukamoto. It also began a series called 'The Retrospective of World Auteurs', the first of which was for the legendary French New Wave director François Truffaut in 1982. Truffaut himself came to Japan to attend Q&A sessions during his film festival, two years before his death. 'The Retrospective of World Auteurs' was highly successful, and *Pia* began to coordinate a festival of British film-makers in 1987 because new British films such as *My Beautiful Laundrette* (Stephen Frears, Film4 Productions, 1985), *A Room with a View* (James Ivory, Merchant Ivory Productions, 1985) and *Mona Lisa* (Neil Jordan, Handmade Films, 1986) had garnered attention at arthouses at the time. Russell was therefore a natural candidate for such treatment.

Takashi Nishimura, a former producer of the event, explained why *Pia* staged a Russell Retrospective:

> Many arthouses were built in big cities like Tokyo in the 1980s and as a result, new British films were introduced into Japan. We talked about who was a pioneer director of British Cinema at the meeting. Somebody said it was Ken Russell and all of us agreed with his comment. Many of us were fans of his work. I enjoyed his films in my youth in the 1970s.

Women in Love was powerful and knocked me out at the cinema. My favourite Russell film was *The Boy Friend* (released in 1971) with Twiggy, a visually stunning film.[25]

Pia Film Festival (PFF) called the project 'The British Film Year in Tokyo' and planned not one but two programs: a Ken Russell Retrospective and a showcase of 'New British Cinema'. The latter introduced recent films from the UK, *Wetherby* (David Hare, Film Four International / Greenpoint Film / Zenith Entertainment. 1985), *A Zed & Two Noughts* (Peter Greenaway, Artificial Eye, 1985), *Sid and Nancy* (Alex Cox, Initial Pictures/Zenith Entertainment, 1986) and *Angel* (Neil Jordan, Channel 4 Films, 1982). It also screened the short films of Russell's former collaborator Derek Jarman.[26] Giving Russell his own retrospective established him as a pioneer of British cinema, leading the charge of newer directors of the eighties. According to Fumio Kurokawa, the former president for the PFF project, one of the most difficult parts was collecting Russell films for the festival because 'Many different companies owned his film rights and we had to negotiate with each company. The hardest negotiation was with Warner Brothers Japan for *Lisztomania* for it was never released at the cinema in Japan.'[27] He had also been a fan of Russell's after being impressed by *The Devils* in the early 1970s: 'It was a revolutionary film and I wanted younger viewers who did not know the name of Russell to discover how great he was like I did in my youth.'[28]

The Ken Russell Retrospective was held from 3 to 9 June 1987 at the Parco Theatre, in the Shibuya area of Tokyo where fashionable younger people would gather. His unreleased films, such as *French Dressing* (Associated British Picture Corporation, 1964), *Savage Messiah* and *Lisztomania* (Goodtimes Enterprises, 1975), were shown for the first time in Japan at the event. Audiences also had the chance to see five of his BBC *Monitor* films: *Elgar* (1962), *Isadora Duncan, the Biggest Dancer in the World* (1966), *Prokofiev* (1961), *Bartók* (1964), and *Delius: Song of Summer* (1968), the only one of the BBC films to have been broadcast on Japanese television via NHK (National Broadcasting Station), on 19 February 1970. They also had the chance to see *Clouds of Glory* (Granada Television, 1978), his double bill presentation for British commercial broadcaster ITV on the Lakes Poets, William Wordsworth and Samuel Coleridge. His newest films, *Aria* (Virgin Vision, 1987, a portmanteau film produced by Don Boyd, to which Russell contributed a section) and *Gothic* (Virgin Vision/Vestron, 1986, which was released in Japan on 1 April 1988), were premiered for Japanese audiences at the festival.

Russell did not come to Japan on 3 June for the festival, although he had planned to give a speech ahead of the *Gothic* premiere. He arrived a few days later, and this author fortunately had a chance to meet him on his first day at the Fairmont Hotel, located near the British Council, which was working with the organisers of the Retrospective. I introduced myself as a member of the Ken Russell Film Club and told him that we had made a booklet on his work. He answered jokingly, 'It might be only one page.' He made a wry face after he discovered I was also a journalist. I heard that he did not like the press. He believed in younger viewers more than the press. When I interviewed with him for *Pigeon* magazine, he commented on a younger generation who were discovering his work:

> Young audiences under thirty, most of them wearing black costumes, came to the preview of *Gothic* in London. I believe these younger viewers became my loyal supporters. They were different from the many critics who always criticized my work whenever they found my name on it.[29]

Russell hoped that he would find new, similar supporters among young Japanese audiences and that the Retrospective would be a catalyst for this. According to Kurokawa, the festival was successful, and Russell's fans also came to the autograph session during the festival. He recalled the event:

> [The] Russell autograph session held at 109 in Shibuya, a shopping building popular among younger people near the theatre hosting the festival, was also successful. I saw many people with the soundtrack album of *Tommy* for getting his autograph. He surely had his loyal fans in Japan at the time and I think the festival contributed to an increase in new supporters in the younger generation.[30]

After three days of the Retrospective, *Mahler* finally began showing at Cinema Square Tokyu in the crowded downtown area of Shinjuku, Tokyo, thirteen years after its first release in the UK. The film was a smash hit, bringing Russell his first success at the Japanese box office, running for eight weeks at Cinema Square Tokyu and then for a further two weeks at another arthouse cinema. So why was the film a hit? Many articles appeared on Russell, including his interview during the Retrospective. One of the biggest newspapers, *Asahi Shinbun*, published his interview on 15 June 1987, and labelled him 'a director strongly supported by the younger generation'.[31] It compared the impressive opening image of the cocoon in *Mahler* to the work of the dancer and director Lindsay Kemp,[32] who also visited Japan for his show that year. The article was great publicity for the film. Mahler was a fad at the time in Japan following Luchino Visconti's film *Death in Venice* (Warner Bros., 1971), which, ironically, Russell's film satirises at one point. Many Japanese people had started to become more interested in European high culture during Japan's economic boom in the 1980s, and Visconti's film was considered a masterpiece of European cinema.

The film and music critic Akiko Kawahara, the first female critic to enthuse about Russell, published the landmark book *Listening to Film Music* in 1981, which included an essay on Russell. She wrote an impressive review of *Mahler* in *Image Forum* in 1987. She had first seen the film in the 1970s in Paris and enjoyed it as an inspiring moment of avant-garde culture in spite of its scandalous content. She formed a different view of the director after seeing the film again in 1987:

> Ken Russell created a Baroque style of beauty with his overpowering energy. I enjoyed its beauty again and realized his sincere attitude, questioning the meaning of life and death, this time. He must have had a complicated internal struggle in himself: love VS death, Eros VS Thanatos. These elements are also essential to the work of Mahler as a composer . . . A male character symbolized death and a female one was a life force in his film . . . The death mask of Mahler contrasted strikingly with the birth of a woman from a cocoon in the opening scene . . . His vision of death was very different to Luchino Visconti's who also used the music of Mahler in *Death in Venice*. Visconti was fascinated with the profound death of the character in his film. On the other hand, Mahler in Russell's film, had two opposite feelings. He romanticized death in the living world, and he resisted death when it was near . . . A couple of years have passed since the music of Mahler became a fad in Japan. The portrait of Mahler that Russell depicted 13 years ago must offer a great opportunity to think about his work and life again.[33]

Image Forum was a new type of critical film magazine which started in the early 1980s. In a special issue entitled 'The Truth of Abnormal and Weird Cinema' in August 1987, film critics and scholars voted for 'the best director of abnormality and weirdness'. Ken Russell came in second place in the poll (Luis Buñuel was in first place and David Cronenberg in third). The interview between Russell and the magazine editor during his stay in Japan appeared in the same issue. Many film viewers had a chance to re-evaluate his work with the Retrospective and *Mahler*, which the poll must have reflected, and Ken Russell was established as a pioneering director from Britain after the success of the Retrospective and the delayed release of this film from the 1970s.

The four films made for (cult) video distribution and production company Vestron had a mixed reception in Japan. The first film, *Gothic*, was released at the same arthouse as *Mahler* on 1 April 1988 and became popular especially among younger audiences, as the director had hoped during the interview. The young manager of the arthouse cinema, Chiaki Ueki, recalled, 'Many stylish younger viewers, who seemed to come from a current fashion magazine, came to see *Gothic*. I heard the topic of the film was spread by word of mouth among them.'[34]

The next Vestron film, *Salome's Last Dance* (1988), was also released at the same pioneering arthouse as *Mahler* and *Gothic* on 23 September 1988 and was highly acclaimed in reviews in the film magazine *Kinema Junpo*. Veteran critic Nagaharu Yodogawa, a rare Russell supporter of the older generation, had admired *The Boy Friend* (MGM-EMI, 1971) as 'the contemporary *Red Shoes*' and also loved *Valentino*.[35] He wrote a rave review of *Salome's Last Dance* for the same magazine in 1988, in which he described it as 'the best *Salome* film ever made':

> When I met Michael Powell and Emeric Pressburger a long time ago, I asked them to make a *Salome* film with the same visual style as *The Tales of Hoffman*. But they showed no interest in the project. I realized I was wrong to ask them because Ken Russell was the right director to do the project . . . Russell noticed that the leading character that Oscar Wilde had described in his story was not a beautiful woman, but a boy . . . It was the best *Salome* film due to the right interpretation of the material.[36]

Although he was the most influential critic at the time, the film had moderate success at the box office.

The next Vestron film, *The Lair of the White Worm* (1987), was released at a small, new cinema without being noticed on 21 October 1989 and it became one of the least popular Russell films in Japan. *The Rainbow* (1989) was shown at the large capacity cinema in the same year and failed to gather much attention. However, though not all the Vestron films were successful, Russell proved he could still make inspiring British films and find younger audiences in the late 1980s.

RUSSELL'S FILMS IN THE 1990S

The influence of the Retrospective had a lasting effect at least until the early 1990s. Russell continued to be regarded as a popular director from Britain, and the pioneering arthouse cinema, Late Show, decided to release his new film, *Whore* (Cheap Date/Trimark, 1991),[37] with a special showcase of four other Russell films: *Mahler*, *Gothic*, *Salome's Last Dance* and *French Dressing*, which were shown as part of a second career retrospective. This arthouse, one of the distributors of *Mahler*, had changed its name from 'Cinema Ten' to 'Cinema Cats' and Russell's films were chosen for the relaunch as the manager of the cinema had been a fan since the 1970s. The four older films were shown between 26 September and 23 October 1992 and *Whore* played from 24 October to 20 November, becoming a box office success. This author wrote an essay on Russell for its release entitled 'Women in Russell Films: Provocative and Defiant Characters in the World of Love and Sexuality' for *Image Forum*, in which I observed:

> In his new film Russell has stepped into the life of a prostitute, an admirer of George Orwell's *Animal Farm*, who wants to be free from

the bondage of a horrible pimp (who is like the pig dictators in the novel) . . . The director depicts the humanity of a tragic woman with his biting sense of humour.[38]

Three years after the release of *Whore*, the 1993 BBC drama *Lady Chatterley's Lover* (based on the controversial 1928 novel by D. H. Lawrence) was edited for the cinema and shown on 3 November 1995 at a large capacity venue, the Miyuki (the same cinema where *Women in Love* was shown in 1970). It did not, however, find a large audience, but Nagaharu Yodogawa, the most influential critic and a Russell supporter, claimed it was 'a vivid adaptation of the great literature' in an advert for the film published in *Asahi Shinbun* (one of the biggest newspapers in Japan) on 2 November 1995.[39] In the same year, there was also a revival of *The Boy Friend*, which had a cult fanbase in Japan, at a small cinema, which did not gather much attention.

In the late 1990s, however, Russell's popularity in Japan began to fade and *Lady Chatterley's Lover* was the last feature film introduced as a new work, though a compilation film, *Tales of Erotica* (Regina Ziegler Filmproduktion, 1996), which included a segment by Russell called 'The Insatiable Mrs. Kirsch', was released at the cinema in 2002.

INFLUENCE ON JAPANESE FILM-MAKERS

The innovative style of Ken Russell films strongly influenced film-makers in Japan. Two in particular admitted to being Russell enthusiasts and to being inspired by his work: film and animation director Macoto (Makoto) Tezuka (born in 1961) and production designer and director Takeo Kimura (born in 1918). Tezuka identified with Russell having started his career making amateur films. His own first professional film was *The Legend of the Stardust Brothers* (Cinesaison, 1985), a rare Japanese rock musical which was at the time influenced by both *Phantom of the Paradise* (Brian De Palma, Harbour Productions, 1974) and *Tommy*. It became a cult movie among younger music fans, and the sequel, *The Brand New Legend of the Stardust Brothers*, arrived thirty-three years later in 2018 (Magic Hour). Tezuka won the Future Film Festival Digital Award at the Venice film festival with *Hakuchi: The Innocent* in 1999 (Shochiku) and was also the winner of Best International Director at LUSCA Fantastic Film Fest with *Tezuka's Barbara* in 2020 (Aeon Entertainment).

Tezuka professed his interest in and admiration for Russell's work in an interview included in a book on the making of *Hakuchi: The Innocent*. He admitted he had been 'fascinated by Russell's work. He made different type of films, but you could still tell they were Russell's by his original styles. I also wanted to create my own film world like Russell's. That is the goal to achieve as a visual artist.'[40]

Tezuka's father, the late Osamu Tezuka, was renowned as the foremost comic (manga) artist of all time in Japan, responsible for creating iconic works such as *Astro Boy* (serialised between 1952 and 1968), and was also a pioneering animator. Macoto Tezuka's career had been largely overshadowed by his father's legacy, which had prompted him towards creating ever more visual film worlds. *Hakuchi: The Innocent* was one of his most ambitious films, inspired by Ango Sakaguchi's 1946 short story *Hakuchi* – itself reflective of the author's own experiences during the war in Tokyo.

The film depicts a retro-futuristic dystopia where the World War has not ended – and neither have the bombings. The only building left standing in Japan is one which broadcasts all entertainment media. It presents a love story between a man named Izawa working at the TV station and an innocent woman during war time. Full of surrealistic images of the past and the future, the film borrows effectively from *Salome's Last Dance*. In one sequence, after her dance, a charismatic pop idol, Ginga (or Salome), asks for the head of Izawa, who has been cool towards her, for a birthday present. She reveals her vulnerable, more human side for the first time later as she talks to his head, which is positioned on a silver plate. Certainly in the visually eccentric and immediate style which defines the film, Tezuka also took from Russell how to use strong and potent images to present character.

Takeo Kimura was another Japanese film-maker and production designer influenced by Russell's work. Kimura had been working for more than sixty years until a year before his death in 2010 and was renowned as one of the best production and art designers in Japanese cinema. He was especially celebrated for his collaborations with Suzuki on films such as *Tokyo Drifter* (Nikkatsu, 1966) and *Zigeunerweisen* (Cinema Placet, 1980). He revealed himself as having been a secret Russell enthusiast in his 1986 memoir *The Movie House is My Real Home*. Choosing his 'ten best films' of all time in the pocketbook *150 Best Foreign Films*, published by Bungei Shunju Sha in 1988, Kimura listed *Tommy* in third place, and he named Russell as best director. In the exciting short essay entitled 'The Inspiring Image of Ken Russell Shot at Me Like a Bullet' in his memoir, he said:

> I was influenced and inspired by many auteurs such as Federico Fellini and Roger Vadim. Ken Russell with his unique sense was also among them. His direction for *Women in Love* was not so impressive to me. There was only lyricism in the film, but I came to understand his real power with *The Devils*. I could not sleep the night when I saw it with my excitement. What a great image maker![41]

There are parallels to be drawn here between the Suzuki–Kimura relationship and that of the relationship between Ken Russell and his protégé, the artist, film-maker and production designer Derek Jarman.[42] Suzuki had impacted similarly on Kimura and just as Jarman produced the sets for *The Devils* and went on to collaborate with Russell further on *Savage Messiah* as production designer, Suzuki and Kimura also collaborated many times, influencing Kimura's own films made in his later years. Kimura also made mention of his favourite film, *Tommy*, in his memoir, stating, 'I was finally lost for words with *Tommy* because all kinds of images were created and spread over the whole screen freely.'[43] Russell's viewers came to understand why Kimura loved the director and came to identify with him: the two were kindred cinematic spirits. There were key similarities between Russell and Suzuki – the prominent use of vivid colours and surreal set designs, for example – and Kimura had also felt a kinship with Suzuki since first working him in 1963.

Kimura and Suzuki's last collaborative film together, *Princess Raccoon* (Suzuki, Shochiku/Nippon Herald Films, 2005), with a Chinese actress, Zhang Ziyi, was a bizarre opera with a touch of *Tommy* and *The Boy Friend*. British film critic Mark Kermode, a prominent defender of and advocate for *The Devils*, referred to the film's 'anarchic explosions of colour' in his review for the *Guardian*.[44] Kimura had finally got a chance to make a colourful, Russell-esque opera with Suzuki, bringing then state of the art computer graphics and digital effects to the film. He also used digital devices in his directorial debut film, *Yume No Manimani* (*Dreaming Awake*, Pal Entertainments Production, 2008),[45] to create dreamy pop art images of Marilyn Monroe which had the power to heal a sensitive young man – a reference to the giant pop art sculpture of Marilyn in *Tommy*. Kimura was regarded not only as a production designer but as an excellent visual artist in his own right, and his work was exhibited at the Kawasaki City Museum between 2002 and 2003.

CONCLUSION: THE GREAT LEGACY OF *TOMMY*

Writing before the release of *Tommy*, Konno proclaimed that Russell's films were ahead of their time. Kimura's favourite film, however, was *Tommy*, which turned out to be the most beloved of Russell's films in Japan, where it was released with great fanfare at large capacity cinemas on 24 April 1976. It was not successful at the box office, however, but became cult hit. It was one of the progenitors of music video and has since been discovered by a younger generation of film and music fans. Norio Nishijima told this author that one of his younger students at Tama Art University, who loved Russell's work, wrote a brilliant graduation paper on *Tommy* in 2018 and was given an award for it by the university,[46] while another student also chose to discuss the film for his graduation paper some years ago. *Tommy* presents a unique fusion of music and image that appeals to younger students in the media-driven twenty-first century.

In 2019 *Tommy* was re-released for the first time in years off the back of the Elton John musical biopic *Rocket Man* (Dexter Fletcher, Paramount, 2019), a film which stylistically and iconographically references and quotes Russell's work throughout. *Tommy* was shown at the new arthouse Uplink Kichijoji in Tokyo on 30 August of that year. I interviewed many of the audience who turned out to be devotees of *Tommy*, including one woman who said she would visit the cinema every day for its five-week run. A young girl wearing a shiny red dress like an Acid Queen appeared when the 'Special Night for Tommy Fans' took place at the cinema on 30 September; various fans of different generations came to see it that night, including the president of The Who fan club of Japan in the 1970s and younger musicians who recreated the *Tommy* show onstage. There was a special atmosphere in the cinema, with the audience singing and shaking tambourines along to the film. Forty-three years after its first release, *Tommy* finally had found the perfect place and a new cult audience.

To conclude, aside from *Tommy*, the chance to see the best of Russell's films in Japan may have passed: *Women in Love* and *The Devils* never got a Japanese home release (although *Mahler* has received a Blu-ray restoration). Russell's work might emerge again with a renaissance of interest in his films. His work awaits a new generation of admirers to appear and support it as the director himself had once hoped.

NOTES

1. Yuji Konno, 'Rhapsody, Tchaikovsky and *The Music Lovers*', *Kinema Junpo*, 1 April 1972.
2. It is interesting to note that despite their scenes of sexual excess and their cult reputation, no one compared or saw Russell's work against the context of 'Pinku Eiga' or 'Pink Cinema'.
3. Yoshio Shirai, interviewed by the author, 27 January 2021.
4. Yoshio Shirai (ed.), '*Women in Love* and Sexuality', special issue of *Kinema Junpo*, 15 May 1970.
5. Ibid.
6. Ibid.
7. Hiroshi Minami, 'Refreshing the Ideas of Lawrence', *Kinema Junpo*, 15 May 1970.
8. Ibid.
9. Kyoko Yamamoto, 'The Bare Truth of Love and Sexuality', *Screen*, July 1970.
10. Nei Kawarabata, *Yomiuri Shinbun*, 11 May 1970.
11. Norio Nishijima, interviewed by the author, 20 August 2021.
12. Yuji Konno, 'The Nature of Politics and the Essence of Madness', *Kinema Junpo*, 1 November 1971.
13. Konno, 'Rhapsody, Tchaikovsky and *The Music Lovers*'.
14. Yuji Konno, 'The World of Ken Russell', in *Three Ground-breaking Directors of Sexually Themed Films* (Tokyo: Kinema Junpo, 1973), 154.
15. Mitsutoshi Ishigami, 'Unique Viewpoints of Ken Russell', in *Three Ground-breaking Directors of Sexually Themed Films*, 170–1.
16. Ibid., 172.
17. See Richard Farmer's chapter in this volume.

18. Masao Fujita, 'Ken Russell and *The Devils*', *Kinema Junpo*, 15 January 1972.
19. Kazuo Takahashi, interviewed by the author, 14 February 2021.
20. Tadanori Yokoo, 'Super Science – Analysing the Mechanism of Love', *Kinema Junpo*, 1 April 1981.
21. Sawako Omori, *'Crimes of Passion'*, *Kinema Junpo*, 1 September 1985.
22. Mitsutoshi Ishigami, 'Bizarre SF Film from the Director with an Obsession with the Past and Death', *Kinema Junpo*, 1 April 1981.
23. Yuji Konno, 'Sex, Drugs and Rock'n'roll: The Last Laugh of the Maverick Director', in *The Ken Russell Film Book* (Tokyo: Uplink), 18.
24. Norio Nishijima, 'Review of *Salome's Last Dance*', in *The Circuit for Film Experience: Collection of Reviews in Art Handbook Magazine 1979–1989* (Tama: Tama Art University, Art Section Laboratory, 2019), 160.
25. Takashi Nishimura, interviewed by the author, 4 February 2021.
26. Jarman's short films *Sloane Square* (1981), *Imagining October* (1984), *Broken English* (Marianne Faithfull, 1979) and *The Queen Is Dead* (The Smiths, 1986) were shown.
27. Fumio Kurokawa, interviewed by the author, 16 February 2021.
28. Ibid.
29. Sawako Omori, 'Interview with Ken Russell', *Pigeon*, August 1987.
30. Fumio Kurokawa, interviewed by the author, 16 February 2021.
31. 'Interview with Director Ken Russell', *Asahi Shinbun*, 15 June 1987.
32. Kemp had also played Angus Corky in *Savage Messiah*.
33. Akiko Kawahara, 'Phantasm: A Dream of the Life and Death of a Great Artist', *Image Forum*, July 1987.
34. Hiroo Otaka and Mariko Inaba (eds), *Welcome to Arthouses* (Tokyo: JICC, 1989), 73.
35. Nagaharu Yodogawa, 'The Boyfriend', *Kinema Junpo*, 1 March 1972.
36. Nagaharu Yodogawa, 'The Best *Salome* Film Ever Made', *Kinema Junpo*, 1 October 1988.
37. Japanese title: *Bondage*.
38. Sawako Omori, 'Women in Russell Films: Provocative and Defiant Characters in the World of Love and Sexuality', *Image Forum*, November 1992.
39. *Asahi Shinbun*, 2 November 1995.
40. Makoto Tezuka and 'The Innocent' Project, 'Makoto Tezuka Interview', in Tatsumi Usihisa (ed.), *The Innocent (Hakuchi)* (Tokyo: Seven Red Mercury, 2000), 57–8.
41. Takeo Kimura, *The Movie House is My Real Home* (Tokyo: Shunju-Sha, 1986), 217–18.
42. Elsewhere in this collection Brian Hoyle explores the influence of Russell's work on Jarman's own film-making style.
43. Kimura, *The Movie House is My Real Home*, 218.
44. Mark Kermode, 'Princess Raccoon', *The Guardian*, 2 July 2006.
45. He was ninety when he made the film, finding a place in the *Guinness Book of Records* as the oldest director to make a debut film.
46. Norio Nishijima, interview.

CHAPTER 14

Nicolas Winding Refn and the Ken Russell Style

Adam Powell

INTRODUCTION

This chapter will provide an analysis of the cinematic style of Ken Russell, a style that led Linda Ruth Williams to declare Russell a 'cinematic brand' and 'almost a genre in his own right'.[1] From the release of *Women in Love* (United Artists, 1969), Russell embarked on a remarkably prolific run of films which crystallised a style of montage editing and a high camp approach to subject, performance and the cinematic image. Throughout the 1970s Russell's work displayed a consistent formal approach in his conceptualisation of a unique type of musical cinema. It was the formation of the more bombastic formal elements of Russell's work which led Williams to propose Russell to be the patron saint and one-man genre of 'British Extreme'.[2]

In 2008 the release of Danish director Nicolas Winding Refn's *Bronson* (Vertigo, 2008) (a film biopic of the man dubbed by the tabloids 'Britain's most dangerous prisoner') caught the eye of critics, as a result of its unusual tone and texture, and drew comparisons with elements of the iconic and controversial British cinema of the 1970s.[3] A comparative analysis of Refn's film and the work of Ken Russell reveals a cross-generational stylistic dialogue between these two auteurs of different eras working with similar modes of style and approaches to adaptation. It is the aim of this chapter, therefore, to consider Refn's work as part of the legacy of Ken Russell in the twenty-first century, and while films like *Bronson* and *Women in Love* (for instance) are clearly very different in a range of ways, this chapter argues that stylistically Refn's work adopts a similar style to Russell. Russell's legacy is (visually) stylistic *and* musical, rather than being in content or text.

THE RUSSELL STYLE: RUSSELL AND REFN

Before becoming a photographer and starting work for the BBC in 1956, Russell secured a scholarship and attended the International Ballet School in South Kensington. Although he did not complete the schooling, he did have a brief stint working with the British Dance Theatre in the early 1950s. From Hermione's (Eleanor Bron) devised entertainments and Gudrun's (Glenda Jackson) encounter with Highland cattle in *Women in Love* to the serpentine movements of Lady Sylvia Marsh (Amanda Donahoe) in *The Lair of the White Worm* (Vestron, 1987), dance is a persistent Russellian device, working in natural partnership with the power of the musical soundtrack. Movement and dance are an organic part of the silent-film style spectacle. The musical soundtrack within Russell's cinema and his artistic disposition evolved this style, which finds its apotheosis in *Tommy* (Columbia, 1975), a feature-length exercise in musical montage with images kept in complete fidelity to the lyrics of The Who's double LP concept album. The group's lead songwriter Pete Townshend frustrated expectations of the band's 1960s pop group heritage towards the end of that decade by experimenting with conceptual ideas and classical arrangements. An epic chronological narrative spanning decades and engaging grand themes (spirituality, messiahs and religious idolatry), *Tommy* (the album), released in 1969, would define the ambitions of the rock opera and evolve popular rock music forms into the 1970s and 1980s. Russell was the ideal candidate to realise a rock opera in cinema, having (inversely) endowed his biopic films of Romantic composers with the contemporary imagery of rock and musical theatre (the marriage of the two worlds would be realised most fully in *Lisztomania* [Goodtimes Enterprises, 1975]). Russell would eventually embark on a significant career in opera away from film-making during the 1980s when he was unable to release films at the rate of the previous decade.

Just as Russell would refer to his childhood memories of the sensorial experience of classical vinyl records as his artistic inspiration, Nicolas Winding Refn would locate music as the primary source of his creativity in a visual medium: 'The images usually come (to me) from music so it becomes very fetishized for me.'[4] Refn's commercial breakthrough film *Drive* (Bold Films, 2011) gained the director a signature musical style from its selection of European electro-pop singles (popularly known as 'Synthwave'), together with the electronic scoring of Cliff Martinez who has worked on all Refn's productions since. In 2014 Refn authorised BBC Radio 1 DJ Zane Lowe to curate a rescoring of the film soundtrack that was subsequently released on DVD/Blu-ray. This unique exercise in creating a type of 'cinematic jukebox' mirrors the imagery Russell conjures when depicting an infant version of himself moving back and forth between projector and gramophone in the autobiographical television film *A*

British Picture (ITV, 1989) as he 'rescored' the silent films he was showing. While some of the original electronic scoring of *Drive* remained, Lowe replaced pop songs on the original soundtrack with different but contemporary artists working within similar genres to those of the original. The result emphasises the dominance of the pop song within the montage and highlights the music video aesthetic of several key scenes in the film gained from the extensive use of the original songs in almost their entirety.

Barry Keith Grant suggests that it was not until the release of *The Music Lovers* (United Artists, 1970) and *The Devils* (Warner Bros., 1971) that Russell's cinema began to display its 'more notorious qualities: bold startling images of eroticism, physical revulsion and violence, a rapid "kino-fist" editing style frequently incorporating unsubtle shock effects'.[5] However, *Women in Love* initiated many of the formal traits and style evident in subsequent films. A lengthy collaboration with editor Michael Bradsell, and eventually Bradsell's assistant Stuart Baird, developed the distinctive montage design of the seventies films. Russell features a signature staccato crosscutting style in moments that reveal the barely concealed violence in the tragic character of Gerald Crich (Oliver Reed): a flurry of quick crosscuts between characters as Gerald thrashes a horse barbarically at a train crossing, incorporating handheld mid-shots, close-ups and crash zooms. The frantic crosscutting alternates with extreme close-ups of Gerald's and Gudrun's faces in the violent culmination of their Alpine bedroom scene during the final act of the film. The shock-cut motif is exhibited in the jump cut from the close-up of Rupert (Alan Bates) and Ursula's (Jennie Linden) love-making in the open air to the drowned lovers' arms entwined amongst the mud of the drained lake. What Grant calls 'shock effects' are previewed in *Women in Love*, but it was Russell's final work for the BBC, *Dance of the Seven Veils* (1970), that would present many images and approaches he would go on to use or even quote directly in the cinema work to follow.

The film is subtitled 'A Comic Strip in Seven Episodes on the Life of Richard Strauss, 1864–1949' and takes the form of a series of music video style montages that would characterise Russell's later films. The film was the director's first major controversy, drawing the ire of Mary Whitehouse and causing Parliament to introduce a motion condemning the BBC for screening it, as well as instigating legal action from the Strauss estate (as a result of the film's accusations of Strauss's Nazism).[6] The film was banned after a single screening on the BBC in February 1970. Choreography in elemental landscapes (both rural idylls and primal deserts), silent film pastiche, and live performance imagery are components Russell would carry over from the Strauss film to his cinema throughout the 1970s – certainly evident in *Mahler* (Goodtimes Enterprises, 1974), whose opening sequence explosively marries fire, water and the landscape – and 1980s.

Russell's montage style often exhibits crash zooms and shock edits framing images of horror, sexuality and trauma, all of which contribute to the overall excess of his visual design. The trip sequences in *Altered States* (Warner Bros., 1980) are a natural development of this. Russell concludes a chapter in *Dance of the Seven Veils* with a sudden cut to a bizarre close-up of a suddenly de-veiled ('devil'd') bald nun. This is echoed in the jump cut close-up of a maggot-ridden skull in the post titles opening shot of the trail up to the city of Loudun in *The Devils*; in the track and zoom on two eyeballs in the box of ashes during the death-dream in *Mahler*; in the sudden image of a snake-entwined human skeleton in the 'Acid Queen' sequence of *Tommy*; or the incongruous cutaways to the erotic art of Aubrey Beardsley in *Crimes of Passion* (New World Pictures, 1984). In *The Devils*, Russell employs his jump cut and crosscutting montage style to frame Sister Jeanne's (Vanessa Redgrave) vision of Grandier (Oliver Reed) on the cross: black and white visuals depict the demented illusion of the nun before closing on a close-up of her gouging a bloody wound into her own palm with a rosary crucifix. Many recurring visual motifs throughout Russell's cinematic oeuvre are iconoclastic images combining the sacred and profane, which led J. Hoberman to align him with a group of cult or avant-garde auteurs with strong surrealist ties: 'a tradition shared by professional symbol-mongers of such varied talent as Alejandro Jodorowsky, Shuji Terayama, Fernando Arrabal, Jean Cocteau, and Ken Russell'.[7]

Refn's *Pusher Trilogy* (Magnolia Pictures, 1996, 2004, 2005) established his career in pioneering a specifically modern Danish crime film and a wider transnational crime genre which has evolved in Europe and globally in the years since. *Bronson* marked a shift into English-language genre film-making and an engagement in popular cinema endowed with cult, counter-cultural and underground qualities. Refn parades Russellian depictions of shocking and oversized sexuality in the poisonous Oedipal mother–son bonds of *Only God Forgives* (Wild Bunch, 2013) and the Amazon Prime series *Too Old to Die Young* (Amazon, 2019), as well as the cannibalistic and vampiric sexuality (à la *Lair of the White Worm*) featured in *The Neon Demon* (Amazon Studios, 2016), whose promotional material's electric blue colour scheme echoed the neon-drenched mise en scène of Russell's erotic thriller *Crimes of Passion*. Refn shares Russell's iconoclastic use of imagery, specifically a freewheeling exchange with art and pop culture combined with autobiographical and fiercely personal expression. *Bronson* is perhaps Refn's most exclusively Russellian film: an insolent biographical film channelling British cinematic and popular culture of the 1970s and 1980s. Using a montage style quite different to the slow cinema-like aesthetic developed in subsequent films, *Bronson* mediates Russell's glam cinematic style at the peak of his cinematic output in the 1970s and 1980s to interpret and completely reimagine the contemporary British hooligan genre (a genre with which, of course, Russell is entirely unconnected).

Camille Paglia states that 'Their reputations as radical liberators were so universally acknowledged that brooding images of Freud and Lawrence in poster form adorned the walls of students in the Sixties.'[8] Paglia claims

D. H. Lawrence's greatest importance to sixties society was as both 'a prophet of sex' and an 'expander of consciousness'.[9] A claim could be made that Russell did much the same for commercial cinema from the style of his own adaptation of the 1920 novel *Women in Love*. Inserting material from a supplementary poem outside of the source novel titled 'Figs' (1917), Russell provides his adaptation with an unrestrained sexuality, including his presentation of the novel's contested homoeroticism (with the first example of full-frontal male nudity in mainstream cinema during the wrestling sequence between Reed and Bates).

Women in Love is a key film in Russell's wider oeuvre in terms of his philosophy towards the classical adaptation as well as his controversial presentations of sexuality. The opening sequence of *The Music Lovers* concludes with Tchaikovsky (Richard Chamberlain) falling into a four-poster bed with his male companion, Count Anton Chiluvsky (Christopher Gable), establishing the central concerns for the film itself. Sexuality and performativity are often naturally combined by Russell as a central element to his spectacle approach, examples include the death-dream music montage sequence in *Mahler* that envisions the composer's wife performing a proactive striptease on top of his coffin; Tommy's mother's sensual convulsions while bathed in floods of baked beans spewing forth from the television in *Tommy*; and Franz Liszt (Roger Daltrey) orally caressing his lover's breasts to the rhythm of a metronome at the beginning of *Lisztomania*. Exuberant and fetishistic depictions of sex provide a recurring sexual anxiety and trauma in Russell's cinema, as seen in the leather-clad femmes fatales of Cosima Wagner (Antonia Ellis) and Lady Sylvia. This is relatable also to the image of Franz Liszt hurtling between a chasm of the vampiric Princess Carolyne's legs before being sucked into a vortex of a giant pair of knickers in imagery echoing that of the train carriage scene of *The Music Lovers*.

From his early television documentaries through to his feature films, Russell's work is synonymous with the artist biopic. The First Piano Concerto scene featured in *The Music Lovers* displays Russell's fluid music montage style together with a tone that anticipates the later films. The sequence is edited rhythmically to a musical soundtrack of the London Symphony Orchestra performing Tchaikovsky's music. A wide shot of the stage and the musicians is presented before the soundtrack is cued by the conductor starting the orchestra onstage (a similar device is used at the start of *Dance of the Seven Veils*, in an ironic filmic quotation of Disney's *Fantasia* [1940]). Russell films the scene frenetically: handheld camera movements follow hands across piano keys, whipping back and forth to the player's arms and head in profile. The composer at the piano dramatically bows his head to the keys and back up again as he straightens his back in rhythm to the music. He performs onstage with the jutting movements of a 1960s/70s rock guitarist, with Russell mimicking contemporary rock music performance imagery. Handheld camera tilts frame hands on piano keys reminiscent of fingers racing over the fretboard of an electric guitar, with the perspective positioned at one end of the keyboard in the fashion a camera would be placed at the end of a guitar neck for a live rock performance. The scene uses quick crosscutting from images of Tchaikovsky pounding the keys to the significant attendees looking up to the stage in rapture as if reacting to a rock music solo. Russell developed this motif in his subsequent features by reimagining Franz Liszt's nineteenth-century concerts as a live rock tour populated by screaming and rioting teenage girls in *Lisztomania*.

Tommy evolves the motif of messianic idolatry. Russell combined the themes of rock performance and religion in the 'Eyesight to the Blind' sequence featuring The Who and Eric Clapton. The montage showcases a merging of live rock performance and religious ritual with the iconographic allusion of huge statues of Marilyn Monroe replacing the figure of the Catholic Virgin to communicate the film's themes with a direct pop symbolism. The track itself adapts the lyrics of the 1951 Blues song by Sonny Boy Williamson II and is emblematic of Russell's postmodern merging or 'remixing' of the classical and popular to remake something old as new. Like the swaying of the prophets and the congregation in *Tommy*, the rhythmic montage of the concerto scene in *The Music Lovers* also reacts to the beat and tempo of the music, often with movement within the frame corresponding to the soundtrack. The instant the music subsides momentarily, and Tchaikovsky meets his sister's gaze in the audience, the image dissolves and we hear a light, high-pitched wind instrument on the soundtrack to cue an image of a bouquet of wildflowers, which then cuts to the composer and his sister walking together in a pine forest; the piano keys cue a further cut to idyllic images of row boats on a lake in summer. Russell constructs music montages for each excerpt in the extended concerto sequence, acting as a flashback or fantasy motif for the significant characters who are shown to be in attendance. In a flurry of crosscutting at the climax of the concert, the scene establishes the three women and one male lover central to the narrative to follow. Russell's experiences of childhood play and exploration playing vinyl records to silent movies crystallised his method in montage. He explained, 'I suddenly realized that Tchaikovsky's symphonic poems could be mini movies.'[10]

While the concerto sequence in *The Music Lovers* visualises the Tchaikovsky soundtrack via live performance imagery and the choreography of heavy flashback scenes, the sequence detailing the composer and his wife's alcohol-drenched train ride back to Moscow from their Saint Petersburg honeymoon uses another Tchaikovsky piece in a similar performative montage style but with a much darker tone. The sequence displays garish expressionist lighting, quick cutting, and handheld close-ups that match the swaying of the violently inebriated and disoriented couple in the claustrophobic confines of the train carriage, choreographing their movements to the musical soundtrack.

Russell scores the scene with Tchaikovsky's Manfred and Pathétique Symphonies (1885 and 1893, respectively), with portions of the same music used for a tragic flashback scene earlier in the film detailing the composer's mother's horrific death by immersion in boiling water. Russell referred to these pieces as 'the most tortured music he wrote',[11] and aligned them with what he viewed as the defining tragedies of the composer's biography. Antonina reaching her arm across the carriage towards Peter's face is punctuated by loud and chaotic brass rising on the soundtrack before a percussive crash in the music prompts her naked body tumbling to the carriage floor. Russell's trademark staccato crosscutting back and forth from her painterly posed naked form to a hysterically perturbed Tchaikovsky creates a blunt statement on repressed (homo)sexuality and trauma. The tone of the train carriage sequence is close to the sexually charged black and white montages featured in *The Devils*, cut to Peter Maxwell Davies's brass-heavy atonal original score with Russell presenting the formal elements of performance, lighting, camera movement and editing he will develop and exaggerate further as he evolves towards more prog rock textures and rock video stylings.

Russell's musical collaboration with rock pianist/keyboardist Rick Wakeman had a significant (and largely unrecognised) influence on the texture and tone of his cinematic style from the mid-1970s. Over the course of the 1980s Russell would turn increasingly to modes of contemporary popular music, engaging with such diverse styles as synth-driven electronic music (e.g. Thomas Dolby's ominous score for *Gothic* [Virgin Vision/Vestron, 1986]), rock, and folk punk (in *The Lair of the White Worm*). Like Russell in cinema, Wakeman would become something of a brand in his own right within popular music and as a member of prog rock monoliths Yes, and would take prog rock to peak grandiosity with bombastic live performances incorporating musical theatre elements 'on ice'. Wakeman's soundtrack for *Lisztomania* evolves the director's previous use of conventional orchestral soundtracks for *The Music Lovers* and *Mahler*. Wakeman's wild reinterpretations of classical pieces with contemporary music forms, including country and western, orchestral jazz, prog rock and the rock ballad, provide the appropriate sonic space for Russell's digressions and escalating use of stylisation. Comparisons may also be drawn with Wendy Carlos's electronic reinterpretations of classical pieces (used prominently in Stanley Kubrick's *A Clockwork Orange* [Warner Bros., 1971] and *The Shining* [Warner Bros., 1980]). Roger Daltrey is another key contributor to Russell's realisation of the rock video visual. As well as contributing to the song writing, Daltrey's soaring rock/blues vocals and performative shape of a rock idol help define the musical and visual texture of *Tommy* and *Lisztomania*. It was Daltrey's physical transition from trim and suited scowling mod to bare-chested, curly-locked rock god that represented the aesthetic evolution of both his own band and the wider rock genre.

By the middle of the 1980s Russell would form his own music video production company and embark on a prolific period producing a series of videos for artists including Elton John, Cliff Richard, Jim Steinman and Sarah Brightman. He integrated the form into his feature work when he produced a music video for Wakeman's *It's A Lovely Life* (1986), a synth and electric guitar driven track incorporating and adapting Dvorak's *New World Symphony* (1893), from the soundtrack to *Crimes of Passion*. It would be played on MTV to promote the film's release. Russell uses it in the film as a framing device, distinct from the fantasy/flashback framing of his previous films' music montages. An excerpt from the video itself is (self-reflexively) cut into the film as a couple passively view it on the television in their living room. Russell uses heavily symbolic imagery to visualise Maggie Bell's screaming rock vocals on the soundtrack. A newly married couple are framed individually diving into a sparkling swimming pool to retrieve their silver cutlery set and decorative birdcage. Quick cuts, crash zooms, slow motion and fast motion, screaming vocal close-ups, and performative movement are stylistic elements Russell has made synonymous with rock music visuals and reflect an overall style developed from *Women in Love* onwards. His direct approach to symbolism in the music video here presents images reflecting the film's characters as they watch the video on television within the diegesis of the story.

Russell deploys a similar rock video style for set pieces involving China Blue's sexual liaisons with clients. While these scenes do not operate as a traditional flashback/memory or a kind of interior psyche/dream as in *Women in Love*, *The Music Lovers*, *The Devils*, *The Boy Friend* (MGM-EMI, 1971) and *Mahler*, an abstraction and distance is attained through theatrical presentation and expressionist spectacle with a similar musical sensibility. The synthesised slow, soulful horns and electronic piano textures of the soundtrack make way for a thrash guitar rock number along with some diegetic grunting and moaning included in the sound mix when China Blue entertains a local cop. Close-ups of bound wrists, stiletto spikes penetrating flesh, faces strained in passion, and still photography cutaways of police violence create a familiar crosscutting montage style. China Blue straddles the naked cop before eventually performing an explicit sex act on the man with an oversized police baton, swaying in a theatrical and sexualised dance movement. The theatrical headbanging movement of the actors alongside the rock music soundtrack and rhythmic editing provide a heightened stylised presentation to the extreme sexual imagery, violence and trauma, and a return to the formal devices and thematic concerns of the aforementioned train sequence in *The Music Lovers*.

The leather S&M costuming of China Blue features prominently again in Russell's music video for the rock group Pandora's Box. The video for 'It's All Coming Back to Me' (1989) features irresistibly camp Russellian imagery in a late example of 'Wagnerian rock', a term coined by the group's creator

Jim Steinman, the creative personality known for being the composer behind Meat Loaf's 1977 album *Bat Out of Hell*, and a musical style which incorporates pop, rock, classical, and musical theatre. The video features a group of bondage-leather-clad dancers undulating on a coffin-like platform (recalling Alma's dance in *Mahler*), classical ballet choreography, as well as the director's familiar symbolic visualisation of the song's lyrics.

NICOLAS WINDING REFN AND THE RUSSELLIAN STYLE

Referring to a key choreographed musical sequence within *Bronson*, Refn has noted:

> that was the first movie I envisioned as if it was a piece of music, and what would it be. I came up with the concept that it must be the Pet Shop Boys [whose music soundtracks the sequence]. It would describe the Bronson character, the sexuality.[12]

Since *Bronson* Refn's films have featured electronic, experimental and classical pieces as well as a continued (Russellian) playful engagement with pop and rock music culture.

Stan Hawkins sees the Pet Shop Boys duo as central to debates around musicology and masculinity in a post-1970s setting. They came to represent a shift in masculinity through strategies of defiance, irony, cynicism, and a new camp sensibility defined by their combination of sullenness and seriousness with the flamboyance of gay disco.[13] The group were previously commissioned to rescore *Battleship Potemkin* (Sergei Eisenstein, Mosfilm, 1925) and performed the score at live screening performances for several years from 2004. Refn initially conceived of having the group score his entire film in this electronic and orchestral hybrid, creating a 1980s pop classical statement comparable to the previously mentioned experiments with classical and popular forms of Wakeman and Carlos during the 1970s. Instead Refn would license their 1987 hit 'It's a Sin' for a music video portion of the sequence set at Broadmoor Hospital, and used a mix of pop and classical soundtrack to support episodic music montages throughout the narrative. The director's conceit of using the Pet Shop Boys as a motif for his main character is one of the film's many examples of camp style, and the extensive use of electronic, pop and classical music throughout the film provides texture to portraits of both masculinity and sexuality.

In the 1964 essay 'Notes on "Camp"', Susan Sontag offers a definition of camp sexuality that delights in exaggeration, common in all varieties of camp behaviour, sensibility and style. An exaggeration of sexual characteristics is coupled with a philosophy analogous to the non-discriminatory 'good–bad axis' approach to popular and classical forms. She writes, 'What is most beautiful in virile men is something feminine, what is most beautiful in feminine women is something *masculine*.'¹⁴ In *Bronson* Refn subverts the ultra-masculine environment of the prison genre and image of the violent prisoner in a Russellian application of music and dance while exploiting the style of experimental biopic pioneered by Russell. Refn utilises a Russellian music montage before the title credit to establish the ongoing theme of performance and artistry via the camp marriage of the popular and classical. Refn's choice of The Walker Brothers' 1978 track 'The Electrician' here is worth noting. Scott Walker holds a unique position within popular music history, combining orchestral, electronic and experimental music with a pop sensibility. After The Walker Brothers disbanded, Scott Walker embarked on a series of increasingly avant-garde solo records with classical influences and covering material ranging from Jacques Brel to Burt Bacharach. 'The Electrician' is used to frame the film's opening title sequence, the slow baritone vocals ('Baby, it's slow. When lights go low') and high-pitched strings accompanying images of Charlie (Tom Hardy) circling a cage, his naked torso bathed in red light and framed in mid-close-ups. The deep red light makes the figure's flesh glow amongst the shadows, endowing him with an almost supernatural or mythical aura. Full-frontal naked shots of the prisoner circling his cell slowly dissolve into one another, cut to the rhythm of the bass tones on the soundtrack. As scores of riot police enter the scene, eventually meeting the prisoner with brutal violence in the confines of the cage, the tone of the song changes as the low vocals turn to a vibrato crooning crescendo. The former discord of the strings turns to a sweeping orchestral melody framing the movement of stomping boots, thrown punches and tumbling bodies into a delicate dance to the soundtrack. The hypermasculine appearance of Charlie, frequently naked throughout the film and always adorned with a Victorian-style strongman bald head and moustache both exaggerates and confounds his masculinity. In the sequence prison brutality is reimagined as an esoteric and sensual dance.

Refn stages Bronson's bare-knuckle fighting career as a burlesque. A jump cut cued by the electronic beat on the soundtrack reveals a slow, tilting close-up of a topless podium dancer bathed in blue light. The next shot frontally frames Charlie in the foreground staring into the middle distance with the topless dancer in the background, side by side, in the promoter's night club. The blue light motif is next used in a scene detailing Charlie's bare-knuckle fighting career, together with the same heavily bass and percussive electro track from the club scene. The track used is 'Digital Versicolour' (2007) by Glass Candy, a track given commercial prominence by Karl Lagerfeld and Chloé when used at runway shows in 2008, further distorting the blending of masculine and feminine as well as the good–bad taste axis in Refn's reimagination of the Bronson character. Charlie stands under a spotlight stripped to the waist and with his back to the camera, staring out into an empty space bathed in projected blue light. His fight promoter moves into frame slowly, passing what looks like rolled or folded bank notes at waist level before cocking a hand on Charlie's shoulder and slowly leaning towards his ear in a whispering motion. The slow, driving percussion and quick, alternating electronic notes of the soundtrack combined with images of naked flesh and currency allude to the sex trade. The staging of the preceding fights (presented in a performance space style, with a small gathering of onlookers positioned in front of the posing fighter) takes on the components of a seedy stage performance. Each blow landed is signified by electronic pulses that register alongside the electronic pop soundtrack and transform the illicit fights into modern dance pieces.

Russell's outrageous portrayal of the France's King Louis XIII in *The Devils* as a cross-dressing sprite recreating Botticelli's *The Birth of Venus* (Figure 14.1) via musical theatre for an audience of drunken clergy intersects with Refn's feminine portrayal of a violent prisoner as performance artist. Kevin M. Flanagan notes that Russell 'can oscillate between aestheticized camp and contemplative silliness in a way that offers a personalised take on cultural commonplaces'.[15] In *Dance of the Seven Veils* Richard Strauss (Christopher Gable) is imagined in a variety of silent film style personas in a style Flanagan correlates to the director's idiosyncratic interpretation of history and cultural memory: 'Russell commonly uses the most pregnant and broadly representative kinds of iconography in order to situate his viewers in relation to specific historical moments.'[16]

Into the 1970s Russell's escalating style and use of allusion developed from the outrageous to the fantastical with an endless stream of reference and allusion that fits Flanagan's remarks. In *Mahler* the composer's real-life conversion to Catholicism is imagined as silent film parody depicting the composer performing

Figure 14.1 Ken Russell's *The Birth of Venus*.
Source: Warner Bros., 1971.

a series of theatrical trials for a dominatrix version of Cosima Wagner, complete with an adapted version of 'Ride of the Valkyries' with additional comedy lyrics. *Lisztomania* co-opts the Nazi symbolism and visual references to Hitler seen in *Dance of the Seven Veils* for the portrayal of Richard Wagner. Russell extends his set of references and allusions to the twentieth-century American comic book using DC Comics' Superman as the visual motif for the Nietzschean Superman, another narrative detail shared with *Dance of the Seven Veils*. The tone of Russell's fantasy adaptation in *Lisztomania* is acknowledged self-consciously when the hero finally starts sniggering at all the horrors of Castle Wagner with the line, 'He looks like a character out of a comic!' Sontag's observation of camp sensibility being 'the metaphor of life as theatre' describes the escalating excesses of this style of characterisation.[17]

Russell's rich and expressive attention to period costume, set design and decor in *Women in Love* and *The Music Lovers* evolves towards a pastiche cosplay, outlandish visual design, and anachronistic approach to history and biography. The piano ballad 'Love's Dream' on the *Lisztomania* soundtrack prompts a non sequitur song-and-dance montage pastiche of *The Gold Rush* (Charlie Chaplin, United Artists, 1925) with Daltrey's Liszt cast as Chaplin. Liszt's concert persona is given visual cues of a sequin stage curtain and a Liberace-esque candelabra, and Wakeman's soundtrack intersperses Wagner's opera *Rienza* (1842) with 'Chopsticks' in a conceit connecting Liszt with 1970s concert pianist Liberace – known for his high camp Las Vegas shows of classical music. Composer Richard Wagner (Paul Nicholas), introduced as a sulky young lad in a sailor suit, is later characterised as a castle-dwelling Dracula cum Dr Frankenstein in *Lisztomania*, before finally morphing into a Nazi officer toting a rifle in the shape and form of an electric guitar. Rick Wakeman cameos as a braindead Frankenstein's monster version of the god Thor, 'animated' by Wagner in a science fiction/orchestral hybrid Frankenstein's laboratory (Figure 14.2).

Russell's silent film avatars of Strauss, Mahler and Liszt echo in the manner in which Refn stages the origin of the relationship between Bronson and his eventual fight promoter/manager (Matt King) as an impromptu rendition of 'Tea for Two (1950)' as performed by Gordon Macrae and Doris Day in the musical of the same name. Russell's pop cultural iconography and characterisation is adopted by Refn through the various guises given to his protagonist. In a black suit, white gloves, and white clown make-up with black detailing in the style of a harlequin, Bronson is presented as a type of one-man Greek chorus in scenes punctuated through the film. These sequences exhibit the same theatrical buffoonery of performance and use of pastiche and allusion as Russell's silent film comic strips; at one point Bronson roars a languid solo vocal of 'Release Me', the Eddie Miller song, to muse on his ongoing incarceration. The opening montage of the protagonist's early childhood and adolescence is presented in ironic mock tone and establishes the playful and

Figure 14.2 Roger Daltrey and Rick Wakeman in *Lisztomania*.
Source: Goodtimes Enterprises, 1975.

excessive imagery to follow. Refn adopts a montage style of jump cuts which truncates time, providing a comic strip of schoolyard fights and petty robbery narrated by Charlie. The director scores the montage with the romanticism of Verdi's 'Va, Pensiero' (1842), which sets a somewhat counterintuitive and cognitively dissonant tone to the scenes of petty juvenile delinquency. The mock heroism of the classical soundtrack reaches natural excesses when 'The Dam Busters March' (1955) accompanies an animated tabloid headline montage referencing the prisoner's historical infamy. Refn uses allusions to both classical and popular forms of music as the motif for the protagonist's 'artistry'. The truncated early biography of the opening scene races immediately towards Charlie's first prison sentence, an image of his mother weeping in the dock leads to a solemn shot following the prisoner to his cell. The shot settles on the back of his bald head before we hear him break into sobs, and just as quickly we cut to the black background and stage setting revealing the harlequin Charlie, white-gloved palms towards the audience with fingers splayed, and open-mouthed grin emanating a hearty chuckle that has replaced the weeping of the previous shot (Figure 14.3). Theatrical camp, parody and allusion combine in Charlie's narration of his biography throughout the film.

In one scene his black and white clown paint is transformed with a pink thunderbolt that recalls David Bowie's 1973 album cover for *Aladdin Sane*. Standing before projected stock footage of the real prisoners' rooftop protest at Broadmoor Hospital in 1983, the now glam rock styled harlequin struts around

Figure 14.3 Tom Hardy as Charlie Bronson.
Source: Vertigo Films, 2008.

the stage singing a karaoke rendition of David Cassidy's 'When I'm a Rock 'n' Roll Star' (1975). Before this Charlie performs a vaudevillian back and forth with himself, his harlequin garb merging with a cross-dress costume in his own rendition of a female prison administrator's confirmation of his imminent transfer to Broadmoor Hospital. His face paint constructs the outline of jet-black women's bob haircut on one side of his dead, with added red lipstick and large painted red nails. Refn's iconographic portrayal of masculinity and Hardy's verbose, physical performance is an exercise in camp taste; 'a relish for the exaggeration of sexual characteristics and personality mannerisms'.[18]

Bronson diverts the visual and narrative conventions of the British crime film and prison drama. Refn's remodelling of the original generic script takes the conventionally low cultural 'folk' icon Charles Bronson and the 'true crime biography' genre and elevates them in a camp and mock-heroic tone with a plot exploring artistic inspiration, artistic expression and the search for fame. The film's opening line of dialogue establishes this plainly: 'My name's Charles Bronson, and all my life I've wanted to be famous.' Refn has confirmed that this opening line frames the perspective as autobiographical. Although not a line added by Refn, the director spoke of how he identified with the opening dialogue and how this led to his own conception of Charles Bronson: 'I just wanted to be famous. I didn't know how to get to it because I couldn't act and

I couldn't sing . . . So, film became what I chose, or it chose me.'[19] This is the crucial point of view of the Russellian biopic and what connects Refn's film to Russell's own highly personal approach to history and adaptation: 'And didn't Tchaikovsky and Mahler say their music is autobiographical, too? Anything happens to me, I find a way of getting it into my films. I can't just depend on historical truth, whatever that is. History is bunk.'[20]

The opening shot of *Bronson* presents a theatrical tableau of the title character, spotlit from above amongst a completely black background. The delivery of the opening lines directly to camera introduces Charlie's omnipotent narration which will continue throughout the film, and the extended credit and post-credit sequence will establish the multi-layered flashback/episodic plot which creates the necessary multifarious and mythic presentation of Charles Bronson. The opening shot of a spotlit Charlie cuts to a mysterious and incongruous space; a long wide shot silhouettes the performer onstage from behind, the golden Art Deco arches of the auditorium filling each side and top of the frame with low light as a capacity black tie crowd looks up to the mystery performer onstage. This cuts to another shot of Charlie, this time framed in mid-shot from the chest up in a corridor of distressed walls. The next cut reveals a more recognisable pose, his bald head tilted forwards and staring blankly again but behind a large pane of glass, which more obviously denotes a prison space. Three more different shots of Bronson follow. These are increasingly more obviously in a prison environment but also present Charlie himself as increasingly iconographic: in one shot he is seated on his bunk, his muscular body framed in a tight vest, a traditional, sailor-style tattoo on each pumped-up forearm, arms crossed in contemplation, and a sideways glance, giving the impression of a strongman variation on Rodin's sculpture *The Thinker* (1880), with the chiaroscuro light and shadow providing a painterly tenderness to the image.

The dialogue throughout this brief montage has Charlie musing about artistic pursuits, stating that his inability to sing or act narrowed the field of pursuit for his life's 'true calling'. We return to the original opening shot of Charlie directly addressing the frontal camera with a hushed, resigned irony as he states, 'Kinda running outta choices, aren't I?' This importantly dissolves back again to the wide shot of the packed auditorium from the stage perspective while strings begin to squeal uncomfortably on the soundtrack as The Walker Brothers montage begins. The deliberate choice of image within the ordered montage establishes the ambiguous space that will be introduced following the title credit and opening montage, and importantly introduces the entire conceit of artistic expression and theatrical performativity. Rather than a realistic and naturalistic presentation of the subject and his autobiography, *Bronson* presents the character as a metaphor and multi-layered, Charlie is presented as the Russellian motif of an artist personifying his art and inspiration, and his violent acts are portrayed as a fantastical artistic spectacle.

'Oh Peter – I felt as if all of last summer was in it.' The reaction of Tchaikovsky's sister (Sabina Maydelle) to his performance alludes to the flashback images accompanying the Piano Concerto in *The Music Lovers* that visualise the composer's iconic music with the idyllic sensorial memories of a family's rural summer. Russell frames the memory as a theatrical choreography and displays the figurative imagery of family members posing balletically before a backdrop of swans upon a peaceful lake. The opening image of *Mahler* presents a lakeside cabin that suddenly bursts into flames at the cue of the orchestral soundtrack. We are later introduced to this space as the composer's work desk, and the surrounding rural setting provides visualisation to excerpts of several of the composer's symphonies in a musical montage sequence that attaches elements of his surroundings to specific instrumentation on the soundtrack. *Mahler* centres its narrative around the factual event of the composer's final train ride that occurred shortly before his death in 1911, although Russell takes licence with the exact historical details of the journey. The shell of the real-life event provides the springboard for a flashback dreamlike narrative and space for the expressive visual performance theatre of Russellian Montage.

Russell is interested less in historical detail and more in myth, the nature of fame and art itself. Tchaikovsky's 1812 Overture (1880) is visualised as a raucous rock performance montage featuring a macabre cartoon fantasy relating the explosion of Tchaikovsky's fame in *The Music Lovers*. The composer's brother Modeste's (Ken Colley) plea for him to conduct ('You could be famous') prompts a musical montage of quick cuts, fast tracks and slow motion, as Tchaikovsky is pursued by the film's supporting cast like a rock idol in scenes anticipating *Tommy* and *Lisztomania*. Flailing limbs grasp surreally out of open windows at him amid screaming close-ups, and his pursuers are shown buffeted with wind in handheld close-up, thick smoke and colourful streamers adding to the rock visual texture. His brother dances in a whirlwind of bank notes, frolicking with can-can dancers, the sequence climaxing with Modeste decapitating the composer's lovers, patron and rivals with canon fire. The composer is shown conducting to hordes of screaming masses standing atop a Russian Palace, an image repeated in *Tommy* when Daltrey addresses the crowds of converts from a rooftop in the 'Welcome' sequence.

The fantastical presentation of Charlie Bronson, and the film's layering of imagined incantations as an alternative to reality, culminates in the final music montage portraying the real-life hostage taking of the art teacher at Hull Prison in February 1999. From the main character's opening refrain, the film details a fantasy perspective that imagines a man searching for his own stage, medium or canvas. Refn reinvents the facts of the hostage situation into a fantasy of artistic creation wherein Charlie himself and the prison environment become his physical art canvas. Bronson is framed in full frontal nudity and covered in black paint with a spotlight making his hulking figure glow, moving in delicate motion to the isolated classical soundtrack of the 'Flower Duet' from *Lakmé*, act 1 by Léo Delibes (1883). Slow, tracking camera movements compliment the delicate classical soundtrack, along with the slow, stylised dance of Charlie emerging towards the tied and restrained prison teacher submerged like an exhibit under a blue velvet cloth. The scene concludes with Charlie placing the sunglasses and bowler hat he is wearing onto the bound teacher's painted visage, his mouth kept agape with an apple, revealing a life model approximation of René Magritte's *The Son of Man* (1964) with an added Dalí moustache. Charlie Bronson the prison artist is given theatrical repurposing in Refn's film, and the concept of artistic creation is used to transcend his biography and the factual events of his acts of violence. Refn's use of montage, a camp style of imagery, performance and soundtrack, as well as his use of parody and allusion align *Bronson* with Russell's approach to the biopic. The film refuses to engage in the nihilism of the prison and true crime genres and instead invents the narrative of the artist in a style which is uniquely and distinctly Russellian.

NOTES

1. Linda Ruth Williams, 'Sweet Swell of Excess: Ken Russell', *Sight and Sound*, vol. 17, no. 7, 2007, 29.
2. Ibid., 30.
3. David Smith, 'Anger at Film about Bronson, UK's Most Violent Prisoner', *Guardian*, 1 March 2009, <https://www.theguardian.com/film/2009/mar/01/charles-bronson-violent-film> (last accessed 4 November 2021).
4. Elizabeth Aubrey May, 'DiS Meets Nicolas Winding Refn', *Drowned in Sound*, <https://drownedinsound.com/in_depth/4151016-film-should-become-like-music-uncontrollable---dis-meets-nicolas-winding-refn> (last accessed 4 November 2021).
5. Barry Keith Grant, 'The Body Politic: Ken Russell in the 1980s', in Lester D. Friedman (ed.), *Fires Were Started: British Cinema and Thatcherism*, rev. edn (New York: Wallflower Press, 2006), 182.
6. Joseph Lanza, *Phallic Frenzy: Ken Russell and His Films* (Chicago: Chicago Review Press, 2007), 88.
7. J. Hoberman and Jonathan Rosenbaum, *Midnight Movies* (New York: Harper & Rowe, 1983), 90.
8. Camille Paglia, 'Tournament of the Modern Personae: D. H. Lawrence's *Women in Love*', in Camille Paglia (ed.), *Vamps & Tramps* (New York: Vintage, 1984), 309.
9. Ibid., 316.
10. John C. Tibbetts, 'Elgar's Ear: A Conversation with Ken Russell', *Quarterly Review of Film and Video*, vol. 22, no. 1, 2005, 40.
11. Lanza, 98.
12. James Hughes, 'The Greatest Music Cue of All Time', *Slate*, 19 July 2013, <https://slate.com/culture/2013/07/only-god-forgives-director-nicolas-winding-refn-discusses-his-favorite-music-in-cinema-history.html> (last accessed 2 June 2022).
13. Stan Hawkins, 'The Pet Shop Boys: Musicology, Masculinity and Banality', in Sheila Whiteley (ed.), *Sexing the Groove: Popular Music and Gender* (London: Taylor and Francis, 1997), 118–33.

14. Susan Sontag, 'Notes on "Camp"', in *Against Interpretation and Other Essays* (London: Penguin Classics, 2009), 279.
15. Kevin M. Flanagan, 'Ken Russell's Wartime Imagery', *Journal of British Cinema and Television*, vol. 12, no. 4, 2015, 542.
16. Ibid.
17. Sontag, 280.
18. Ibid.
19. Ken Guidry, 'Nicolas Winding Refn Says Jason Statham & Guy Pearce Turned Down "Bronson," Talks Influence of Stanley Kubrick and More', *IndieWire*, 9 June 2015, <https://www.indiewire.com/2015/06/nicolas-winding-refn-says-jason-statham-guy-pearce-turned-down-bronson-talks-influence-of-stanley-kubrick-and-more-263167/> (last accessed 2 June 2022).
20. Tibbetts, 37.

PART 5

A Word from the Editor . . .

CHAPTER 15

Ken Russell's *Song of Summer*: The Virtue of Restraint

Roger Crittenden

INTRODUCTION

> The film to me is not just a portrait of Delius and the working relationship with Eric Fenby, but it is also about the creation of a work of art - because I really think this film is a work of art - I think it is the best film I ever made.
>
> (Ken Russell - BBC DVD Commentary)

This chapter is a personal reflection on Ken Russell's *Delius: Song of Summer* (BBC, 1968) and its production from my perspective as the editor.

Of all the films Ken Russell made, *Song of Summer* was one of the most carefully conceived and executed: the film's discipline stems partly from respecting Eric Fenby's 1937 memoir, *Delius as I Knew Him*, an approach made more likely by the fact that the author was still living. Everyone involved in *Song of Summer* shared in creating an authentic account of the contribution of an unassuming but gritty young man from Yorkshire to the realisation of major compositions during the final years of Delius's life to the almost complete obliteration of his own artistic development.

Eric Fenby's collaboration with Ken on the screenplay created a rigorous blueprint for the film since it focused so strongly on the tensions arising from Delius's illness and inability to communicate his creative ideas, and his relationship with the willing but nervous young Fenby. The casting proved immaculately felicitous despite the complete absence of familiar faces from Ken's previous work. The choice of Max Adrian as Delius may have seemed obvious because of his uncannily similar appearance to the composer, but his performance carried impressive gravitas even though at the time he had a reputation for comedy and revue which had tended to obscure the fact that he had been a founding member of both Peter Hall's Royal Shakespeare Company and Laurence Olivier's National Theatre. Maureen Pryor shared the fact with Max Adrian of being born in Ireland, but her career had none of his stardom. Instead, she was a constant as a supporting actor on stage and screen. In a way this made her ideal for the role of Jelka, a woman living in the shadow of a self-obsessed artist. The real coup in the casting, however, was Christopher Gable as Fenby. I had the luck some years later to work again with Chris when I edited a film about his favourite dance partner at the Royal Ballet, the incomparable Lynn Seymour. Observing his generous and enthusiastic spirit in rehearsals with Lynn served to underline for me his natural sensitivity so apparent in *Song of Summer*. It was not surprising that Ken subsequently cast him in several films. Even the casting of David Collings in the cameo part of Percy Grainger brought a necessary energy at a crucial point in the story.

In retrospect it is arguable that budgetary constraints preventing French locations made necessity the mother of invention with studio sets and English exteriors. It certainly brought out the creative talent of Judy Steel as designer and the lighting craft of Dick Bush behind the camera. I also had reason to be grateful to John Murphy, the sound recordist, who went beyond the bounds of professional application in recording wild tracks at dawn and dusk to compensate for the main location's being under the flight path into Heathrow, which made the sync recordings of dialogue unusable.

Despite knowing what a great team Ken had gathered together around the project, the intense week that I spent viewing the rushes with him made me surprisingly anxious. The serious intensity of scene after scene played out over many takes made me feel that I had stumbled upon the raw material for a film so uncharacteristic of Ken that his many fans would find it strangely disappointing. The truth is that there have always been a considerable number of aficionados who may respect *Song of Summer* but will always prefer his more baroque inventions. However, what the Delius film proved beyond a doubt was that Ken had a unique mastery of his craft that could be applied to spare and unembroidered storytelling when the subject demanded. It was only as I put the film together that I realised that I had suffered from a preconceived expectation based on the work of Ken's that I had been involved in before. In the end my admiration for his work was greatly enhanced by this particular film.

IN THE BEGINNING: THE MISSING LAUREL AND HARDY SEQUENCE

In the sequence that opens *Song of Summer*, the composer Frederick Delius's (future) amanuensis Eric Fenby is seen providing the musical accompaniment to the Laurel and Hardy film *Way Out West* (James W. Horne, MGM/Hal

Roach Studios, 1937), which had to be excised from the BBC DVD release due to copyright issues, since that footage had not been cleared for use beyond the original television transmission. It has rarely been seen as intended since its original transmission, though at the time of writing a pirated recording is available on YouTube. For the DVD release, however, Ken returned to the film and forged a replacement sequence using footage salvaged from a silent comedy, *What Next?* (Walter Forde, Nettlefold Films, 1928), and using the original shots of Christopher Gable (Fenby) at the organ as well as library footage of a cinema audience. While this substitution is more coherent than the original, it also spoils the link to Laurel and Hardy made by Fenby's comment during his first meeting with Delius, when he remarks that he has been accompanying silent films at his local cinema, 'mainly Laurel and Hardy's'.

The fact that the Laurel and Hardy sequence was from *Way Out West*, with the Avalon Boys singing whilst the duo dance, was no inhibition for Ken, who reimagined it as silent with live musical accompaniment. Cinema enjoys ignoring the three dramatic unities of time, place and action, insisted on by Aristotle in his *Poetics*; however, in this sequence we, ironically, built a filmic reality that ostensibly observes those unities whilst simultaneously ignoring them: the film on the screen was made in America in 1937; the audience was filmed somewhere in England, probably in the 1950s; and Christopher Gable as Fenby playing the organ was shot in 1968 in London. Edited together they represent an event in the 1920s in a cinema in Scarborough, North Yorkshire.

FENBY'S MUSICAL BACKGROUND

It was, perhaps misleading on Ken's part to imply at the beginning that Fenby's musical activity was limited to the accompaniment of silent films. The script originally included voice-over, which came after the cinema scene, stating:

> I had also held an organ post at Holy Trinity Church where my father was a chorister, since I was twelve. Besides the usual repertoire I played several pieces of my own including a little organ sonata. I also found time to conduct a local madrigal group and once had conducted the Spa Orchestra when they had played a piece of my own.[1]

This confirmation of Fenby's musical experience and knowledge was never recorded. These facts would have made us more confident of his ability to transcribe Delius's musical thoughts, but then his ability to do so would not have appeared quite the miracle it does. Nevertheless, every shot from the end of the opening cinema sequence to Fenby arriving at the Delius house in France is exactly as originally conceived in the script. Nothing was added, and nothing was moved from its intended position although the scripted 'montage of crossing the channel' was never shot.[2]

Yet the individual shots are hardly ever tied together by strict continuity of action. The juncture between shots is a manipulation of space and time 'rhythmed' to provide a seamless progression. We move from a hillside to a living room to a seascape to a train to a station to a car to an interior of the house without any pause or artificial effect. The habitual use of continuity of action to bridge each cut that I had become familiar with at the BBC had made me nervous of abandoning that safety net. In Ken's case, the instinctive application of rhythmically effective juxtapositions allowed him to create whole visual scenarios that slotted together without a single jarring edit. This reminded me of the first film I edited, *The Market* made in the Portobello Road in 1962 by myself and friends of the director Ron Porter. It was shot mute and structured around image subject rather than continuity. The memory of that experience, edited at night in borrowed Soho cutting rooms, encouraged me to feel comfortable in overriding BBC conventions.

In the early part of *Song of Summer* voice-over narration plays a significant part in bridging transitions. Even so the combining of images represents a subtle balancing act on the tightrope of filmic construction because they underline the function of rhythm. For instance, the cut from Fenby rising from his seat on the train to his case hitting the platform, or the servant picking up the case to the moving car interior, or the cut from the car squeaking to a halt and cutting to the doors opening in the house all depend on control of rhythm. In a well-shot film the 'style' will often largely dictate itself, and often in editing *Song of Summer* each proceeding shot was anticipated and self-evident. This meant that the task of editing was to find the ideal 'frame' (since I was cutting on film) to end one shot and which frame to start the next, rather than choosing from alternative shots that covered the same moment.

The mistake we make, as my editor friend Claire Atherton has emphasised to me, is to talk about what we do as 'cutting'.[3] The last frame or digital scan we use is only the final fraction of a second of the shot. It is as if we are putting all the emphasis on the dying moment of the last note of a musical phrase when the whole phrase is where the meaning or feeling is contained. The effect of the shot or musical phrase almost invariably resonates beyond that last moment and across the junction with its neighbour. Visual resonance is not a concept regularly discussed, perhaps because it is easier to understand the persistence of a sound than the way images survive their apparent disappearance and replacement with another.

Our anxiety as film-makers about the audience being secure in the visual world we present is most cogently demonstrated by the convention of the 'over the shoulder shot', something you will not find in *Song of Summer*. In a conversation between two characters, the 'presence' of the other person is proved by showing the back of their shoulder to one side of the frame whilst the camera faces the person with whom they are conversing. It is as if we assume the observer can't maintain the knowledge of the other character's presence without a visual hint. It is also a false angle, possible only from a camera and not from

Figure 15.1 Fenby and Delius.
Source: BBC, 1968.

a character's point of view. To another friend and editor, Yann Dedet,[4] this is an ugly anathema – a feeling I share and, on the overwhelming evidence of his films, so did Ken Russell.

Genuine two-shot alternatives to the over the shoulder shot are many and varied. Take, for instance, Figure 15.1 from *Song of Summer*: images such as this all have a dynamism that is absent from the crude over the shoulder shot and, more importantly, make the intercutting of matching shots of the two characters unnecessary.

POINT OF VIEW

The driving force of Ken's visual vocabulary was an imaginative articulation of pictorial narrative made magic by montage. I was lucky enough to observe this in infinite detail during the editing of *Isadora Duncan, the Biggest Dancer in the World* (BBC, 1966) and *Dante's Inferno: The Private Life of Dante Gabriel Rossetti, Poet and Painter* (BBC, 1967). Let me give you an example. In the case of *Isadora* I was thrust into a ridiculous argument when the film was being approved for transmission and, in the absence of the editor Mike Bradsell, I had to supervise the completion. The film ends with the death of the dancer when her scarf catches in the wheel of a car and strangles her. This is followed by a marvellous sequence of Isadora and her pupils running together down a country hill to the strains of Beethoven's 'Ode to Joy'. The combination successfully melds the tragedy of her death with the ecstasy of her life. In a meeting of executives, Ken was being asked to choose between the two endings, as though the combination offended good taste. Sitting silently in a corner of the office, I was so irritated by this discussion that I suddenly blurted out, 'Are you really asking Ken to choose between French and German Romanticism when the combination is so potent?' To my surprise there was no further discussion, and the edit was approved. Frankly, Ken's craft never needed such quasi-intellectual explanations or justifications.

In *Song of Summer* this visual lexicon has a specific dimension because the whole film is told from the point of view of Fenby. We are watching either him or what he sees. It is a technique more familiar from film noir, where the detective's or protagonist's point of view usually dominates. *Chinatown* (Roman Polanski, Paramount, 1974) provides an example of this, where Jack Nicholson, as Jake Gittes, is either onscreen or the observer of what we see – something that was always visualised in the immaculate screenplay of Robert Towne, as can be confirmed in print as it was published in 2000 by Faber and Faber.[5] *Song of Summer* exhibits the same intense concentration on one point of view, with little deviation except for the visit of Percy Grainger.

According to the screenplay, Fenby and Grainger play *Song of the High Hills*, then they go through to Delius's bedroom and the story is told of carting Delius up the mountain to see the sunset, after which the incident is shown in flashback. Hence, the story is told to Fenby before it is illustrated, maintaining the point of view. We cut the film accordingly, but it was clear that this linear treatment was ineffective. Part way through the recital on the two pianos, Ken identified a point at which we would fade across to the orchestral version and begin the visualisation of the journey up the mountain, saving the climax of the sunset until the story is related to Fenby. It was a good decision, but I remember feeling uncomfortable that we were asking the audience to embark on the journey up the mountain before that event had been introduced in the narrative.

PAUSING FOR MEANING

Returning to the detail of an edit, the weight that should be given to the end of a shot and the best point to enter the next is not necessarily in harmony; often, the tighter a cut (that is, using less of each shot), the smoother the transition, leaving no breathing space for the tightrope to go slack. But the value of a shot can be in the pause before or after the essential action or dialogue. Anecdotally, Ken once told me that on one of his early feature films, when the cut was longer than the producers wanted, the editor worked on his own over a weekend and proudly presented Ken with a version on the Monday morning reduced to the required length, and explained to him that he had managed it by removing all the pauses, at which, Ken told me, he exploded and after calming down supervised the restoration of those meaningful moments.

The value of this 'pause' can be seen at the end of the early dinner scene in *Song of Summer* when we kept every usable frame of Christopher Gable alone at the table, nervously eating and observed by the maid after Jelka and Delius have left. When I showed my cut of this scene to Ken he made no suggestion that we should shorten the ending, and it remains for me one of the most affecting moments in the film. Habitually, Ken didn't call cut until well after the essential action of a shot had been completed, knowing that magic often occurs in that tense hiatus.

Beginnings of scenes or shots are even more important. If we examine the complete scene that Ken extracted from the opening of *Way Out West*, nothing is happening when we first see Laurel and Hardy observing the Avalon Boys making their music outside the saloon. They watch and listen, then very slowly begin to sway and then tap their feet before eventually essaying dance 'moves'. The surreal appearance of these two dressed entirely out of place and time creating their own theatrical event in the dirt of an old West street set is definitely 'way out'. Without the winding up from inaction to full on 'choreography', the comedy would lack finesse. Often in editing too much weight is given to the kernel of a scene without letting the audience absorb the shell or context first.

MUSIC AND FORM

The music of Delius is introduced the way Fenby first heard it, in his home on the radio whilst playing chess with his father. Ken directed the camera to subtly isolate Fenby in the frame to allow us to listen with him. True or not, the idea that Fenby's future life was decided between moves in a game of chess is a nice touch. We are first given a taste of Delius's music quite subtly when Jelka leads Fenby into the music room and, as the camera pans off him, we hear a section of ethereal choral music which stops when he recognises the photo of the young Delius, underlining how Fenby is drawn to Delius by his music.

The visit of Percy Grainger integrates his compositions into the storytelling. Ken's attitude to music was always flexible: if throwing a tennis ball over the roof of a large house and running through it to catch it the other side is impossible, careful editing of image and music makes the sequence so seamless it appears possible in a film. But the music itself is not sacrosanct; we made several cuts in Grainger's composition 'Country Gardens', which accompanies his dramatic arrival, purely to accommodate the needs of the visual sequence. Nor was Delius himself safe from similar treatment: the repetitive musical phrase that accompanies Fenby's voice-over describing the years which resulted in the completion of several pieces of music is a loop made by Ken himself from a 35 mm recording on magnetic tape of a Delius composition. Making such a loop so that the repeated phrase did not hiccup at the join on the primitive machine we were working with required patience and persistence, but he knew instinctively that the phrase we looped would suit the purpose.

Just as significant is resisting the use of music. When Fenby fails in his first attempt to take down a melody and rushes from the room out of the house and up the hill to the railway as if he is about to throw himself under a train, many a director would have used a score to emphasise the emotion and cover the lack of any visual continuity between shots. However, natural effects and the doubling of the actual length of the passing train by editing sleight of hand raise the tension so effectively, as Fenby attempts to escape the man whose music is the source of his anxiety, that to have added music would have been to slip into melodrama.

On two occasions we observe Delius, Jelka and Fenby listening to recordings of music but there is no resorting to visual illustration. However, such images were contemplated. When they listen to a Delius composition we zoom into his face and the shooting script stated:

EXT; MOORS: MUSICAL MONTAGE
The young Delius escaping from the smog of Bradford to the fresh air of the moors (see Appendix).[6]

This 'Appendix' contained the additional material to be shot illustrating episodes from Delius's youth. First was Ken's elaboration of the scene he actually shot of the young Delius escaping Bradford on a canal barge and encountering a young woman in the countryside. I cut this together but resisted inserting it in the film. Ken viewed it and without comment never asked me to include it in the assembly.

Second, the 'Appendix' details the following:

SCENE 43A: FLASHBACK DURING SONG OF THE HIGH HILLS
A) Tilt down from mountain. Young Delius and girl run nude into the water
B) Young Delius and girl going up mountain
C) Mountain top. Young Delius and girl reach summit
D) Close shot young Delius; close shot young girl back-lit laughing.[7]

Considering the context of Fenby and Grainger, playing the music and the subsequent retelling of the story of carrying Delius up the mountain to see the sunset, it was never going to make narrative sense to insert these images. The lacuna that remains is the photo of the actor who played young Delius that Fenby spots on first entering the house.

When Delius talks about his time in Florida, since there was no budget for location shooting, a research assistant had been detailed to source library footage of orange groves, alligator swamps and the singing 'Negroes' (as Delius calls them in the film). In this case there is no reference in the script to illustrative images, and once I had assembled the scene of them listening, and Ken had viewed it, he never referred to the potential use of library footage. When I was editing the film whilst Ken was away preparing *Women in Love* (United Artists, 1969), the material itself convinced me that it needed no ornamentation, and I knew I would want to argue against it on his return. I needn't have worried since in the event Ken didn't even discuss the option, though I imagine he might have had a debate with himself.

ANOTHER KIND OF FILM

Yet that Florida episode in Delius's life contained the potential for a Ken Russell film much closer to his usual style. As researched more recently by Tasmin Little in the film directed by Michael Darlow, *The Lost Child* (BBC, 1997), there is hardly a doubt that Delius fathered a child by an African American woman during his time there, and despite returning to Florida some years later he apparently failed to make contact with either the mother or their offspring. Little points out that Delius's mature musical style owes much to being strongly influenced by the music he encountered in America, and this adds weight to the idea of quite another film.

The extent to which Ken struggled with the opportunities presented by Delius's life for more sensual, even erotic imagery can be illustrated by the fact that he did shoot a sequence of the maid and the 'bruder' enjoying sex next to the dying body of Delius. Whilst this occurrence was apparently confirmed by Fenby, it still felt incongruous within the context of the film. Incidentally, regarding historical accuracy, whilst the spreading of rose petals around the corpse of Delius that ends the film is based on fact, the combination with the radio broadcast of his music that actually happened a few days after is a neat juxtaposition conceived by Ken to give the piece its climax.

Yet a scene of greater pathos was available to Ken. Fenby had to escort the coffin from Grez-sur-Loing in France to England for reburial after it had been exhumed. It was Delius's wish to be buried in England. After an exhausting journey there was a brief ceremony at midnight in the churchyard at Limpsfield in the south of England, and the coffin was left overnight to be interred the next day. It is easy to see the images Ken's imagination might have conjured up. Fenby thought that Delius's body should have remained in Grez with his spirit, and perhaps this is why the return of his corpse to England was never dramatised. After all, even if Limpsfield was a favoured burial place for musicians, it was neither birthplace nor spiritual home for Delius. Ken's 'novelisation' of

Delius's life, *Delius: A Moment with Venus*,[8] in depicting a series of tabloid revelations, seems to suggest he was still carrying a frustration about the more colourful film he could have made. On the other hand, Ken's circumstances at the time could easily have led to someone else making the Delius film.

BIG SCREEN, LITTLE SCREEN

When Ken's feature *Billion Dollar Brain* (United Artists, 1967), an adaptation of the Len Deighton novel, was released in January 1968 the expectation was that he would immediately move on to another film for the big screen – his project on Nijinsky starring Rudolph Nureyev. Ken anticipates this ultimately unmade project in archived correspondence in the Delius file, at the BBC Written Archives Centre; he would later go on to cast Nureyev as Rudolph Valentino in the film *Valentino* (United Artists, 1977). The box office returns on *Billion Dollar Brain* were poor and that project stalled. In the meantime, the BBC had assumed that Ken, who had previously been in development on the Delius project and had had discussions with Fenby, would not be returning to the small screen and so had encouraged another director, Anthony Wilkinson, to develop a script. Wilkinson's nine-page treatment is still lodged in the BBC Written Archives Centre.[9] It is a thorough and insightful portrait of Fenby's years with the composer, with suggestions for multiple flashbacks. It includes the exhumation in Grez and the reburial in Limpsfield. Wilkinson had by this time met with Fenby himself and even approached Max Adrian to play the composer.

As documented in archived correspondence, when Ken demanded he be given the Delius project back, saying if he didn't get it he would never work at the BBC again, the powers that be did not take long to cave in and grab the opportunity to back another project by their most successful film-maker. Wilkinson's treatment contains everything that the Russell film dramatised and more, and it would have been available to Ken when developing his own version (although the main source for both was Fenby's 1938 memoir, *Delius as I Knew Him*[10]). Ironically, the result of being gazumped from the project led to Wilkinson's being supported by the BBC in making an ambitious co-production with CBC and NET about Richard Wagner called *The Siegfried Idyll* (1969), which I also edited.

LISTENING FOR CLUES

I had been lucky enough to work on earlier Ken Russell films alongside Mike Bradsell (*Isadora Duncan, the Biggest Dancer in the World* and *Dante's Inferno*). In both cases Mike was the editor but had to leave the work before it was completed because he was committed to other projects and Ken, not unusually, had overrun his schedule. Thus it became my task to add the finishing touches and to see the film through to final print. So in a way I served an apprenticeship under Mike, and it was my great good luck to be trusted by Ken to edit the Delius film since by then Mike had left the BBC primarily to work on Ken's features.

I say good luck because Mike was a consummate editor from whom I learnt an enormous amount about the craft and above all else the importance of being 100 per cent committed to the work. Apart from the films by Ken that I assisted him on, there were others in which I was involved. Mike had been Peter Watkin's editor on both *Culloden* (BBC, 1964) and *The War Game* (BBC, 1965). The latter became notorious when it was banned from transmission due to concerns over its possible effects on public fears about a nuclear war. Bowing to media pressure, the BBC agreed to a screening at the National Film Theatre for an invited group of journalists. On the day, since Mike was too busy with his current editing task, I was delegated to accompany the print to the NFT, watch from projection, and immediately after the screening carry the film back to the BBC. Believe it or not, the risk of someone stealing the print or, as happened often in those days, a pirated copy being made for subsequent illegal circulation made that the most nerve-wracking day of my career in the cutting rooms.

A more specific example of Mike's commitment to a project was on a film by Barrie Gavin about the composer *Gustav Holst* (BBC, 1966). Mike convinced Barrie that the montage to cover the sequence of music from a particular composition needed more evocative images. The following weekend I found myself acting as driver and assistant as we journeyed to the Cotswolds so that Mike could shoot mute tracking shots from my trusty Austin Farina of landscape in the lanes around the villages of Upper and Lower Slaughter. The next week, after processing, these images became part of the film. The only comparison I can make for this example of such dedication to the work is that of Stewart McAllister as editor of Humphrey Jennings's classic wartime film *Listen to Britain* (Crown Film Unit, 1942), when the two collaborators agreed on shooting additional material to provide effective visual embroidery to the structure. In that case McAllister was rewarded with a co-director credit. In my opinion, Mike Bradsell has often deserved a similar approbation.

There were other incidents that prepared me for the particular nature of working with Ken. On the *Isadora* film we had to post-sync the voices of her pupils for sequences which had been shot mute. A dozen teenage girls were herded into a dubbing theatre and coaxed to scream and shout whilst observing the footage on a screen. It was not long before Ken decided he had better things to do and with a casual 'You can supervise this, Roger', he disappeared. I was flabbergasted and lost for words. The girls were already out of control.

Fortunately, Vivian Pickles, who played Isadora, was also present at the session and came to my rescue, 'acting' as the girls' supervisor as she did in the film, and we eventually recorded the necessary 'wild' tracks. Incidentally, Vivian quite rightly received the award for Best Actress at the 1967 Monte Carlo International Festival.

Ken would always continue refining the edit of a film right up to the last possible minute before the sound mixing. On *Isadora* we were still making minor alterations on the day before the scheduled dub. It came to past midnight and Ken suddenly succumbed to hunger since none of us had eaten all that day. Off he went home to have a steak, as he put it, and I confided to my assistant that we would have to begin the track laying and writing of the dubbing charts, or we would have nothing ready for the mixing in the morning. I steeled myself to tell Ken on his return that no more changes to the picture cut could be contemplated. An hour later he appeared carrying a large bag of crisps and a magnum of Champagne. I crumbled and we carried on cutting whilst I sent my assistant to another room to start preparations for the mixing session. Without sleep and with only one reel of the eight ready, we staggered into the dubbing theatre, my assumption being that Ken could supervise the session whilst we tried to keep up with preparing other reels. Unfortunately, the tape splicer we used to join the sections of soundtrack had become magnetised, which meant every time a join went over the sound heads it emitted a loud click. The session had to be abandoned and all the sound relayed, a mammoth task since every track had to be retransferred from the original tapes and each section identified so that it could be laid again in complete synchronisation with the picture. After a confrontation with front office, I was given a further two weeks to prepare the sound on the understanding that Ken was not allowed to continue re-cutting. Those tracks were the best I have ever prepared.

I hope that describing this episode gives a graphic picture of Ken's single-minded dedication to his work. If not, one more example should clinch it. In the case of *Dante's Inferno*, I had not been Mike Bradsell's assistant when I was delegated to take over the film's completion. This meant I was not familiar with the material in the way the assistant had to be when the editing was on film in order to immediately supply the editor with any shot or trim they required. It is not unusual for there to be a hundred hours of shot material for a feature film, so you can appreciate the need for familiarisation before the editing begins.

Ken seemed very happy that I had been made available when Mike had to go off; this is not to flatter myself, simply to underline the trust necessary in the intensely close and pressured work of the cutting room that means a familiar face is more welcome than a stranger. He said there was very little polishing to be done to the edit. What happened over the next two days was the most uncomfortable forty-eight hours I have ever experienced as an editor. Not once but several times Ken asked me to find a particular shot that he wanted to insert in a sequence. First, I had to familiarise myself with the way the material had been organised and then to identify the can or trim bin the required shot should be in. In each case it took hours to reach the conclusion that the shot could not be found, whilst Ken got more and more exasperated and insistent. I resorted to the continuity notes, which are the record and description of each shot, to try to identify the material that Ken was describing. At the end of the first day we had achieved nothing. The following morning I came to work early to see if I could be successful without the looming pressure of Ken's presence. No such luck. Ken arrived and insisted that I order reprints of the rolls of film which contained the scenes that would have included the shots he was after. The material arrived on the third day and we viewed it together. None of the shots was there. I had the bright idea of talking to Mike and contacted him on the phone. He had no memory of the shots. A frustrated Ken reluctantly abandoned the search and we concluded the work amicably over the next week or so.

My conclusion then and now is that Ken had conceived these images vividly in his mind's eye and they had become part of the imagined fabric of his film. They were details he had intended to shoot that were actually never committed to celluloid. If nothing else, this is a measure of the intensity of his visual creativity. At the time I would have given anything to have had the power to conjure those images into reality because I wanted to be an integral part of bringing his imagination to life. This is what all editors wish to share with their director.

In any case, when it came to editing *Song of Summer*, from these previous experiences of observing him at work I knew Ken was disinclined to elaborate on the details of the film we were constructing together. It was clear in his head so why shouldn't it be clear in mine? When there were choices to be made I could only conclude that he was happy to leave things as they were if no comment was forthcoming. He was truly inside the film and you were looking through a frosted window or listening at the crack in a door, eager to give of your best. This was true for everyone involved. Some actors are on record as experiencing a method of his that involved numbers. 'Give me a four' might mean tone it down a bit, or 'Give me a nine' implied heightening the performance. I would like to think that Ken knew how Fenby felt in struggling to understand Delius's intentions and secretly sympathised with similar difficulties his own collaborators had in trying to interpret his wishes. It was a struggle in particular for Maureen Pryor, who played Jelka in *Song of Summer*; there was one occasion when Ken went to over thirty takes of a shot without ever being able to explain to Maureen what he was looking for in her performance.

My fellow technicians had to visualise what Ken had in mind. The designer Judy Steel was assigned to the project by the BBC, although Ken had wanted Luciana Arrighi, with whom he had worked before, including on both *Isadora* and *Dante's Inferno*. Luciana won the Academy Award for her work on *Howards End* (James Ivory, Merchant-Ivory, 1992) and continues to design feature films to this day. She just happens to be the sister of Nike Arrighi, who starred in the first film I ever edited.

In the event, despite being a substitute for Luciana, Judy Steel rose magnificently to the challenge. The main set of the music room was constructed with the help of a photograph of the original, but Judy would have noticed the clear reference to rooms on two floors. Indeed, we frequently see the exterior of a two-storey house. Yet the interior sets did not include a staircase. Characters are either upstairs or down: never in transition. It would be so easy to construct dramaturgical reasons for this, but I am sure it was a budgetary consideration. At one point on an exterior shot we pan down from an upstairs window to Jelka listening below as Delius and Fenby strive to communicate effectively.

CONTRIBUTING TO THE WHOLE

Judy Steel's sets are very impressive. The huge double doors into the living room are reminiscent of expressionist sets from Scandinavian films of the 1920s. I admired Judy's work tremendously and regretted that it was let down acoustically in the shooting on the set in Ealing Studios by the floors not being wooden and the doors being made of plywood so the sound of footsteps and closures were wrong. We re-recorded every footstep and replaced every door opening and shutting, both in shot and off-screen, with the right sound, to support the feeling that the 'house' was real.

We can easily underestimate the contribution of the cinematographer Dick Bush whose lighting, especially in bringing 'sunlight' into studio sets, is another reason for the feeling of authenticity. The image of Delius, when Fenby first meets him, surrounded by a screen but with light filtering through, in a natural chiaroscuro, is particularly effective as seen in 35 mm black and white. Ken had to fight a long battle to resist the BBC's preference for 16 mm colour film, which by then had become the norm.

The exteriors of the Delius house were shot in Surrey close to an airport with take-offs and landings occurring every minute. Clean dialogue and effects were impossible. John Murphy, the sound recordist, did two things which made my work so much more satisfying. First, he re-recorded all the dialogue close-miked at the end of the shooting of each scene. The actors were still in the rhythm of their delivery, and it all fitted beautifully. But second, he and his assistant got up at dawn several times and recorded equivalent footsteps and atmosphere sound for those scenes before the airport became busy again. Even when we had to record post-sync dialogue, the sound effects were invaluable. It is easy to underestimate the importance of convincing sound, since it has to be authentic but an integrated part of the fabric of the film. In this case, our efforts were effective enough to contribute to the fact that several people asked me after transmission where that beautiful house was. This is one measure of the quality of the work by Judy, Dick and John to which I was happy to add my contribution.

THE PRIMACY OF THE ACTOR

The unselfish ensemble of performers Max Adrian, Maureen Pryor and Christopher Gable was such a joy for me, even though their individual experiences and approaches to acting varied enormously. As mentioned before, Max was a classical actor, whose technique was to decide his approach and to make minor modifications if necessary on subsequent takes. Appropriately, he was the fixed point around which the other two revolved. Maureen, on the other hand, was more the 'method' actor, which meant that every next take was an opportunity to try something different. Chris, a consummate performer as a dancer but new to acting, took his cues from the other two. I observed this most keenly when they recorded dialogue replacement. Chris was initially nervous of the technique required but he was coaxed and coached to perfection by the others. Their generosity with each other was in part a reflection of the fact that Ken largely left them to their own devices and devising.

You can always tell how supportive actors are of each other by the way they 'feed' lines in a dialogue scene whilst their fellow actor is in a single close-up. For some reason, on a couple of occasions during the shooting of this film the off-screen actor was replaced by a production assistant. You could hear the PA delivering the lines in a neutral tone, giving nothing for the on-screen actor to feed off. This only underlined to me how the nuances of performance gain from the sympathy between actors, and the quality of Chris's performance in particular owes much to Max and Maureen. This benefit of mutual support demonstrated itself most strongly in the composing scenes, which were shot on two cameras. Despite the edginess implicit in the situation and Chris having to listen *and* play, these scenes were so effective and demanded but little adjustment in editing between cameras. This is where the intermingling of rhythms shows itself most strongly, and the editor would be insensitive to think he or she could improve it.

The moment that epitomises why the detail of a memory, if faithfully executed, can seem more real and valuable than any invention or over-dramatisation is when Fenby misinterprets what Delius means by a quarter note and realises it is because he was brought up the 'English way' as opposed to the 'German nomenclature' familiar to Delius. It is the way Chris as Fenby pauses to think this through despite Delius (Max) being eager to get an idea down that seems so authentic and seems on the screen to be internalised. The dawning of a perception conveyed to the audience is one of the best frissons you can offer. Onstage the actor controls it completely, unless sabotaged by their fellow performers. In the edit suite it can be either respected or destroyed, and sometimes improved if the actor fails to allow for this thought process in his or her pacing and pausing. It is an underestimated part of the craft of acting, and therefore editing, that listening and reacting are more difficult to pace than dialogue itself.

Some years ago I remember being disappointed by the performance of an actress as Helena in a West End production of *A Midsummer Night's Dream*. She had recently starred in a TV drama series and this was her first leading role on the stage. When she had lines to deliver she became vividly animated but inbetween she switched off, so much so that she might have been a disinterested observer, not even as involved as someone in the audience. It spoilt the whole effect and was a disservice to her fellow actors. But then TV is mostly a close-up medium, and allows you to get away with spasmodic 'Acting'. Onstage she was only on camera, so to speak, when she had lines to deliver. Even then only her face had to act.

Laurel and Hardy both acted and interacted continuously – audibly and visually, which their humour depended on. Christopher Gable's skill in performing was partly to do with being a dancer. Louise Brooks, who starred as Lulu in G. W. Pabst's classic *Pandora's Box* (Nero-Film, 1929), once said to me, 'Dancers are the best actors – they perform with their whole being – body and soul.' Such integrated acting is a gift to the editor, who knows that at any given moment there will be electricity of sufficient voltage on the screen.

Compared with TV's reliance on the close-up, in Ken's expansive style there is nowhere to hide for the actor. The intensity that has been so admired in *Song of Summer* does not depend on the closeness of the camera to the actor or indeed on colourful renderings of artificial settings. It was not surprising to those who knew Ken that when he was asked in 2007 to list his top ten films, not only were six in black and white but they all took full advantage of a mise en scène that privileged the inclusive shot over the fracturing of cinematic space. Orson Welles's *Citizen Kane* (RKO, 1941) is there but so are Fritz Lang's *Metropolis* (UFA, 1927), Federico Fellini's *La Strada* (Ponti-De Laurentiis Cinematografica, 1954), Jean Cocteau's *Beauty and the Beast* (Les Films André Paulvé, 1946), Alfred Hitchcock's *The 39 Steps* (Gaumont-British, 1935) and the Marx Brothers' *A Night at the Opera* (MGM, 1935). We should remember that in the 1960s, at a time when the normal TV screen was only 20 inches across, the received wisdom was that audiences wouldn't watch if the camera was too far away from the action. It was also considered a turn-off to film in black and white.

Ken was working against the grain and the enemy were visible at every turn. This included the preparation for transmission. As editors we were always instructed to order prints on TV stock, which produced images of lower contrast to match the parameters the engineers felt the medium could cope with. This meant that in black and white there were no actual blacks or whites but a range of greys, often referred to by film buffs as soot and whitewash. Ken always insisted that the order to the laboratory must be for printing on 'cinema contrast stock'. Even then one of us would always be detailed to be in the control room for transmission to prevent engineers adjusting the image to fit their predetermined limits. The machine involved had the acronym TARIF, which stood for 'technical apparatus for rectifying indifferent film' – a clear indicator that electronic engineers considered their medium superior. This was not true then, and for some of us never will be. As you can imagine, this whole set-up was anathema to Ken, but he stood out in this as in so many ways as a beacon of visual artistry, making films that could stand with the best of cinema rather than be reduced to the mediocre fare usually seen on television.

In the case of *Song of Summer*, this insistence on such standards was publicly vindicated when it was finally shown in the cinema in 2001 in Ken's presence at the Telluride Festival in Colorado, and he received a standing ovation.

I would dearly love to have been there.

NOTES

1. Author's personal shooting script material.
2. Ibid.
3. Film editor Claire Atherton is best known for her collaboration over many years with Chantal Akerman. She is the subject of an interview in my book, Roger Crittenden, *Fine Cuts: Interviews on the Practice of European Film Editing*, 2nd edn (New York: Routledge, 2018).
4. Yann Dedet first edited with François Truffaut, including *La Nuit Americaine* (Day for Night, 1973). He has garnered many awards, in particular for his work with Maurice Pialat. See also Crittenden, *Fine Cuts*.
5. Robert Towne, *Chinatown* (London: Faber and Faber, 2000).
6. Author's personal shooting script material.
7. Ibid.
8. Ken Russell, *Elgar: The Erotic Variations and Delius: A Moment with Venus* (London: Peter Owen, 2007).
9. BBC Written Archives Centre, *Delius* file, T53/118/2.
10. Eric Fenby, *Delius as I Knew Him* (London: Charles Birchall and Sons, 1948).

Index

The 39 Steps (1933), 296
42nd St (1933), 152

adaptation, 2, 15, 17, 61, 69, 70, 71, 73, 78, 76, 121, 145, 155, 166, 169, 181, 220–1, 243, 255, 260, 264, 271, 274, 290
Adderley, Julian 'Cannonball', 114
Adrian, Max, 152, 230, 281, 290, 295
Ai No Corrida / In the Realm of the Senses (1972), 245
Alexander Nevsky (1938), 70, 246
Alfie (1966), 53
All Talking, All Singing, All Dancing (1971), 145, 158
Altered States (1980), 13, 14, 19n, 33, 43, 59, 70, 71, 172, 214, 222, 224, 229, 249, 250, 262
Altman, Rick, 180, 181
Altman, Robert, 242
Always on Sunday (BBC, 1965), 11, 116–19, 122, 126, 131, 232
Amelia and the Angel (1958), 29, 44, 169, 171, 214, 221, 248
Amiel, Jon, 214, 218
Anderson, Lindsay, 5, 6, 15, 19, 186
Angel (1982), 251
Angels are So Few (BBC, 1970), 216
Anger, Kenneth, 163
Antonioni, Michelangelo 46 (*Blow-up* [1966]), 163
Apollinaire. Guillaume, 117
architecture, 57, 70, 80, 84, 132
Aria (1987), 38, 72, 174, 251
Art Deco, 148, 151, 152, 153, 154, 158, 159
Artillerymen (1893–5), 118
asylums, 14, 35, 80–1, 86, 133, 165
At Eternity's Gate (2018), 122
Attenborough, David, 7, 19
Avant-garde, 80, 83, 85, 134, 139, 152, 163, 167, 253, 263, 26

Bacon, Francis, 6, 110
The Band, 185
Baird, Roy, 4
Baird, Stuart, 43, 262
Bal du moulin de la Galette (1876), 130
The Balcony (1868), 113
Barr, Charles, 163
Bartók (BBC, 1964), 82, 83–5, 251
Bat out of Hell (Meat Loaf album, 1977), 268
Bates, Alan, 48, 55, 244, 262, 264
Battleship Potemkin (1925), 268
Baudelaire, Charles, 58
Baxter, John, 7, 58, 95, 156
BBC, 7, 8–10, 16–18, 24
  Monitor, 2, 24, 43–4, 79, 99, 109–10, 112, 116, 119, 125–6, 113, 115, 162–3, 214–15, 222, 251
  Omnibus, 2, 43, 1
Beardsley, Aubrey, 56, 86, 87, 154, 249
A Beast with Two Backs (BBC, 1968), 219
Beaton, Cecil, 154–5, 158
Beauty and the Beast (1946), 296
Beckett, Samuel, 84
Beethoven Confidential (novel, 2006), 230, 231
Bellocchio, Marco, 163
Berkeley, Busby, 14, 27, 70, 147, 152, 155
Betjeman, John, 57, 214
Betty Boop (animated cartoon), 27
Between Two Rivers (BBC, 1960), 215
BFI Experimental Film fund, 29, 169, 214, 248
Biba, 157–8
Big Eyes (2014), 122
Biller, Anna, 13, 185
Billion Dollar Brain (1967), 51, 53, 70, 97, 101, 239, 246–7, 290
The Black Maskers Suite (1923), 131
Blake, Peter, 56, 112, 113, 122

INDEX 299

The Blood on Satan's Claw (1971), 58
Blue (1993), 171
Bonnie and Clyde (Warner Bros., 1967), 151
Bookstand (BBC), 215
Boorman, John, 5, 43, 140, 162, 170, 231
Boreas and Oreithyia (1896), 127
Boshier, Derek, 56, 112, 114–15
Boty, Pauline, 72, 85, 112, 115
Boudica Bites Back (2009), 12, 13, 34, 88
Bowie, David, 272
The Boy Friend (1971), 2, 17, 27, 28, 29, 36, 51, 70, 115, 120, 145–6, 147–9, 151, 152–3, 154–8, 158–9, 169, 226, 251, 254, 255, 257, 267
Boyd, Don, 38, 43, 174, 175, 177, 251
Bradsell Mike, 12, 43, 262, 285, 290–1
Bragg, Melvyn, 2, 3, 8, 11, 12, 43, 101, 116, 139, 229
Brahms Gets Laid (novel, 2014), 41, 230, 231
Brakhage, Stan 163
Branded to Kill (1967), 247
The Brides of Dracula (1960), 219
Bright, John, 150
Brightman, Sarah, 267
Brimstone and Treacle (BBC, 1976), 216, 222, 223
British Film Industry/establishment, 3, 117, 172, 249
British Film Institute (BFI), 11, 156, 197, 208, 215
A British Picture (1989), 262
A British Picture (Russell biography), 5
Bronson (film), 18, 260, 263, 268–9, 271–6
Bronson, Charles (criminal), 273, 275
Buñuel, Luis, 253
Burton, Humphrey, 3, 43
Bush, Dick, 32, 43, 102, 282, 294
Butterfield, Cleo, 150, 153
Byrne, Gabriel, 54, 56, 72
Byron, Lord, 54, 72, 73, 77
Byronic Performance, 48, 50, 53, 54–65

C20 Vintage Fashion (shop), 150
Cabaret (1972), 157
The Cabinet of Dr. Caligari (1920), 77, 121
Calvino, Italo, 26
Camille (1921), 203
Cammell, Donald, 59
Caravaggio (1966), 164, 166, 167, 168, 170, 173–4, 229
Casanova (BBC, 1971), 217, 218
Castle (Rowntree's Black Magic advert), 102–4
The Castle of Otranto (1764), 75
Cathy Come Home (BBC, 1966), 137
Cavani, Liliana, 245
Cézanne, Paul, 168
Channel 4, 34
  Big Brother, 2, 10, 43
  I-Camcorder, 12; 164, 171
Chaplin, Charlie, 27, 271
Chayefsky, Paddy, 33, 36, 71, 214, 224
Un Chien Andalou (1929), 80
Christ in the House of His Parents (1849–50), 135
Cinema Museum, London, 11

Citizen Kane (1941), 82, 296
Clapton, Eric, 265
Clarke, Ossie, 151, 152
Clerk Saunders (1857), 121
Climax (2018), 14
Clouds of Glory (ITV, 1978), 35, 121, 251
Cobra (1925), 200
Cocteau, Jean, 44, 77, 163, 263, 296
Cohen, Sheila, 150
Coleman, Ornette, 114
Collings, David, 81, 282
Colour Me Kubrick (2005), 15, 35
Colquhoun, Robert ('The Two Roberts'), 110, 111, 123n
counterculture, 16, 55–61, 63, 150
Cox, Alex, 177, 251
Crimes of Passion (1984), 11, 13, 35, 63, 74–6, 81, 87, 172, 222, 232, 248–50, 263, 267
Crimes of Passion (2016), 231
Cry of the Banshee (1970), 58
Crittenden, Roger, 9, 18, 43
Cronenberg, David, 14, 231, 253
Culloden (BBC, 1964), 291
Cyr, Miriam, 77, 120

Daltrey, Roger, 43, 88, 264, 266, 272, 275
Dance of the Seven Veils (BBC, 1970), 2, 7, 11, 23, 29, 30, 31, 75, 120, 130, 135, 175, 176, 177, 222, 223, 262, 263, 264, 270, 271
Dante's Dream at the Time of the Death of Beatrice (1869–71), 121
Dante's Inferno (BBC, 1967), 11, 29, 42, 48, 49, 54, 55–61, 62, 65, 66, 91n, 109, 115, 119–12, 126, 130–1, 132, 134, 136, 139, 165, 239, 285, 290, 292, 294
Daughtry, J. Martin, 182, 183
De Morgan, Evelyn, 126–9; 133
De Palma, Brian, 255
Death of Marat I (1907), 109
The Debussy Film (BBC, 1965), 2, 4, 11, 33, 38, 54, 76, 79, 80, 82, 84, 85, 91n, 103, 104, 116, 121, 126
Decadent Movement, 55, 58, 86
Le Déjeuner des canotiers (1881), 130
Le Déjeuner sur l'herbe (1863), 137
Del Toro, Guillermo, 13, 14
Delius, As I Knew Him (memoir by Eric Fenby, 1937), 235, 281
Delius: A Moment with Venus (novel, 2007), 228, 230, 235–41
Delius: Song of Summer (BBC, 1968), 4, 18, 109, 125–6, 146, 171, 228, 237–40, 251, 281–3, 286, 287–9, 289–90, 290–4, 295
Derbyshire, Delia, 80
Deren, Maya, 163, 167
The Devil's Violinist (2013), 14
The Devils (1970), 3–4, 9, 10, 11, 13, 14, 17, 30, 34, 48, 49, 54, 55, 58, 62, 63–4, 65, 66, 70, 74, 75, 77, 81, 120, 135–6, 146, 147, 152, 155, 156, 163–7, 169, 171–2, 176, 185, 203, 221, 222, 223, 232, 240, 242, 245, 247–8, 251, 256, 257, 258, 262, 263, 266, 267

The Diary of a Nobody: The Domestic Jottings of a City Clerk (BBC, 1964), 29
Dickinson, Thorold, 162, 163
Die Nibelungen (1924), 121
Disney, 32, 114, 264
documentary, 1, 2, 11, 15, 17, 18, 24, 34, 84, 86, 100, 109, 110, 112, 116, 126, 129, 131, 133, 137 138, 139, 145, 158, 171, 176, 186, 196, 202, 203, 215, 222
Dolby sound, 182
Dolby, Thomas, 80, 266
The Dotty World of James Lloyd (1964), 116
Double Dare (BBC, 1976), 216, 219
Dracula, 33, 71, 72, 78, 87–8, 271
Dracula (1958), 73
Dracula (1979), 87
The Dream (1910), 118
Dreyer, Carl, 77, 163, 172
Drive (2011), 261–2
Durgnat, Ray, 163

Ebert, Roger, 228
Ecce Ancilla Domini! (The Annunciation, 1849–50), 119
editing, 87, 104, 105, 113, 114, 122, 127–9, 169, 175–6, 207, 220–1, 260, 262, 284
Edward II (1991), 164, 166
Eidsheim, Nina Sun, 181
Eisenstein, Sergei, 70, 111, 163
The Electrician (Scott Walker song), 269
electronic music, 80, 115, 262, 266–70, 197
Elgar (BBC, 1962), 4, 11, 19n, 23, 29, 30, 81, 123nn, 126, 134, 137, 138, 171, 173, 176, 214, 215, 218, 222, 232, 251
Elgar: Fantasy of a Composer on a Bicycle, 30, 232
Elgar: The Erotic Variations (novel, 2015), 230, 231, 232–5, 236, 238, 239, 240
England's Glory (1961), 114
English, Michael, 150
Enter the Void (2009), 14
The Entombment of Christ (1604), 170, 172
Evans, Lloyd, 231

The Fall of the House of Usher, 25, 76, 82
The Fall of the Louse of Usher (BBC, 2002), 14, 25, 33, 35, 85, 86, 88
Fantasia (1940), 264
Felix the Cat, 27
Fellini, Federico, 1, 138, 163, 242, 256, 296
Fenby, Eric, 109, 171, 228, 235–236, 238–9, 281–3, 284–6, 287, 287–90, 293–4, 294–5
film clubs, 242, 247–8, 250
Fists in the Pocket (1965), 163
Flanagan, Kevin M., 6, 7, 9, 69–70, 71, 113, 270
Flying Down to Rio (1933), 152
Footlight Parade (1933), 152
The Four Horsemen of the Apocalypse (1921), 199, 203
Frankenstein, 15, 70–4, 82, 86, 88–9, 271
French Dressing (1964), 75, 78, 101, 251, 254
Freud, Lucien, 110

Freud, Sigmund, 62, 80, 263
Funeral in Berlin (1966), 53
Fuseli, Henri, 70, 119

Gable, Christopher, 28, 154, 264, 270, 282, 283, 287, 295, 296
The Garden (1990), 170
Garris, Mick, 43
Gaslight (1940), 162
Gaudier-Brzeska Henri, 29, 111, 118, 119, 167–8, 221, 222
Gauguin, Paul, 109
Genet, Jean, 163
Gibbs, Christopher, 50
The Girlhood of Mary Virgin (1848–9), 119
Glass Candy (group), 269
The Gold Rush (1925), 271
The Good Ship Venus (2005), 13, 88
Gothic (1986), 9, 11, 14, 26, 27, 28, 33, 48, 54, 56, 69–70, 71–3, 77–8, 80, 83, 86–7, 89, 115, 119–20, 172, 214, 251–2, 253, 254, 266
Grainger, Percy, 228, 238, 282, 286, 287, 288
Granny Takes a Trip (shop), 150
Grant, Barry Keith, 72, 153, 262
The Great Gatsby (1974), 157
Greenaway, Peter, 43, 127, 177, 251
Guadagnino, Luca, 14

Hale, Georgina, 11, 36, 81
Hall, Peter, 281
Hamilton (2015 musical), 181
Hammer Studios, 54n16, 67, 73, 219
Hanke, Ken, 7, 64, 80, 97, 168, 169, 172, 180
Hardy, Tom, 269, 273
Hare, David, 251
Hawkes, Jacquetta, 79
Häxan (1922), 77
Hearst, Stephen, 130
Herne Bay, Kent, 78
Hill, Benny (comedian), 5, 30
Hitchcock, Alfred, 15, 74, 296
The Hitchhiker's Guide to the Galaxy, 230
Hockney, David, 114, 115, 152, 154
Hodges, Mike, 231
homosexuality 16, 51, 64, 110, 152, 170, 174, 229, 230, 268
horror and the supernatural, 11, 13–14, 15, 19n, 33–4, 50, 55, 58, 67n, 69, 70, 71–5, 77, 79n, 80, 81–9 83, 85, 119, 131, 185, 219–20, 224, 246, 269
A House in Bayswater (BBC, 1960), 11, 43, 79, 83
Hulanicki, Barbara, 157, 158–9
Hung On You (shop), 150
The Hurdy-Gurdy Man (2018), 14
Hurt, William, 23 19, 43, 49, 249
Huxley, Aldous, 30, 64, 75, 165
Huysmans, Joris-Karl, 55

Immortal Beloved (1995), 15
The Ipcress File (1965), 53, 246

Ireland, Dan, 13, 43
Isadora, the Biggest Dancer in the World (BBC, 1966), 11, 70, 78, 81, 91n, 115, 126, 151, 216, 251, 285, 290, 291–2, 293
Ishigami, Mitsutoshi, 246–7, 248
It's All Coming Back to Me (music video, 1989), 72, 267
ITV, 2, 35, 99, 100, 106n, 177, 218, 251
Ivan The Terrible (1944–6), 164

J. Walter Thomson Agency, 98, 99, 102
Jackson, Glenda, 11, 26, 61–2, 81, 243, 245, 249, 261
Jagger, Mick, 50, 59, 154
James, M. R., 78
Japan, 10, 18, 40, 242–58
Jarman, Derek, 17, 70, 162–77, 231, 251, 257
Jarry, Alfred, 232
jazz, 112, 114, 156, 266
Jennings, Humphrey, 163
Joe's Ark (BBC, 1976), 216
John, Elton, 2, 99, 258, 267
Jones, Gemma, 65, 165
Jordan, Neil, 251
Joyce, James, 232
Junkopia (1981), 79

Kael, Pauline, 223
Kawarabata, Nei, 244
Kemp, Lindsay, 168, 252
Ken Russell Retrospective (Japan), 249–54
Kermode, Mark, 11, 13, 43, 257
The Kids Are Alright (1979), 185
Kimura, Takeo, 255, 256–7
A Kind of Loving (1962), 100
Kinema Junpo (Japanese film publication), 18, 242, 243–4, 246, 247, 249, 250, 254
The Kiss (1897), 109
Kitaj, R. B., 114
A Kitten for Hitler (2007), 12
Konno, Yuji, 244, 245–7
Kramer, Larry, 214, 220
Kubrick, Stanley, 8, 13, 15, 19n, 35, 51, 61, 243, 266

La Strada (1954), 296
Laban, Rudolph, 50
Lacan, Jacques, 186
Lacey, Bruce, 84, 88
The Lair of the White Worm (1987), 11, 13, 14, 15, 26, 32, 34, 71, 73, 75, 172, 219, 220, 222, 254, 261, 263, 266
Lake District, 7, 120, 191
lakes and boats, 77–80
Lamour, Dorothy, 27, 40
Lang, Fritz, 77, 121, 166, 217, 296
Langley Moore, Doris, 149, 150
Lanza, Joseph, 8–9, 71, 96, 131, 201, 230
'Last of the Teddy Girls' (photographic series), 70
Last Picture Frock (Shop), 150

Last Tango in Paris (1972), 245
The Last Waltz (1978), 185
Laurel and Hardy, 282–3, 287, 296
Lawrence, D. H., 2, 9, 44, 54, 61, 65, 70, 121, 200, 220, 232, 243, 244, 246, 255, 263–4
Lay Down Your Arms (ITV, 1970), 218
Lean, David, 97, 242
Lee, Christopher, 73
Levy, Don, 163
Liden, Jenny, 55, 61, 200, 262
Lipstick on Your Collar (BBC, 1993), 216
Lisztomania (1975), 10, 23, 29, 31, 37, 69, 70, 88; 113, 166, 172, 181, 217, 225, 229, 234, 251; 261, 264–6, 271–2
Littlewood, Joan, 50
Litvinoff, Si, 53
Loach, Ken, 137–8, 213
London, 6, 8, 11, 41, 43, 53, 56, 57, 64, 70, 76, 83, 84, 110, 113, 114, 115, 126, 134, 139, 149, 150–3, 154, 155, 162, 163, 167, 229, 236, 252, 283
London Moods (1961), 57
The Lonely Shore (BBC, 1962), 1, 37, 79, 109
The Love Witch (2017), 13
Loving Vincent (2017), 122
Lowe, Zane, 261
Lowry, L. S., 135
Luckhurst, Roger, 72

MacBryde, Robert ('The Two Roberts'), 16, 110, 123n
McCartney, Paul, 157
McClelland, Alan, 110
Madonna, 14
Mahler (1974), 31, 36–7, 48, 77, 78; 81, 84, 120, 121, 129, 166, 171, 173, 174, 177, 181, 182, 217–18, 221, 234, 248, 252–3, 254, 258, 262–3, 264, 266, 267, 268, 270, 271, 274, 275
Malcolm, Derek, 43, 229
Man Playing Snooker and Thinking of Other Things (1961), 114
Manet, Édouard, 113, 133, 137
Manfred Symphony (1885), 81, 174, 266
Marker, Chris, 79
Marx Brothers, 27, 166, 296
masculinity *see* sex and sexuality
Maxwell-Davies, Peter, 43, 266
The Mayor of Casterbridge (BBC, 1978), 221
Melvin, Murray, 29, 49, 50–1, 65, 87, 89
Midnight Movie (1994), 219, 220
Mike and Gaby's Space Gospel (novel, 1999), 230, 231
Millais, John Everett, 57, 119, 122, 134, 135, 136
Miller, Jonathan, 3, 78
Minami, Hiroshi, 244
Mindbender (1994), 36, 221
Mingus, Charles, 114
Mizuno, Haruo, 243
modernism, 17, 69–71, 77, 78–89
Monitor (BBC), 2, 24, 43, 44, 79, 99, 109, 110, 112, 116, 119, 125, 126, 133, 135, 162, 163, 214, 215, 222, 251

Monsieur Beaucaire (1924), 201
montage style, 263, 264, 267, 272
Moran of the Lady Letty (1922), 200, 204
Morley, Carol, 13
Morgan, Evelyn De, 126–33
The Most Handsome Hero of the Cosmos and Mr Shepard (1962), 114
Mr Nice (2010), 15
Mr. Turner (2014), 122
MTV, 180, 267
multi-modal listening, 182–3, 193
Munch, Edvard, 109
Murphy, John (sound recordist), 282, 294
The Music Lovers (1970), 2, 11, 27, 30, 36, 48, 51, 52, 70, 80–1, 96–7, 120, 129, 132, 147, 174, 175, 185, 203, 219, 220, 223, 230, 239, 242, 245, 262, 264–6, 267, 271, 275
The Mystery of Dr Martinu (BBC, 1992), 2, 35, 80
The Mystery of Mata Hari (2004), 13, 88

National Theatre, 281
The Neon Demon (2016), 263
Nevermore (O Taïti) (1897), 109
A Night at the Opera (1935), 296
The Night Porter (1972), 245
The Nightmare (1781), 119
Nijinsky, Vaslav, 41, 53, 195, 204–5, 290
Nishijima, Norio, 244, 250, 257
Noe, Gaspar, 14
Nolin, Michael, 16, 83, 85–8
Nosferatu (1922), 121
nostalgia, 17, 111, 146, 152, 153, 154–8, 159
novels, 228–40
Nureyev, Rudolph, 195, 196, 197, 198, 200, 203, 205, 208, 290

Offscreen Film Festival, 8
Old Battersea House (BBC, 1961), 17, 126–35, 140
Old Junior's Cart (1908), 118
Olivier, Laurence, 281
Olympia (1865), 137
Omnibus, 2, 43, 119
On the Balcony (1955–7), 113
Only God Forgives (2013), 263
Ophüls, Max, 163
Ormsby-Gore, Jane, 150
Orridge, Genesis P., 152
Oshima, Nagisa, 245
Our Lady of Peace (1907), 127

Paglia, Camille, 263
Palmer, Tony, 162
The Party's Over (1965), 64
Pasolini, Pier Paolo, 163, 170, 229, 245
The Passion of Joan of Arc (1929), 172
Pathétique Symphony (1893), 50, 81, 174, 266
Peepshow (1946), 146
Pennies from Heaven (BBC, 1978), 216, 219, 226

Performance (1970), 59, 154
Perkins, Anthony, 35, 63, 74, 75, 76
Pet Shop Boys, 176, 268
The Phantom of the Opera (1987), 224
Phantom of the Paradise (1974), 255
Phillips, Gene D., 98, 171
Phillips, Peter (pop artist), 56, 112, 114
Picasso, Pablo, 109, 110, 117
Pickles, Vivian, 81, 292, 78
Pinewood Studios, 163, 164, 166
Pink Floyd, 181
Play for Today, 137
Poe, Edgar Allan, 4, 33, 49, 77, 82, 83, 84, 85–6, 86–8
A Poet In London (BBC, 1959), 11, 57
Pollack, Leonard (costume designer), 15
Pop Art, 56, 77, 80, 85, 112–16, 133, 158, 249, 257
Pop Goes the Easel (BBC, 1962), 11, 56, 109, 112–16, 122, 133, 215
Portobello style, 147–53
Portrait of Madame M (1895–7), 118
postmodernism, 16, 17, 71, 72, 86, 88, 153, 265
Potter, Dennis, 17, 213–26
Potter, Sally, 177
Powell, Michael, 15, 137, 170, 174, 231, 254
Pre-Raphaelite Brotherhood, 6, 16–17, 42, 55, 57, 58, 86, 119–21, 122, 125–40, 165
The Preservation Man (BBC, 1962), 29, 88
Pressburger, Emeric, 137, 174, 254
Princess Raccoon (2007), 257
Prokofiev (BBC, 1961), 214, 251
Pusher Trilogy (1996–2005), 263
Pushkin (1986), 224–55

Quant, Mary, 157
Queen of Spades (1949), 162
Quintaphonic sound, 182, 186

Rabelais, 169, 230, 232
The Rainbow (1989), 37, 70, 71, 120, 254
Rainey, Michael, 150
Rais, Gilles de, 84
Realism, 17, 58, 135, 137, 138, 147, 217
The Red Cross (1914–16), 127
Redgrave, Vanessa, 49, 165, 263
Reed, Oliver, 16, 34, 38, 48, 49, 50, 51, 53, 54–66
  performances in Russell's films; masculinity, 72, 82, 116, 139, 191, 244, 245, 262, 263
Renoir, Jean, 163
Renoir, Pierre Auguste, 130
Resnais, Alan 79, 83, 129
Retrochic 146, 150, 151–3, 154
Revenge of the Elephant Man (2004), 13, 35, 88
Reynolds, Joshua, 121
Richard, Cliff, 99, 267
Richardson, Natasha, 77
Richardson, Tony, 97
Rime of the Ancient Mariner (ITV, 1978), 35
Rocketman (2018), 258

Roeg, Nicolas, 5, 14, 15, 43, 59, 140, 154, 229, 249
Romantics and Romanticism, 2, 3, 5, 6, 27, 48, 49, 51, 54–5, 55–61, 69–71, 72, 111, 122, 173, 199–200, 201, 220, 240, 253, 261, 272, 286
Roszak, Theodore, 56
Rose, Bernard, 1, 14–15
Rosen, Jelka, 281, 287, 288, 293, 294
Rossetti, Dante Gabriel, 58, 119
Rousseau, Henry, 116–19, 122
Royal Shakespeare Company, 281
Rumley, Simon, 177
The Russia House (1992), 15
Russell, Elize, 3, 7, 9, 14, 15, 16, 18
Russell, Ken
  advertising, 95–109;
  amateur/ early filmmaking, 2, 5, 12, 19n, 43–4, 76, 83, 88, 96, 120, 145, 146, 167, 171, 248
  ballet, xiv, 3, 28, 32–3, 39, 41–2, 53, 84, 99, 111, 195, 204–5, 261, 268, 282
  Catholicism 76, 120, 171, 270
  censors, 11, 49, 105, 137, 170, 172, 217, 223, 229, 231, 243–5
  childhood, 5, 16, 24–8, 85, 153, 261, 265
  collaboration, 10, 16, n32 20, 48, 50–4, 54–6, 71–7, 82, 85–9, 101–4, 146–59, 163–72, 262, 266, 281, 285–97
  critics, 2, 3–7, 13, 18n25 19, 24, 34, 43, 44, 80, 83, 88, 95, 96, 97, 117, 118, 136, 139, 166, 167, 171, 174, 180, 213, 223, 225, 228–9, 242, 243–7, 252–7, 260
  education, 39–44
  'Enfant Terrible', 1–5, 23, 225
  'Madman', 3, 35, 88
  mother (Ethel), 24–6, 31, 36–7, 41–2, 45
  music, 1, 3, 4, 7, 14, 18, 24, 29, 38, 41–2, 43, 80, 81, 82, 88, 99, 109, 110, 111, 113, 116, 119, 125–6, 129, 131, 138, 145, 147, 152, 153, 173–4, 174–8, 180–93, 213–14, 216–17, 217–19, 220, 221, 223, 224–5, 236, 237–8, 253, 260, 264–76, 283–90
  (rock) opera, 3, 17, 34, 83, 172, 174, 176, 177, 181–1, 183, 186, 224, 257, 261
  photography, 2, 3, 42, 43, 70, 76, 130, 147, 267
  Russellian style, 6, 15, 17, 18, 24, 36, 48, 50–1, 70, 72, 74, 83, 88, 97, 99, 102, 105, 111, 113, 114, 120, 121, 127, 137, 145, 146, 150, 151, 152, 158, 196, 214, 216–217, 225, 229, 243, 245, 247, 253, 254, 255–6, 260–76
  Southampton and Southampton Solent University, 5, 8, 15, 24, 26, 27, 32, 38–45;
  unmade films and projects, 82; *Pretty Boy Floyd*, 35; *Ten Times Poe/Horrible Beauty*, 16, 85–8; *Dracula*, 33, 71, 73, 83, 87–8; *Elgar: Land of Hope and Glory*, 19n; *Trees*, 37; *The Beethoven Secret*, 15, 81; *The Angels*, 96; *Music, Music, Music*, 96; *Van Gogh*, 124n46
Russell, Shirley (née Kingdon), 8, 14, 17, 20n, 43, 61, 146, 147–59
Russell, Victoria (daughter), 73, 147, 150, 156

Salome's Last Dance (1988), 28, 29, 30, 43, 71, 74, 86, 87, 110, 172, 228, 253, 254, 256
Saltzman, Harry, 53, 101
Sandler, Barry, 74–6, 214
Sands, Julian, 77
Satie, Eric, 110, 111, 123
Savage Messiah (1972), 11, 17, 29, 36, 40, 111, 118–19, 132, 147, 156, 163, 167–9, 169–70, 223, 224, 248, 251, 257
Schlesinger, John, 100, 162
Scott, Ridley, 43, 100
Scott, Tony, 43
Scottish Painters (BBC, 1959), 16, 109, 110–12, 113, 118
seaside 78, 123n
Sebastiane (1976), 169–72
The Secret Life of Arnold Bax (BBC, 1992), 16
The Secret of the Loch (1934) 31, 76
set design 10, 17, 70 72, 163, 229, 257, 271
sex and sexuality, 6, 14, 27–8, 28–9, 48–50, 51–5, 56, 61–6, 74–6, 77, 80–1, 86, 87, 104, 110, 118, 119–20, 136, 170, 171, 196, 197, 201, 206, 207, 213, 219–220, 222, 223, 224, 228–240, 243–5, 254, 262, 263–4, 266–7, 268, 270, 273, 289
The Sheik (1921), 200–1, 203, 205
Shelley, Mary, 59, 73, 79, 115, 119, 120
Shelley, Percy Bysshe, 59, 77, 78, 120
Shirai, Yoshio, 243, 244–5, 247
Shostakovich, Dmitri, 175
Sid and Nancy (1986), 251
Siddal, Elizabeth, 16, 56, 58, 59, 115, 119, 120–1, 131
Silence (2016), 171
The Singing Detective (1986), 214, 218, 219, 222
Slade School of Fine Art, 162, 162, 167
The Sleeping Gypsy (1897), 118
Slocombe, Dougie, 43
Sontag, Susan, 152, 266, 271
sound design, 169, 180–93
The Spear of Ithuriel (1890), 128
stardom, 17, 195–208
Steinman, Jim, 72, 90n, 267, 268
Stevenson, Robert Louis, 71
Stirling, Wilhelmina, 126, 131–4
Stoker, Bram, 72, 73, 87, 220
Strachey, Lytton, 70, 214
Strauss, Richard, 4, 7, 130, 177, 222, 223, 224, 262, 270, 271
Stravinsky, Igor 41
Strickland, Peter 13
Surrealism 2, 78, 79, 80, 117, 217, 242, 247, 256, 263
Suschitzky, Peter (set designer), 15, 102
Suspiria (2018), 14
Suzuki, Seijun, 247, 256–7

The Tales of Hoffman (1951), 174, 254
Tchaikovsky, Pyotr Ilyich, 2, 30, 41, 50, 51, 81, 120, 129, 173, 174, 175, 219, 220, 221, 230, 246, 264, 265, 266, 274, 275

304 INDEX

Teddy Girls (post war youth subculture), 43, 70, 151
Tezuka, Macoto, 255–6
Tezuka, Osamu, 256
Three Ground-breaking Directors of Sexually Themed Films (Japanese film publication), 246, 246
Throbbing Gristle, 152
Too Old to Die Young (2019), 263
Tommy (1975), 4, 5, 6, 9, 10, 11, 14, 17, 23, 30, 31–2, 34, 35, 45, 48, 70, 72, 73, 76, 77, 96, 112–13, 120, 137, 157, 169, 171–2, 177, 180–93
   hermeneutics and 'The Amazing Journey', 183–93, 217, 222, 224
   in Japan, 248, 252, 255, 256–8
   Russell style, 261, 263, 264, 265, 266, 275
Townshend Pete, 43, 180, 181, 185, 186, 187, 188, 189, 190, 191, 261
transgression, 17, 74, 201
Trapped Ashes (2006), 'The Girl With the Golden Breasts', 15
The Trial of Joan of Arc (1962), 171
Turner Kathleen, 74, 249
Tutti, Cosey Fanni, 152
Twiggy (model and actress), 28, 146, 149, 154, 155–6, 157, 159. 251

UK Gay Liberation Front, 152
Uncharted Seas (1921), 200

Valentino (1977), 11, 12, 17, 29, 43, 71, 195–207
The Vampyr (1932), 77
Van Gogh, Vincent, 109, 122, 124n, 129
Venus and Cupid (1878), 127
Vestron Video, 11, 13, 71, 72, 86, 251, 253, 254
Violation (novel, 2005), 230
Visconti, Luchino, 1, 170, 252, 253
Volk, Stephen, 33, 72, 73, 214

W.R.: Mysteries of the Organism, 246
A Waiting Game (1975), 231
Wakeman, Rick, 266–8, 271, 272
Walker, Alexander, 3, 34, 40, 199, 223
Walker, Scott, 269
The Wall (1982), 181
Walpole, Horace, 75
Walton, Tony, 158
War (1894), 118

The War Game (BBC, 1965), 291
War Requiem (1989), 174
Warhol, Andy, 133, 163, 167
Watch the Birdie (BBC, 1963), 43, 75
Watching the Wheels Come Off (2010), 231
Watkin, David, 43, 102
Watkin, Peter, 291
Way Out West (1937), 282–3, 286
The Wedding of St George and Princess Sabra (1857), 120
Wetherby (1985), 251
What My Heroes Think of the Space Race (1962), 114
What Next? (1928), 283
Wheatley, Ben, 14, 140, 177
Wheldon, Huw, 2, 35, 44, 79, 113, 125–6, 131, 162–3, 214
Where Adam Stood (1976), 222
Whitehead, Peter, 97, 106n, 163
Whitehouse, Mary, 7, 137, 222, 262
The Who, 172, 180, 181, 182, 185, 258, 261, 265
Whore (1991), 29, 220, 254–5
The Wicker Man (1973), 219
Wiene, Robert, 77, 121
Wilde, Oscar, 55–6, 70, 74, 86, 87, 172, 254
William and Mary (ITV, 1978), 120
Williams, Billy, 43, 61, 100, 101
Williams, Linda Ruth, 9, 61, 65, 167, 260
Wilson, Colin, 232, 239
Wilson, Sandy, 145
Winding-Refn Nicolas, 10, 18, 185, 260–276
Windsor, Barbara, 152
Witchfinder General (1968), 58
The Wizard of Oz (1939), 164
Women in Love (1969), 9, 11, 18, 27, 34, 44, 48, 50, 54, 55, 61–3, 64–5, 66, 70, 78, 96, 100, 103, 115, 147, 170, 213, 220, 242, 243–7, 251, 255, 256, 258, 260, 261, 262, 264, 271, 289
Woolf, Virginia, 70
World War I, 118
wrestling, 48, 64, 115, 243, 244, 264

Yodogawa, Nagaharu, 254, 255
Yume No Manimani (*Dreaming Awake*, 2008), 257

A Zed & Two Noughts (1985), 251